MATTHEW

The Hodder Bible Commentary

Edited by Lee Gatiss

MATTHEW

BEN COOPER

HODDER &
STOUGHTON

The Hodder Bible Commentary
Series Editor: Lee Gatiss

First published in Great Britain in 2024 by Hodder & Stoughton
An Hachette UK company

I

The Hodder Bible Commentary: Matthew copyright © Ben Cooper 2024

A CIP catalogue record for this title is available from the British Library

Hardback ISBN 9781473695030
ebook ISBN 9781473695214

Typeset in Bembo Std and Utopia by Palimpsest Book Production Ltd, Falkirk, Stirlingshire

Printed and bound in Great Britain by Clays Ltd, Elcograf S.p.A.

Hodder & Stoughton policy is to use papers that are natural, renewable and recyclable products
and made from wood grown in sustainable forests. The logging and manufacturing processes
are expected to conform to the environmental regulations of the country of origin.

Hodder & Stoughton Ltd
Carmelite House
50 Victoria Embankment
London EC4Y 0DZ

www.hodderfaith.com
www.hodderbiblecommentary.com

Contents

PART FOUR: THE PATTERN OF JESUS'S
MINISTRY – MATTHEW 4:12–10:42

PART FIVE: JESUS'S MINISTRY IN GALILEE –
MATTHEW 11:1–16:20

PART SIX: JESUS'S MINISTRY FROM GALILEE
TO JERUSALEM – MATTHEW 16:21–20:34

PART SEVEN: JESUS'S MINISTRY COMPLETED
IN JERUSALEM – MATTHEW 21–8

Series Preface

The unfolding of your words gives light
(Psalm 119:130)

The Hodder Bible Commentary aims to proclaim afresh in our generation the unchanging and unerring word of God, for the glory of God and the good of his people. This fifty-volume commentary on the whole Bible seeks to provide the contemporary church with fresh and readable expositions of Scripture which are doctrinally sensitive and globally aware, accessible for all adult readers but particularly useful to those who preach, teach and lead Bible studies in churches and small groups.

Building on the success of Hodder's NIV Proclamation Bible, we have assembled as contributors a remarkable team of men and women from around the world. Alongside a diverse panel of trusted Consultant Editors, they have a tremendous variety of denominational backgrounds and ministries. Each has great experience in unfolding the gospel of Jesus Christ and all are united in our aim of faithfully expounding the Bible in a way that takes account of the original text, biblical theology, the history of interpretation and the needs of the contemporary global church.

These volumes are serious expositions – not overly technical, scholarly works of reference but not simply sermons either. As well as carefully unpacking what the Bible says, they are sensitive to how it has been used in doctrinal discussions over the centuries and in our own day, though not dominated by such concerns at the expense of the text's own agenda. They also try to speak not only into a white, middle-class, Western context (for example), as some might, but to be aware of ways in which other cultures hear and need to hear what the Spirit is saying to the churches.

As you tuck into his word, with the help of this book, may the glorious Father 'give you the Spirit of wisdom and revelation, so that you may know him better' (Ephesians 1:17).

Lee Gatiss, Series Editor

Consultant Editors

The Series Editor would like to thank the following Consultant Editors for their contributions to the Hodder Bible Commentary:

Shady Anis (*Egypt*)
Kirsten Birkett (*UK*)
Felipe Chamy (*Chile*)
Ben Cooper (*UK*)
Mervyn Eloff (*South Africa*)
Keri Folmar (*Dubai*)
Kerry Gatiss (*UK*)
Kara Hartley (*Australia*)
Julian Hardyman (*Madagascar*)
Stephen Fagbemi (*Nigeria*)
Rosanne Jones (*Japan*)
Henry Jansma (*USA*)
Samuel Lago (*USA*)
Andis Miezitis (*Latvia*)
Adrian Reynolds (*UK*)
Peter Ryan (*Australia*)
Sookgoo Shin (*South Korea*)
Myrto Theocharous (*Greece*)

Acknowledgments

Many thanks to my excellent and attentive editor, Lee Gatiss, who has been thoughtful and insightful throughout (and remarkably patient with my late submissions). Thanks too to my consultant editor, Kerry Gatiss, for her attention to detail. And thanks to Chris Moore for careful reading and numerous helpful comments and suggestions.

I would like to thank my boss at The Proclamation Trust, Nigel Styles, for his patience with me as I've been writing and editing this.

Many thanks to the students I've taught Matthew to over the years: for your attention, enthusiasm and engagement.

Most of all, thanks to my wife Catherine – my wonderful helper and companion.

But glory be to God alone.

Abbreviations

BDAG W. Bauer, F. W. Danker, W. F. Arndt, F. W. Gingrich, *A Greek–English Lexicon of the New Testament and Other Early Christian Literature* (Third edition; Chicago: University of Chicago Press, 2000).

LSJ   Henry George Liddell and Robert Scott, *A Greek-English Lexicon*, revised and augmented throughout by Sir Henry Stuart Jones with the assistance of Roderick McKenzie (Oxford: Clarendon Press, 1940).

PART ONE

....

INTRODUCTION

I

Orientation

> Then the eleven disciples went to Galilee, to the mountain where Jesus had told them to go. When they saw him, they worshipped him; but some doubted. Then Jesus came to them and said, 'All authority in heaven and on earth has been given to me. Therefore go and make disciples of all nations, baptising them in the name of the Father and of the Son and of the Holy Spirit, and teaching them to obey everything I have commanded you. And surely I am with you always, to the very end of the age.' (Matthew 28:16–20)

It is generally frowned upon to flick to the end of a detective story to see what happens. It means missing out on much of the suspense, surprise and drama the author wanted us to experience. But with a Gospel, and Matthew's Gospel in particular, turning to the end turns out to be a very good strategy, and an excellent way to get our bearings. This is where the Gospel is heading. And at the end, Matthew shows us Jesus on a mountain, commissioning his disciples to 'go and make disciples of all nations' (verse 19). Everything he has said is building to this – to what is almost universally now known as the 'Great Commission'. This is where the narrative ends, leaving room for our narratives to fit in, as readers. Potentially, this is where we may join the story as disciples of Jesus. Matthew would love to see us right there in verse 19: among those people in the nations, made into disciples of Jesus. We live in the period of history that began at this moment on the mountain in Galilee, from which the task of disciple-making has cascaded down through generations of disciples ever since. Teaching or preaching this Gospel is going to encourage further disciples of Jesus to join in, making new generations of disciples, all of whom know that Jesus is with us every day until the end of the age.

Here we find the big themes of Matthew's Gospel coming together one last time. We see the concern Matthew has shown throughout the Gospel for history. Indeed, he is showing us a major turning point in history. In fulfilment of all that God has promised in the past, something has happened to begin a new age. Jesus has now been given all authority in heaven and on earth. *What* has just happened, to bring about such a huge change? The answer Matthew will give is: the suffering, death and resurrection of Jesus, and it has been the key moment in all of history. Moving to another theme, we see that central to Matthew's understanding of history is the person of Jesus. We see in these verses the authority of Jesus, the worship of Jesus, the command given by Jesus, the teaching of Jesus and the enduring presence of Jesus. And we also see Matthew's deep concern for discipleship. The central, enduring command to his disciples is to 'go and make disciples of all nations'.

These three great themes – history (past, present and future, centred on the death and resurrection of Jesus), the person of Jesus, and discipleship – will prove helpful categories for orientating ourselves as we prepare to read and process Matthew's Gospel. Matthew has written in and about a particular historical context, which includes a deep understanding of the past and a very clear vision of the future. He has structured and arranged his Gospel around the person of Jesus. And he has done it all with a purpose orientated towards discipleship.

1. Historical context and perspective

Modern biblical scholarship does have a view on how Matthew's Gospel relates to history, although only according to its own (somewhat arbitrary) standards, conventions and concerns. I shall highlight here a few useful things we can learn from this material, but we shall see it is much more important for the reader of this Gospel to align themselves with Matthew's view on history – past, present and future.

We can divide the questions scholars ask into two kinds. The first kind concerns the history of the Gospel: the origins of Matthew's Gospel and the historical context in which it was written. The second concerns the history *in* the Gospel: the historical claims Matthew makes in the Gospel, and the wider context in which they take place.

The history of the Gospel

On the history of the text of Matthew's Gospel, the kinds of questions of interest to scholars can be found in the introductory section of pretty much any serious commentary on Matthew.[1] Who wrote this document we know as the Gospel of Matthew? Was it Matthew the tax collector

---

[1] Or, better still, a book-length introduction to Matthew, such as R. T. France,

and apostle (10:3)? Is this the same person as Levi the tax collector mentioned in Mark 2:14 and Luke 5:27–32? Even if, as seems likely, these are one and the same, could it have been written by someone else altogether? Was he Jewish? Was he a 'teacher of the law' (a scribe)?[2] What were his sources? *When* was it written? Was it written before or after Mark's Gospel? Was it written before or after the siege of Jerusalem and the partial destruction of the Temple in AD 70? Where was it written? For whom was it written?

There are no explicit, watertight answers in the text of Matthew's Gospel to most of these questions. The author chooses not to identify himself clearly in the body of the text. We should acknowledge this, and his desire not to draw attention to himself. His desire, as we might expect, is to draw our attention to someone else, namely Jesus. Nevertheless, I shall continue to call the author 'Matthew' – partly because it would be odd and confusing to call him anything else, but also because every surviving manuscript or fragment (the earliest being from the late second century) has the name Matthew in the title. This is also the name used by Papias, a bishop of Hierapolis in Asia Minor, in connection with the Gospel in a passage usually dated to around AD 140.[3] So, Matthew it is.

From the very earliest times, the assumption has been that this 'Matthew' was the apostle and tax-collector of 10:3, although there is little further evidence to support or contradict this. Personally, I think it unlikely. If he was, it's a puzzle that he chooses to use and condense Mark's accounts of many events rather than give his own personal eyewitness testimony (as we find in the alternative eyewitness perspective given in John's Gospel, for example). But I wouldn't want to insist on this – it's quite possible he *was* Matthew the apostle. Whether he was or not, I, like Raymond Brown, suspect he may have come from some kind of scribal background – one of those Jesus describes as 'a teacher of the law [scribe] made a disciple for the kingdom' (13:52, my translation).[4] He has a deep, intimate and respectful knowledge of the Jewish Scriptures.

Matthew: Evangelist and Teacher (London: Paternoster Press, 1989), especially chapters 2 and 3.

[2] The NIV translation we are using in this commentary prefers 'teacher of the law' to 'scribe', and this is the terminology I shall be using in what follows.

[3] This is in a passage quoted by Eusebius (AD 300–400) in Book III of his *Ecclesiastical History*. Eusebius, *Ecclesiastical History, Volume I: Books 1–5*, trans. Kirsopp Lake, volume 153, Loeb Classical Library (Cambridge, MA: Harvard University Press, 1926). See the discussion in France, *Matthew: Evangelist and Teacher*, 53–60.

[4] Raymond E. Brown, *The Birth of the Messiah: A Commentary on the Infancy*

His meticulous compositional structures suggest a high degree of literary ability. So, perhaps, a teacher of the law who became a disciple. There are limits, however, to how much we gain from speculation along these lines.

Most scholars suggest that Mark's Gospel was one of Matthew's sources, and was written earlier. Certainly, we can say it's less likely that Matthew was one of Mark's sources and that Matthew was written first. When we compare, say, the episode of the woman with bleeding who touched Jesus's garment and was healed, we find that Mark 5:25–34 is much longer and more detailed than Matthew 9:20–22. There are sufficient points of contact to suppose that one author was using the other (or had access to similar sources). But why would Mark use Matthew if he also had access to all the other details he shows he knows?

Most likely, Matthew has taken Mark's account (or one of his sources) and summarised the key features, stripping out all the details. The question of what other sources Matthew had access to (and how they overlap with Luke's, for example) has occupied an extraordinary amount of scholarly time and attention, but with no concrete evidence to draw on, any conclusions are necessarily speculative. It's likely in any case that the history of composition of the Gospels was quite complex, that they are, as France says, 'partially parallel developments of the common traditions, rather than placed in a simple line of "dependence"'.[5]

There also seems to be no way of firmly fixing *when* the Gospel was written. The fact that there's no explicit, detailed description of the tumultuous events of the siege and sacking of Jerusalem in AD 66–70 (for example) doesn't necessarily suggest a date earlier than this. Matthew could have been writing after AD 70, but with those events in the past and therefore no urgent need to issue a direct warning about them, he may well have wanted to focus on different, future tribulations of a similar kind. Finally, Matthew says nothing direct about *where* the Gospel was written and does not specify the addressees. This is not a letter.

Having said all this, it does seem reasonable to suppose Matthew composed his Gospel with a particular group of first readers and hearers in mind, even if it would be unreasonable to fix the boundaries of this group. The potential audience of Matthew's Gospel is unbounded, deliberately so. The same could be said of the other Gospels. In Matthew, we see this unboundedness in the Great Commission, where the disciples are

---

Narratives in the Gospels of Matthew and Luke (Updated edition; New York: Yale University Press, 1993), 46.

[5] R. T. France, *The Gospel of Matthew* (Grand Rapids: Eerdmans, 2007), 21.

commanded to teach what Jesus has commanded in the nations – the teaching Matthew has recorded for us earlier in his Gospel. Matthew's hope and expectation was therefore that his Gospel would ultimately reach a non-Jewish audience.

Nonetheless, I have found it helpful to imagine Matthew thinking of his very first (but not only) readers and hearers as Greek-speaking Jewish people (or Gentile God-fearing synagogue attenders) living somewhere like the city of (Syrian) Antioch, some 700km north of Jerusalem and near the coast, whose ruins lie near the modern city of Antakya in southern Turkey. This might sound overly specific, so let me explain!

Why do I imagine Matthew had in mind Jewish people (or Gentile God-fearing synagogue attenders) as readers and hearers of his Gospel first and foremost? Because the Gospel seems to expect an extensive knowledge of the Hebrew Scriptures. Part of the argument (as we shall see) is that everything God is doing through Jesus is in fulfilment of these Scriptures, which is not much of an argument for those who don't know or care about them.

Why *Greek-speaking* Jewish people? Well, most obviously, like the rest of the New Testament, Matthew was written in Greek. (Papias claimed it was originally written in Hebrew/Aramaic, but it doesn't read like a translated text. And even in the unlikely event that it was originally written in Hebrew or Aramaic, someone saw fit to translate it into Greek, which is how it was used in the early church, and how it has survived to today.) It is also worth remembering that Greek-speaking (Hellenised) Jewish people were the primary mission field for the early church, closely followed by Gentile God-fearing synagogue attenders. There were about five million Jewish people scattered around the Mediterranean in the first century, compared to a million or so in Palestine.

Why do I suggest (Syrian) Antioch as a first setting? It is the view of some scholars that Matthew's Gospel was written in Antioch, although there's little explicit evidence for this.[6] But even if the Gospel wasn't written in Antioch, this was exactly the sort of place Matthew would have wanted it circulated, read aloud and heard by as many people as possible. Antioch was a centre of Hellenistic Judaism, and (as we have

---

[6] · The claim goes back to B. H. Streeter, *The Four Gospels: A Study of Origins* (London: Macmillan, 1924), 500–527. Streeter argued that 'the Gospel would not have been generally accepted as Apostolic unless it had been backed by one of the great Churches' (*The Four Gospels*, 501). In his view, the church in Antioch was the most likely candidate.

confirmed in Acts 13–14) quickly became a centre of Christian mission. Matthew would have wanted his Gospel hard at work in such a place, as an instrument to make Greek-speaking Jewish people into disciples of Jesus – and as an instrument to enthuse, train and equip many of these disciples to become disciple-makers themselves, engaged in the mission of the early churches out into the Mediterranean world.

Imagining ourselves in ancient Antioch is therefore a helpful place to orientate ourselves. This was a city – as one writer sums it up – 'filled with misery, fear, despair and hatred'.[7] Ancient cities were essentially large forts, the ancient world being a dangerous and violent place. The small space behind the fortified walls was unhealthily crammed with people looking for protection as they desperately tried to work out some kind of livelihood. Water was scarce, food was scarce and work was scarce. There was no sewage system to speak of, there was no soap or other kinds of modern hygiene, and medical practice generally did more harm than good. There were no building regulations, the risk of fire was extreme and the population density was staggeringly high. The average life expectancy in the ancient world was between twenty and twenty-five years, owing mostly to massive infant mortality rates. If you made it to twenty-five years, you had a reasonably good chance of reaching old age. On the other hand, one-third of children died before the age of six. The rate of female infanticide stood at a horrific 20 per cent.[8] The Roman philosopher Seneca (4 BC–AD 65) said this of the Graeco–Roman world in the first century: 'Most men ebb and flow in wretchedness between the fear of death and the hardships of life.'[9] In short, the presence and threat of death would have felt frighteningly close to Matthew's first readers – a reality confirmed for us in the desperate people Jesus meets in chapters 8–9 of the Gospel.

It is into such a world that Matthew speaks, claiming that Jesus has come to fulfil what was said through the prophet Isaiah:

---

[7] Rodney Stark, *The Rise of Christianity: A Sociologist Reconsiders History* (Princeton: Princeton University Press, 1996), 160.

[8] For more on this, see Peter Bolt, 'Life, Death and the Afterlife in the Greco-Roman World', in *Life in the Face of Death: The Resurrection Message of the New Testament*, ed. Richard N. Longenecker (Grand Rapids: Eerdmans, 1998).

[9] Seneca, *Epistolae 4*, 'On the Terrors of Death', 5, in *Epistles: Volume I: Epistles 1–65*, trans. Richard M. Gummere, volume 75, Loeb Classical Library (Cambridge: Harvard University Press, 1917), 12–19.

the people living in darkness
   have seen a great light;
on those living in the land of the shadow of death
   a light has dawned.

(Matthew 4:16)

For a Greek-speaking synagogue attender (whether Jewish or Gentile God-fearer) feeling the weight of the shadow of death in a city like first-century Antioch, this should have had a profound impact. It would have been a claim worth investigating.

The history in the Gospel

The events Matthew describes in the Gospel take place largely in Galilee and Judea, beginning with the birth of Jesus in Bethlehem in Judea and ending with his resurrection appearance before the eleven remaining disciples on a mountain in Galilee. We can pick up most of what we need to know about the immediate historical context of these events from the Gospel itself. This includes the tensions surrounding the Roman occupation and the Herodian Tetrarchy. We can even pick up some of the tension existing between the centre of first-century Judaism in Jerusalem and the Judaism that survived in the northern outpost of Galilee.[10] The disdain that Jerusalem felt towards the north is palpable in the exchanges between Peter and those in the courtyard of the high priest in 26:69–75. Jesus is identified as Jesus of Galilee (26:69) and Jesus of Nazareth (26:71). Peter's northern accent gives him away (26:73). There is further historical evidence to explore in some of these areas, but our concern here will be more firmly focused on what we have before us in the text of Matthew.

Jesus's opponents

It is worth saying a little more, however, on some of the opponents Jesus faces in the Gospel and their historical background. We can broadly and roughly divide these opponents into two groups. The first is those who are part of the religious and cultural establishment. These include the chief priests, the elders of the people and the Sadducees. It's hard to say much about the Sadducees with any certainty. Josephus (AD 37–97) associated

---

[10] As explored in France, *The Gospel of Matthew*, 5–7.

them with the upper social classes in Judean society.[11] In the New Testament, their main distinctive is not believing in the resurrection from the dead (Matthew 22:23–33; Mark 12:18–27; Luke 20:27–40; Acts 23:6–8).[12]

The second group – given more prominence by Matthew – are the Pharisees, which Jesus frequently links with the 'teachers of the law', especially in Matthew 23. The word 'Pharisee' may originally have meant something like 'separate one' or 'separatist', although this is contested.[13] Indeed, the origins of this group are obscure, possibly coming around the time of start of the Hasmonian Dynasty (which began in 141 BC), and possibly from a scribal background.[14] They had a clear interest in ritual purity, even for people not involved in the Temple system, but this may have been a common view across many Jewish people at the time. Their most important distinctive was actually one widely commended in the New Testament: a firm belief in the resurrection to come (based on texts such as Daniel 12:1–4).

The Pharisees were an important group not just during the time of Jesus's earthly ministry, but also later, as we see in the book of Acts (Acts 15:5; 23:6–8). After the end of the Temple in AD 70, the Pharisees became a dominant group in Judaism, even if their influence on Rabbinic Judaism has been exaggerated.[15] It seems likely that, at the time of Matthew writing his Gospel, those obeying the call to 'make disciples of all nations' (28:19) would have encountered the opposition of the Pharisees.

There have been many recent attempts by New Testament scholars (and others) to rehabilitate the Pharisees, in part motivated by the claim that 'negative descriptions of Pharisees bleed over into antisemitic discourse'.[16] For example, Kent Yinger concludes that the Pharisees were not widely considered hypocrites in the first century and that Christians have largely

---

[11] Josephus, *Jewish Antiquities, Volume V: Books 12–13*, trans. Ralph Marcus, volume 365, Loeb Classical Library (Cambridge: Harvard University Press, 1943), 13.298.

[12] N. T. Wright, *The Resurrection of the Son of God*, Christian Origins and the Question of God (London: SPCK, 2003), 131–40.

[13] See Craig E. Morrison, 'What's in a Name? Interpreting the Name "Pharisee"', in *The Pharisees*, ed. Joseph Sievers and Amy-Jill Levine (Grand Rapids: Eerdmans, 2021), chapter 1.

[14] Vasile Babota, 'In Search of the Origins of the Pharisees', in *The Pharisees*, ed. Sievers and Levine, chapter 2.

[15] Gunter Stemberger, 'The Pharisees and the Rabbis', in *The Pharisees*, ed. Sievers and Levine, chapter 13.

[16] Joseph Sievers and Amy-Jill Levine, 'Preface', in *The Pharisees*, ed. Sievers and Levine.

misunderstood them.[17] We can agree that it is good, of course, to avoid over-generalising or stereotyping. After all, the New Testament includes two Pharisees – Nicodemus (John 3:1–21; 7:50–51; 19:39) and Gamaliel (Acts 5:34–9) – who, whatever their faults, are not portrayed as legalistic, money-loving, xenophobic or hypocritical.

Nevertheless, we cannot get away from the fact that Matthew's portrait of the Pharisees is unremittingly negative.[18] It may well be that some Pharisees were not nearly as bad as the particular Pharisees described in Matthew's Gospel, but the disputes and encounters Matthew describes still expose the fatal flaw in the Pharisaical reform movement. When John and then Jesus proclaim that the kingdom of the heavens is near (3:2; 4:17), the Pharisees are shown (beginning in 3:7–12) to be dangerously unresponsive, apparently secure in their Abrahamic heritage and their obedience to the Law. The events of the Gospel expose the dangerous complacency in this attitude, the flaws in their interpretation of the Law and (for some, at least) the selective application of the Law to their own advantage. Ultimately, they are shown to be no different from God's people in the past, with nothing more to offer. Just like the people of Isaiah's day, their hearts are 'far from' the Lord (15:8). They are the 'descendants [literally, "sons of"] those who murdered the prophets' (23:31). Just as the failure to love the Lord and obey him led to covenant curse, exile and wrath in the past (as Matthew reminds us at the beginning of the Gospel, 1:11–12), so it will lead to the Pharisees and teachers of the law failing to enter the kingdom of heaven (as implied in 5:20, for example). Something new is needed to bring a different outcome: a new, merciful intervention from the Lord. This is indeed what the Lord has promised through the prophets (in, for example, Ezekiel 36–37 or Jeremiah 31:31–4), but Matthew's portrait of the Pharisees shows that as a whole they were failing to acknowledge this or to be humble in their desperate need for mercy. They showed no eagerness to look for the merciful intervention of the Lord, or indeed to recognise it coming in Jesus, and they thereby missed the extraordinary good news of the Lord fulfilling his promises.[19]

---

[17] See Kent L. Yinger, *The Pharisees: Their History, Character, and New Testament Portrait* (Eugene: Cascade Books, 2022).

[18] It is not, however, anti-semitic. We must insist that the faults of the Pharisees are by no means portrayed anywhere in the New Testament as ethnic or racial faults. This should be obvious, given that the critique is coming through ethnically Jewish writers.

[19] Although there are, of course, some exceptions to this bleak conclusion in the wider New Testament, Nicodemus and Paul being obvious examples.

Indeed, the characteristic uniting all Jesus's opponents is their failure to recognise the Lord at work in and through Jesus, which may be why Matthew is happy to lump both Pharisee and Sadducee together (3:7; 16:1, 11–12), despite their many differences.

Matthew's perspective on history

It is helpful to put ourselves in the shoes (or sandals) of the very first readers and hearers of Matthew's Gospel if we are to understand him rightly and the historical context and setting of the Gospel. But attempting to pin these things down – to find the history behind the text, as it were – is an imprecise and speculative exercise. We can only take things so far.

We find ourselves on much more solid ground when we turn to Matthew's own perspective on the significance of the history he was writing about. We might not know very much about Matthew and where he was writing, but from his Gospel we can piece together what *he* thought about history – past, present and future. For Matthew, the past was a place of both great failure and darkness, even shame; but also of great promise, ready to be fulfilled. For Matthew, the present was the time of fulfilment, realised in the birth of Jesus and his life, ministry, death and resurrection. Jesus came to fulfil the Law and the Prophets. For Matthew, the future was dominated by the kingdom of the heavens – heaven and earth reunited into one renewed cosmos.[20] This shaped Matthew's understanding of the present again: the time after the resurrection of Jesus but before the 'end of the age' (28:20). This is the age of disciple-making in all the nations (20:19). Matthew always intended the audience of his Gospel to be an expanding one. As Stephen Barton notes, many scholars too quickly dismiss 'the possibility that the Gospels are open texts intended, not only for audiences of believers, but for audiences of unbelievers as well'.[21] In the case of Matthew, we suspect

---

[20] In common with every other English translation I know, the 2011 NIV uses 'the kingdom of heaven [singular]' throughout Matthew's Gospel. This is despite Matthew using the plural, 'the kingdom of the *heavens*'. Jonathan T. Pennington has convincingly argued that Matthew uses the plural *heavens* to denote the place of divine ruling activity, while he uses the singular *heaven* to talk about the sky, or within the pairing 'heaven and earth'. So the plural is significant: it's part of the way Matthew shows there is a 'standing tension between the realms of heaven and earth'. Jonathan T. Pennington, *Heaven and Earth in the Gospel of Matthew* (Leiden: Brill, 2007), 209. There is more on Matthew's understanding of the kingdom below.
[21] Stephen C. Barton, 'Can We Identify the Gospel Audiences?', in *The Gospels*

that most of the very first readers and hearers would have been Jewish, but the moment they started to obey Jesus's command, making disciples in the nations and using the Gospel to pass on Jesus's teaching, the next generation of readers and hearers would have included more and more Gentiles. Indeed, this is where many of us fit in – part of Matthew's ever-expanding audience, to the end of the age.

2. Structure

Various proposals have been made for the structure of Matthew's Gospel.[22] This might suggest a high degree of uncertainty or disagreement, but actually there is a high level of agreement about the basic data. For example, one of the things we notice on a first reading is the large quantity of uninterrupted teaching from Jesus. The narrative about Jesus (which we find in different forms in all the Gospels) alternates with long blocks of teaching from Jesus. Matthew is building his account around the person of Jesus, but the structure of his Gospel more especially highlights Jesus as teacher. And if Jesus is highlighted as teacher, then we as readers of the Gospel are being cast by Matthew as disciples (or potential disciples) – people who learn though instruction from another. (We shall see that being a disciple of Jesus means more than this, but never any less than this.)

There is teaching from Jesus spread throughout the Gospel, but five longer blocks of teaching end with a phrase along the lines of, 'When Jesus had finished saying these things . . .' (7:28; 11:1; 13:53; 19:1; 26:1). The starting point of some of these five blocks of teaching is debated, but it is generally agreed that they constitute one of the main features of Matthew's Gospel. Roughly, they cover chapters 5–7, 10, 13, 18 and 24–5.

On closer inspection, there are other structural markers, showing that these blocks of teaching fit into wider patterns. For example, Matthew groups chapters 5 to 9 together by repeating an almost identical summary of Jesus's ministry of proclaiming the kingdom at 4:23 (at the end of chapter 4) and then again at 9:35: 'Jesus went through all the towns and villages [/throughout Galilee], teaching in their synagogues, proclaiming

---

for All Christians: Rethinking the Gospel Audiences, ed. Richard Bauckham (Grand Rapids: Eerdmans, 1998), 194.

[22] There is a good survey in Wilhelmus Johannes Cornelis Weren, *Studies in Matthew's Gospel: Literary Design, Intertextuality, and Social Setting* (Leiden: Brill, 2014), 13–41. Weren's own proposal has much in common with the one suggested here.

the good news of the kingdom, and healing every disease and illness [among the people]'. Chapter 10 is then basically concerned with Jesus multiplying this ministry twelve-fold (by sending out the Twelve to the lost sheep of the house of Israel). What's more, Jesus's proclamation of the kingdom actually begins in 4:17, in a section beginning at 4:12. So Matthew 4:12–10:42 is all concerned with setting a pattern of kingdom proclamation – Jesus first; then multiplied by his disciples.

Before 4:12–10:42, Matthew 1–2 stand apart by containing background material. With Matthew 1–2 grouped together and 4:12–10:42 grouped together, we can see the Gospel divided is into four basic sections:[23]

Background

1–2 Jesus comes to fulfil the Law and the Prophets

Body

3:1–4:11 Jesus is commissioned by his Father, with a mandate to complete *before* the judgment

4:12–10:42 Jesus proclaims the nearness of the kingdom in word and deed

11–28 Jesus completes his role as the Servent of the Lord

Figure 1

There is plenty more fine structure in Matthew, most of which we shall see as we work through the Gospel. But it's worth pausing here to give a brief overview of how these four main sections work together to tell Matthew's account of Jesus, noting some of the more important structural features along the way.

---

[23] Some proposals for Matthew's structure put heavy emphasis on the phrase 'From that time on . . .', which we find at 4:17 and 16:21. These can then be used to divide the Gospel into three parts. This approach was popularised by Jack D. Kingsbury, *Matthew: Structure, Christology, Kingdom* (Philadelphia: Fortress Press, 1975), 1–39, but goes back at least to Edgar Krentz, 'The Extent of Matthew's Prologue: Towards the Structure of the First Gospel', *Journal of Biblical Literature* 83 (1964). The problem is that this repeated phrase doesn't work well as an inclusion, because the material in between lacks a unifying idea. It is better to take the phrase as marking two transitional sections (as below and in Weren, *Studies in Matthew's Gospel*, 22–41).

Chapters 1–2: Jesus comes to fulfil the Scriptures

This section has two parts: the genealogy (1:1–17), followed by the birth of Jesus and his rescue from the murderous intentions of Herod (1:18–2:23). The genealogy has a threefold structure, a simple structural pattern we'll see Matthew likes to use wherever he can.

The genealogy connects us to the Old Testament storyline, gives us the background crisis facing the nation of Israel and acts as a departure point for the rest of the Gospel. Since the exile to Babylon, Israel has fallen back to the level of the nations and has no king. In this desperate situation, Matthew presents Jesus as son of David (a king able to fulfil God's promises to David) and son of Abraham (a saviour able to fulfil God's promises to Abraham). He is born to fulfil the need for someone who can 'save his people from their sins' (Matthew 1:21). Right from the beginning, he is ignored by those who should welcome him, and his life is in danger. But God has been powerful in the past to provide both leadership and rescue for his people, and this power will find its fulfilment in Jesus. Some ten times across the Gospel, Matthew makes an editorial comment to say something along the lines of, 'This was to fulfil what had been spoken by the Lord through the prophet . . .', and four of them come in these first two chapters.

Chapters 3:1–4:11: Jesus is commissioned and tested

This section has three parts: the proclamation of John (3:1–12), the baptism of Jesus (3:13–17) and the testing of Jesus (4:1–11).

John proclaims the nearness of the kingdom of the heavens (on which more below), rightly associating this with the closeness of the coming wrath of God and the crushing of God's enemies. Indeed, he seems to be expecting the one coming after him – the one he is preparing the way for – to bring this wrath and judgment right away. The surprise is then that when Jesus arrives, he comes with neither wrath nor axe nor winnowing shovel. Instead, he does something very strange, getting baptised alongside the sinners coming out to the Jordan river. There are only hints at this stage as to what is going on. But these are the first clues that Jesus is taking on the role of Isaiah's Servant figure, here being 'numbered with the transgressors' (Isaiah 53:12). The voice from the heavens at his baptism confirms the approval of his Father, using similar words to those used to commend the Servant in Isaiah 42:1. We can begin to conclude that Jesus is responding to the will of his Father, taking on a task or mandate from his Father, to complete before the Judgment. This will be to save the people from the coming wrath and so prepare them for the coming kingdom. He stands alongside them here, and will later bear their sin (Isaiah 53:12). His resolve as Son of God to complete this task (rather than use his authority for his own benefit) is then tested by the devil in the wilderness (and will be tested again at 16:22–3 and 27:38–44).

Chapters 4:12–10:42: Jesus proclaims the kingdom

4:12–17 is a transitional section, giving Matthew's understanding that the coming of Jesus fulfils Isaiah's prophecy of light dawning 'in the land of the shadow of death' (citing Isaiah 9:1–2). It ends with 4:17:

> From that time on Jesus began to preach, 'Repent, for the kingdom of [the heavens] has come near.'

Jesus then calls the first four disciples to follow him, to become those who 'fish for people' (4:18–22). Later, he will send these four, plus eight others, to proclaim the nearness of the kingdom to the lost sheep of the house of Israel (10:1–15).

Jesus's own proclamation of the kingdom is expressed alongside and through his teaching (5:1–7:29) and his healing and exorcism ministry (8:1–9:34).

As Jesus proclaims the kingdom, he teaches his disciples what it will mean to live in the light of the kingdom – for the glory of their Father in the heavens (5:16) and in close, secret relationship with him alone (6:1–7:11). As Jesus proclaims the kingdom, he shows us something of what the kingdom will be like through his healing and exorcism ministry. He gives multiple illustrations of lifting people from the shadow of death, teaching along the way that the key thing that needs dealing with is people's sin. He then sends the Twelve to replicate twelvefold across the towns of Israel what he has been proclaiming and doing (chapter 10).

Chapters 11:1–28:20: Jesus is resisted but victorious

If 4:12–10:42 sets a pattern of kingdom proclamation – a repeatable pattern, to be multiplied by the disciples – then chapters 11–28 of the

Gospel show this ministry worked out in the particular, personal narrative of Jesus as he completes the mandate given to him by his Father at his baptism. Early on in these chapters, we encounter Matthew's own commentary on what's happening, in the longest quotation from the Old Testament in the Gospel (12:17–21). This confirms explicitly that Jesus has taken on the role of Isaiah's Servant of the Lord. He is the one chosen by the Lord God to proclaim coming justice to the world (12:18), who has come for now in gentleness, not responding to opposition with judgment at this time (12:19–20a). Rather, he will persist in his task until he achieves a victory to bring hope to the nations (12:20b–21).

This is basically what we then see worked out in the rest of the Gospel.

Not surprisingly, Matthew has also given this long section some structure. One-third of the way through, we find ourselves at Caesarea Philippi (16:13–28), where Peter confesses Jesus to be the Christ. This is another transitional section, including the phrase, 'From that time on . . .' (16:21, as in 4:12–17 above). This begins a subsection structured around three passion-vindication predictions from Jesus (16:21; 17:22–3; 20:17–19) – a subsection that runs to the end of chapter 20. There is in fact fine structure right across Matthew 11–28 (often involving groups of three), but for the moment it will suffice to note the three main subsections, with 16:13–20:34 in the middle, roughly corresponding to geographical location (as in the diagram below). Matthew 11:1–16:12 takes place in Galilee, 16:13–20:34 begins in Caesarea Philippi but emphasises Jesus heading for Jerusalem, and Matthew 21–8 takes place in Jerusalem itself (with a brief return to Galilee at the end).

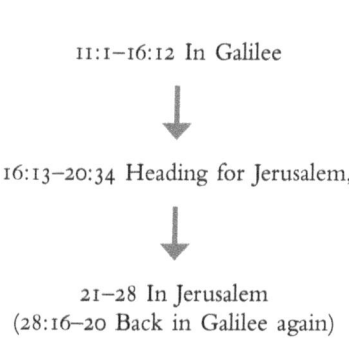

11:1–16:12 In Galilee

16:13–20:34 Heading for Jerusalem,

21–28 In Jerusalem
(28:16–20 Back in Galilee again)

Figure 2

R. T. France helpfully reminds us of the very strong social and political north–south divide between Galilee and Judea/Jerusalem.[24] Jerusalem was the undisputed centre of Judaism; Galilee, a backwater, frequently mocked by those in the southern province. The journey from Galilee to Jerusalem in the Gospels is therefore quite a drama. The pride of the religious establishment faces a challenge from a surprising source – from a Nazarene (2:23), a Galilean (26:69).

Jesus's ministry in Galilee (11:1–16:12) follows immediately from the comprehensive proclamation of the kingdom described in 4:12–10:42. The response to the proclamation is, at best, mixed. Israel fails to recognise the deeds of the Christ and repent. Beginning with John the Baptist, questions are raised and opposition increases. This, however, is to be expected, as Jesus explains in the teaching of Matthew 13. And, despite the opposition, Jesus himself does not falter in compassionate, powerful outreach as Servant. This is even as his own disciples fail to recognise him properly, as they are shown to be those of 'little faith'. Some partial resolution is found as they recognise him as the Son of God (14:33) and as the Christ, the Son of the living God (16:16).

As Jesus heads towards his execution (and resurrection) in Jerusalem (16:13–20:34), the disciples (and Peter in particular) fail to recognise the necessity of his suffering and death, and so unwittingly find themselves aligned with Satan (16:23). In response, Jesus presses home both the necessity of his death and the necessity of following his lead – in practical expressions of servanthood within the assembly of his disciples.

Jesus then arrives in Jerusalem (21:1–11) and enters the Temple courts to confront the false authority of the religious establishment. This sets in motion the events leading to his death.

The final resolution of Matthew's narrative comes in the handing over, death and resurrection of Jesus (Matthew 26–28). These chapters show his vindication in resurrection and therefore where true authority lies (resolving the conflict over authority begun in the Temple courts). They confirm the necessity of his death (against the misunderstandings of the disciples). They truly reveal him as the Son of God and sin-bearing Servant of the Lord (addressing any doubt there may have been about his identity). And they show Jesus fulfilling his mandate to bring forgiveness of sins through his death (hence dealing with the fundamental problem he came to solve).

Finally, we briefly return to Galilee (28:16–20). With the crises of

---

[24] France, *The Gospel of Matthew*, 5–7.

the Gospel dealt with at such a deep level, the victory of God and the forgiveness of sins can be proclaimed globally, making disciples in every nation.

3. Purpose

This commentary is written under the conviction that Matthew's Gospel is more than a merely human document. I would like to echo Howard Marshall's words in the Preface to his commentary on the Pastoral Epistles, that 'I write from a self-consciously Christian set of presuppositions'.[25] As Holy Scripture, I take it that this is part of 'God's Word written' (as Article 20 of the *Anglican Thirty-nine Articles* describes it); that God himself was sovereign over its inspiration and composition, in a manner that by no means replaces or suppresses the role of its human author. The texts of Holy Scripture were written in particular, ancient contexts, but I take it that this is not a barrier to the Holy Spirit speaking through them to people today. And if Matthew's Gospel is in some profound way God speaking (present tense), then we can take it that he does so with reason and purpose. The question is: what purpose?

This is a more straightforward question to address for Matthew's Gospel than it might be for other parts of Scripture. We can begin with Matthew, the human author, and take his pastoral purposes and intentions as a starting point. Seeking to discern God's purposes and intentions then means reading this within the context of the whole of the Holy Scriptures. But, actually, this will not hugely change our assessment of the Gospel's purpose. From the very first verses, we find Matthew is already concerned to place his account firmly within the context of the Hebrew Scriptures.

Reading Matthew alongside other texts in the New Testament canon also doesn't much modify our assessment of its divine purpose. It might of course help us to understand Matthew's purpose. It means any claims Matthew might make – historical or theological, explicit or implicit – will not contradict similar claims elsewhere in the New Testament. If we do find an apparent contradiction, then our default position will be that the problem is with us as readers, that we have misundersto something somewhere. But once we're clear on Matthew's purpose, th New Testament does not supply any event or further revelation th comes after he wrote his Gospel that should cause us to modify great

---

[25] I. Howard Marshall, *The Pastoral Epistles* (London: T&T Clark, 1999), xiv.

our assessment of its purpose for today.[26] We speak different languages, in all sorts of different social and cultural contexts, with many conventions that are different from those in the ancient world – and all these things need to be considered. But, essentially, the purpose of the Gospel remains the same as it was when it was written.

Matthew's purpose – a brief summary

So what were Matthew's pastoral intentions and desires as he composed and wrote his Gospel? Most commentaries ignore this question altogether. R. T. France does at least have a go at answering this question in his introduction to Matthew.[27] However, his conclusion – that the pastoral function of the Gospel has something to do with providing teaching for Christian disciples – is a start, but hardly ground-breaking.

What, then, is it that unites the whole book and gives it one overarching, controlling purpose? We have already seen that Matthew has structured his Gospel around the person of Jesus; in particular, Jesus as teacher. Even from the brief overview above, we have also begun to see that:

- He came to fulfil the Law and the Prophets;
- He came like light into a world under the shadow of death – bringing salvation to sinners by dying as sin-bearer under the curse of God;
- He came to do this before the End of all things – before the Judgment of the world and the final restoration of the cosmos in the kingdom of the heavens;
- He came to call people to follow him as his disciples;
- And he came to send them to make disciples in all nations.

We might then begin to conclude that the overarching purpose of Matthew's Gospel is to make disciples of Jesus, who are in turn disciple-makers.

This is very much a short-form summary of Matthew's purpose. It leaves much of the detail to be expanded. To become a disciple of Jesus, for example, means acknowledging all sorts of radical truths about the course of history, about the coming kingdom and about the person of

---

[26] The one possible exception to this is the partial destruction of the Temple in Jerusalem in AD 70, but we shall deal with this in the more detailed commentary later on.

[27] France, *Matthew: Evangelist and Teacher*, 251–60.

Jesus. We shall uncover plenty more detail in the commentary below. But as a rough guide, it helps to give a clear focus to the main thing the Gospel is about. Its purpose is to make disciples of Jesus who are in turn disciple-makers.

My claim is that this was Matthew's pastoral intention for his very first readers and hearers, whom I take to be (as discussed above) in large part fellow Greek-speaking Jewish people. His intent was to present them with Jesus. And his desire was that they would become disciples of Jesus, responsive to news of the kingdom and shaped and transformed by his teaching. That is, transformed individually and corporately to live in the light of the coming kingdom of the heavens, persevering to the End.

But the climax of Jesus's teaching was a command to go and make disciples in all nations. It was Matthew's intention right from the beginning that the influence of his Gospel would be ever-expanding, crossing the boundary from Jew to Gentile, making disciples in every generation – who in turn become disciple-makers. So the basic purpose of the Gospel for these later generations of readers remains the same: to make disciples of Jesus who are in turn disciple-makers.

To make disciples of Jesus

Before we look more closely at the detail of the Gospel, it's worth pausing to say a little more by way of introduction and overview on the two component parts of this basic purpose, beginning with Matthew's concern to make those who are not disciples of Jesus into disciples of Jesus.

Like the other Gospels, Matthew's Gospel functions to create disciples by bringing its readers and hearers into a close personal encounter with Jesus himself. As we become immersed in the Gospel narratives, it is as if we are back there in the first century, amazed by the words and deeds of Jesus, hearing his proclamation of the gospel of the kingdom, having to respond one way or another to his call to come to him and follow.

Background   **Body**

1–2 Jesus comes to fulfil the Law and the Prophets

3:1–4:11 Jesus is commissioned by his Father, with a mandate to complete *before* the judgment

4:12–10:42 Jesus proclaims the nearness of the kingdom in word and deed

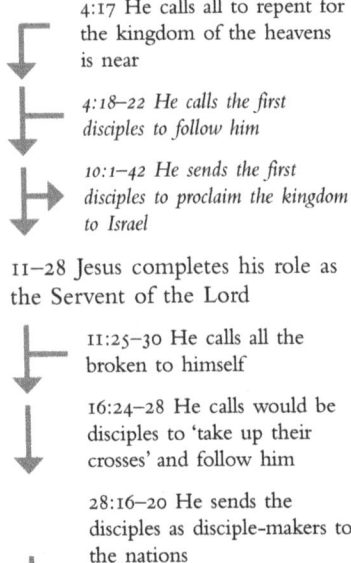

4:17 He calls all to repent for the kingdom of the heavens is near

4:18–22 He calls the first disciples to follow him

10:1–42 He sends the first disciples to proclaim the kingdom to Israel

11–28 Jesus completes his role as the Servent of the Lord

11:25–30 He calls all the broken to himself

16:24–28 He calls would be disciples to 'take up their crosses' and follow him

28:16–20 He sends the disciples as disciple-makers to the nations

Figure 3

Each of the Gospels does this in a different way. In Matthew's Gospel, there is a clear order and process whereby a reader or hearer is drawn to become a disciple of Jesus. The diagram above outlines how this fits into the structure. Some of the steps are quite specifically focused on particular disciples at the time (indicated by text in italics). They set a pattern – which we can expect to be repeated in some way – but first they concern named disciples: for instance, the first four disciples (4:18–22), and then the Twelve (Matthew 10). Some, on the other hand, have a broader target. There are four calls or commands with a much wider scope to them, placed at significant moments in the Gospel account and forming a sequence. They are:

Repent, for the kingdom of [the heavens] has come near. (4:17, repeating 3:2)

Come to me, all you who are weary and burdened, and I will give you rest. Take my yoke upon you and learn from me, for I am gentle and humble in heart, and you will find rest for your souls. For my yoke is easy and my burden is light. (11:28–30)

Whoever wants to be my disciple must deny themselves and take up their cross and follow me. (16:24)

Therefore go and make disciples of all nations, baptising them in the name of the Father and of the Son and of the Holy Spirit, and teaching them to obey everything I have commanded you. And surely I am with you always, to the very end of the age. (28:19–20)

The last of these looks at first glance like it is directed specifically to the Eleven. But Matthew has generalised the command by deliberately calling them disciples in 28:16. Disciples are being called to make disciples, who will be commanded to make disciples, and so on. As Peter O'Brien puts it, 'the Eleven are to make men and women as they themselves are'.[28]

We shall look at these in context in the detailed commentary below. Here, it is just worth noting the progression in the sequence. Matthew begins with a very broad and general call to respond to the nearness of the kingdom (4:17). This becomes much more personal and Jesus-centred when Jesus calls the weary and burdened to himself (11:28–30). By 16:24, it is clear that discipleship cannot be a merely passive alignment with Jesus, but must involve actively following in Jesus's footsteps. And in 28:19–20, disciples are called to join and participate in the global task of disciple-making.

Matthew is clearly not interested in making half-hearted 'disciples': unconvinced and unconvincing, conflicted in their devotion to the Father, cowardly in proclamation, full of doubt and little faith, uncaring and unforgiving, lacking perseverance, passive and unengaged when it comes to service and mission.

---

[28] Peter O'Brien, 'The Great Commission of Matthew 28:18–20: A Missionary Mandate or Not?', *Reformed Theological Review* 35 (1976): 73–4.

To make disciples who are disciple-makers

So, like the other Gospels, Matthew brings us into a close encounter with the real Jesus and calls us to follow him. But what makes Matthew's Gospel distinct and unique is its focused ending:

> Therefore go and make disciples of all nations, baptising them in the name of the Father and of the Son and of the Holy Spirit, and teaching them to obey everything I have commanded you. And surely I am with you always, to the very end of the age.

It is clear that the kind of disciples Jesus wants to make are those who go on to be disciple-makers. But is there more we can say about the kind of disciple Jesus wants to make? Similarly, is there more we can say on in what way, and how, they should be disciple-makers? Jesus seems to teach on both these subjects. Indeed, he seems to do so at length in the other distinctive feature of Matthew's Gospel: the long blocks of teaching from Jesus in chapters 5–7, 10, 13, 18 and 24–5.

But how should we process Jesus's teaching?

The difficulty we face as we process this material is that, chronologically, Jesus is speaking well after the teaching of the prophets (and the giving of the Law), but before his own death and resurrection. Should we then classify what he says alongside Old Testament ethical teaching, or alongside the teaching of the New Testament epistles? Or does it fall into a category of its own, such that it is now of merely historical interest? It was quite common in the late nineteenth and twentieth centuries, for example, for scholars to classify Jesus's teaching as an 'interim ethic' – one that applied to the disciples before Jesus's death and resurrection, but not after.[29] Is this teaching intended for our ears, or not?

Take Jesus's teaching to his disciples in 16:24 – 'Whoever wants to be my disciple must deny themselves and take up their cross and follow me.' Most contemporary readers of Matthew don't hesitate to take this as an enduring call to sacrificial and costly discipleship in the pattern of Jesus. But not all. A little while ago, I came across someone preaching this as a deliberately impossible literal demand to be crucified alongside Jesus for

---

[29] This was the view of the liberal German scholar Johannes Weiss (1863–1914), for example.

our salvation. The function of the teaching is then ultimately to show us we cannot 'pick up our cross'. He has to do it for us.

Some have adopted a similar approach to teaching the Sermon on the Mount (Matthew 5–7). Jesus, it is claimed, sets an ethical standard for his disciples that is deliberately impossible. Hence the 'greater righteousness' in 5:20: 'For I tell you that unless your righteousness surpasses that of the Pharisees and the teachers of the law, you will certainly not enter the kingdom of heaven.' Hence the extraordinary demand in 5:48: 'Be perfect, therefore, as your heavenly Father is perfect.' The main function of the Sermon, in this view, is to convict us of our inability to achieve sufficient righteousness and perfection to enter the kingdom.

I would want to agree wholeheartedly that Matthew presents Jesus as taking on something utterly unique. When Jesus himself 'takes up his cross', he is the Servant of the Lord taking on the role of curse-bearer for his people. Matthew presents him clearly as such as he dies. He then shows Jesus as the Son of Man vindicated in his resurrection. This is a vindication won and achieved by Jesus alone, on behalf of his disciples, which he then draws them into, saving them from their sins. The disciples made precisely zero contribution to any of this. They were profoundly unable to do so. Likewise any other reader, no matter how hard they work on their behaviour.

But despite the fact that, chronologically, Jesus's teaching in the Gospel is given mostly before the events of his death and resurrection, this unique work of Jesus is presupposed in his teaching, such that it really is intended to be applied to post-resurrection disciples. The clearest indication of this is in the Great Commission itself, the last part of which is a call by Jesus for the Eleven to teach the disciples they are making 'to obey everything I have commanded you'. Where do we find what he has commanded them? We turn back in the Gospel to Jesus's teaching. As Peter O'Brien puts it, 'Jesus is the authoritative Lord whose commands are to be kept, the content of which may be discerned from the rest of the Gospel'.[30] The things Jesus taught them, they are to pass on and teach as they make new disciples. Likewise, Terence Donaldson, who argues from the Great Commission that Matthew's readers are invited to learn alongside the disciples in the Gospel, 'joining with them as they listen to Jesus's teaching'.[31]

---

[30] O'Brien, 'The Great Commission', 77.
[31] Terence L. Donaldson, 'Guiding Readers – Making Disciples: Discipleship in

The internal evidence of the teaching itself also strongly implies that the unique work of Jesus in his death and resurrection is presupposed – even though the teaching is given before the event. When Jesus says, 'Whoever wants to be my disciple must deny themselves and take up their cross and follow me' (16:24; compare 10:38), it makes most sense to take this as a command for a post-resurrection context. It really cannot make much sense at the time. Why is Jesus talking about the cross? Crucifixion was an extreme form of execution designed by the Romans to extract maximum public shame, and was not usually mentioned in polite conversation. At this stage, Jesus hasn't even told his disciples this is how he is going to die. Only after his death on a cross (and his subsequent resurrection) would this start to make any sense. Jesus also says here his disciples must take up their crosses 'and follow me' – again, presupposing that Jesus has already taken up his cross and died for them.

Likewise, it is presupposed throughout the Sermon on the Mount that Jesus is directing his teaching at people who are already of the kingdom. In the Beatitudes (5:3–12), Jesus describes people who already in some sense possess the kingdom of the heavens (5:3, 10). That is, people who already have a real, deep, dependent relationship with their Father in the heavens – who can be taught to pray to him daily (6:9–13) and who can ask him for anything as their Father and expect the most loving of responses (7:7–11). And I don't think it could be clearer that Jesus expects what he commands to be actually taught (5:19) and expects what he has said to be not just heard but also put into practice (7:24–7).

Now it may well be that 'righteous' works done by Jesus's disciples in response to his teaching (which, as we shall see, in Matthew basically means works that align with the will of the Father) will serve on the Day of Judgment as evidence of their relationship through him with the Father. Jesus expects his disciples to be accumulating such evidence in a way that the Pharisees and Scribes cannot (because they have no such relationship). Hence 5:20 and the expectation of a greater righteousness. On the last day, to those without such evidence, Jesus will say, 'I never knew you' (7:23). That is, for such people there never was any relationship. But this emphatically is not the same as saying that such works formed or constituted the relationship in the first place – or that

---

Matthew's Narrative Strategy', in *Patterns of Discipleship in the New Testament*, ed. Richard N. Longenecker (Grand Rapids: Eerdmans, 1996), 41

such works earn someone the right to enter the kingdom. We shall see that in the Sermon on the Mount these works serve a different purpose altogether: a missionary purpose, to spread the light of the Father's glory in the world (5:16).

So the default answer to the question 'Does Jesus's teaching apply to a post-resurrection disciple today?' is basically, 'Yes.' Having said this, as with all ethical teaching given in a particular situation, we may have to factor in some of the changes between that situation and its point of application today. Jesus's teaching may not disappear down some theological black hole as a result of his death and resurrection, but there may be some changes in circumstances to ponder. For example, in 5:23–4 Jesus addresses the case of someone offering a gift at the altar and remembering some wrong they have done, and in 17:24–7 he suggests his disciples should pay the Temple tax. We know that by the end of the Gospel the Temple has been rendered useless (27:51), and within a generation it ceases to operate altogether. So we don't apply this teaching directly – just the principles it embodies.

Matthew 10 presents another very particular situation. We know that by the end of the Gospel the mission Jesus sends his disciples on will have expanded from just Israel to all the nations. So this teaching doesn't apply to a post-resurrection setting directly (even if, again, the principles are intended to apply). Hence we can expect some of the details in 10:5–15 to be peculiar to mission to fellow Israelites.

The purpose of Jesus's teaching

The upshot of this discussion is that I shall take Jesus's teaching in the Gospel as intended for post-resurrection readers, including us today. It serves a key purpose in making and forming authentic disciples. And it serves a further purpose in shaping those disciples as disciple-makers.

Jesus's teaching is spread throughout the Gospel, but is most especially concentrated in the five main speeches found in (roughly) chapters 5–7, 10, 13, 18 and 24–5. These fit into the structure of the Gospel as in the diagram below:

Background	**Body**
1–2 Jesus comes to fulfil the Law and the Prophets	3:1–4:11 Jesus is commissioned by his Father, with a mandate to complete *before* the judgment
	4:12–10:42 Jesus proclaims the nearness of the kingdom in word and deed

 5–7 Teaching on mission foundations (Sermon on the Mount)

 10:1–42 Teaching on proclaiming the kingdom

11–28 Jesus completes his role as the Servant of the Lord

 13 Teaching on a kingdom perspectivce in mission

 18 Teaching on community care, discipline and forgiveness

 24–5 Teaching on perserverance to the end

Figure 4

We have already seen that the Great Commission at the end of the Gospel encourages us to go back and read the Gospel again. The task of 'making disciples' has two components to it, the second of which is:

> . . . teaching them to obey everything I have commanded you. (Matthew 28:20a)

This points us to look again at what Jesus taught and commanded the first disciples – and most especially points us back to the five main speeches. These will build new disciples in authentic discipleship in all sorts of ways, not least of which will be building them as disciple-makers:

- Matthew 5–7 (the Sermon on the Mount) sets the foundations. Jesus encourages his disciples to have deep trust in their heavenly Father and the reality of the coming kingdom, such a deep trust that this is visible in radical new behaviour (5:21–48). This brings glory to the Father (5:16), proclaims the reality of the kingdom and makes

28

it compelling and attractive to those on the outside. This display of light to the world is undergirded by a prayerful, exclusive, authentic relationship with their Father (6:1–7:11). Realising that the Sermon on the Mount has this missionary focus and purpose transforms what would otherwise be a very confusing or discouraging text into something much more positive.

- Matthew 10 teaches and motivates the disciple-making disciple to proclaim the kingdom in the face of persecution.
- Matthew 13 encourages the disciple to remain confident in the kingdom despite appearances. This is most especially as the 'word of the kingdom' (which makes disciples) is sown with apparently mixed results.
- Matthew 18 (together with the other teaching in 16:13–20:34) teaches that discipleship (and disciple-making) takes place in a community – one that should be characterised by humility, care, discipline and forgiveness.
- Matthew 24–5 teaches and motivates the disciple to persevere through tribulation to the end, with vigilance and diligence. By the end of the Gospel, we know that a primary aspect of this diligence is to be in the task of disciple-making.

In the scholarly debate on the genre of the Gospels (what kind of literature they are), the most common view is that they are in many ways similar to ancient biography, or *bios*. As Richard Burridge explains, this 'is a type of writing which occurs naturally among groups of people who have formed around a certain charismatic teacher or leader, seeking to follow after him'.[32] Ancient biography was much looser than modern biography – less systematic, precise or comprehensive. A *bios* of a famous philosopher, such as Socrates for example, might include various random anecdotes showcasing his teaching, and may even include an extended account of his death as a way to disclose his full character. All of this was intended to promote aspects of the teaching of the dead philosopher for a new generation.

These may be the closest points of comparison to the Gospels in the ancient world, but the differences are also quite stark. The Gospels are much more tightly composed and arranged. The intent is to bring the reader to follow the teaching of Jesus in every respect. And not just his

---

[32] Richard A. Burridge, *What Are the Gospels? A Comparison with Graeco-Roman Biography* (Second edition; Grand Rapids: Eerdmans, 2004), 76.

teaching, but also to follow him – the extraordinary claim of a Gospel being that the Teacher is not dead! (And that he is much more than a teacher.) But in the case of Matthew's Gospel, we can go further still. The narrative and teaching are also training and equipping the disciple for the specific task of disciple-making. The extended teaching material makes Matthew's Gospel what we might call a missionary training narrative.

In this, narrative sections and the pure teaching sections work together. The narrative draws readers in to become disciples, and Jesus's teaching functions to form and grow them. The teaching also equips them to be disciple-makers. And the narrative plus teaching then becomes a primary tool for disciple-makers. As disciple-makers teach the Gospel to others, those who are not yet disciples of Jesus will hear his call to rethink everything about the world and themselves, challenged and convicted by the nearness of the kingdom of the heavens. They will hear his gentle appeal to come to him and have the burden of living as sinners under the shadow of death lifted from them. They will hear his challenge to deny themselves, take up their crosses and follow him – a call to an authentic discipleship of sacrificial service. And they will hear his commission: to go and make further disciples. They will concurrently become responsive to Jesus's teaching, growing in depth as disciples, equipped as disciple-makers. And so on, to the end of the age.

If we come across disciples of Jesus who are indistinguishable from those in the world around them – lethargic, conflicted, prayerless, passive, flaky, proud, careless, self-promoting, unforgiving, demotivated or unengaged with evangelism and mission – one reason might be that they haven't been taught (or have been mistaught) this amazing God-given missionary training resource.

From text to purpose

As previously mentioned, this commentary is written from an unashamedly Christian point of view. I take Matthew's Gospel to be part of Holy Scripture; that through this ancient text, God, by means of his Spirit, is speaking, present tense, to the churches.

If it is true that this is ultimately God speaking (through Matthew), then he has reasons, intentions and purposes for the readers of the Gospel. I have argued that because this is a New Testament text, and because it is a text with an unspecified, unbounded audience, we can take God's wider purposes for this Gospel to be closely aligned with Matthew's purposes as he composed and wrote it. We just need to consider the fact that Matthew knew and understood his very first readers much better than any future potential readers. In other words, to understand Matthew, it will help to put ourselves in first-century sandals. And perhaps, as I suggested above, to imagine ourselves as Greek-speaking people living somewhere like the city of Antioch. It makes more sense to suppose that Matthew had someone like this in mind, rather than, say, a Brazilian disciple from the sixteenth century (or from any other place or time in history – past, present or future). This is even though he wrote in the expectation that many future, foreign readers would be discipled by Jesus's teaching (as 28:16–20 implies).

We have already addressed in sketch form above the overall purpose of Matthew's Gospel. The overarching purpose is to make disciples who are disciple-makers. The aim of the section-by-section commentary below is to show how each section of the Gospel makes its individual contribution to this overall purpose. Since the purpose is in part to make disciples, I shall also be aiming to summarise what we should be learning as disciples from each section.

The commentary is written to outline the steps I conclude Matthew wants us as readers to go through as we process his text – either as potential disciples or disciples looking to learn and grow. In other words, I want to sit alongside you as you read, study and reflect – pointing out various features in the text and encouraging you to ask what Matthew wants us to infer from them. I want to help you sit alongside the first readers of the Gospel, and the first disciples as they listened to Jesus himself, as we put ourselves in first-century sandals, so we can understand clearly what's being said. And we want to see not just what Matthew has done in composing and constructing the Gospel, but also why he has done so. This commentary will differ from other approaches by asking the 'why?' questions much earlier and much more often. This is under the conviction that only then – as we grapple to discern God's living and active intentions through Matthew – will we grasp the full richness of the Gospel.

4. Theology

I have talked already about how reading Matthew from the point of view of Christian faith, in the wider context of the biblical canon, can and should affect our understanding of the claims Matthew makes. Any claims Matthew might make – historical or theological, explicit or implicit – will not contradict similar claims elsewhere in the New Testament. If we do find an apparent contradiction, then our default position will be that the problem is with us as readers: that we have misunderstood something somewhere.

This is not (or shouldn't be) a question of massaging our reading of the text until it conforms with what we already thought. It is rather a question of taking the courtesy we should already show towards Matthew and extending it to include the rest of the New Testament. We read each part of Matthew in the light of the other parts of Matthew. Now we extend this to read each part of Matthew alongside a wider set of texts (while acknowledging differences in authorship, genre and circumstance).

If we do this, then our understanding of theological issues and concepts should no longer be stubbornly stuck at some fixed point, but rather open to correction and fine tuning as we listen to Matthew's distinctive voice and contribution. If done carefully, we have nothing to fear from doing this. If our convictions are that all true theology comes from the Bible, then this approach will not lead us away from the truth, only closer towards it. This is how theology should be done. Not with a fixed and immovable standard that restricts, obscures or distorts Matthew's voice. But inductively: with convictions that are both strong and flexible, responsive to what Matthew has to say.

Reading Matthew theologically

In the detailed commentary in Part 2, I shall pause from time to time to reflect on Matthew's contribution to an area of doctrine or a doctrinal discussion. For example, this could be taking a commonly understood doctrinal concept, such as 'repentance', and then seeing how Matthew actually uses the language associated with this concept in a given context. It is relatively unusual to do this in a commentary.[33] The tendency is to stick within one book without much reference to the wider biblical context. We might find comments on what Matthew thinks, but very rarely is this discussed in relation to what, say, the apostle Paul thinks. Frequently, the working assumption seems to be that Matthew has little to say on certain topics – on the atonement, for example (something we shall find is very far from the truth). In this commentary, I won't shy away

---

[33] It is more common to treat Matthew's theology separately, as in Terence L. Donaldson, *Jesus on the Mountain: A Study in Matthean Theology* (Sheffield: JSOT, 1985); Ulrich Luz, *The Theology of the Gospel of Matthew* (Cambridge: Cambridge University Press, 1995); or Mark Allan Powell, *God with Us: A Pastoral Theology of Matthew's Gospel* (Minneapolis: Fortress Press, 1995). There is little attempt in these books to integrate Matthew's theology with the rest of the New Testament.

from theological reflection. I have suffered too often the frustration of wanting to know what Matthew says in connection with some doctrinal issue and then turning to the commentaries only to find it hasn't even been addressed, let alone been given a satisfactory treatment. The further frustration is that theologians throughout Christian history have indeed frequently engaged with Matthew's Gospel and these contributions are also not well represented in modern commentaries.

The topics in Part 2 will be addressed as they come up and as they are suggested by the unfolding of the Gospel. This will keep any discussion controlled by context and narrative development. There are a few useful things to say in advance, however, by way of preview and introduction. Roughly, these relate to the areas of Christology, eschatology and discipleship.

Christology

There is much to say about Christology (the doctrine of the identity of Jesus) in Matthew. Most of this is communicated through the unfolding of his narrative, and we shall be seeing how this works in the commentary below. It will be helpful, however, to say a little here about the overall shape of Matthew's presentation. For one thing, it is quite different from the approach taken by John in his Gospel. John begins at the beginning of all things, with the divine Word (John 1:1–2) and at the Creation (John 1:3), and then tells us that 'the Word became flesh and made his dwelling among us' (John 1:14). This incarnate Word is then identified as 'the one and only Son' (1:14, 18), who is Jesus Christ (1:17–18). In other words, it is explicit in John's Gospel right from the beginning that Jesus is both 'flesh' (that is, fully human) and fully God – fully part of the divine identity.

Matthew's presentation (and similar things could be said of Mark and Luke) that Jesus is fully part of the divine identity is more gradual. He begins with Jesus as the Messiah, the son of David (1:1). That is, he begins with Jesus as the promised human descendant of David, called Messiah, who will save and rescue God's people, leading them to victory. As we shall see, only as the narrative unfolds do we get a gradual unveiling of the divine identity of Jesus. From the beginning we get suggestions, hints, implications that Jesus is much more than a merely human king like David. Only at the end do we see the identity fully revealed, as Jesus is given full, divine authority over heaven and earth (28:18).

Part of this presentation of the identity of Jesus is through the titles Matthew gives him and shows Jesus giving himself. We shall be seeing how these work in context later, but it's worth stepping back briefly here to get something of an overview. There are broadly three groups of titles used of Jesus and one strong association to a title, each with its own background in the Old Testament.

The first group relates to the title 'Christ' or 'Messiah' that Matthew gives Jesus in 1:1. It is used of Jesus just fourteen times in the Gospel (and never directly by himself). 'Christ' is Greek for 'Anointed One', and in the context of the genealogy of 1:1–17 this is a reference back to the anointed kings of Israel. (The 2011 NIV translation of Matthew prefers the Hebrew title 'Messiah' to the Greek title 'Christ', partly for this reason, and I shall follow its practice in what follows.) Most especially, Matthew links Jesus to King David. Jesus is born of Mary, wife of Joseph, son of David. This suggests Jesus is the fulfilment of the Lord God's promises in, for example, 2 Samuel 7:1–17, where David is promised a descendant whose kingdom will be established for ever (2 Samuel 7:13).

This group includes the title or designation 'Son'. The voice from the heavens in Matthew 3:17 says of Jesus, 'This is my Son . . .' – a strong allusion to Psalm 2:7, where the 'son' is also the Messiah, the king anointed by the Lord who will crush his enemies and inherit the nations. 'Son' is also one of the ways the Lord God talks about his people, the nation of Israel, in the Old Testament (Exodus 4:22; Hosea 11:1 (quoted by Matthew in 2:15)).

First and foremost, then, the titles 'Messiah', 'Son' and even 'Son of God' are human titles.[34] But we shall quickly see in Matthew's unfolding narrative that for Jesus to be 'son' is more than merely being a human king like David, or merely representing God's people. There is a unique, individual intimacy and closeness with his Father in the heavens that goes far beyond this. He is 'the Messiah, the Son of the living God' (16:16).

There is a similar ambiguity when people address Jesus as 'Lord'. The word in Greek is used of someone who is an owner, is a master or has some other kind of acknowledged authority.[35] But it is also the word used to translate the Hebrew name YHWH in the Greek version of the Old Testament, the name uniquely revealed to Israel by God to know him by.[36] For example, 'Lord' in Matthew 3:3, a quotation of Isaiah 40:3, is YHWH in the Hebrew text. Frequently, 'Lord' used to address Jesus in

---

[34] Compare Luke 3:38, where Adam is son of God.

[35] BDAG, 'kurios'.

[36] The name YHWH is typically displayed in most English translations of the Old Testament using small capitals: 'Lord'.

Matthew's Gospel could simply be a term of respect, like 'Sir' in English. Sometimes it is linked to the first group of titles above, as in 'Lord, son of David, have mercy' (Matthew 15:22; 20:30–31). But sometimes it very clearly suggests someone beyond mere human. In Matthew 3, John is preparing the way for the 'Lord' (3:3; YHWH in Isaiah 40:3); the one who appears is Jesus (3:17). In Matthew 12:8, Jesus is Lord of the Sabbath. When Peter cries out, 'Lord, save me!' in 14:30, he is echoing the appeal of the psalmists to YHWH in Psalms 116:4 and 118:25.

As we noted above, Matthew uses the title 'Messiah' relatively sparingly. This is perhaps because of potential misunderstanding – as we witness in 16:13–28, where Peter seems to think that to be the Messiah is incompatible with suffering and death. Jesus's preferred title for himself is 'Son of Man' (used some thirty times, beginning at 8:20). 'Son of Man' in the Hebrew Scriptures can just mean 'human' or 'human being' (as in Psalms 8:4; 80:17; 144:3 146:3, or extensively in Ezekiel, for example).[37] Hence some have argued that the title 'Son of Man' is never used by Jesus to explain who he is, just to refer to himself.[38] But Jesus's usage suggests he wants to allude to the shadowy human figure, the 'one like a son of man', in Daniel 7:13. This is most obvious in 26:64, where Jesus says, 'From now on you will see the Son of Man . . . coming on the clouds of heaven,' closely echoing the language of Daniel 7:13. In the partial interpretation of the vision in Daniel 7:15–27, he learns that the holy people of the Most High are being and will be crushed and devoured by the tyrannical kingdoms of the earth, represented in the vision by beasts from the sea. But in the end they will be vindicated (Daniel 7:26–7). The 'one like a son of man' in the vision represents these people – those who have come through the tribulation, finally vindicated by the Ancient of Days and given all authority and a kingdom that will never be destroyed. By coining the title 'Son of Man' for himself, Jesus indicates that he is taking on this role on behalf of God's people. More so than the title 'Messiah', it's a title that clearly shows that opposition, suffering and death are part of the package – while insisting that divine vindication and victory will be the final outcome. As R. T. France puts it, 'After his humiliation and

---

[37] Compare Richard Bauckham: 'The term "son of man" is not a title, a conventional expression, or a technical term. It is an ordinary way of saying "man" or "human" in Semitic languages.' Richard Bauckham, *'Son of Man', Volume 1: Early Jewish Literature* (Grand Rapids: Eerdmans, 2023), 109.

[38] For example, Kingsbury, *Matthew: Structure, Christology, Kingdom*, 114–17.

suffering, Jesus will receive from his Father the vindication, enthrone-
ment, glory and judgment which are given to "one like a son of man"
in Daniel 7.'[39]

While 'Son of Man' first and foremost suggests someone human, Jesus
also (as with the other titles above) suggests that for him it means much
more. The Son of Man has authority on earth to forgive sins (9:6). The
Son of Man is Lord of the Sabbath (12:8). In 26:62–66, the high priest
takes Jesus's claim to be the Son of Man (and 'Lord' of Psalm 110:1) as
blasphemy.

The role of 'Son of Man' is closely related to the fourth way Matthew
wants to portray Jesus in his Gospel. This is not so much a title used
of Jesus. But what we do find across the Gospel is a sequence of Old
Testament quotations and allusions where Matthew is encouraging us to
connect Jesus to the Servant figure of Isaiah 40–55. The direct quotations
from the Servant songs are in 8:17 (quoting Isaiah 53:4) and 12:18–21
(quoting Isaiah 42:1–4). But the voice from heaven in 3:17 and 17:5 also
picks up some of Isaiah 42:1, suggesting the Father is commending Jesus
in our hearing for taking on the Servant role. This is the point in the
plot of Matthew where, as Terence Donaldson argues, Jesus is taking on
a mandate from his Father as God's Son, but it becomes clear that this
will involve fulfilling the role of Isaiah's Servant.[40] There are other, broader
allusions. Matthew presents Jesus dying on the cross under the curse of
God as sin-bearer, fulfilling the Servant's role as sin-bearer in Isaiah 53:12.
But the Servant in Isaiah is not just sin-bearer for God's people. He is also
to be a light for the nations (Isaiah 42:6), taking God's salvation to the
ends of the earth (Isaiah 49:6). This is a role Jesus draws his disciples to
participate in, as he hints at in 5:14 ('You are the light of the world') and
makes explicit in 28:19 ('Therefore go and make disciples of all nations').

Eschatology

Matthew also has much to teach us about eschatology: the doctrine of
the last things in earthly history. As with his Christology, this is largely
taught through the unfolding narrative.[41] But one thing is very obvious

---

[39] France, *Matthew: Evangelist and Teacher*, 292.

[40] Terence L. Donaldson, 'The Vindicated Son: A Narrative Approach to Matthean
Christology', in *Contours of Christology in the New Testament*, ed. Richard N.
Longenecker (Grand Rapids: Eerdmans, 2005).

[41] As explored in Ben Cooper, 'Adaptive Eschatological Inference from the Gospel
of Matthew', *Journal for the Study of the New Testament* 33, no. 1 (2010).

right from the beginning of the Gospel, and that is the importance of the proclamation of the nearness of the kingdom of the heavens. The term 'kingdom of the heavens' comes some thirty-two times in Matthew's Gospel. What is this 'kingdom' – first referred to by John the Baptist (3:2) and then taken up in the proclamation of Jesus from 4:17?

This is a question where we may be coming to Matthew's Gospel with some presupposed ideas. There's not the space here to go through all the different possibilities and suggestions that have been made. In short, I shall be agreeing with Jonathan T. Pennington in the commentary that the term 'kingdom of the heavens' is not merely a way of talking about the rule or reign of God (as in, for example, Psalm 145:11).[42] That is, it is not identical to the term 'kingdom of God'. Matthew is happy to use 'kingdom of God' – and does so on four occasions (12:28; 19:24; 21:31, 43). In these cases, we *can* argue that Matthew is wanting to talk about the present experience of the rule of God. God does reign now. Similarly, as we have declared in Matthew 28:18, Christ does reign now. But when Matthew uses 'kingdom of the heavens' he is referring to something at least slightly different, and quite specific. The *heavens* (plural) in Matthew refer not to God himself, but to the realm of God above – a spatial idea. (Sadly, the plural gets lost in our English translations, so we can easily miss its significance.) The kingdom of the heavens, then, seems to be referring to a future reality where the kingdom established in the heavens comes down from the heavens, and so heaven and earth are reunited in one unified realm.[43] This is what Jesus teaches his disciples to pray for in the Lord's Prayer:

> Our Father in [the heavens],
> hallowed be your name,
> your kingdom come,
> your will be done,
>   on earth as it is in heaven.
>   (Matthew 6:9–10)

This kingdom will come from heaven. As Pennington concludes, 'it is not like earthly kingdoms, stands over against them, and will eschatologically replace them (on earth)'.[44] It is not so much about God's rule now, but

---

[42] Pennington, *Heaven and Earth*, 281–5.

[43] Which is also Paul's understanding of the future: that God's purpose is 'to bring unity to all things in heaven and on earth under Christ' (Ephesians 1:10).

[44] Pennington, *Heaven and Earth*, 321.

about something to be established by God, as promised (for example) in 2 Samuel 7. And it will ultimately replace every false and tyrannical kingdom on earth, as in the interpretation of Nebuchadnezzar's dream in Daniel 2:44–5 and in Daniel's own vision and its interpretation in Daniel 7:13–14, 26–7. Now that all authority in heaven and on earth has been given to Jesus (28:18), this kingdom is closer than ever. When the kingdom fully comes, it will be nothing less than a new heaven and a new earth.

Discipleship

The proclamation of the kingdom of the heavens provides the context within which Jesus calls people to come and follow him. The calling of Simon Peter, Andrew, James and John in 4:18–22 immediately follows the proclamation of the nearness of the kingdom in 4:17. These four plus others Matthew calls 'disciples' for the first time in 5:1.

The word 'disciple' simply means someone who learns from another, in distinction from the teacher who instructs them. In 5:1–2, the disciples come to Jesus and he begins to teach them. In 10:24, Jesus teaches the Twelve, saying 'The student is not above the teacher.' (The 2011 NIV has 'student' here, but the word is 'disciple'.)

It will also be clear from the detail of the Gospel that to be a disciple of Jesus means more than being just a good student, pupil or apprentice. In the same verses that talk of Jesus as teacher and the Twelve as disciples, he is also 'master' and they are 'bond-servants' (10:24–5). As we've already seen, being a disciple of Jesus will involve taking up one's cross and following him (16:24) – equivalent to 'losing one's life' (16:25). Indeed, we'll see that Matthew's portrayal of the wider concept of discipleship will encompass much more than those moments where he chooses to employ the word 'disciple'.

A key feature of Matthew's presentation is worth flagging up in advance. As I have already suggested, Matthew's portrayal of discipleship is very closely linked to his Christology. What Jesus does, the disciples are to do (10:7–8, 24–5). But this is more than mere imitation. The disciples participate in what Jesus is doing – and continues to do – incorporated into the role he has taken on.[45] Jesus is Isaiah's Servant of the Lord, a light for the nations (Isaiah 42:6), taking God's salvation to the ends of the earth (Isaiah 49:6). Jesus draws the disciples in to participate in this,

---

[45] As argued at greater length in Ben Cooper, *Incorporated Servanthood: Commitment and Discipleship in the Gospel of Matthew* (London: Bloomsbury T&T Clark, 2013).

as he hints at in 5:14 ('You are the light of the world') and as he makes explicit in 28:19–20 ('Therefore go and make disciples of all nations . . . And surely I am with you always, to the very end of the age').

Having 'ears to hear'

Finally, before turning to the more detailed commentary in Part 2, I do want to acknowledge that understanding the Gospels and teaching them to others is not at all straightforward. We can find it pretty hard work. The temptation when we are a bit stuck or confused (and no doubt hard pressed in other ways) is to take an apparently low-risk approach and simply repeat what we have heard someone else say. The danger is that we then perpetuate something that really isn't there in the text, and miss out on some of the riches that are.

So we need to read a little more slowly and carefully, ready to be challenged or surprised. Here is a brief taster of some of the potential surprises we shall encounter as we work though the Gospel:

- When John and Jesus proclaim the general command, 'Repent, for the kingdom of heaven has come near' (3:2; 4:17), they are not calling the people to turn their lives around. Not first and foremost, anyway.
- The 'kingdom of heaven' (or, better, 'the kingdom of the heavens'), as I have already hinted, does not refer to something that can grow – even in Matthew 13:31–2. If you were somehow able to talk to Matthew about 'growing the kingdom' or 'expanding the kingdom' or 'kingdom growth', he would give you a very puzzled look.
- The Beatitudes (5:3–12) are not blessings.
- Most of us are clear that when Jesus calls his disciples 'the salt of the earth' (5:13), he doesn't mean what the phrase has come to mean in common English usage – that is, the common folk, the ordinary people, etc. But we should also be clear that what he does mean has very little to do with politics or social action – with Christians being some kind of salt-like preservative in non-Christian society.
- There is much in Matthew's Gospel about the reality of future judgment and the awfulness of hell. But this is never presented as a choice between 'heaven and hell'. On the other hand, there is much in the Gospel about a different pairing: the contrast between 'heaven and earth'.
- The man building on the rock (7:24) does not represent someone

building their life on Jesus's. (At least, it's a bit more specific than that.)

- Jesus does not instruct his disciples to ask the Lord of the harvest to raise up leaders for the harvest field (9:38). When Christians pray for God to raise up leaders (or paid or full-time workers) for the harvest, they are not accurately echoing Jesus's words.
- There is more than one reason why Jesus speaks in parables (Matthew 13).
- There is nothing very triumphant about Jesus entering Jerusalem (21:1–11). And when he goes to the Temple (21:12–17), he doesn't cleanse it.
- In his speech in Matthew 24, the fate of the Temple isn't the focus of Jesus's attention. He really doesn't want us to be distracted by the physical destruction of the Temple that took place in AD 70.
- Matthew does not include Barabbas as a character in his account of Pilate before the crowd (27:15–26) to teach us about penal substitutionary atonement.
- When Matthew describes Jesus crying out, 'My God, my God, why have you forsaken me?' shortly before he dies (27:46, the 'cry of dereliction'), he is by no means implying that at that moment (or at any other moment) the Trinity was torn asunder.
- When Matthew describes the tearing in two of the curtain of the Temple from top to bottom (27:51), he is not using this to symbolise a new access to God.

Indeed, if we have ears to hear and eyes to see, then we shall find Matthew's theology of the atonement in chapters 26–28 of his Gospel (which, yes, does encompass and strongly affirm the doctrine of penal substitutionary atonement) so wonderfully rich and comprehensive that there is really no need to flail around desperately searching for verses on which to hook a theology of the atonement imported from elsewhere.

We could say something similar of Matthew's Gospel as a whole. The preacher or teacher of Matthew's Gospel is very much like the teacher of the law made a disciple for the kingdom of the heavens in 13:52 – like the owner of a house bringing out of his storeroom great treasures, new as well as old. And my hope and prayer is that the preaching of Matthew's Gospel will more than ever be used by God to enrich communities of disciples in all the nations – making authentic disciples of Jesus who are disciple-makers for the kingdom.

PART TWO

....

THE BACKGROUND TO JESUS'S MINISTRY

MATTHEW 1–2

2

Jesus Comes to Fulfil the Scriptures

MATTHEW 1–2

In the structure of Matthew's Gospel, as we discussed above, the first two chapters set the background for the main account of Jesus.

1. History so far • Matthew 1:1–17

Matthew's genealogy of Jesus sets a departure point for the rest of his account. It puts everything that follows into context. Looking back, it connects his account of Jesus to the storyline of the Hebrew Scriptures. It reminds us of the background problem of unfulfilled promise and national failure. Looking forward, it will connect this storyline seamlessly into the rest of Matthew's narrative, pointing forward to where all these problems find their resolution and all the promises find their fulfilment, in 'Jesus who is called the Messiah' (verse 16).

The genealogy of Jesus the Messiah

1 This is the genealogy[a] of Jesus the Messiah[b] the son of David, the son of Abraham:

2 Abraham was the father of Isaac,
Isaac the father of Jacob,
Jacob the father of Judah and his brothers,
3 Judah the father of Perez and Zerah, whose mother was Tamar,
Perez the father of Hezron,
Hezron the father of Ram,
4 Ram the father of Amminadab,
Amminadab the father of Nahshon,
Nahshon the father of Salmon,
5 Salmon the father of Boaz, whose mother was Rahab,
Boaz the father of Obed, whose mother was Ruth,
Obed the father of Jesse,
6 and Jesse the father of King David.

David was the father of Solomon, whose mother had been Uriah's wife,
7 Solomon the father of Rehoboam,
Rehoboam the father of Abijah,
Abijah the father of Asa,

8 Asa the father of Jehoshaphat,
Jehoshaphat the father of
Jehoram,
Jehoram the father of Uzziah,
9 Uzziah the father of Jotham,
Jotham the father of Ahaz,
Ahaz the father of Hezekiah,
10 Hezekiah the father of
Manasseh,
Manasseh the father of Amon,
Amon the father of Josiah,
11 and Josiah the father of Jeco-
niah[c] and his brothers
at the time of the exile to
Babylon.

12 After the exile to Babylon:
Jeconiah was the father of
Shealtiel,
Shealtiel the father of
Zerubbabel,
13 Zerubbabel the father of Abihud,
Abihud the father of Eliakim,

Eliakim the father of Azor,
14 Azor the father of Zadok,
Zadok the father of Akim,
Akim the father of Elihud,
15 Elihud the father of Eleazar,
Eleazar the father of Matthan,
Matthan the father of Jacob,
16 and Jacob the father of Joseph,
the husband of Mary, and
Mary was the mother of
Jesus who is called the
Messiah.

17 Thus there were fourteen generations in all from Abraham to David,
fourteen from David to the exile to
Babylon, and fourteen from the exile
to the Messiah.

_____

a 1 Or *is an account of the origin*
b 1 Or *Jesus Christ. Messiah* (Hebrew) and
Christ (Greek) both mean *Anointed One;*
also in verse 18.
c 11 That is, Jehoiachin; also in verse 12

We might find this a strange way to introduce things! Why choose to begin with a genealogy? To begin with, genealogies connect real people (here: Jesus) to real people in past generations. In many cultures, genealogies or family trees establish an enduring family identity.[1] Within this, an individual's identity can also be established – where they 'come from', so to speak. Likewise here: Matthew is establishing for us the true identity of Jesus.[2]

_____

[1] Roland Bishop, 'In the Grand Scheme of Things: An Exploration of the Meaning of Genealogical Research', *Journal of Popular Culture* 41, no. 3 (2008). Kiem-Kiok Kwa comments, 'Just as Matthew starts his gospel with Jesus's ancestors and locates him in a family within time and space, so we all are part of extended biological families.' Samson Uytanlet and Kiem-Kiok Kwa, *Matthew: A Pastoral and Contextual Commentary* (Carlise: Langham Global Library, 2017), 42.
[2] Jane Tooher recounts the story of a man from the Balangao tribe in the northern Philippines in the 1960s who accepted that the Gospel of Matthew must be true when he was first shown it begins with a genealogy. Jane Tooher, 'Hearing the Old

We may go further: the genealogy describes a royal lineage. There is a repeated emphasis on King David throughout. Matthew strongly wants to make the point: Jesus is a 'son' of David (a descendent of David). This is part of his evidence that Jesus is the Messiah (verses 1 and 16–17). But Matthew is doing more than this. He is using the genealogy to remind us of some basic theology and some essential, foundational history.

Some of the theology is built into the nature of a genealogy. Genealogies are reminders that people die, but that someone's death is not the end of the story. A window of hope is left open in the next generation. Matthew seems to have in mind the great genealogies of the book of Genesis.[3] These make a similar point. When Adam sinned, death came into the world and his own death became certain. But in God's patient mercy, death did not come to Adam and Eve instantly. They lived long enough to have children, thus perpetuating life and hope into the future, even in the presence of death. This is what we see in the genealogy of Genesis 5, with its repeated refrain 'and then he died', for example. Some family lines from Adam led nowhere but to further curse and wickedness. Some of them led to new possibilities of blessing, most especially the line that passed through Abraham.

This line through Abraham is the line Matthew picks up here (1:2), as he begins to relate the history of God's people. He expects us to know from Genesis 12:1–3 that this line will build down the generations into a nation, finally spilling out in blessing to all the families of the earth. The genealogy is 'an outline of salvation history which traces the line of God's promise and the unfolding of his purposes'.[4] It is guaranteed to end in blessing for the world – but how? That is the history Matthew will begin to tell through the carefully chosen and arranged material in the rest of the genealogy, and will continue to tell in the rest of the Gospel.

The genealogy has a rhythm to it: Abraham was the father of Isaac, Isaac the father of Jacob . . . and so on. This is especially obvious when it is read out loud, as most people would have encountered it originally. But Matthew occasionally breaks the rhythm. He does it by mentioning extra men, like Judah's brothers in verse 2. And he does it by mentioning

---

Testament Women in Matthew's Genealogy: Tamar, Rahab, Ruth and the Wife of Uriah the Hittite', in *Listen to Him: Reading and Preaching Emmanuel in Matthew*, ed. Peter Bolt (London: Latimer, 2015), 120–21.

[3] Brown, *Birth of the Messiah*, 66.

[4] John Nolland, *The Gospel of Matthew: A Commentary on the Greek Text* (Grand Rapids: Eerdmans, 2005), 73.

significant women, like Tamar in verse 3. The convention in the ancient world was to present the male line of descent, so including women was highly unusual and significant. It's important not to treat these women simplistically or salaciously. They are not merely 'sexual sinners' as is sometimes said[5] – the reality is more complex and positive. They may be unexpected and unusual additions to the genealogy, but they were also women of faith. And whether the additions are male or female, Matthew wants us to ask, 'Why? Why is this person or these people mentioned here?' (We shall consider some examples shortly.)

The genealogy illustrates Matthew's taste for triads – grouping material into threes. We shall see him using this structural device liberally throughout the Gospel. The main part of the genealogy is divided into three panels of fourteen generations (as in Table 1 below).

1:1 The title: A book of the origins of Jesus the Messiah, son of David, son of Abraham		
1:2 From Abraham . . . (not kings) . . . to David the King (1:6a)	1:6b From David . . . (kings) . . . to the exile to Babylon (1:11)	1:12 From the exile . . . (not kings) . . . to Jesus, called Messiah (1:16)
1:17 The summary: three groups of fourteen generations from Abraham to the Messiah		

Table 1

Just in case we missed this, Matthew makes the 3x14 pattern crystal clear in verse 17. Triads are well known rhetorical devices, especially in oratory.[6] A list of three is short enough to process easily and keep in mind all at once. And a list of three is long enough to show a pattern and a progression, often with an emphasis on the final item. Here, Matthew tells a three-part theological history, culminating in the birth of Jesus.

---

5 Most commentators dismiss the suggestion that sexual sin is the main reason for including the women. But in a survey of recent preaching on the genealogy, Jane Tooher found undue weight given to the sexual sin of the women. Tooher, 'Hearing the Women in Matthew's Genealogy', 122–34.

6 For example, orators from ancient days to the present have made extensive use of the tricolon – 'a set of three units of speech put in a row'. Sam Leith, *You Talkin' to Me? Rhetoric from Aristotle to Obama* (London: Profile Books, 2011), 276.

The heading (1:1)

The genealogy begins and ends in a similar fashion. This is another of Matthew's favourite structural devices, known as inclusion: using repeated material to bracket together material into sections. Thus 'Messiah', 'David' and 'Abraham' appear in the first verse and are then repeated in verse 17. This confirms that Matthew wants us to read 1:1–17 as a unit. From the beginning and the end, we can also see this is all about Jesus. It is Jesus who is called the Messiah who tops and tails these verses (1:1 and 1:16–17). The word here is 'Christ', Greek for 'Anointed One'. Matthew wants us to connect this back to the anointed kings of Israel, for whom the equivalent Hebrew term is 'Messiah'. In particular, Matthew connects Jesus with King David – Jesus is 'son of David' (verse 1). And he takes us back still further – Jesus is 'son of Abraham'.

From Abraham to David (1:2–6a)

The first block of names covers the generations from Abraham to David. God's promises to Abraham raised a new hope for humanity, which was partially experienced under the kingship of David. The promises were of a nation (Genesis 12:2) – offspring and a land to live in (Genesis 12:7) – and a line of kings (Genesis 17:6, 16). This was a period of rising hope. There are fourteen generations presented here, so long as we count Abraham in verse 2.

At the end of verse 2, the first break in the rhythm of the genealogy reminds us of the birth of the nation of Israel: Judah and his brothers were the heads of the twelve tribes. Matthew wants us to note the beginning of national blessing for Israel – the first stage of the blessing promised to Abraham. He then takes us through Isaac, Jacob and Judah, and eventually to David. David is given special emphasis.[7] He is mentioned more than anyone else in the genealogy as a whole – five times. Here, there is also a break in the regular pattern: in verse 6 he is not just 'David' but 'King David'. He is the first fulfilment of the promises. With David as king, the promises became an observable reality, at least for a time. Only the promise of blessing spilling out to all the families of the earth (Genesis 12:3) remained unseen (and even this was hinted at).

---

[7] He is 'the central figure throughout the genealogy', as Craig Blomberg puts it, and most other commentators also note. Craig L. Blomberg, *Matthew* (Nashville: Broadman and Holman, 1992), 53.

The other breaks in the rhythm of these verses remind us this was very far from a smooth and easy process. Matthew mentions Tamar (1:3), Rahab (1:5) and Ruth (1:5). These women provide examples of those who come under God's promises of blessing by faith. All three were marginal and vulnerable. The story of Tamar and Judah was messy, to say the least (Genesis 38). Yet Judah came to see how Tamar was more righteous than himself (Genesis 38:26). Rahab and Ruth were outsiders and yet were drawn into the family and became instruments in the divine plan. Rahab was a prostitute (Joshua 2:1). Yet she also had great faith (Hebrews 11:31) and was considered righteous (James 2:25). All three are not only examples of faith, but also evidence of the sovereign grace of God, able to fulfil his promises against the apparent odds: through the difficulties, awkwardness and messiness of life.

From David to the Exile (1:6b–11)

The second block of names covers the generations from David to Jeconiah. Matthew is selective in the kings he chooses to mention here, leaving out four he could have included from Israel's history. (He can do this legitimately because 'was the father of' is a flexible way of speaking and can mean 'was the grandfather of' or even 'was the ancestor of'.) He seems to do this to hold the number of generations to fourteen. In the first block of names we saw rising hope, but here we see it dashed by the failure of David and his descendants, leading to exile.

This block is topped and tailed by two significant breaks in the rhythm. After introducing Solomon, Matthew adds, 'whose mother had been Uriah's wife' (1:6). This draws our attention not to Bathsheba (who is not named at all), but to David and his moral failure. It is a stinging reminder of both the adultery he committed and (by naming Uriah) the innocent blood he shed. This is the fault line that opens up over the coming generations. There are some relatively good kings in the list (such as Jehoshaphat, Hezekiah, Josiah), but the overall trajectory is downwards. Matthew breaks the rhythm again in verse 11 with 'and his brothers at the time of the exile to Babylon'. The words 'and his brothers' should remind us of the same phrase back in verse 2. That marked the beginning of blessing for Israel as a nation – the first stage of the blessing promised to Abraham. By using the same phrase in verse 11, Matthew may well be telling us that this is when the age of national blessing effectively came to an end. He then explicitly reminds us of the exile to Babylon, which is another of the emphases in the genealogy, being mentioned three times in total (1:11, 12, 17).[8] It is also the only event Matthew refers to – otherwise we just have names and relationships. This is the crisis point in the dramatic history he is telling. This is the moment when all hope seemed lost.

From the Exile to Jesus the Messiah (1:12–16)

The final block of names covers the generations from Jeconiah to Joseph. As with the first block of names, there are fourteen generations here so long as we count the first name (Jeconiah) as well as the last. The difficulty is that we have already counted Jeconiah in the second block of names in 1:6a–11. Many commentators think Matthew made a mistake,[9] but it could be deliberate. The Exile is so destructive, so catastrophic, so cuts through the history of Israel that it puts everything back to square one. The continuity is lost. We have to start counting again. The discontinuity is stressed through the prominent break in rhythm at the start of this block, 'After the exile to Babylon . . .' (1:12).

The Exile began a period of deep distress for God's people. This is reflected in the names here, many of which are obscure and unfamiliar. These are no longer the names of kings, despite God's promise to David that even after he died, his 'throne shall be established for ever' (2 Samuel 7:4–17). Every name here after Jeconiah therefore represents a disturbing apparent contradiction. (Psalm 89:30–51, written in this period, articulates some of the anguish and confusion the people were going through, processing what seemed at the time to be the breaking of God's promises.)

Hope is rekindled suddenly when the line reaches Joseph (who then becomes a main character in the next section, 1:18–2:23, showing us how to respond to it). Joseph is 'the husband of Mary', another break in the regular patterns. In the next section (1:18–25), we shall see Joseph grappling with the awkwardness of Mary becoming pregnant before they 'came together' (1:18). But just as God worked through Tamar, Rahab and Ruth, so he works through Mary. And the big questions raised by the genealogy – 'What about the promises to Abraham?' and 'What about David's throne, established forever?' – are now answered in Jesus who is called the Messiah.

---

[8] David Bauer, 'The Literary and Theological Function of the Genealogy in Matthew's Gospel', in *Treasures New and Old: Recent Contributions to Matthean Studies*, ed. David Bauer and Mark Allen Powell (Atlanta: Scholar's Press, 1996), 144–6.

[9] For example, W. D. Davies and Dale C. Allison, Jr., *Matthew 1–7* (London: T&T Clark, 1988), 186.

The summary (1:17)

In verse 17, Matthew confirms the threefold pattern of the genealogy and reminds us that he has arranged each part into fourteen generations. Why is Matthew putting so much stress on the number fourteen? The most plausible explanation is that this is another way of emphasising the importance of David in the genealogy. Matthew is modelling his genealogy to some extent on those in the book of Genesis. The genealogy in Genesis 46, for instance, is organised around the name Gad. It was common in the ancient world to use the numerical values of names to make a point. The name Gad has two letters in Hebrew: G and D. We can assign numbers to these, based on their location in the Hebrew alphabet. So G has value 3 and D has value 4, making the value of Gad 3+4=7. Gad appears seventh in the list (and has seven sons).[10] Matthew has done something similar here with David. The name David has three letters in Hebrew: D (value 4), V (value 6) and D (value 4), making the value of David 4+6+4=14. And David appears fourteenth in the list.

SUMMARY AND PURPOSE

So this is the history Matthew is telling through his opening genealogy. There has been hope raised through Abraham, to whom God made the promises. There has been hope partially realised in the nation briefly united and under God's blessing through David. Much in the genealogy emphasises David and the hope he represents. He is the model of the one who fulfils God's promises: his victories, won through great personal affliction and rejection, brought the first stage of God's promised blessing, and for a short time turned hope into a reality. But this hope was eroded by David's own failure and his descendants' progressive descent into wickedness. It was apparently extinguished in the exile to Babylon and the long period of national shame that followed. But now there is a new hope, the prospect of radical change in the fortunes of God's people and the fulfilment of all that he has promised. A hope focused on the son of David, the son of Abraham, who is called the Messiah.

The overall purpose of Matthew is to make its readers who aren't disciples of Jesus into disciples of Jesus, and to motivate and equip its readers who are disciples of Jesus to be disciple-makers. What the genealogy in 1:1–17 contributes to this is a heightened expectation of radical

---

[10] Davies and Allison, *Matthew 1–7*, 164.

change in the fortunes of God's people – a hope focused on Jesus, who is Messiah. This draws those who engage with it towards discipleship. But the genealogy also reminds us of the promises to Abraham of global blessing, highlighting some of the unexpected people who have been drawn into God's purposes. It therefore also begins the task of motivating disciples to be disciple-makers.

In short, the purpose of the genealogy is (with other hopes dashed) for us to place all our hopes for the blessing promised by God on Jesus, who is Messiah. This hope is founded on the promises of God to Abraham. It is hope raised by and experienced in King David – hope dashed by national failure and exile, but restored in the birth of Jesus. It is hope accessible to all kinds of people – even to outsiders – because of the unstoppable, sovereign grace of God, powerful to fulfil promises of blessing that will spill over into the whole world.

2. Jesus has come to fulfil the Prophets • Matthew 1:18–2:23

What we shall see in this section is the arrival of Jesus into the world as the climax of a true historical drama, and at the same time generating a true drama that we as readers are being invited to engage with. The true historical drama is the one Matthew has already introduced and sketched for us in the genealogy in 1:1–17. The hopes raised by the promises to Abraham and David, crushed through the failures of Israel's kings, are now rekindled through Jesus, who is called Messiah (1:16).

Joseph accepts Jesus as his son

18 This is how the birth of Jesus the Messiah came about[d]: his mother Mary was pledged to be married to Joseph, but before they came together, she was found to be pregnant through the Holy Spirit. **19** Because Joseph her husband was faithful to the law, and yet[e] did not want to expose her to public disgrace, he had in mind to divorce her quietly.

20 But after he had considered this, an angel of the Lord appeared to him in a dream and said, 'Joseph son of David, do not be afraid to take Mary home as your wife, because what is conceived in her is from the Holy Spirit. **21** She will give birth to a son, and you are to give him the name Jesus,[f] because he will save his people from their sins.'

22 All this took place to fulfil what the Lord had said through the prophet: **23** 'The virgin will conceive and give birth to a son, and they will call him Immanuel'[g] (which means 'God with us').

24 When Joseph woke up, he did what the angel of the Lord had commanded him and took Mary home as his wife. **25** But he did not consummate their marriage until she gave birth to a son. And he gave him the name Jesus.

The Magi visit the Messiah

2 After Jesus was born in Bethlehem in Judea, during the time of King Herod, Magi[a] from the east came to Jerusalem **2** and asked, 'Where is the one who has been born king of the Jews? We saw his star when it rose and have come to worship him.'

3 When King Herod heard this he was disturbed, and all Jerusalem with him. **4** When he had called together all the people's chief priests and teachers of the law, he asked them where the Messiah was to be born. **5** 'In Bethlehem in Judea,' they replied, 'for this is what the prophet has written:

6 ' "But you, Bethlehem, in the land of Judah,
are by no means least among the rulers of Judah;
for out of you will come a ruler who will shepherd my people Israel." [b]'

7 Then Herod called the Magi secretly and found out from them the exact time the star had appeared. **8** He sent them to Bethlehem and said, 'Go and search carefully for the child. As soon as you find him, report to me, so that I too may go and worship him.'

9 After they had heard the king, they went on their way, and the star they had seen when it rose went ahead of them until it stopped over the place where the child was. **10** When they saw the star, they were overjoyed. **11** On coming to the house, they saw the child with his mother Mary, and they bowed down and worshipped him. Then they opened their treasures and presented him with gifts of gold, frankincense and myrrh. **12** And having been warned in a dream not to go back to Herod, they returned to their country by another route.

The escape to Egypt

13 When they had gone, an angel of the Lord appeared to Joseph in a dream. 'Get up,' he said, 'take the child and his mother and escape to Egypt. Stay there until I tell you, for Herod is going to search for the child to kill him.'

14 So he got up, took the child and his mother during the night and left for Egypt, **15** where he stayed until the death of Herod. And so was fulfilled what the Lord had said through the prophet: 'Out of Egypt I called my son.' [c]

16 When Herod realised that he had been outwitted by the Magi, he was furious, and he gave orders to kill all the boys in Bethlehem and its vicinity who were two years old and under, in accordance with the time he had learned from the Magi. **17** Then what was said through the prophet Jeremiah was fulfilled:

18 'A voice is heard in Ramah,
weeping and great mourning,
Rachel weeping for her children

and refusing to be comforted,
because they are no more.'^d

The return to Nazareth

19 After Herod died, an angel of the
Lord appeared in a dream to Joseph
in Egypt 20 and said, 'Get up, take the
child and his mother and go to the land
of Israel, for those who were trying to
take the child's life are dead.'

21 So he got up, took the child and his
mother and went to the land of Israel.
22 But when he heard that Archelaus
was reigning in Judea in place of his
father Herod, he was afraid to go there.

Having been warned in a dream, he
withdrew to the district of Galilee,
23 and he went and lived in a town
called Nazareth. So was fulfilled what
was said through the prophets, that he
would be called a Nazarene.

———

d 18 Or *The origin of Jesus the Messiah was
like this*
e 19 Or *was a righteous man and*
f 21 *Jesus* is the Greek form of Joshua,
which means *the LORD saves.*
g 23 Isaiah 7:14
a 1 Traditionally *wise men*
b 6 Micah 5:2,4
c 15 Hosea 11:1
d 18 Jer. 31:15

As we now zoom in for a close account of the origins of Jesus, Matthew
shows us things that connect with this prior history: things happened
to fulfil the word of the Lord spoken previously through the prophets
(1:22–3; 2:15, 17–18, 23; note also 2:4–6). The arrival of Jesus generates
a new drama: a conflict between those who want to serve and honour
him and those who are not interested or want to kill him. God reveals
to us through this drama more of the main character: Jesus himself. And
the waves from the arrival of Jesus continue to generate a challenge
for us today. Will we respond to him with indifference, like the experts
in Jerusalem, or with worship and joy, like the Magi? Will we respond
to him with fear and hatred, like Herod, or with unreserved trust and
obedience, like Joseph?

The section 1:18–2:23 picks up from 1:16, expanding the brief mention
of the birth of Jesus and giving particular prominence to Joseph, 'son of
David' (1:20). In some ways, Matthew shows Jesus arriving quietly, but
he also wants to hint that this stands in line with God's mighty deeds
in Israel's history, even surpassing them all. The God who rescued his
people from the tyranny of Egypt and Pharaoh in Exodus is beginning
an even greater rescue in Jesus. Matthew 1:1–17 showed us how Jesus
fits into a sketch of the history of God's people. Now, 1:18–2:23 shows
us more about Jesus and the first steps in a right response to what God
is doing through him (or, from Joseph's perspective, a response to what
God is about to do). Matthew encourages us to respond wholeheartedly,
whether we are Jewish (like Joseph) or Gentile (like the Magi). And he

exposes the ugliness and irrationality of a negative response: whether it's murderous hatred (like Herod) or snobby indifference (like 'all Jerusalem', the chief priests and the teachers of the law).

The section can be seen as composed of five scenes (1:18–25; 2:1–12; 2:13–15; 2:16–18; 2:19–23), each with its own reference to the prophets (1:22–3; 2:6, 15, 18, 23), and with the focus alternating between Joseph and Herod.[11] But the first two of these have multiple parts to them, and the final three are short and seem to work together, telling the complete story arc of going down to Egypt and then returning. It may be best, then, to see this as composed of three main sections, each with three parts.[12] In the genealogy, we saw that Matthew likes to arrange things in threes. As we work through the Gospel, we shall also see that Matthew often likes to arrange his groups of threes into broader structures – 3x3 structures, for example. If that is the case here, then the 3x3 structure looks like this:

1:18–25 Joseph	2:1–12 The Magi and Herod	2:13–23 Joseph and Herod
1:18–21 Joseph is introduced, and then addressed by an angel	2:1–2 The Magi confront Herod concerning the King of the Jews	2:13–15 Joseph is addressed by an angel; goes down to Egypt (Scripture fulfilled)
1:22–3 (Scripture fulfilled)	2:3–8 Herod and all Jerusalem are disturbed (Scripture quoted)	2:16–18 Herod is furious (Scripture fulfilled)
1:24–5 Joseph believes and obeys	2:9–12 The Magi are overjoyed when they see Mary's child	2:19–23 Joseph is addressed by an angel; comes back from Egypt to Nazareth (Scripture fulfilled)

Table 2

Joseph (1:18–25)

This section of the Gospel is about the genesis or origin of Jesus the Messiah (1:18) – that is, not just about his birth.[13] His origin in the

[11] This is the first of the structures considered by Brown, *Birth of the Messiah*, 51.
[12] The main section corresponds to the second of the structures considered by Brown, *Birth of the Messiah*, 52. But he does not notice the three-part nature of what he labels scenes one and two, and hence how the two structures can be reconciled.
[13] France, *The Gospel of Matthew*, 46.

world is 100 per cent the initiative of God, to fulfil what he has spoken through the prophets. To bring this about, Jesus is born of Mary through the Holy Spirit, to be Immanuel, 'God with us'. The main characters in the narrative then show us how to respond to God's initiative in Jesus: like Joseph, not Herod; like the Magi, not like the chief priests, teachers of the law and 'all Jerusalem'.

We begin with Joseph. The difficulty and awkwardness of the situation Joseph finds himself in continues a theme from the genealogy, found in the extra comments that reminded us of the extraordinary stories of Tamar, Rahab, Ruth and the wife of Uriah. This raises the expectation that God will again intervene with unexpected blessing and grace into a messy or irregular situation. Joseph is presented positively as 'faithful to the law'. More literally, he is a 'righteous man', but not in the superficial, merely external fashion Jesus will later expose in the Pharisees. He really does want to do the right thing, and it is clear Matthew wants us to identify with him. It will be clearer still as the narrative unfolds.

In verse 20, an angel of the Lord breaks into the awkwardness of Mary's pregnancy and reveals the truth behind the situation: God is amazingly at work in her. The source of the one conceived in her is none other than the Holy Spirit. He is to be given the name Jesus, 'because he will save his people from their sins' (1:21).

So who is this one conceived in Mary, exactly? And what has he come to do? And for whom? It is here that the name given to him is so significant: Jesus, which is the Greek form of Joshua, meaning (roughly) 'YHWH saves'.[14] The name communicates that YHWH is a saving God. But, more specifically, the prophets expected YHWH to save his people *from their sins* (see, for example, Ezekiel 36:29a; 37:23b). That is, they expected YHWH to address the crisis Matthew has highlighted three times in the genealogy: the national dishonour and uncleanliness caused by the sin of the people, leading to their exile to Babylon (1:11–12, 17). This makes the 'he' in 1:21 ambiguous. Is 'he' the one conceived in Mary, to be called Jesus? Or is 'he' YHWH, the one who has personally promised to save his people from their sins? Matthew is already beginning to strongly imply that they are one and the same. In and through Jesus, YHWH has come to save his people from their sins.

First and foremost, 'his people' in 1:21 must refer to ethnic Israel: what Jesus later calls 'the lost sheep of Israel' (10:6). But we shall see, as the Gospel unfolds, that Jesus will work a salvation from sins at such a

---

[14] As explained, for example, by Davies and Allison, *Matthew 1–7*, 209.

deep level that its light will flood out beyond Israel to the nations (Isaiah 42:6; 49:6), addressing not just the dishonour of Israel but also the sin and shame of all humanity.

That in and through Jesus YHWH has come to save his people from their sins prompts Matthew's editorial comment in 1:22–3. Jesus is nothing less than 'God with us': included within the divine identity but relationally present to his people. This, says Matthew, took place to fulfil Isaiah 7:14, 'The virgin will conceive . . .' etc. This is a good example of some of the complexities of Matthew's use of the Old Testament. The section following this one briefly gives more detail on how to understand 'fulfilment' in Matthew, and his 'fulfilment formulae'. But to cut a long story short, in 1:22–3 Matthew wants us know that the birth of Jesus was no accident! It happened to fulfil the expectations raised by God through the prophet Isaiah that a child will be born to be 'God with us', a sign of salvation even at a time when faith is lacking.

As we began to see in the Introduction on Christology, Matthew begins with Jesus the Messiah (1:18) – Jesus as the promised human descendant of David, called Messiah, who will save and rescue God's people, leading them to victory. But we are seeing in 1:18–23 that Matthew begins his gradual unveiling of the divine identity of Jesus without delay. That Mary is pregnant by the Holy Spirit (1:18, 20) doesn't prove or necessitate that the person conceived in her has a divine nature, but it does at the very least suggest the personal involvement and intervention of God at the most intimate level. And we can certainly say that it is consistent with God becoming incarnate in Jesus, and indeed a 'fitting' way for him to do it – as Anselm (and, more recently, Oliver Crisp) have suggested.[15] Jesus will save his people from their sins, but his very name reminds us that it is YHWH who saves. What's more, his birth will bring about 'God with us' (1:23).

Joseph's response to all this is exemplary (verses 24–5). He does exactly what he has been told to do, taking Mary as his wife (while refraining from sexual union), and then naming the child Jesus.[16]

---

[15] In Anselm's *Why God Became Man* and *On the Virgin Conception and Original Sin* (See *Anselm of Canterbury, the Major Works*, eds. Brian Davies and Gillian Evans (Oxford: Oxford University Press, 1998)). Also Oliver Crisp, *God Incarnate: Explorations in Christology* (London: T&T Clark, 2009), 77–102.

[16] It surprises many people that Matthew seems utterly unconcerned and unembarrassed that Joseph is not physically or genetically Jesus's father, while also insisting that Jesus is 'son of David' through Joseph's line (1:16, 20). It may be that conventions at the time meant that an adopted child really was considered equivalent

Herod and the Magi (2:1–12)

Now we are introduced to a new set of characters: the Magi and Herod. The location in 1:18–25 was unspecified, but in 2:1–8 the location is Jerusalem, in the royal court. It is another awkward moment. Herod is the king – the king of the Jews, he would have said. A delegation of Magi from the east appears at the court of King Herod and ask, 'Where is the one who has been born *king of the Jews*? We saw his star when it rose and have come to worship him' (my emphasis). Not surprisingly, Herod is disturbed – affronted and afraid – and all Jerusalem with him (2:3).

We must quickly forget images some of us may have picked up from watching nativity plays. This is not a delegation of foreign kings. It is also not quite right to call them 'wise men'. They are Magi. The word is used elsewhere in the Bible of magicians, manipulators of the underworld. They are, perhaps, court magicians with some sort of advisory capacity (as in Daniel 2:2, for example). So maybe we could think of them as *representatives* of kings.[17] But nonetheless, they are magicians, astrologers and idolaters. These are the sorts of people despised and ridiculed in the books of Exodus and Daniel.[18] What is more, we do not know how many there were. There are three gifts mentioned in verse 11, but why should we assume one gift per person? There is no mention of any camels.

Herod was a 'client king' of Judea, crowned in Rome in 40 BC.[19] That is, although he had the title 'king', his relationship with Rome was asymmetrical, and his 'rule depended on Rome's continued approval'.[20] Matthew portrays him as in the dark, having to search for answers from his experts. He assembles the chief priests and teachers of the law, those

---

to a biological child. (This is how Jesus is seen in Matthew 13:55, for example.) By telling us that *Joseph* was the one who named Jesus (1:25), Matthew may be suggesting this act declares the close connection between them – that Jesus is fully part of Joseph's family line.

[17] If Matthew intended us to pick this up, it may suggest an allusion to Isaiah 60:3 and explain the prevalence of kings in the history of interpretation of these verses (along with Psalm 72:10).

[18] Mark Allan Powell, *Chasing the Eastern Star: Adventures in Biblical Reader-Response Criticism* (First edition; Louisville: Westminster John Knox, 2001), 156.

[19] According, that is, to the account of Herod the Great we find in Josephus, *Jewish Antiquities, Volume VI: Books 14–15*, trans. Ralph Marcus and Allen Wikgren, volume 489, Loeb Classical Library (Cambridge, MA: Harvard University Press, 1943).

[20] Julia Wilker, 'Client kings', Oxford Classical Dictionary (online),. https://doi.org/10.1093/acrefore/9780199381135.013.1677 (accessed 27 February 2024).

who know the prophets and their hopes and expectations. From them, Herod wants to know where the Messiah is to be born. The experts give the answer from the prophet Micah: the Messiah, the true shepherd of Israel, will come from Bethlehem (2:6; quoting Micah 5:2).

Herod sends the Magi to Bethlehem. And he says he wants them to investigate. 'As soon as you find him,' he says, 'report to me, so that I too may go and worship him.' But Matthew also makes it clear he does not go with them. Neither do the chief priests or the teachers of the law. Neither does anyone from Jerusalem. This is despite the fact that it is less than nine kilometres from Jerusalem to Bethlehem – not much more than an afternoon stroll.[21]

The Magi do not seem to mind and are not at all disturbed by this. They leave the client king in his darkness, and the light guides them to the true King. When they see the star they are, says verse 10, 'overjoyed'. Literally: they rejoiced greatly with great joy. They do not then respond with passive disrespect, like those in Jerusalem. They come to the house, and when they see the child they fall to the ground in worship. Their hearts are not cold and closed. They open up their treasure boxes and, even though they are not themselves kings, they give kingly gifts, fit for a king (2:11, as in Psalm 72:10–11, 15; Isaiah 60:3, 5–6). And they leave under the favour of God, who gives them safe passage back home (2:12).

Matthew's first readers would have been shocked and shamed by the contrast he is making. Ignorant, pagan idolaters have taken the lead in the response to God's initiative in Jesus. They have responded to a sign in the night sky, a 'star'. In the ancient world, astrological signs were frequently associated with great events and new kings.[22] Jewish experts would have regarded this as dangerous superstition, and yet the God of the heavens graciously uses it to guide these pagans to the truth. Their response goes over and above those with the privileges of God's revelation in the Scriptures – those who, to say the least, should know better. Even if the contrast does not strike us with quite the same force today, the response of the Magi remains a deeply attractive example to follow.

---

[21] Davies and Allison, *Matthew 1–7*, 226.
[22] Davies and Allison, *Matthew 1–7*, 233.

Joseph and Herod (2:13–23)

Matthew then contrasts Joseph and Herod directly. The energy pent up by the awkward incident in Jerusalem has not yet fully worked itself out. It has put Jesus in danger. In verse 13 the story cuts back to Joseph. The Magi have just left, and suddenly an angel of the Lord appears to Joseph in a dream, saying, 'Get up, take the child and his mother and escape to Egypt.' And he does.

All this, Matthew comments, was to fulfil what the Lord said through the prophet [Hosea]: 'Out of Egypt I called my son' (2:15; quoting Hosea 11:1). That is, the withdrawal is part of an exodus-like pattern, within which they all need to go to Egypt so that God can call them out again, rescued from Pharaoh-like Herod. Matthew is implying that Jesus is therefore one like Moses, but greater than Moses.[23]

The narrative cuts back to Herod (2:16). He has, literally, been made to look a fool by the Magi. And he still fears the child they were looking for. He orders the murder of every child in Bethlehem, two years old or under, just to make sure. Matthew portrays Herod as a deeply troubled man in this chapter, full of turmoil and anger – presumably fearful for his position. He is like Pharaoh, targeting Hebrew baby boys to destroy the threat he feels against himself (compare Exodus 1:15–16). He disbelieves what he has been told by the Magi and the experts in Jerusalem about the coming King of the Jews. At least, he disbelieves the full import of it. In fact, whatever he believes, he is profoundly irrational. If the Magi are wrong, he has nothing to worry about. If they are right, what he does is remarkably stupid, acting defiantly towards God, with violence and hatred. But that is where his instincts take him.

All this, Matthew comments, was to fulfil what was said through the prophet Jeremiah (2:17–18). The grief in Bethlehem provoked by the violence of 2:16 corresponds to the grief felt in Ramah at the time of Jeremiah, as the lost children of Judah were exiled to Babylon. Matthew is saying that grief has now been fulfilled in Bethlehem, a prelude to the joyful new thing the Lord is beginning in Jesus. That is, not even the reckless violence of 2:16 can check what God is doing. Certainly, a mere client king like Herod cannot stand in his way. By verse 19, Herod is dead. The narrative cuts back to Joseph again. The situation has moved

---

[23] As argued at length in Dale C. Allison, Jr., *The New Moses: A Matthean Typology* (Edinburgh: T&T Clark, 1993), 140–65.

on. So, says Matthew, an angel of the Lord appears to Joseph in a dream, and the angel sends them back to the land of Israel.

Even this is not the end of it. There remains the danger of hostility from Herod's brutal son, the tyrant Archelaus. Joseph has one last dream. We see the pattern for the fourth and last time: the Lord speaks and Joseph responds. The contrast between Joseph and Herod (and son) could not be stronger. Unlike Herod, Joseph has an authentic royal background: he is a 'son of David'. Unlike Herod, flailing around in the dark, he is in the light, 'in the loop', as it were – told directly by the Lord what is going on. Most importantly, he believes what he hears and he acts obediently.

Joseph responds to the warning in the last dream (2:22), and the family end up settling in Nazareth, where Jesus can grow up untroubled – until he is finally ready to fulfil the purpose for which he has come.

All this, Matthew comments, was to fulfil what was said through the prophets: 'he would be called a Nazarene' (2:23). There is more on this below, but most likely, since Nazareth was taken to be a place of scorn and dishonour (compare John 1:46), this is an indirect way of alluding to what the prophets said about the one to come. For example, there is Isaiah 53:3 on the Servant of the Lord: 'He was despised and rejected by mankind . . . and we held him in low esteem'. In other words, Jesus is bringing about a new and greater exodus rescue than the one God accomplished through Moses. Moses (like Joshua and David) was known as 'the servant of the Lord' (the first of seventeen examples being Deuteronomy 34:5). But Jesus is *the* Servant of the Lord, who will take on the shame of his people and rescue them by dying as 'sin-bearer' for many (Isaiah 53:12).

SUMMARY AND PURPOSE

The overall purpose of Matthew is to make its readers who are not disciples of Jesus into disciples of Jesus, and to equip its readers who are disciples of Jesus to be disciple-makers. Building on the genealogy in 1:1–17, the section from 1:18–2:23 contributes to this by drawing those who engage with it further towards discipleship by showing more of the greatness of the event of Jesus's birth, the rightness of aligning oneself to what God is doing and the awfulness of opposing or dismissing him.

Matthew is showing God fulfilling in Jesus not just what he promised to Abraham and David (which he showed in the genealogy), but also what he spoke through the prophets. He wants us to see that, in Jesus, God is doing something extraordinary – something history-changing – and therefore something we as readers should not miss or ignore.

Matthew's comments in the 'fulfilment formulae' (1:22–3; 2:15, 17–18, 23), plus the quotation in 2:6, give his own interpretation of what happens in this section. A comprehensive understanding of these requires a thorough knowledge of the original contexts and some careful thought. But the main point of them should be clear even without comprehensive explanation. Taken together, we can see that the hopes and expectations of the prophets (even when they are more implied than explicit) are fulfilled in Jesus. In Jesus, Matthew is claiming, God is with us and for us, a true king and shepherd, bringing about a new exodus and rescue – through hostility, grief and shame.

In short, the purpose of 1:18–2:23 is to bring about a trusting, obedient, joyful alignment with what God is fulfilling through Jesus, born to save his people from their sins. We should not miss the very clear response Matthew is encouraging here. He wants us to associate with the unreserved trust of Joseph and the overflowing joy of the Magi – while dissociating from the irrational hatred of Herod and the indifference of 'all Jerusalem', the chief priests and teachers of the law.

Fulfilment

How is Matthew thinking about 'fulfilment'? In his understanding, how is prophecy fulfilled? We might expect it to work like this: in the past, the Lord speaks through a prophet to make or repeat an explicit promise or to make a verifiable prediction. Then, later, whatever was promised or predicted happens. And a New Testament author reports it, effectively saying, 'Ta-dah! There you go!'

There is a good example of this in Matthew 2:5–6. In the past, the Lord spoke through the prophet Micah. Now, through the chief priests and teachers of the law, Matthew reminds us what the Lord said about a ruler to come from Bethlehem in the land of Judah (Micah 5:2). Matthew has already told us that Jesus was born in Bethlehem (2:1). There is a promise/prediction. And then, in Jesus, it happens.

But it is very striking that Matthew doesn't use the language of fulfilment in 2:5–6. Instead, he talks about 'fulfilment' extensively elsewhere in 1:18–2:23, in what have become known as his 'fulfilment formulae' or 'formula-quotations'. There are ten of these across the Gospel (1:22–3; 2:15, 17–18, 23; 4:14; 8:17; 12:17; 13:35; 21:4; 27:9). These are moments in the narrative when Matthew pauses and comments on what is happening with a formal quotation from the Hebrew Scriptures, each following a very similar format. Four of them appear in this early section of the Gospel. We quickly realise that these are quite different from the promise/

prediction-now-come-true pattern we saw in 2:5–6. Something much more subtle is going on.

The key is to remember the pattern Matthew has already established in the genealogy of 1:1–17. In the genealogy, Matthew was reminding us of the promises in the Law to Abraham, and in the (former) prophets to David. The three panels of generations then reminded us of the history of Israel, where the content of the promises began to be seen (especially in the reign of King David, first panel) but only temporarily (second and third panels), until the birth of Jesus (1:16). We see this same pattern in the fulfilment sayings: Matthew notices a 'correspondence in history' (as Klyne Sndograss puts it) between an Old Testament context and the narrative he is telling of Jesus, inviting a comparison.[24] The comparison shows that something hinted at but unrealised (or only partially, temporarily realised) in an old context becomes full and real (fulfilled) in the coming of Jesus.

As the genealogy suggests, Matthew could have dug anywhere into the history of Israel to show us this pattern at work. The connections he chooses to make are raised by the events he is narrating: the unusual conception of Jesus by the Spirit in Mary, for example (1:18–21). At first glance, some of the connections might seem to us slight and superficial. This accusation might be fair of other interpreters of the Hebrew Scriptures (in the ancient community of Qumran, for example,[25] or among some of the rabbis, or in some early Christian interpretation). But closer inspection shows that Matthew has chosen his connections very carefully. When we consider the original context of the quotation, we get a very rich picture of the new thing the Lord God is bringing about through the coming of Jesus.

Take the first fulfilment saying, quoting Isaiah 7:14, 'The virgin will conceive and give birth to a son, and they will call him Immanuel.' If we go back and read the context in Isaiah, it doesn't take long to work out that Matthew is not saying this was a simple, long-range prediction. He is not saying, for example, that by using the word 'virgin', Isaiah was making a mere prediction of the miraculous nature of the birth in 1:18–25. Rather, what Matthew is describing as a whole in these verses mirrors and greatly magnifies what happened in Isaiah 7. The Immanuel

---

[24] Klyne R. Snodgrass, 'The Use of the Old Testament in the New', in *New Testament Criticism and Interpretation*, ed. D. A. Black (Grand Rapids: Zondervan, 1991), 416.
[25] The *Habakkuk Commentary* (1QpHab), one of the original seven Dead Sea Scrolls discovered in 1947, is a notorious example.

child in Isaiah 7:14 was first and foremost expected to be born before the coming of the Assyrians, as 7:15–17 indicates. He was to be a sign to Ahaz and the house of David in response to Ahaz's lack of faith (Isaiah 7:1–9). Ahaz's lack of faith would result in him missing out on the salvation of the Lord; judgment would come from Assyria (Isaiah 7:17). And yet the Immanuel child still points to salvation: from Rezin and Syria first and foremost (Isaiah 7:16); and then in Isaiah 8–10, the prophet will go on to hint of a much greater subsequent deliverance and blessing. It's these hints that are ultimately fulfilled in the Immanuel child of Matthew 1. At a similar time of darkness and lack of faith, Matthew is saying, Jesus will be 'God with us' in a greater way – the Lord personally here to save, born to save his people from their sins – completing the expectations that were unfinished in Isaiah's day.

The second fulfilment saying in 2:15 follows a withdrawal, a fleeing to Egypt from the threat of Herod. This may look like God on the defensive, but no, says Matthew, this was to fulfil what the Lord had said through the prophet: 'Out of Egypt I called my son' (2:15b; quoting Hosea 11:1). As with the quotation of Isaiah 7:14 in 1:23, Matthew is not taking Hosea 11:1 as a simple, long-range prediction. After all, in this verse the prophet was looking backwards in history, to the exodus of Israel, God's 'firstborn son', from Egypt. In context, Hosea was looking back to the first exodus as a historical pattern he was confident the Lord would repeat in a second, greater exodus (Hosea 11:10–11). It is this second exodus Matthew claims is being fulfilled by the withdrawal of Joseph, Mary and Jesus to Egypt. Or rather, the withdrawal is part of an exodus-like pattern, within which they all need to go to Egypt so that God can call them out again, rescued from Pharaoh-like Herod. (This points to the bigger exodus Matthew will go on to show accomplished through Jesus: nothing less than a rescue of a global people – from sin, shame and the shadow of death.)

In 2:17–18, Matthew comments on the violence brought by Herod into Bethlehem, quoting this time from the prophet Jeremiah (Jeremiah 31:15). Again, Matthew is not taking this as a simple, long-range forecast or prediction of what he has just described in 2:16. In the verse from Jeremiah, the prophet is using Rachel, Jacob's wife, to personify Israel and to express the grief she feels for her lost children as they are deported to Babylon via the staging post of Ramah, some eight kilometres north of Jerusalem. The grief in Bethlehem provoked by the violence of 2:16 corresponds to that grief felt in Ramah all those years before. But the grief in Ramah was the prelude for the joy felt in Jeremiah 31:16–17, when the prophet looked forward to the tears being wiped away. The grief is the background for the announcement of a new covenant in Jeremiah 31:31–4. So, Matthew is saying, that grief has now been fulfilled in Bethlehem, a prelude to the joyful new thing the Lord has begun in Jesus.

Matthew comments with a fulfilment saying one last time in 1:18–2:23, that the return to Nazareth fulfilled what was spoken by the prophets: 'He shall be called a Nazarene' (2:23). This time we do not have a quotation! Is what Matthew says a reference to the Nazirite sect of the book of Numbers 6? Is it an allusion to a similar-sounding word in Isaiah 11:1, which would link Jesus to David again? Or to a different, similar-sounding word in Isaiah 42:6; 49:6, which would link Jesus for the first time to Isaiah's Servant figure? Or is Nazareth so closely associated with Galilee in Matthew's mind that the text he has in mind is the one he later quotes in 4:14–16, about the light dawning in Galilee (Isaiah 9:1–2)? There have been many suggestions.[26] Most likely, 2:23 links to Isaiah's Servant in a different way. To be a Nazarene was despised and shameful in the first century (see, for example, John 1:46), and (as R. T. France notes) this negative tone seems to be reflected in the words of the servant girl speaking of 'Jesus of Nazareth' in 26:71.[27] In Matthew's understanding, 'Nazarene' is an indirect way, then, of alluding to what the prophets said about the one to come – such as Isaiah 53:3:

> He was despised and rejected by mankind . . .
> Like one from whom people hide their faces
>   he was despised, and we held him in low esteem.

In all these cases, understood rightly, Matthew is teaching us how to read the Scriptures. He doesn't want us to do it clumsily, reading in ideas that are not there. It has sometimes been suggested that Matthew was doing just this.[28] A caricature of Matthew's handling of the Old Testament claims he rode roughshod over what the original authors had in mind, to show us something that can only be seen with Christian hindsight. That is, there was a hidden 'fuller', 'spiritual' meaning in the original text, brought to light by the revelation of new truth to the New Testament

---

[26] Most are outlined in Davies and Allison, *Matthew 1–7*, 275–81.

[27] France, *The Gospel of Matthew*, 94.

[28] For example, the Swedish theologian Krister Olofsson Stendahl, *The School of St. Matthew and Its Use of the Old Testament* (Lund: Gleerup, 1954); or, more recently, Richard N. Longenecker, *Biblical Exegesis of the Apostolic Period* (Grand Rapids: Eerdmans, 1999). But many others too.

authors like Matthew. The new truth is effectively read back into the old text with the claim it was there all along, even if hidden. The result is different from any 'fuller meaning' that comes from reading an Old Testament text in context, and in the light of its fulfilment in Jesus. In the caricature, the 'spiritual' senses implied by Matthew's quotations seem to be derived in a way that is entirely independent of their human authors. But the caricature is false. As Paul Williamson notes on Matthew 2:15, 'Matthew is not suggesting that Hosea 11:1 was really all about Jesus; nor is he bringing out a "fuller meaning" *(Sensus Plenior)* that Hosea never saw or intended.' Rather, 'Matthew is once again interpreting this [Old Testament] text in light of its wider context.'[29]

Finding a 'fuller meaning', in the sense of 'spiritual' meaning derived independently of the implied intentions of the human author, did become quite common in the early history of Christian interpretation of the Old Testament, and it has become fashionable in some circles to suggest we ought to recover some variation of this interpretative approach today.[30] But this will not do. The problem is that one cannot learn anything new from a 'reading backwards' strategy – you only get out what you put in. Even some of this gets lost in the mental gymnastics needed to establish all the connected patterns. And if this is what Matthew is doing, it would leave the fulfilment sayings devoid of content, saying nothing in terms of commentary on the unfolding narrative, rendering them utterly unpersuasive. Hopefully, we have seen that Matthew is doing something much more sophisticated, and that he is encouraging us to do the same. He is wanting us to remember the whole background history, and specific episodes in that history, in context, read with due respect for the arrow of time, as the grand narrative of the Scriptures unfolds to reveal its fulfilment in Jesus.

---

[29] Paul R. Williamson, 'What Was Said through the Prophet(s): Matthew's Use of the OT', in *Listen to Him: Reading and Preaching Emmanuel in Matthew*, ed. Peter Bolt (London: Latimer, 2015), 34.

[30] See, for example, Craig A. Carter, *Interpreting Scripture with the Great Tradition: Recovering the Genius of Premodern Exegesis* (Grand Rapids: Baker Academic, 2018).

PART THREE

THE ORIGINS OF JESUS'S MINISTRY

MATTHEW 3:1–4:11

3

Jesus Is Commissioned and Tested

MATTHEW 3:1–4:11

So far in Matthew's Gospel we have been introduced to Jesus as the one who will restore hope to a fallen people (1:1–17) and who will save them from their sins (1:21). He has come in fulfilment of the prophets: God with us (1:23) – with us as Saviour, not (yet) as Judge – the shepherd born in David's town (2:6), who will bring about a new exodus from and through grief and shame (2:15, 18, 23). We have been encouraged to respond to him with unconditional trust, like Joseph, and an overflowing joy, like the Magi. The first two chapters have been concerned with the origin of Jesus in his birth. Now, at the beginning of Matthew 3, we fast forward to the background and origins of Jesus's ministry.

There are three main sections in 3:1–4:11. Although the second section is shorter than the others, we shall find the density of theological content there outdoes them both. Each section divides quite nicely into three:

3:1–12 John prepares the way	3:13–17 Jesus, the Son, is commissioned as Servant	4:1–11 Jesus, the Son, is tested as Servant
3:1–2 John proclaims the nearness of the kingdom of the heavens	3:13 Jesus arrives – to be baptised!	4:1–4 Jesus is led to the wilderness and tested for the first time
3:3–6 John is a herald and a prophet	3:14–15 John tries to dissuade him	4:5–7 Jesus is tested a second time
3:7–12 John warns the Pharisees and Sadducees of imminent judgment . . .	3:16–17 Jesus is baptised and confirmed as Son and Servant	4:8–11 Jesus is tested for a third time

Table 3

1. *Change your mindset* • *Matthew 3:1–12*

The world is not as it seems (to most people). Its history is not as it seems. Its future is certainly not as it seems. We shall see this in multiple ways in this passage.

John the Baptist prepares the way

3 In those days John the Baptist came, preaching in the wilderness of Judea **2** and saying, 'Repent, for the kingdom of heaven has come near.' **3** This is he who was spoken of through the prophet Isaiah:

> 'A voice of one calling in the wilderness,
> "Prepare the way for the Lord,
> make straight paths for him." '**a**

4 John's clothes were made of camel's hair, and he had a leather belt round his waist. His food was locusts and wild honey. **5** People went out to him from Jerusalem and all Judea and the whole region of the Jordan. **6** Confessing their sins, they were baptised by him in the River Jordan.

7 But when he saw many of the Pharisees and Sadducees coming to where he was baptising, he said to them: 'You brood of vipers! Who warned you to flee from the coming wrath? **8** Produce fruit in keeping with repentance. **9** And do not think you can say to yourselves, "We have Abraham as our father." I tell you that out of these stones God can raise up children for Abraham. **10** The axe has been laid to the root of the trees, and every tree that does not produce good fruit will be cut down and thrown into the fire.

11 'I baptise you with**b** water for repentance. But after me comes one who is more powerful than I, whose sandals I am not worthy to carry. He will baptise you with**b** the Holy Spirit and fire. **12** His winnowing fork is in his hand, and he will clear his threshing-floor, gathering his wheat into the barn and burning up the chaff with unquenchable fire.'

---

a 3 Isaiah 40:3
b 11 Or *in*

Matthew 3 begins with John the Baptist crying out to a general, unspecified audience the command, 'Repent!' (3:2). Matthew comments that John is preparing for a momentous moment in history as the 'voice of one calling in the wilderness' spoken of by Isaiah (Isaiah 40:3). So the command 'Repent' is parallel to 'Prepare the way for the Lord, make straight paths for him' (Matthew 3:3).

There is more on the meaning of the command 'Repent!' in the section following this one, where I shall argue that the word John uses here has the same meaning in this context as it does more widely in Greek usage at the time. That is, John is calling people to change their hearts or minds in preparation for the kingdom and the coming of the Lord, a change that includes coming to feel remorse, regret, sorrow or contrition about sin. That they will come to see that they have refused 'to acknowledge God's rule over them'[1]. We shall see in the following verses that there is an expectation built into this call that the change of heart or mind will inevitably lead to conviction of sin and a change of allegiance, and should follow through into changes in behaviour – what John himself calls 'fruit in keeping with repentance' in 3:8. But first and foremost John is calling for a change in how people view reality and their place within it – what we might now call a 'mindset' change. This is in response to news concerning the kingdom. Change your heart, mind or mindset, says John, because the kingdom of heaven has come near (3:2). As we began to see in the Introduction, the heavens (plural) in Matthew refer not to God himself, but to the realm of God above. The kingdom of the heavens then seems to be referring to a future reality where heaven and earth are reunited in one unified realm. As Jonathan T. Pennington concludes, 'It is not like earthly kingdoms, stands over against them, and will eschatologically replace them (on earth).'[2] It will fill the cosmos, heaven and earth.[3] It is not so much about God's rule now, but about something to be established by God. Hence Matthew's comment that John was fulfilling the role of the 'voice' in Isaiah 40:3, preparing the way for the Lord.

This immediately shakes up anyone thinking that the physically observable world, as we can see it now before us, is all there is. There are also the heavens. This is the place where God's presence is manifest through his unopposed rule. John is drawing people's attention to a deeply uncomfortable, inconvenient truth. God exists, he is the one and only God, the one who created this world, and he cares about the cosmos he created. Humanity has rejected his rule, splitting and separating earth from heaven. This state of affairs cannot last forever. He will act to bring earth and heaven back together in a new kingdom – the kingdom of heaven. And John has burst into history to say, 'You need to be ready for that now.'

---

[1] Uytanlet and Kwa, *Matthew*, 64.
[2] Pennington, *Heaven and Earth*, 321.
[3] As Samson Uytanlet notes, 'Perhaps it would also be good to stop using the expression "expanding God's kingdom." Christians are called, not to expand God's kingdom, but simply to proclaim it!' Uytanlet and Kwa, *Matthew*, 194.

Matthew has already told us, in verse 3, that he understands John to be a herald, preparing the way for the Lord. Next, he portrays John as a prophet. He is dressed like the prophet Elijah, verse 4, in camel hair and leather (compare 2 Kings 1:8). And he is credible. People are listening. If the kingdom of the heavens is near, then the sin of the people, their rebellion against God, is a problem. They are flooding out to John, confessing their sins and publicly acknowledging their need for cleansing by being baptised in the Jordan. Going out to the Jordan, where God's people entered the Land (Joshua 3:1), is like saying, 'We don't deserve to be here!' Getting baptised in the Jordan – that is, dipped and cleansed in water – is like saying, 'I'm not truly of Abraham's family – I need to be washed of my uncleanliness like the Gentile commander Naaman' (2 Kings 5).

John's preaching is even attracting members of the religious elite (verse 7) – of all colours. It is here that John's warning gets amplified. It is clear he thinks these people, no matter how well thought of, are not ready for what is coming. They are no better than a 'brood of vipers' (verse 7).[4] (Jesus will apply this same phrase to the Pharisees in Matthew 12:34 and 23:33.) We can see here that John links the nearness of the kingdom with the 'coming wrath [of God]'.

But the Pharisees and Sadducees are at risk of this wrath because they are not producing 'fruit in keeping with repentance' (verse 8). That is, they are not behaving in a way that is in keeping with believing in the nearness of the kingdom of the heavens. John is clear that the acceptability of the change of heart or mind he has called for (repentance, verse 2), even if marked by baptism, is, as Nolland says, 'subject to the reality of that repentance coming to expression in subsequent life'.[5]

Without such fruit, they cannot rely on their ancestry going back to Abraham. This is simply not enough if, as John says, verse 10, the axe is at the root of the tree, such that every fruitless tree will be cut down and burnt. John baptises with water, so that people can express their change of heart or mind in the light of news of the kingdom (verse 11). But the one coming after him will baptise with Holy Spirit and fire. As Wesley Olmstead argues, we should probably take this as a single

---

[4] The word suggests false witness and deception. This is a common way of thinking about snakes across cultures. Samson Uytanlet comments that in the Central Luzon dialect of Tagalog, 'the word ahas (or snake) does not only refer to the crawling creature with split-tongue, it is often used metaphorically to refer to traitors'. Uytanlet and Kwa, Matthew, 65.

[5] Nolland, Matthew, 143.

'Holy Spirit-and-fire' baptism, which will burn in judgment to leave the cosmos purified.[6]

In verse 12, the picture broadens with a new image. The one coming after John has a winnowing shovel in his hand.[7] Wheat and chaff have been separated from one another on the threshing floor, and he will use the shovel to gather the wheat into a barn. The remaining chaff will be burned with unquenchable fire. The burning is thus just one side of a separating process at the Judgment. John is warning the Pharisees and Sadducees that, as things stand, they will find themselves on the wrong side of the separation.

SUMMARY AND PURPOSE

The purpose of 3:1–12 is approximately the same as John's purpose as he proclaimed the nearness of the kingdom of heaven. Matthew at this stage wants his readers and hearers to change their minds, hearts and 'mindset' about the world they live in (if they have not done so already) and the future that is coming their way. The kingdom of the heavens is near. God exists. God cares about the cosmos he created. He rules now from the heavens, and will one day rule unopposed in a new cosmos where heaven and earth are reunited – with all that this implies about the false kingdoms and darkness of the world swept away in judgment by a heavenly kingdom. Within this change of mind about the state and future of the world will be a change in how we view ourselves – a conviction of sin. Teaching or preaching on 3:1–12 will therefore be teaching or preaching aiming for a radical change in worldview and deep conviction. The exchange between John and the Pharisees and Sadducees especially targets anyone presuming upon salvation through the coming judgment without such a radical change in heart and mind.

Like the people of John's day, many people in our day, and especially in

---

[6] Wesley G. Olmstead, *Matthew 1–14: A Handbook on the Greek Text* (Waco: Baylor University Press, 2019), 49.

[7] Commentators and translators continue to call it a winnowing 'fork', despite careful work by Gustav Dalman, *Von Der Ernte Zum Mehl*, Arbeit Und Sitte in Palästina, III (Hildesheim: Georg Olms, 1964), 116–25. Although BDAG hedges its bets by describing it as 'a fork-like shovel', all the evidence points to it being a tool that looks nothing like a fork and very much like a shovel. This makes sense: it's hard to imagine how one would gather wheat into a barn using a fork! See also Jane Ellen Harrison, 'Mystica Vannus Iacchi (Continued)', *The Journal of Hellenic Studies* 24 (1904): 245–7, which includes a picture and an explanation of how it came to be confused with a fork.

western culture, have also stopped thinking about the bigger questions of life: the existence of a God who actually cares about the world, whether there might be anything beyond the observable universe, or whether history is going anywhere (rather than just petering out in a far-distant heat death). The assumption is that this is all there is, things will always be like this and all the key consequences are under our control. Preaching about the kingdom, like John does here, is then a wake-up call to a bigger reality and a radically different future.

From this should come a conviction of sin or feeling of shame. There is a wider context to our existence, all humanity has dishonoured God and there is a reckoning to come. Some, of course, partially accept this, like the Pharisees and Sadducees in this passage, but, also like them, presume upon their status, heritage or background. John exposes them as just as fruitless as those who deny and dishonour God altogether.

Repentance

In Matthew 3:2, John preaches, 'Repent, for the kingdom of heaven has come near.' Jesus will preach exactly the same message in Matthew 4:17. But do they mean exactly the same thing contemporary Christians mean when they think about the concept of 'repentance' or use the word 'repent' or 'repentance'? I think we shall see: not quite. So, then, what do John and Jesus mean?

Certainly, before the Reformation, people would have read the command in Matthew 3:2 and 4:17 quite differently from modern readers. In the Latin Vulgate, the command is, 'Do penance!' In medieval (and modern Roman Catholic) theology, this would have been taken as a call to seek forgiveness of sins through the sacrament of penance. To 'do penance', a penitent person would confess their sin to a priest, expressing sorrow and a desire to make amends for it – that is, to make 'satisfaction' for it. The priest would then pronounce an absolution, declaring the sin forgiven. (Works of penance might also be suggested, but these would not strictly be part of the sacrament.)[8]

We might say that the Reformation began in 1517 with Martin Luther's challenge to this reading and understanding in his Disputation

---

[8] Richard A. Muller, *Dictionary of Latin and Greek Theological Terms: Drawn Principally from Protestant Scholastic Theology* (Carlisle: Paternoster, 1985), 18, 229–30, 271. The Latin word used in the Vulgate of Matthew 3:2 and 4:17 is *paenitentia*. In late vulgar Latin, this became *repoenitentia*, which became in Old French *repentance* and which then lies behind the English words repentance and repent.

on the Power and Efficacy of Indulgences, more commonly known as the Ninety-Five Theses.[9] In Luther's view, Jesus in Matthew 4:17 was calling believers to a lifelong contrition or sorrow for sin (thesis one), an attitude that has nothing to do with the sacramental penance administered by priests (thesis two). This inner contrition, if genuine, will show itself in outward mortification of the flesh (that is, actually putting some sins to death – thesis three). It will continue in believers until they enter the kingdom of heaven (thesis four).

Later Reformers preferred a different Latin word to translate the call in Matthew 3:2 and 4:17: *resipiscentia*, meaning a change of mind or heart.[10] But they agreed with Luther that this included a lifelong contrition or sorrow for sin.

But it has become common in more recent times to explain the command we have in 3:2 and 4:17 using the concept of *turning*. The suggestion has some plausibility to it. After all, Matthew presents John in the clothes of a prophet (Matthew 3:4). Could it not be, then, that John the Baptist in Matthew 3:2 was repeating the call of the prophets to an apostate people to turn? The prophetic call to turn had two elements to it. First, there was a relational aspect to turning: the call to turn back to the Lord, away from false gods and idols (e.g., Isaiah 31:6; 44:22; Jeremiah 3:12, 14, 22; Ezekiel 14:6; Hosea 14:1–2; Joel 2:12–13; Zechariah 1:3; Malachi 3:7). Then there was the behavioural aspect to turning: to turn from wicked practices (e.g., Jeremiah 18:11; 25:5; 35:15; Ezekiel 18:30; 33:11; Zechariah 1:4).

If John was repeating the call of the prophets, then we should also be clear that he would have been following the prophets in giving priority to the *relational* aspect of turning. The Lord calls on the people through the prophets to turn back to him, turning from idols or false gods. Inseparable from this, but depending upon it, the people should ask the Lord for forgiveness and then start listening to him again and obeying what he says, thus turning from wickedness towards righteousness. But the turning back to the Lord has priority. So it might then make sense to paraphrase Matthew 3:2 as, 'Turn back to the Lord your God, for his kingdom has come near.'

But modern evangelicals tend to use the word 'repent' exclusively to talk about the second kind of turning, saying that what we call

---

[9] Martin Luther, *The Ninety-Five Theses and Other Writings*, trans. William R. Russell (London: Penguin, 2017).

[10] Muller, *Dictionary of Latin and Greek Theological Terms*, 264.

'repentance' is 'turning from sin'.[11] In the context of Matthew 3 and 4, this would give us a problem. Then we would have something like, 'Turn from your sins, for the kingdom of heaven has come near.' Since this call precedes any other in Matthew's Gospel, we would then risk falling into what Sinclair Ferguson has called 'preparationism'.[12]

Preparationism is when we say or imply that someone needs to 'sort their life out', turning from sin, before they can come to Christ and find forgiveness. Sadly, a great deal of evangelistic preaching I have heard on Matthew 4:17 (or the equivalent verses in Mark 1:14–15) has fallen into this trap.

As it happens, the link between the commands in Matthew 3:2 and 4:17 and the prophetic call to turn is not as direct as it appears in English translations. The Greek verb in 3:2 and 4:17 is *metanoeō*. The Hebrew verb used in all the examples of the prophetic call to turn cited above is *šūb*. English translations sometimes use the word 'repent' for these, just as they do for *metanoeō*, so it is not surprising that English readers link the two. But in each and every one of these examples, in the Greek translation of the Hebrew Scriptures (the LXX), the verb used to translate *šūb* is a different one – either *epistrephō* or *apostrephō*. (These are the normal Greek words for 'turn'.) The verb *metanoeō* does appear in the LXX, some nineteen times, in fact.[13] In fifteen of these cases, it translates the Hebrew verb *niham* – to regret or be sorry. Only once is it clearly used to translate *šūb*, in the text of Isaiah 14:6. In this verse, *šūb* is used to describe the turning of the heart – to admit transgression and to remember who the Lord is (Isaiah 46:8–11).

All of this suggests the Reformers were right to take *metanoeō* to mean specifically a change of heart, mind or mindset – a change often associated with sorrow or regret – rather than simply a synonym for turning. A 'change of heart or mind' was also how the word was used in the wider Greek literature of the time.[14]

We can even see from the context in Matthew 3:2 and 4:17 what kind of change of mind John and Jesus have in view: it is, 'Change your mind, for the kingdom of the heavens is near!' That is: change your minds about

---

[11] For example, Wayne Grudem, *Systematic Theology: An Introduction to Biblical Doctrine* (Leicester: Inter-Varsity Press, 1994), 709.

[12] Sinclair B. Ferguson, *The Whole Christ: Legalism, Antinomianism, and Gospel Assurance: Why the Marrow Controversy Still Matters* (Wheaton: Crossway, 2016), 57.

[13] Excluding examples from the Apocrypha.

[14] LSJ, '*metanoeō*.'

God and the future he is bringing about. Doing this will then bring about the deep shame and remorse for sin we observe in the people in 3:6.

Indeed, let me be clear: the change of mind *should* show itself in visible action. Change of mind and the action associated with a change of mind may even happen in what is basically the same event. The people respond to John's preaching about the kingdom and the future, changing their hearts and minds, and they get baptised and confess their sins (Matthew 3:6) all as one event, even if the mind and heart response has logical priority. What's more, John would certainly say that a true change of heart or mind will always show itself in visible 'fruit'. Hence his rebuke of the Pharisees and Sadducees in 3:8: 'Produce fruit in keeping with repentance.' John may be implying that although they have come to observe his baptism, they are not actually getting baptised or confessing their sins. Or he may have in mind the absence of the kind of behavioural changes Luke records him describing in Luke 3:10–14. Either way, the important point is that change of heart or mind (with sorrow and regret) is the right response to the news of the kingdom, and John knows that the Pharisees and Sadducees haven't responded this way because of the absence of visible 'fruit' in their lives and behaviour.

In Matthew 11:20–21, Jesus denounces towns like Chorazin and Bethsaida because the people there did not change their hearts or minds in response to his mighty works. Had the same works been done in wicked cities like Tyre or Sidon, he says, they would have changed their hearts or minds long ago and shown their contrition and sorrow at their sin 'in sackcloth and ashes'. Similarly, in Matthew 12:41, Jesus reminds the Pharisees and teachers of the law about how the people of Nineveh changed their hearts and minds in response to the preaching of Jonah. (Jonah's preaching, like John's, warned of future judgment. Their response also showed itself in sorrow and contrition: in fasting, sackcloth and sitting in the dust. And, indeed, in action: in turning from evil ways: Jonah 3:6–10.)

In Matthew 27:3, Matthew describes the change of mind experienced by Judas when he sees Jesus condemned by the chief priests and elders. Judas comes to realise that he has 'betrayed innocent blood' (27:4). Matthew uses a related but different word here, *metamelomai*, perhaps to indicate that his change of mind is very different from that called for in 3:2 and 4:17, in that it doesn't lead him to seek the forgiveness of his sins in Jesus.

Putting this all together helps us recover the priority of the heart and mind in what we conceptually call 'repentance'. It turns out that the Reformers had better instincts on how to read 'repent' in 3:2 and 4:17 than some modern evangelicals. We could add that the Puritans had better instincts when it came to developing the concept and doctrine of repentance. For example, Thomas Watson (1620–86) maintained that repentance is a 'spiritual medicine' made up of six special (and ordered) ingredients: 1) sight of sin; 2) sorrow for sin; 3) confession of sin; 4) shame for sin; 5) hatred for sin; 6) turning from sin.[15] As with Matthew, conviction comes before behavioural change. But better still to have ears to hear Matthew's portrayal of a right response. This begins in 3:2 and 4:17 with convictions about the kingdom and personal sin, then moves to coming to Jesus (11:28–30), then following him on the path of the cross (16:24) and culminates with disciple-making in all nations (28:16–20).

2. Jesus's baptism and commissioning • Matthew 3:13–17

John has just warned that someone greater than him will come after him, someone who will baptise with a 'Holy Spirit-and-fire' baptism (Matthew 3:11). This, then, is what happens:

The baptism of Jesus

13 Then Jesus came from Galilee to the Jordan to be baptised by John. 14 But John tried to deter him, saying, 'I need to be baptised by you, and do you come to me?'

15 Jesus replied, 'Let it be so now; it is proper for us to do this to fulfil all righteousness.' Then John consented.

16 As soon as Jesus was baptised, he went up out of the water. At that moment heaven was opened, and he saw the Spirit of God descending like a dove and alighting on him. 17 And a voice from heaven said, 'This is my Son, whom I love; with him I am well pleased.'

In verse 13, someone does come after John: Jesus comes from Galilee. And John clearly recognises him as the baptiser he is preparing the way for. We can see this in verse 14. John says, 'I need to be baptised by you.'

We must not miss the massive and wonderful surprise here! Jesus is the one John has been preparing the way for. But there is no axe, no winnowing shovel and, most importantly, no fire (at least, not yet).

The second major surprise is that Jesus doesn't do any baptising but

---

15 Thomas Watson, *The Doctrine of Repentance* (Edinburgh: Banner of Truth Trust, 1987), 18.

instead gets baptised by John. We can see from verse 14 that John knows Jesus doesn't need to be baptised: it should be the other way round. So what is Jesus doing? To be baptised means acknowledging one's sin (3:6). Jesus doesn't need to be baptised, but here is willing to be identified and associated with those who came to the Jordan confessing their sins. He is getting alongside them, much as he will do with the 'tax-collectors and sinners' later in the Gospel. And this identification with sinners will prove to be crucial for saving them. This is to 'fulfil all righteousness' (3:15). We shall see that 'righteousness' in Matthew can be equated to conformity to the will of God the Father.[16] The immediate narrative context has highlighted the will of the Father to deal with the sin of his people (Matthew 1:21). How, then, will this serve to fulfil this aim? Matthew has already been drawing our attention to the prophet Isaiah. We should therefore be able to see fairly readily that Jesus here is taking on the Servant role of being 'numbered with the transgressors' – to bear 'the sin of many' (Isaiah 53:12).

So, yes, the kingdom of the heavens is near. Judgment is coming. But Jesus has come to deal with sin before the Judgment. John's expectation was that the one coming after him would be bringing an 'axe' to bear soon – 'the axe has been laid to the root of the trees' (Matthew 3:10). This expectation of arrival and judgment as one event is resolved in the narrative into two parts. Jesus comes to be 'numbered with the transgressors' first, to prepare his people for the coming wrath.[17]

Terrence Donaldson helpfully identifies this moment as the point in Matthew's narrative where the main character is identified and 'accepts a mandate to do what needs to be done'.[18] The mandate here is to save his people from their sins (Matthew 1:21).

As Jesus publicly takes on this task, heaven opens and rejoices (verses 16 and 17). The Spirit of God comes down on Jesus, marking him as the one through whom God will act (verse 16). The Spirit rests upon the Servant in Isaiah 42:1, so this is another sign pointing to Jesus as the Servant. The sense of divine approval is reinforced as the voice of the Father expresses his delight: 'This is my Son, whom I love; with him I am well pleased' (verse 17).

Matthew cannot be said to be supporting 'adoptionism' here.

---

[16] We can see this, for example, by comparing Matthew 5:20 with 7:21.

[17] This concept of 'temporal resolution' in narrative is expanded in Cooper, 'Adaptive Eschatological Inference from the Gospel of Matthew', 59–80.

[18] Donaldson, 'Vindicated Son', 112.

Adoptionism is the doctrine that Jesus was adopted as Son of God only at his baptism and prior to this had no divine nature. But we have already been shown the Holy Spirit involved supernaturally with the birth of Jesus (Matthew 1:18, 20). Matthew has also already depicted Jesus as worthy of divine worship, even as a child (Matthew 2:11). His account is entirely consistent with a Trinitarian understanding.[19] The point here is to show us signs (visible and audible) of approval from both Spirit and Father as the Son takes on the mandate to deal with sins. The descent of the Spirit also shows us that Jesus has been divinely equipped to complete his task, much as a hero might be equipped and armed at a similar moment in a quest story. (That Jesus is equipped by the Spirit to complete his task will be confirmed later in Matthew 12:28.)

The heavenly voice commends Jesus using words from Psalm 2:7, 'This is my Son.' In Psalm 2, the Lord is addressing the king he has installed on Zion to destroy his enemies. In other words, Jesus has just been declared to be the 'Psalm 2 King' – the Anointed, the Messiah (to use the Hebrew term) or Christ (to use the Greek). He also represents and embodies God's rescued people, who are also called God's 'Son' in the Scriptures – Exodus 4:22 ('Israel is my firstborn son') and Hosea 11:1 ('When Israel was a child, I loved him, and out of Egypt I called my son'; quoted by Matthew back in 2:15).

To this the heavenly voice adds words from Isaiah 42:1, 'whom I love' (or 'the beloved'), 'with him I am well pleased'. (The words match exactly those Matthew uses in 12:18 to quote from Isaiah 42.) This reinforces the picture Matthew is building of Jesus as Isaiah's Servant of the Lord – taking on the Servant role of dying as sin-bearer for God's people (Isaiah 53:12), the one who will be the means whereby the light of salvation will reach the nations of the world (Isaiah 42:6; 49:6).

So the mandate from the Father which Jesus takes on here is as the Son who is Servant, to be a sin-bearer for the people and to take the light of salvation to the nations.

SUMMARY AND PURPOSE
The overall purpose of Matthew is to make its readers who aren't disciples of Jesus into disciples of Jesus, and to motivate and equip its readers who

---

[19] Not just against adoptionism. The simultaneous appearance of all three Persons counters Sabellianism too (the view that the three Persons of the Trinity are not distinct, but there is just one Person with three modes of appearance).

are disciples of Jesus to be disciple-makers. The early chapters prepare the way for this by restoring hope, changing our minds about the future. They also introduce Jesus and begin to clarify how he is going to bring all these things about.

For these verses, the immediate context is hugely important: the expectation of judgment raised by John in 3:7–12. John has been preaching the kingdom but is expecting the one coming after him to bring a separating judgment. These verses about Jesus's baptism should change our expectations, just as John's expectations had to change. The absolutely huge surprise to pick out is that when Jesus comes, he comes without an axe, fire or winnowing shovel – he comes not to baptise (yet), rather to be baptised. There is a massive sense of relief and joy that Jesus chose to stand alongside sinners and to take on the task of bearing the sin of his people. The purpose of these few verses, then, is to bring us to focus on Jesus as the one to come before the Judgment, the one taking on the mandate to deal with the problem of sin, and to join the divine celebration as he does so.

Complacency and indifference towards God may be the dominant notes of many cultures in the world today (especially western ones), but a conviction of sin or shame and a fear of judgment will catch up with all of us sooner or later. But here is Jesus, who willingly stands alongside the sinners who have come out to the Jordan. Here is the great comfort of this passage: that for those willing to acknowledge their sin and shame, Jesus is on their side. And in Matthew's account, he will go on to bear these burdens for them.

3. The Son, tested as Servant • Matthew 4:1–11

In the background to Jesus's arrival and the start of his ministry sketched in Matthew's genealogy (Matthew 1:1–17) lies the failure of Israel's kings, beginning with David (Matthew 1:6), and the past failure of God's rescued people, beginning in the wilderness after their rescue from Egypt, but culminating in the exile or deportation to Babylon (Matthew 1:11–12). Matthew has been telling us and showing us that Jesus has come to correct and address these past failures, restoring hope in the promises to Abraham and David.

But Matthew is presenting Jesus as much more than a merely human king like David. He is 'God with us' (Matthew 1:23). The Magi have worshipped him (Matthew 2:11) and John has been introduced as the one preparing the way for 'the Lord' (Matthew 3:3) – that is YHWH or the LORD in Isaiah 40:3. So the eternal Son has, by the Spirit, been born as a human of Mary (Matthew 1:16, 18–25), and as an adult has just been declared to be the 'Son' of Psalm 2. Confirmation has come visually – the Spirit descending on him like a dove (Matthew 3:16) – and audibly, from the voice of the Father from the heavens.

What does it actually mean for Jesus to be 'Son' or 'Son of God'? Matthew has already suggested the answer is, 'Not what you might expect!' (In particular, not quite what many at the time, even John, are expecting.) Jesus has come with a specific task to complete: to save his people from their sins (Matthew 1:21). He has not (yet) come with the judgment John has been expecting (Matthew 3:7–10). He has not (yet) come to baptise with fire (Matthew 3:11–12) but to be baptised, standing in solidarity with sinners (Matthew 3:13–15) – 'numbered with the transgressors' (Isaiah 53:12). In Matthew 3:17, the voice from the heavens says, 'This is my Son, whom I love; with him I am well pleased,' quoting from Isaiah 42:1 – a further suggestion that Jesus has come as Isaiah's Servant of the Lord.

In Matthew 4:1–11 we shall get further clarification on what it means to be 'Son' or 'Son of God'. The Spirit sends Jesus (God's beloved Son) into the wilderness, to be 'tested' – into an experience that deliberately follows the patterns of Israel (God's firstborn Son) in the wilderness. Here, the 'tempter' (verse 3), the 'devil' (verses 5, 8, 11), Satan himself (verse 10), challenges Jesus with three false ways of understanding what it means to be 'Son of God'.

Jesus is tested in the wilderness

4 Then Jesus was led by the Spirit into the wilderness to be tempted[a] by the devil. ²After fasting for forty days and forty nights, he was hungry. ³The tempter came to him and said, 'If you are the Son of God, tell these stones to become bread.'

⁴Jesus answered, 'It is written: "Man shall not live on bread alone, but on every word that comes from the mouth of God."[b]'

⁵Then the devil took him to the holy city and set him on the highest point of the temple. ⁶'If you are the Son of God,' he said, 'throw yourself down. For it is written:

" He will command his angels
    concerning you,
and they will lift you up in their
    hands,
so that you will not strike your
    foot against a stone."[c]'

⁷Jesus answered him, 'It is also written: "Do not put the Lord your God to the test."[d]'

82

8 Again, the devil took him to a very high mountain and showed him all the kingdoms of the world and their splendour. 9 'All this I will give you,' he said, 'if you will bow down and worship me.' 10 Jesus said to him, 'Away from me, Satan! For it is written: "Worship the Lord your God, and serve him only."e'

11 Then the devil left him, and angels came and attended him.

_____

a 1 The Greek for *tempted* can also mean tested.
b 4 Deut. 8:3
c 6 Psalm 91:11,12
d 7 Deut. 6:16
e 10 Deut. 6:13

Jesus led out to be tested as true Israelite and human (4:1)

After the opening of the heavens in Matthew 3:16, we get a slightly different kind of narrative in 4:1–11. It has a visionary feel to it, more like the visionary experiences of one of the prophets, such as Ezekiel or Zechariah, but none the less real for that. What we have unveiled for us here is the beginning of the cosmic battle taken on by Jesus on behalf of his people. The role of the Spirit, seen resting on Jesus in Matthew 3:16 (as per Isaiah 42:1), is to facilitate and empower his Servant ministry. This begins by taking him to the wilderness to be tested (verse 1). The Father declared of Jesus, 'This is my Son' (Matthew 3:17). But what does this really mean?

We have had numerous hints already that it means coming before the Judgment, standing with sinners (rather than judging them at this stage), to save them from their sins (Matthew 1:21), as Isaiah's Servant of the Lord. This is what gets tested and revealed even more clearly here. We might have certain expectations about what it means to be 'Son of God' – that it will mean coming with power, confrontation and judgment, for example. But this would destroy people in their sins, not save them. The Servant of the Lord in Isaiah, on the other hand, will be numbered with the transgressors and bear their sin (Isaiah 53:12). The test then is: is Jesus, as Son, worthy to take on the Servant task given to him by his Father?

This testing is 'by the devil', verse 1.[20] That is, it is by the one who through lies, accusations and slander opposes God. 'Devil' means slanderer in Greek, just as 'Satan' means adversary in Hebrew. So the testing is done with malicious intent, meaning it's not entirely wrong to call them 'temptations'. But while the devil's intent might be to tempt through

_____

[20] 'Testing' here is different from the language of trials to build character found in many cultures, and is more than simply being tempted to sin. Uytanlet and Kwa, *Matthew*, 73

these interactions with Jesus, God's intent is to test – to demonstrate, for our benefit – the worthiness of his Son.

In these verses, Jesus demonstrates his worthiness under test as the true Israelite. Matthew draws our attention to the number forty in verse 2, reminding us of Israel's forty years of testing in the wilderness. Jesus then quotes throughout from the book of Deuteronomy in response to the devil, words from God originally addressed to a failing and struggling Israel. But behind this lies another confrontation with the devil/Satan: between humanity and the serpent in the garden of Genesis 3. The serpent tempted the man and woman to doubt God's word and provision, to test his love and to exchange his love for something else (fruit from the tree of the knowledge of good and evil). They failed, and that pattern of failure is a pattern shared by all humanity. Israel should have been the new Adam, rescued from slavery, placed in a new garden (the Promised Land). But they too failed, and were expelled from the Land – much as Adam and Eve were expelled from the garden. Post-exile, 'Israel' is really no different from the rest of humanity. So although the contrast in these verses looks particular (Jesus contrasted with Israel), it is actually quite universal (Jesus contrasted with everyone).

But Matthew is showing Jesus as more than just a true Israelite, more even than a true human. Jesus is also the beloved Son, given a particular task by his Father. The tests in 4:1–11 demonstrate his worthiness to complete this – the Servant task of saving his people from their sins. And these things are demonstrated for us here so that, aware of our own failings, whether Jew or Gentile, we then pin all our hopes on Jesus.

The first test: Jesus, truly responsive to God's word of love (4:2–4)

Jesus shows himself as the only true Israelite and the only true human, the only one who is perfectly responsive to the word of God. (In particular, believing the word of love from his Father in Matthew 3:17, so he can go on to endure human suffering and death.)

After fasting for forty days and nights (verse 2), Jesus is hungry (not surprisingly!). He is thereby tested: will he use his power as Son of God to turn stones into bread (4:3)? Will he grumble at having no food, like the Israelites in the wilderness? Will he doubt the love of his Father expressed in 3:17 and put aside his humanity to use his power as Son of God to make bread, just like that? Will he follow the woman and the man in Genesis 3 and get what he wants to eat, right now? Will he transgress the bounds of the task his Father has given him, making it impossible for him to go on to die as a curse-bearer on behalf of God's people? The fasting has taken him to the edge of death, foreshadowing the bearing of death he will face on the cross. Will he pull out from the task he has taken on?

In response to all these implied questions, Jesus quotes Deuteronomy 8:3: 'Man shall not live on bread alone, but on every word that comes from the mouth of God.' Bread comes second to obedience to the word of God.

The second test: Jesus, fully confident in the care of his Father (4:5–7)

Jesus shows himself as the only one who truly trusts God with full confidence, and will not test him by putting his life on the line. (Rather, he will go on to lay down his life voluntarily – not as a test, but as a ransom for many, Matthew 20:28.)

The devil tests him a second time (4:6). Will Jesus follow the Israelites in what they did, testing the Lord their God? The devil suggests a scriptural warrant for doing so, in the protection promised in Psalm 91:11–12 for the one who dwells in the shelter of the Most High and trusts the Lord as refuge and fortress (Psalm 91:1–2). If Jesus is the Son of God, the one to whom the Psalms point forward, then surely he will be safe if he falls from the pinnacle of the Temple? But will he put his life on the line to win a debating point with the devil, rather than going on lay down his life to win the lives of many? In response, Jesus quotes Deuteronomy 6:16: 'Do not put the Lord your God to the test'. To test would show a lack of confidence. It would be a blasphemy to imply God's faithful promise is untrue. It would show a distrust in God's promises and purposes for him.

The third test: Jesus, the only true worshipper (4:8–11)

Jesus shows himself as the only one whose devotion to God remains constant and exclusive. (And his obedience and faithfulness will be vindicated when his Father gives him all authority in heaven and on earth: Matthew 28:18.)

The devil tests Jesus a third time, showing him the kingdoms of the world and offering them all in exchange for worship. The drama this time is in wondering whether Jesus will compromise in his worship, submitting himself to someone or something other than the God who is Lord and Creator, as Israel eventually did. Will he follow the man and woman in the garden of Genesis 3, exchanging the love of God for something else? Here, the devil offers Jesus dominion over all the kingdoms of the world, subject to being subservient to him. Will Jesus believe this scam and put aside the kingdom of the heavens? Will he put aside the path his Father has placed him on for this unseemly shortcut?

As Joe Kapolyo puts it, 'God's will must be fulfilled by appropriate means.'[21] Faced with all these possibilities, Jesus addresses the devil using his Hebrew name, Satan, and quotes from Deuteronomy 6:13: 'Worship the Lord your God, and serve him only.'

Matthew tells us the devil left Jesus, verse 11. But as we read on, we shall find that this is only the beginning of the battle between them. As Powell notes, 'This challenge represents Satan's first, albeit unsuccessful, attempt to dissuade God's agent and thwart the divine plan.'[22] The tests will continue. When Peter says in the middle of the Gospel, in response to Jesus talking about his suffering and death, 'This shall never happen to you!' Jesus replies, 'Get behind me, Satan!' (Matthew 16:22–3) – very much like verse 10 here. When he is on the cross, the people mock: 'Come down from the cross, if you are the Son of God!' (Matthew 27:40) – much as Satan taunts him here. But he stays on the cross, and saves his people from their sins.

In other words, we shall see the righteousness of Jesus as he perseveres in obedience through all these tests. And his determination to do as his Father wants will be seen to be completely vindicated. His trust in God's love and his love for God his Father is well founded. We can see this even here. Jesus is desperately hungry but, verse 11, the Father sends angels to attend him – literally, to feed him. As per the promises in Psalm 91. Later in the story, Jesus will lay down his life – not by throwing himself off a building, but on the cross, in obedience to his Father. Not as a test, but as a ransom for God's people. Jesus's victory over sin, death, evil and the devil will be so complete that on a mountain at the other end of the Gospel, all authority in heaven and on earth will be given to him (Matthew 28:18). It will not be given

---

[21] Joe Kapolyo, 'Matthew', in *Africa Bible Commentary*, ed. Tokunboh Adeyemo (Grand Rapids: Zondervan, 2006), 1142.

[22] Mark Allan Powell, 'The Plots and Subplots of Matthew's Gospel', *New Testament Studies* 38, no. 2 (1992): 200.

by the devil, as in the scam promise of verse 9 here, but given by the Father. In other words, Jesus is proving himself worthy not only to resist the devil, but also to defeat him.

SUMMARY AND PURPOSE

The purpose of 4:1–11 is threefold:

- To convince us of Jesus's determination to obey his Father's will, to defeat Satan and to complete the task he has been given.
- To remind us, and make us acutely aware, of our own failures to listen, trust and worship – seen relative to the perfect obedience of Jesus.
- Thereby to bring us to pin all our hopes on Jesus, the only true Israelite, the only true human, through whom alone Satan can be defeated and our humanity restored through his incarnation, death and resurrection.

Here we should find further conviction of sin, shame and failure – and therefore conviction of our profound need of Jesus. In his complete and uncompromised dependency, trust and worship, Jesus exposes failures that have inflicted all humanity since Genesis 3, and have been especially and painfully apparent in the history of Israel.

When it comes to our own struggles with temptation and sin, memorising Scripture can be a very effective strategy, reshaping our thoughts and instincts according to God's will. The verses can also often prove to be powerful when recalled in vulnerable moments. However, there is more to this passage than Jesus simply setting us a good example in this regard (although he does do this). After all, not many of us will ever face the peculiar kinds of testing described in these verses. (Not many have been tempted to turn stones into bread or jump off a temple, and very few in practice face the temptation to become a global dictator.) The main focus here is on Jesus's victory, and this is then the foundation for us approaching our own struggles as his disciples. If we consider ourselves connected to Jesus in these verses, as his disciples, with an identity rooted in him and the task he completed on our behalf, saved by his victory over evil, then our own listening, trust and worship can grow, and we shall then be in a better place to battle sin in our lives. (Compare Romans 6:10–12.) In particular, Jesus will call and teach us to depend upon our Father alone, trust him alone and worship him alone (e.g., Matthew 6:19–34).

The main thrust of these verses is about finding renewed confidence in our Saviour. He is tested so we can know he is more than worthy for the task he has taken on. And we shall see the determination he shows here to do his Father's will for the sake of others continue and follow through to the end of the Gospel.

PART FOUR

....

THE PATTERN OF JESUS'S MINISTRY

MATTHEW 4:12–10:42

4

Calling and Proclamation

MATTHEW 4:12–25

The overall structure of this section can be pictured like this:

> 3:1–4:11 Jesus proclaims the kingdom
> of the heavens in word and deed
>
> 4:12–17 A summary of the transition from John to
> Jesus, with a repeat of the call to repent
>
> > 4:18–22 Jesus calls the first
> > disciples to follow
> >
> > > 4:23 Summary: teaching,
> > > proclaiming
> > >
> > > (4:24–5 Huge crowds follow
> > >
> > > > 5:1–7:29 Jesus teaches his disciples in the
> > > > hearing of the crowd
> > > > (kingdom proclaimed in word)
> > > >
> > > > 8:1–9:34 Jesus demonstrates in advance the
> > > > lifting of the shadow of death
> > > > (kingdom proclaimed in deed)
> > >
> > > 9:35 Summary: teaching,
> > > proclaiming, healing
> > >
> > > (9:36–8 Jesus has compassion on the crowds,
> > > and calls his disciples to pray for more
> > > workers)
> >
> > 10:1–42 Jesus sends the first disciples to
> > proclaim the kingdom to Israel

Figure 5

At the centre is Jesus's proclamation of the kingdom in word (Matthew 5–7) and deed (Matthew 8–9). Around this in the concentric structure are the repeated summaries at 4:23 and 9:35, each immediately followed by a description of the crowd. Around this are two sections dealing with the first disciples. In 4:18–22, the first disciples are called. In Matthew 10, they are sent out to proclaim the kingdom to Israel.

91

1. *Calling* • *Matthew 4:12–22*

These are transitional verses, taking us from the ministry of John (described by Matthew in 3:1–12) to the ministry of Jesus (which begins formally at verse 17), accompanied by his first followers.

Jesus begins to preach

12 When Jesus heard that John had been put in prison, he withdrew to Galilee. **13** Leaving Nazareth, he went and lived in Capernaum, which was by the lake in the area of Zebulun and Naphtali – **14** to fulfil what was said through the prophet Isaiah:

15 'Land of Zebulun and land of
    Naphtali,
  the Way of the Sea, beyond the
    Jordan,
  Galilee of the Gentiles –
16 the people living in darkness
  have seen a great light;
on those living in the land of the
    shadow of death
a light has dawned.'[f]

17 From that time on Jesus began to preach, 'Repent, for the kingdom of heaven has come near.'

Jesus calls his first disciples

18 As Jesus was walking beside the Sea of Galilee, he saw two brothers, Simon called Peter and his brother Andrew. They were casting a net into the lake, for they were fishermen. **19** 'Come, follow me,' Jesus said, 'and I will send you out to fish for people.' **20** At once they left their nets and followed him.

21 Going on from there, he saw two other brothers, James son of Zebedee and his brother John. They were in a boat with their father Zebedee, preparing their nets. Jesus called them, **22** and immediately they left the boat and their father and followed him.

---

f 16 Isaiah 9:1,2

The sequence of events is easy to follow. John is arrested, and this prompts Jesus to withdraw into Galilee (verses 12–13). Matthew then makes two comments. First, he says, this fulfils what Isaiah said about where the light will dawn in the darkness (verses 14–16). Second, from this time on, Jesus began to preach (verse 17), picking up John's message to repent in the light of the nearness of the kingdom.

Jesus's ministry is then mapped out in more detail from verse 18. He calls his first followers (verses 18–22). He then, accompanied by them, begins his ministry throughout Galilee: teaching, proclaiming and healing (verse 23). This attracts great crowds from all around who also follow him (verses 24–5), which sets the stage for the beginning of the Sermon on the Mount (Matthew 5:1).

Breaking the verses into sections is tricky. The most obvious division is into three parts: verses 12–17, on the dawning of light in Galilee; verses 18–22, on the calling of the first followers; and verses 23–25, on Jesus's ministry in Galilee.[1] The difficulty is that verse 17, which begins, 'From that time on . . .', sounds like it is starting something new (rather than ending a section). Also, the continuity between verses 18–22 and 23–5 in the original Greek text is stronger than these divisions imply.

We get more clarity by stepping back and seeing how Matthew 4:12–10:42 works as a larger section. We have already noted that 4:23 is matched by 9:35, summarising Jesus's ministry in Galilee. In between these, the proclamation of the gospel of the kingdom is shown in Jesus teaching his disciples (Matthew 5–7, the Sermon on the Mount) and his healing and exorcism ministry (Matthew 8:1–9:34). Outside the markers at 4:23 and 9:35, there is Jesus calling the first followers in 4:18–22, then calling them to pray for extra workers in 9:36–8, and sending them out to multiply his ministry in Matthew 10. Verses 12–17 of chapter 4, then, stand as a summary of the transition from the ministry of John to the ministry of Jesus. This is expanded in 4:18–10:42 in such a way that we can begin to see how Jesus's proclamation of the gospel of the kingdom, and his 'fishing for people', will continue and multiply through the ministry of his followers and disciples.

The traditional divisions (verses 12–17, 18–22, 23–5) are fine, so long as we recognise the relationships between them. Jesus 'withdraws' to Galilee, where Isaiah has said the light will dawn in the darkness, and this is where he begins his ministry. We then see the first responders to Jesus in verses 18–22, who join Jesus in the ministry of verses 23–5 as his disciples. That is, as followers whom he will teach as disciples (Matthew 5:1–2).

From the arrest of John to the dawning of the light in Jesus (4:12–17)

The moral darkness in Jerusalem has led to the arrest of John, so Jesus doesn't go there, but instead withdraws back home to Galilee. At first, it seems a surprising move. After all, there is plenty of darkness and death here too, as we shall see. It is also hardly at the centre of things, not where many people would expect a world-changing ministry to begin. It is almost out in the nations, with the Gentiles.

---

[1] Nolland, *Matthew*, 171.

We have come across this pattern of withdrawing already in Matthew's Gospel. In 2:12, the Magi were warned to avoid Herod, and so withdrew to their home by another route. In 2:13–4 Joseph was also warned about Herod, so the family withdrew to Egypt. In 2:22 he was warned about Herod's son, and so withdrew to Galilee. Later in the Gospel, Jesus will continue with the pattern of withdrawal in the face of persecution and opposition (Matthew 12:15; 14:13; 15:21). This seems to be a positive missionary strategy. There may be a time to face and confront opposition, but (in general) actively hostile opposition will impede or slow down gospel proclamation. Jesus moves to places where he can speak freely and be heard. (This principle will later on drive Jesus's teaching in 10:23: 'When you are persecuted in one place, flee to another.')

But if we know the prophet Isaiah, the move to Galilee shouldn't surprise us at all. In Isaiah 9, the prophet sings a song of hope for a future generation, and he locates the focus of this hope in exactly the place Jesus has chosen. In Isaiah, the prophet was using 'darkness' and the 'shadow of death' to talk about the political oppression and violent death resulting from the Assyrian invasion of the northern tribes of Israel. Here, Matthew seems to be thinking about much more than the end of the eighth-century BC 'Assyrian crisis'. He is talking about the 'darkness' and 'shadow of death' brought upon the earth by humanity's sinful rebellion against their God.

Hence the beginning of Jesus's preaching in Matthew 4:17, which is like light breaking into the darkness because it proclaims the nearness of the kingdom of the heavens, where sin and death is dealt with, every false kingdom is swept away, and heaven and earth are reunited in a new cosmos.

We have heard these words before, of course (see above on 3:2 and the meaning of 'repent'). But on the lips of Jesus they should evoke a different response. When John was preaching the kingdom, he was expecting one to come after him who would bring fire and judgment (Matthew 3:7–12). We can imagine the people responding with some anxiety as they went out to the Jordan to be baptised, understandably uncertain about whether anything they could do as sinners could prepare them for what was coming. But then Jesus came without judgment, to stand alongside and for sinners (Matthew 3:13–17). So now, when Jesus proclaims the nearness of the kingdom and calls the people to repent, the response can be more positive and hopeful. As with John's preaching, our world view is changed and we are convicted of our sin – but now we have Jesus. There is a little breathing space, a window of opportunity to get ready for the kingdom, and someone here before the Judgment with the express purpose of preparing us for it – by bearing our sins.

The calling of the first followers (4:18–22)

There is a window of opportunity: Jesus has come before the Judgment, to prepare his people for it. But how, exactly, does someone make use of this window of opportunity? Matthew shows us. These verses show us a model response to Jesus and his proclamation. This is not just because of their placement just after the command in verse 17, but also because the pattern of getting up and following is repeated. We see it twice. (We shall see it again with Matthew the tax collector in chapter 9 and with the two blind men at the end of chapter 20.) The repetition suggests that this is not a one-off; this is a regular pattern that others can be involved in too.

The pattern is the same both times. Jesus calls them and everything they once depended on for their lives and livelihood they leave behind. Now they depend on Jesus. First it happens to Simon Peter and Andrew (verses 18–20); then it happens to James and John (verses 21–2).

We learn that responding to the light means a radical break and a radical, urgent realignment behind Jesus and his mission. Following Jesus means placing your life in his hands, going where he goes, doing as he does and learning from him (which, as we will see shortly in the Sermon on the Mount, is what it means to be a 'disciple'). In the 2011 NIV, Jesus says here, 'I will send you out to fish for people' (verse 19). More accurately, Jesus says, 'I will make you *fishers* of people' (my emphasis).

Jesus will send out these followers (with eight others) in Matthew 10, but only after teaching them (Matthew 5–7) and showing them what it looks like (Matthew 8–9). And he will send them out to the nations (Matthew 28:16–20), but only after he has suffered, died and been raised to life.

It might help to know that in some ways this is very similar to Elijah calling Elisha in 1 Kings 19. Elijah passes by and calls him, and Elisha ends up following him and going after him. But there is a key difference too: Elisha goes and says goodbye to his father and mother. The implication is: when Jesus calls you, when the kingdom is near, there is no time for any of that.

SUMMARY AND PURPOSE

The overall purpose of Matthew 4:12–10:42 is to evoke response to Jesus's proclamation, in word and deed, of the gospel of the kingdom of the heavens: to follow him, to trust him and to be instructed by him to go and proclaim the gospel.

The purpose of Matthew 4:12–23 within this is for people who know they are living in darkness to respond to Jesus's proclamation of the kingdom as light, with hope, to drop everything and follow him, eager to learn from him and participate as he gathers people to himself. Matthew wants his readers to acknowledge they live 'in darkness' and 'under the shadow of death' (4:16). We repress this inconvenient truth, fill our lives with things to distract ourselves from it and push the reality and inevitability of death out of sight as much as we can. But the reality will hit us sooner or later. Much better, of course, if we face up to it sooner. This is a great passage to encourage people to acknowledge the reality while there is still time.

As we saw in Matthew 3, for those who do accept that they live in darkness and under the shadow of death, and who have become convicted of their sin, hearing about the nearness of the kingdom might well bring anxiety or panic rather than comfort. But now that Jesus has come to stand with sinners (3:13–17) and has been tested in his resolve to complete the task his Father has given him (4:1–11), we can see the news of the kingdom as light dawning in the darkness.

The simple wholeheartedness of the first disciples, dropping everything to follow Jesus, is a huge challenge. (And we have much more of this challenge to wholeheartedness to come – e.g., Matthew 5:8; 6:19–24; 8:18–22; 9:9; 13:44–6; 16:24–8; 20:29–34.)

These verses summarise the beginning of Jesus's ministry of gospel and kingdom proclamation, inspiring us with their cosmic, history-changing scope and encouraging us to respond to the light of the kingdom by copying the very first disciples in their eagerness to follow him.

2. Proclaiming the kingdom • Matthew 4:23–5

These verses summarise Jesus's ministry in Galilee for the first time.

Jesus heals the sick

23 Jesus went throughout Galilee, teaching in their synagogues, proclaiming the good news of the kingdom, and healing every disease and illness among the people. 24 News about him spread all over Syria, and people brought to him all who were ill

with various diseases, those suffering severe pain, the demon-possessed, those having seizures, and the paralysed; and he healed them. **25** Large crowds from Galilee, the Decapolis,**g**

Jerusalem, Judea and the region across the Jordan followed him.

_____

g 25 That is, the Ten Cities

We have noted already that Matthew 4:23 is virtually identical to Matthew 9:35, meaning we can take this as a summary of everything that happens in between: teaching, preaching or proclaiming the gospel of the kingdom, and healing and exorcism. The emphasis in Matthew 5–7 is on Jesus's teaching. The emphasis in Matthew 8–9 is on his healing and exorcism ministry. And in everything Jesus does he is accompanied by his disciples – to learn from him. Everything Jesus does in Matthew 4:23–9:35 he will send his disciples to do in Matthew 10, and all of his teaching in Matthew 5–7 and Matthew 10 is training them in preparation for this task.

In Matthew 4:24–5 we begin to see the urgent need for this expanded ministry. What Jesus is doing is drawing people to himself like a magnet. People struggling in many severe ways under the shadow of death have been attracted by his healing and exorcism ministry (verse 24). Matthew tells us they come from every direction. Jesus is gathering a people around himself, rather like God did through Moses at Mount Sinai. We shall return to the healing and exorcism ministry in Matthew 8–9, and to the large crowds in 9:36–8, where Jesus will call his disciples to pray for more workers cast into the harvest field, just before sending them out with news of the kingdom in Matthew 10.

But just looking ahead to 5:1–2, the striking thing here is that Jesus doesn't respond to the crowds by addressing them. Instead, although he remains aware of the presence of the crowds, he sits down to address and to teach his disciples. We see here the principle of facing urgent need through teaching and training. If he were like us, Jesus might have been distracted by the crowds and given them all his attention.[2] But his first priority is to establish and train his disciples – a strategy of multiplying ministry and mission in the face of urgent need.

_____

[2] Samuel Uytanlet notes that in Filipino culture, the _masa_ (or 'masses') hold the key to political power. They are the ones the candidates at election time appeal to. Uytanlet and Kwa, _Matthew_, 79. Similar things could be said about other cultures. The contrast with Jesus's approach is very striking.

5

Proclaiming in Word

MATTHEW 5–7

1. An Introduction to the Sermon on the Mount • Matthew 5–7

It is with some trepidation that we turn next to what is almost universally called 'the Sermon on the Mount' (Matthew 5–7), knowing just how important these chapters have been in Christian history, tradition and thought – but also knowing just how much difficulty and confusion they have caused.

The history of interpretation of the Sermon on the Mount is enormously complicated.[1] As Ulrich Luz noted, there is also a strong connection between an interpretation and the historical situation in which it was made. The interpretations are 'expressions of the church's understanding of itself and of the proper church reality at a given time'.[2] But despite the complexity, we can tease out three main approaches to the Sermon on the Mount:

- Perfectionism. The Sermon is an ethical system setting out (perfect) standards for kingdom entry, contrary to kingdom entry by faith.
- A *deliberately* unattainable standard. The Sermon is setting a high ethical standard (as in the first approach), but a deliberately impossible one. It then functions to convict us of sin and to lead us to (an imputed) righteousness in Christ by faith.
- Grace is presupposed. The disciples are taken to have already a strong faith relationship with Jesus as their teacher and a living

---

[1] There are brief surveys in Ulrich Luz, *Matthew 1–7* (Minneapolis: Augsburg, 1989), 218–23 and Joachim Jeremias, *The Sermon on the Mount* (Philadelphia: Fortress Press, 1963), 1–6.
[2] Luz, *Matthew 1–7*, 218

relationship with the Father through him. The Sermon then maps out what it means to live by faith as a disciple of Jesus in the light of the kingdom.

The first approach has been very common at various times in history, especially before the Reformation. Some more recent versions of this have set up Matthew as an opponent of the teaching of the apostle Paul. Matthew is taken to be pro-Law in reaction to Paul's alleged (over-) insistence on grace and faith.[3]

We have already come across the second approach in the Introduction above (in the section titled 'But how should we process Jesus's teaching?'). This approach became more common after the Reformation, and then even more so in modern evangelicalism (partly in reaction to the nineteenth-century 'holiness' movements which took something much more like the first approach). A significant proportion of the teaching and preaching I've heard personally on the Sermon on the Mount over the last thirty years has been some variation on this second approach. It certainly results in a nice simple message to preach. In my experience, the basic message is often then supplemented in the more detailed teaching of the Sermon with some cherry-picked applications of some things Christians ought *not* to do (like get angry, be lustful or worry), and a few things they really *ought to do* (such as tell the truth, love their enemies and pray). These are implicitly presented as behaviours we somehow *should* control and *are able* to control, rather than as unattainable ideals. Listeners are unsurprisingly left somewhat confused.

Not that this second approach is entirely wrong. For the crowd listening in to the Sermon (5:1), its standards would have seemed both amazing and unattainable (7:28–9). The disciples would also have found it convicting, challenging and humbling – and so should we. Nevertheless, as an overall approach it really doesn't make much sense. It doesn't fit with the context of the Sermon in Matthew's Gospel or the content of the Sermon itself – not least how emphatic Jesus seems to be that he expects his teaching actually to be put into practice (5:19; 7:21–7).

I shall be following the third approach in what follows. Grace is presupposed for the disciples. As we noted in the Introduction under

---

[3] For example, David C. Sim, *The Gospel of Matthew and Christian Judaism: The History and Social Setting of the Matthean Community* (Edinburgh: T&T Clark, 1998), 123–39.

'Discipleship', the word 'disciple' presupposes a teacher–disciple relationship. By employing (for the first time) the label 'disciples' here in 5:1, Matthew is indicating this already-existing relationship. This is confirmed as we read on. These are people who are already 'salt' and 'light' (5:13–17) and who already have a relationship though Jesus with God as Father (5:16, 45, 48; 6:1, 4, 6, 8, 14–15, 18, 26, 32) – relating to their Father in prayer as his beloved children (6:9–13, 7:7–11).

We might miss this because we don't have an explicit description of the application of this grace to the disciples in the Sermon itself. It's implied – presupposed – rather than spelled out. It's not explained, for example, how such grace could come to people Jesus candidly describes as 'evil' (7:11). We only get this fully explained as we witness and process the sin-/curse-bearing death of Jesus later in the Gospel. But for the moment it should be clear: Jesus is addressing his disciples as disciples – not as potential disciples.

Context

The background to the Sermon is that the kingdom of the heavens is near (3:2; 4:17) and that Jesus has come as Son and Servant to fulfil a mandate given to him by his Father. Matthew has compared his arrival to light breaking into the darkness of the 'shadow of death' (4:15–16). If we know Isaiah, we should be asking, how is this light going to spill out into the nations? (And the Sermon will begin to give us some answers.)

Jesus has also just called his first disciples and promised to make them 'fishers of people' (4:18–22). We should be asking, 'What does it actually look like to follow Jesus as one of his disciples?' and, 'What are the first steps in becoming a "fisher of people"?' (Again, the Sermon will begin to give us some answers to these questions.)

We noted above the repetition of a similar summary of Jesus's ministry in Galilee – almost word for word – in 4:23–4 and 9:35. This keeps this material together as a unit: the first part focused on Jesus's teaching (Matthew 5–7); the second on his healing and exorcism ministry (Matthew 8–9). (For a reminder of how the Sermon fits into the context of 4:12–10:42, see Figure 5 above.) These are both components of what it means for Jesus to be proclaiming 'the good news of the kingdom' (4:23; 9:35). As we come into the Sermon on the Mount, we can expect Jesus to be teaching his disciples in the light of the reality of the kingdom.

The situation Jesus is speaking into is set up in the first two verses of

Matthew 5. Jesus sees the crowd, but then sits and teaches his disciples. We shall find this double audience very important when it comes to processing and teaching the Sermon. The teaching is *primarily* for the disciples, and Jesus expects them to hear it and put it into practice. But it is also intended to be overheard by the crowd.

If we then read right through to the end of Gospel – through the giving over and arrest of Jesus, his crucifixion and curse-bearing death, and his vindication in resurrection – we end at the Great Commission, and Jesus's command to 'go and make disciples of all nations' (28:19). The final component of this is '. . . teaching them to obey everything I have commanded' (28:20). As we've noted before, this encourages us to go back and read the Gospel again, taking particular note of everything Jesus has commanded – the Sermon on the Mount being where the bulk of this teaching begins.

That means, from a second reading of the Sermon onwards, the fact that grace is presupposed in Jesus's teaching of his disciples is far less puzzling. Reading the Sermon again, having read through to the end of the Gospel, clarifies things enormously, because it means we can read it as those who have been:

- humbled to acknowledge personal failure (like Peter, for example). We do then indeed begin reading the Sermon in the state of being 'poor in spirit' (5:3);
- served by Jesus the Servant, for the forgiveness of their sins and the wiping away of curse and shame. Hence being in a place where we can daily ask for the removal of our 'debts' (6:12);
- adopted into God's (missionary) family. Hence being able to call God our Father, in covenant relationship;
- adopted into the Servant task of taking the light of salvation to the nations (Isaiah 42:6; 49:6). Hence the strong missionary component we see throughout the Sermon, on the vocation of Jesus's disciples as 'light of the world' (5:14–16).

The purpose of the Sermon

The overall purpose of Matthew is to make its readers who aren't disciples of Jesus into disciples of Jesus, and to motivate and equip its readers who are disciples of Jesus to be disciple-makers.

For the crowds listening in (5:1a; 7:28–9), the Sermon is part of Jesus's proclamation of the coming kingdom. It presents an astonishing moral vision of what it means to live in the light of the kingdom – an implicit invitation to join in by becoming disciples of Jesus. It stirs the 'moral imagination' of anyone who hears it.[4] It is important to keep this in mind (especially for those teaching or preaching the Sermon to mixed audiences, where many are not disciples of Jesus). But this is not the primary purpose of the Sermon, which is clearly focused on the disciples (5:1b–2).

The purpose of the Sermon on the Mount for the disciples of Jesus is, then, a deep, humble, heart-based, exclusive dependence on God as Father, flowing out into radical behaviour that brings others to praise him, setting the foundations for a disciple-making discipleship.

Here, then, are five consequences for reading the Sermon on the Mount:

- Don't slip into reading this as a 'works righteousness' (as in the first approach to the Sermon outlined above). It should be impossible to read it this way. In the Sermon, it is the Pharisees (and 'hypocrites' of 6:2, 5, 16) who represent the pursuit of a phony 'righteousness' based on external works, not Jesus and his disciples. Jesus is implacably opposed to the Pharisees throughout the Sermon, as he is throughout the Gospel.
- Look for a conviction of a sin (as in the second approach to the Sermon outlined above). But look for much more than a conviction of sin. Keep looking for the missionary purpose driving Jesus's teaching – being light to the world to the glory of the Father (5:16).
- Indeed, notice (and delight in) the emphasis on God the Father throughout.
- But don't miss the (slightly hidden) centrality of Jesus. He is speaking to *his* disciples (5:1), who will be persecuted on *his* account (5:11). He is the one who speaks with ultimate authority ('But I tell you . . .', 5:22, 28, 32, 34, 39, 44) and will judge the world with ultimate authority (7:21–3). This is where the grace presupposed in the Sermon comes from – it comes from following him.
- Keep coming back to 5:3–6. When the moral challenge and vision of the Sermon seem too much, remember that the kingdom of the heavens belongs to the poor in spirit, those in mourning, the meek and those who hunger and thirst for righteousness.

---

[4] This helpful expression comes from Dale C. Allison, Jr., *The Sermon on the Mount: Inspiring the Moral Imagination* (New York: Crossroad, 1999).

Structure

The Sermon on the Mount begins with favourable value judgments on certain characteristics (5:3–10) and ends with exhortations and appeals (7:13–27). The material in between deals first with the nature and identity of the disciple of Jesus (summed up in 5:13 as 'the salt of the earth'). Building on this, Jesus then deals with the function and vocation of his disciples (summed up in 5:14 as 'the light of the world'). The middle section fits together like this:[5]

A You are the salt of the earth (5:13)

    B You are the light of the world (5:14–16)

    B' This is how, in fulfilment of the Law and the Prophets, to be 'light' (5:17–48)

A' This is how to be 'salt', and act in a way that is consistent with the Law and the Prophets (6:1–7:12).

Or, for more detail, see the diagram below:

---

[5] This structure joins many from scholars who have suggested some kind of concentric arrangement to the Sermon. Most of these try to place the Lord's Prayer at the centre (e.g., Daniel Patte, *The Gospel According to Matthew* (Fortress, 1987), 65; Luz, *Matthew 1–7*, 211–13; Günter Bornkamm, 'Der Aufbau Der Bergpredigt', *New Testament Studies* 24 (1977–8); Robert A. Guelich, *The Sermon on the Mount: A Foundation for Understanding* (Waco: Word Books, 1982), 324–5). The proposal here (and in Ben Cooper, 'Following and Fishing 101: Revisiting and Expanding William Dumbrell on the Logic and Structure of the Sermon of the Mount', *Journal for Gospels and Acts Research* 3 (2019)) is much simpler, and aims to work with the microstructures of the Sermon more effectively than these suggestions.

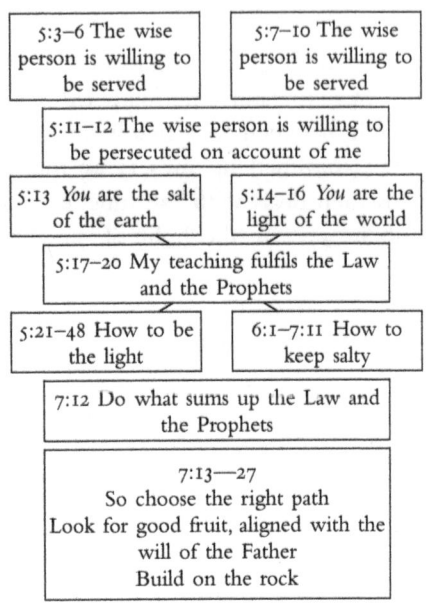

Figure 6

2. Identity and vocation • Matthew 5:1–20

The overall context of 4:12–10:42 is that, building on the proclamation of John, Jesus is now proclaiming the nearness of the kingdom of the heavens (4:17). He has called his first disciples to follow him, promising to make them fishers 'of people' (4:18–22). He has begun a ministry of proclaiming the gospel of the kingdom in Galilee, attracting great crowds of people from all the surrounding regions (4:23–5).

Introduction to the Sermon on the Mount

5 Now when Jesus saw the crowds, he went up on a mountainside and sat down. His disciples came to him, **2** and he began to teach them.

The Beatitudes

He said:

3 'Blessed are the poor in spirit,
　　for theirs is the kingdom of
　　　heaven.
4 Blessed are those who mourn,
　　for they will be comforted.
5 Blessed are the meek,
　　for they will inherit the earth.
6 Blessed are those who hunger and
　　　thirst for righteousness,

for they will be filled.

7 Blessed are the merciful,

for they will be shown mercy.

8 Blessed are the pure in heart,

for they will see God.

9 Blessed are the peacemakers,

for they will be called children of God.

10 Blessed are those who are persecuted because of righteousness,

for theirs is the kingdom of heaven.

11 'Blessed are you when people insult you, persecute you and falsely say all kinds of evil against you because of me. **12** Rejoice and be glad, because great is your reward in heaven, for in the same way they persecuted the prophets who were before you.

Salt and light

13 'You are the salt of the earth. But if the salt loses its saltiness, how can it be made salty again? It is no longer good for anything, except to be thrown out and trampled underfoot.

14 'You are the light of the world. A town built on a hill cannot be hidden. **15** Neither do people light a lamp and put it under a bowl. Instead they put it on its stand, and it gives light to everyone in the house. **16** In the same way, let your light shine before others, that they may see your good deeds and glorify your Father in heaven.

The fulfilment of the law

17 'Do not think that I have come to abolish the Law or the Prophets; I have not come to abolish them but to fulfil them. **18** For truly I tell you, until heaven and earth disappear, not the smallest letter, not the least stroke of a pen, will by any means disappear from the Law until everything is accomplished. **19** Therefore anyone who sets aside one of the least of these commands and teaches others accordingly will be called least in the kingdom of heaven, but whoever practises and teaches these commands will be called great in the kingdom of heaven. **20** For I tell you that unless your righteousness surpasses that of the Pharisees and the teachers of the law, you will certainly not enter the kingdom of heaven.

William Dumbrell's article on the logic of Matthew 5:1–20 provides a very good starting place for thinking about the structure and flow of argument in these verses.[6] Matthew begins in 5:1–2 with the crowds, prompting Jesus to sit down with his disciples in a prominent place to teach them. This gives the situational setting of the Sermon on the Mount: Jesus teaching his disciples in the sight and hearing of the crowds.

---

[6] William J. Dumbrell, 'The Logic of the Role of the Law in Matthew 5:1–20', *Novum Testamentum* 23, no. 1 (1981). There is a summary, critique and expansion of his arguments in Cooper, 'Following and Fishing', 41–55.

Jesus's actual teaching begins with a sequence of nine wisdom sayings, in an 8+1 pattern:

> 5:3–10: an eight-part description of truly wise people, who are living the best possible life (and the reasons why it is the best life).

> 5:11–12: this description applied directly to the disciples, who take on the role of the prophets, suffering on account of Jesus.

The main block of eight wisdom sayings runs from 5:3 to 5:10, with both these verses including the phrase 'for theirs is the kingdom of [the heavens]'. This then seems to divide into two blocks of four, each ending with a saying about righteousness (5:3–6, 7–10).

But in 5:11–12, Jesus applies this teaching directly to the disciples in front of him: blessed are *you* when others revile you . . . This focus on direct, second-person address is what continues into 5:13–16.

Verses 13–16 divide into two sayings. In each part, there is an emphatic declaration ('*You* are . . .'), followed by reasons and encouragement to persevere in this identity or function:

	5:13	5:14–16
Declaration:	*You* are the salt of the earth	*You* are the light of the world
Support:	Seasoning is useless if it loses its saltiness.	Lights are useless if they are hidden. So let your light shine . . .

Table 4

Jesus then moves straight on to verse 17 without pausing. Verses 17–18 also divide into two. In each part, Jesus makes clear what he has not come to do and won't encourage, followed by a statement making it clear what he has come to do and what he will encourage. In each case, this is followed by an emphatic statement of support (5:18, 20):

	5:17–18	5:19–20
Negative:	Do not think I have come to abolish . . .	Anyone who sets aside one of the least of these . . . and teaches others accordingly . . .
Positive:	. . . but to fulfil	Whoever practices and teaches these
Support:	For truly I tell you . . .	For I tell you . . .

Table 5

'Blessed' (Greek: *makarios*)

The wisdom sayings in 5:3–12 have long been known as the Beatitudes – *beatus* being the Latin word for 'blessing'. English translations have almost always gone for 'blessed'. But this is misleading if it's taken to indicate an explicit act of blessing from God on a person – or an explicit declaration of being under God's favour.[7] There's a different word in Greek for this (*eulogētos*), with a different Old Testament background. The Old Testament background to *makarios* (found throughout the Psalms, for example) is a word that declares a favourable value judgment on someone in the happy state of living wisely. Psalm 1:1 is a good example: '"Blessed"/"happy" is the one who does not walk in step with the wicked.' In wider Greek usage at the time Jesus was speaking, it was a word used to describe 'the good life'. It applies therefore to the person who is truly wise, with a character that is truly human, living the best kind of life. It remains a very hard word to translate. A possible paraphrase might be: the person who is living the best possible life is actually the one who is poor in spirit, because . . . and so on.[8]

The best life you can live (5:1–12)

Note the double audience in 5:1–2. If we listen to what Jesus says in this passage standing alongside someone in the crowd, then we are likely to find the description of someone 'blessed' in 5:3–12 challenging rather than encouraging. But if we listen alongside the disciples then it reads very differently. As discussed above, Matthew seems to be taking it as given that Jesus is talking to his disciples as true disciples, who have been humbled and incorporated into Jesus's Servant work in the nations. He's anticipating both everything Jesus will do for them to save them from their sins and the commissioning in 28:16–20.

---

[7] As Pennington notes, 'One misreads the Beatitudes if they are taken as mere statements of God's blessing without recognizing that inherent in a *macarism* [beatitude] is an appeal to live in a certain way that will result in our flourishing.' Jonathan T. Pennington, *The Sermon on the Mount and Human Flourishing: A Theological Commentary* (Grand Rapids: Baker Academic, 2017), 160.

[8] Similarly in African culture, where to 'bless' is often what socially superior people do to show goodwill to those below them. But as Joe Kapolyo notes, 'the Beatitudes are not talking about this kind of blessedness! . . . They teach that blessedness results from the cultivation of certain attributes that are approved of by God.' Kapolyo, 'Matthew', 1143.

The surprise here is that, faced with a crowd of needy people, Jesus's first instinct is to sit down and teach his disciples. As we shall see further, the strategy is to teach and train the disciples (Matthew 5–7, 10) in the context of Jesus's own ministry (Matthew 8–9), so that workers for the harvest can be multiplied (9:35–8) and then sent out (10:5, anticipating 28:16–20). The way Jesus begins his teaching is also a surprise: eight slightly enigmatic wisdom sayings (5:3–10) that are only directly applied to the disciples in a final, ninth saying (5:11–12).

These Beatitudes are a gentle, indirect encouragement on (or invitation to) the life Jesus is commending. This is the life of the truly humble, wise person – a disciple of Jesus, as it turns out (5:11–12). Jesus begins his teaching by commending certain foundational attitudes (5:3–6), moves on to encourage conduct that flows from these attitudes (5:7–10) and then explicitly encourages his disciples to endure the suffering that will come from this prophet-like ministry (5:11–12).

The first part of each Beatitude describes the character of the truly wise people Jesus is commending. The first four describe their identity and attitudes. This will be further developed in the salt metaphor (5:13) and the second half of the main body of the Sermon (6:1–7:11). Jesus uses language from Isaiah 61:1–3. In Isaiah, the prophet is announcing good news to a crushed community. These are people living under thick darkness but waiting upon God (Isaiah 60:2), recalling the darkness of Isaiah 9:2, which Matthew has quoted in 4:16, describing the condition of the people as under 'the shadow of death'.

The 'poor in spirit' (5:3) are therefore those who are acknowledging their struggle under the shadow of death, convicted of their culpability (like the people flooding out to John in 3:5–6) but now accepting the light that has arrived in Jesus.

'Those who mourn' (5:4) are those not just mourning their sin (though that is a part of it), but simply mourning – crushed under the reality and awfulness of death.

Meekness (5:5) is a quality Matthew also uses of Jesus (11:29, 21:5; compare 12:19–20). As we've seen in Matthew 3–4, Jesus has not come (yet) to fight or judge, but with an offer of peace. Likewise, his disciples are those who have put down their weapons in the human fight for supremacy and have instead entrusted themselves to God.

Those who 'hunger and thirst for righteousness' (5:6) are aware of their own moral shortcomings in this broken world, but are also longing for 'righteousness' more generally – justice and peace flooding into a broken world to repair and realign it with its God.

These first Beatitudes thus work something like this: Jesus says knowingly to his disciples, 'Let us consider truly wise people, those living the best possible life. They are poor in spirit, they are in mourning, meek, etc. And yet they are still living the best possible life! Why? Because (implied: as my disciples) the kingdom of the heavens is theirs, etc.' The second part of each Beatitude, giving the reason why such people are truly wise, emphasises the future – when heaven and earth are reunited, death and mourning taken away, the whole earth given to God's people, the whole cosmos put right.[9] But these also have some impact in the present. Jesus says that 'theirs is the kingdom of heaven' (5:3, present tense; and again in 5:10). From the future certainties Jesus has spoken of come assurance, hope – of comfort and inheritance – and an alignment with God even now as a follower of Jesus.

The first four sayings emphasise brokenness and humility. For those before you willing to acknowledge these things in themselves, they act as an encouragement – you can stress the good things Jesus promises such people. To the dispirited and broken disciple, they are an assurance and comfort. To a growing disciple, they are a different kind of encouragement: to seek depth in humility and dependence, and to seek to express conduct appropriate to true discipleship. For those 'in the crowd', or for 'disciples' with a false humility still not recognising their brokenness, they act as both a challenge and an invitation to discipleship. To the false disciple – self-sufficient, proud, hard-hearted, unmerciful, aggressive and lawless – they act as a warning.

If 5:3–6 describe a humble identity and humble attitudes, then 5:7–10 describe conduct based upon this foundation. This is further developed in 5:11–12, the light metaphor (5:14–16) and the first half of the main body of the Sermon (5:21–48). These are people beginning to show some of the characteristics of their heavenly Father and their allegiance to Jesus.

So they are 'merciful' (5:7), just as their Father has been to them. They are 'pure in heart' (5:8): displaying good conduct that is not just on the surface but has been interiorised, flowing from the heart, just like Jesus. They are 'peacemakers', also just like Jesus. Building on the meekness of 5:5, they act to bring about peace. The emphasis later will be on spreading the peace of God (see 10:12–13), not necessarily bringing other kinds of peace (see 10:34–6). And they are persecuted for their righteousness (5:10), just like Jesus.

---

[9] As Mark Allan Powell puts it, 'All of the first four beatitudes speak of reversal of circumstances for those who are unfortunate.' Mark Allan Powell, 'Matthew's Beatitudes: Reversals and Rewards of the Kingdom', *Catholic Biblical Quarterly* 58, no. 3 (1996): 469.

This second set of Beatitudes thus work something like this: Jesus says, 'Let us consider truly wise people, those living the best possible life. They are showing conduct that is merciful, pure in heart, peace-making, etc. These things are hard, and provoke hostility and persecution. And yet they persevere because this is the best possible life for them to live. How so? Because (implied: as my disciples) they will be shown mercy, they will see God, etc.' Again, the second part of each Beatitude emphasises future certainties – the disciples shown mercy at the Judgment, able to see God, fully adopted (compare Romans 8:23) and living in the kingdom. But, again, these have some impact in the present. The certainty of future mercy is itself a mercy. Jesus's disciples can already 'see' God in him. They can already call God 'Father'. The kingdom of heaven is even now 'theirs' – present tense.

The final Beatitude 5:11–12 links what Jesus has just said to the disciples and provides the transition into the rest of the Sermon. The 'righteous-ness' of 5:10 is in fact conduct that links a disciple to Jesus – Jesus says it provokes hostility 'because of me' (5:11). Hostility is in itself nothing to rejoice in. But if it confirms a connection to Jesus, then it confirms a 'reward in heaven'. That is, a reward kept in heaven until the full coming of the kingdom of heaven. This then also connects the disciples to the prophets, who were likewise persecuted in the past. That is, the identity, ministry and vocation of the prophets is now fulfilled in Jesus's disciples, as he will go on to explain at greater length.

The second set of four sayings (with the last one expanded in 5:11–12) spell out in broad terms how Jesus's disciples are to live in the world: acting with mercy, from a pure heart, to bring about peace (with God) even when such action results in persecution. There will be more detail about such things as the Sermon unfolds. Remember: these things don't result in becoming a disciple; they are addressed to people who are already disciples. Even so, they are challenging: hard because they don't come naturally to us; hard because they are costly and provoke persecution. So, again, this is a place to remind disciples where they are heading as they do these things because of Jesus.

Salt and light (5:13–16)

To describe the disciples as 'the salt of the earth' is an obscure metaphor. On its own, it could mean many things, and has been interpreted in many ways. But Jesus is addressing his disciples as those who have some kind of new relationship with God, under what we might call (although Jesus doesn't use the word) a new covenant. From this moment, the Gospel is heading towards a denouement where the disciples will be sent out to make disciples of the nations under what is recognisable from the rest of Scripture as a 'covenant oath': '. . . and surely I am with you always, to the very end of the age' (28:20b). It therefore makes most sense to take Jesus to be building on the Old Testament association between salt and the covenant.[10] That is, the reference in 5:13 is an allusion to 'the salt of the covenant' (Leviticus 2:13; Exodus 30:35; Numbers 18:19; 2 Chronicles 13:5). In the last of these references, Abijah appeals to the enduring and permanent relationship the Lord has established with David and his descendants (compare 2 Samuel 7), calling it a 'covenant of salt'. A big question left hanging at the end of the Old Testament was: what has happened to this covenant of salt with David, which was supposed to be enduring and permanent? The genealogy in 1:1–17 has reminded us of this question and pointed us to Jesus as the key to the answer. Now Jesus looks his disciples in the eye and says, '*You* are the salt of the earth.' That is, 'As my disciples, the covenant continues with you.'

Why 'earth', rather than 'world', as in 5:14? Because the covenant relationship established by Jesus between God and his disciples operates until 'the very end of the age' (28:20b). In this time, before the final coming of the kingdom, as heaven and earth remain separated, it's their concern that the will of God is done on earth as it is in heaven (look ahead to 6:10). But lose this covenant identity, and the disciples will be useless and worthless (5:13b).

Quite what it means to be 'salt' in practice is something on which Jesus will have much more to say (in 6:1–7:11) – so we can let people know that there will be much more detail to come when it comes to application! Here, it's the sense of a precious and special identity that's worth dwelling on. If we are the 'salt of the earth', then we are part of the enduring covenant God made with David and we are heirs to the promises to Abraham. That is, as disciples of Jesus (but only as disciples of Jesus), whether Jew or Gentile, we have the genealogy of 1:1–17 as our heritage. We have a strong connection to what God has been doing, deeply rooted in his plans and purposes, stretching right back to the beginning. What's more, we are representatives of what God is doing on the earth right now. This makes any other self-identity we might have (or foolishly yearn for) pale into relative insignificance.

---

[10] This was one of Dumbrell's most innovative and helpful suggestions. Dumbrell, 'Logic', 12.

To be 'the light of the world' (5:14a) is more obviously an allusion to the expectation of the prophets that from God's people the light of salvation will come to flood the whole world. For example, the Servant of Isaiah 49:6 is told:

> It is too small a thing for you to be my servant
>> to restore the tribes of Jacob
>> and bring back those of Israel I have kept.
> I will also make you a light for the Gentiles,
>> that my salvation may reach to the ends of the earth.

(See also Isaiah 42:6.) The 'town built on a hill' (5:14b) sounds much like Zion in Isaiah 2:1–4, the mountain to which all the nations will come, streaming to its light (Isaiah 60:1–2). Now Jesus looks his disciples in the eye and says, '*You* are the light of the world.' That is, 'As my disciples, the prophetic expectation that light will flood to every corner of creation is going to be fulfilled in you.' Why 'world', rather than 'earth'? Probably because this light is to be seen in the whole cosmos: not just the earth, but visible in the heavenly spaces too.

If being 'light' is the disciples' vocation, function and purpose in the world, then it makes no sense to hide it. Lights or lamps are not for hiding, but for putting on a stand to shine brightly (5:15). Likewise, you should let your light shine before others, says Jesus (5:16a). The means by which the light shines is through certain good deeds (5:16b), but note carefully the purpose of these. They are not done to establish a relationship with Jesus or the Father. That is taken as given. Rather, they are done to bring glory to our Father in the heavens. While 'light' understood this way doesn't establish a relationship with the Father or gain access to the kingdom, it is evidence that someone has such a relationship and is part of the kingdom – just as bright light from a torch is evidence of fresh batteries. We would expect the 'light' coming from one who has such a relationship to be brighter than that coming from one who doesn't. Getting this straight will help with understanding 5:20.

Jesus will also have much more to say on what it means to be 'light' – especially in the rest of Matthew 5. So the detail can wait. Here, again, it is worth dwelling on the basic idea and the enormous privilege of having such a role in the world. All other vocations, if they are to mean anything at all, must be subsumed under this one. There is nothing more purposeful and noble, or indeed truly human, than this role of shining light in the darkness of the world to the glory of the Father.

Fulfilling the Law and the Prophets (5:17–20)

Without a pause, Jesus immediately begins to talk about the Law and the Prophets. The disciples know that the Law has always been central to the identity of God's people, and to the covenant between God and his people. They also know that the prophets, as they have called the people to turn back to the Lord, have also called them to show this through a renewed obedience to his Law. What's more, the prophets have also suggested that when the nations flock to Zion, then the Law will go out, bringing justice and peace (Isaiah 2:3–4).

Jesus moves to shut down the thought, before it even comes to mind, that in following him the disciples will have to abandon these convictions. He has not come to abolish the Law or contradict what the prophets have said, but to fulfil them (5:17). I arguedabove that the context and flow of thought in Matthew 5 strongly suggest this will be fulfilment though his authoritative ethical teaching, expounding and building upon the teaching of Moses and the prophets.

It is very much worth having in mind here how Matthew has used the word 'fulfil' so far in the Gospel, especially in the 'fulfilment' of Scripture (which is also what Jesus is talking about here). In the so-called 'fulfilment formulae' so far (1:22–3; 2:15, 17–18, 23; 4:14–16), Matthew has considered an Old Testament text in the light of the wider context of Scripture, especially in the light of the great promises to Abraham and David. Whatever was lacking, incomplete or unrealised in the original context is now brought to completion ('fulfilled') through what God is doing in Jesus. This is what Jesus is claiming he is doing here in relation to the whole of the Law and the Prophets.

This still leaves the question: how is Jesus bringing to completion what was incomplete in the Law and the Prophets? The answer in the second of the four approaches to the Sermon on the Mount we looked at above is that what was lacking in the Law and the Prophets is now realised ('fulfilled') in the perfect obedience of Jesus (which his disciples can now have access to by faith). This sounds theologically plausible, but the difficulty is that there's nothing in the Sermon about Jesus's obedience. Jesus doesn't say, 'I have not come to abolish them but to fulfil them *in myself.*' The context of this verse and the flow of thought in the Sermon suggest a different answer.

The immediate context is the 'good deeds' the disciples are encouraged to perform to the glory of the Father in 5:16. Jesus continues on into verse 17 without a pause: what he says flows from the question implied in verse

16: 'Which good deeds?' Jesus is then emphatic that he is not abandoning what God has said about good deeds to his glory in the past – what he said through Moses and what he said through the prophets (about what he had previously said through Moses). Rather, he has come to 'fulfil' what was said previously. And the context and flow of thought strongly suggest this will be fulfilment though his authoritative ethical teaching.[11] This is what Jesus goes on to talk about: he wants the disciples to put into practice and teach 'these commands' (5:19; compare 28:20). He wants them to listen carefully and respond as he says (six times), 'But I tell you . . .' in 5:21–48.

Because Jesus has come to fulfil the Law, the disciples can listen to and obey what he will go on to say without reservation, confident that the good purpose of the Law will remain fully intact (5:18). This will remain true 'until heaven and earth disappear' (or, more literally, 'pass by' – perhaps when heaven and earth are transformed by the final coming of the kingdom), or until 'everything is accomplished'. This must at least include what the disciples are to accomplish as 'salt' and 'light' – which will continue to the 'end of the age' (28:20b).

Jesus then exhorts his disciples to listen to him, practise what he says and teach others to do the same (5:19). This will fulfil their function as the 'light of the world', consistent with their membership of the kingdom, where such things will be commended. If they don't, and they set aside what he says and teach others likewise, the inconsistency will be jarring. Jesus doesn't spell out what it means to be 'called least' in the kingdom in 5:19. But the example of the Pharisees and scribes in the next verse – who, as Jesus will show, fall short in both practice and teaching – is a sobering one.

Jesus then backs this up with the warning of 5:20. Far from promoting a kind of 'legalism', this is warning *against* legalism. Legalism, properly understood, is the misuse of the law in a way that leads to destruction and exclusion from the kingdom – which is what the Pharisees and teachers of the law are in danger of. Jesus is saying to his disciples, 'Don't be like them!' And if the disciples are not like them, this will be visible (as 'light') in their behaviour – shown in their alignment with their Father (to his glory). But if they were to be like them, their entry to the kingdom would likewise be in question.

SUMMARY AND PURPOSE

The overall purpose of Matthew is to make its readers who aren't disciples of Jesus into disciples of Jesus, and to motivate and equip its readers

---

[11] So also Dumbrell, 'Logic', 18–19.

who are disciples of Jesus to be disciple-makers. The overall purpose of 4:12–10:42 is to respond to Jesus's proclamation, in word and deed, of the gospel of the kingdom of the heavens: following him, trusting him and being instructed by him to go and proclaim the gospel in our turn.

The overall purpose of the Sermon on the Mount for a disciple is a deep, humble, heart-based, exclusive dependence on God as Father, flowing out into radical behaviour that brings others to praise him, setting the foundations for a disciple-making discipleship. (It functions in a different way for the crowd looking on and listening in – see the introductory comments above.)

The purpose of the wisdom sayings in 5:1–12 is to introduce the Sermon on the Mount by addressing those who have been drawn into all that Jesus is doing in the world with wise words of encouragement. These encourage disciples of Jesus in their brokenness by reminding them of the future ahead, but also bring them to feel some of the weight and responsibility of what they have been brought into.

The huge danger with these verses is of teaching them as if these were obstacles to overcome in order to enter the kingdom, or 'eight steps to fulfil your true potential'. That, of course, would be hugely discouraging, robbing the true disciple of assurance and motivation. The dominant note here is one of encouragement for the true disciple. True disciples continue to experience brokenness and longing (5:3–6). True disciples are engaged in a hard struggle to be like Jesus in a hostile world (5:7–12). They might well wonder, 'Is this right? Should it be this hard? Am I on the right path?' Jesus's answer is an emphatic 'Yes! You are on the best possible path, living the best possible life. Yours is the kingdom of heaven.'

The section 5:13–20 is foundational to the rest of the Sermon, sketching out the basic claims Jesus wants to present to his disciples and to help them to take what he is going to teach them seriously, to be ready to put what he says into action (and to teach what he says too; compare 28:20). The basic purpose is to change what the disciples think about themselves and to open their ears. They are to think of themselves as 'salt' – heirs of the enduring covenant promises God made in the past – and 'light' – the means by which praise of God will be restored in people across the world. And they are to listen seriously to what Jesus teaches: far from being 'out of the blue', it is the culmination and fulfilment of hundreds of years of God speaking to his people. And the expectation is clear that they should do as he says and teach others to do likewise, making their lives noticeably more to the praise of the Father than those who won't listen to Jesus (5:20).

Righteousness

There is a deep concern throughout the Sermon for righteousness (5:6, 10, 20, 45; 6:1, 33). This is also a word capable of causing some confusion. The key thing to note is that when Jesus uses the word he isn't using it or applying it to the same issue the apostle Paul frequently applies it to in his letters. In Galatians and Romans, Paul is famously concerned with justification: how someone comes to be counted righteous in a relationship with God through faith. As we have already noticed, this status is presupposed in the Sermon for the disciples of Jesus. Hence why he can say of them 'theirs is the kingdom of [the heavens]', and hence why he can encourage them to address God as Father in prayer.

In Matthew, 'righteousness' is a word used much as the equivalent Hebrew term is used in the Psalms. In Psalm 1, for example, the righteous person delights in God's word and is 'like a tree planted by streams of water, which yields its fruit in season' (Psalm 1:3). The heart or will of the righteous person is aligned with the will of God, and this can be seen and heard in what they say and do. As Pennington puts it, 'I define "righteousness" in Matthew as *whole-person behaviour that accords with God's nature, will, and coming kingdom*.'[12]

We can think about this alignment at two different levels. First, this can be a heart-based alignment with the will of God to bring about his saving purposes through Jesus. Jesus has used the word 'righteousness' to talk about such an alignment in 3:15. To stand alongside the sinners in baptism was 'proper . . . to fulfil all righteousness'. This was Jesus aligning himself to the will of his Father to save such people. We then align ourselves with this saving will by believing and trusting in Jesus and following him as one of his disciples.

Then we can think about the moral will of God regarding day-to-day behaviour. We'll see that this is a subset, a component, of his wider saving purposes. This is what he has saved disciples of Jesus to be and do. This is what he has saved them *for*.

Once we have understood better how the word 'righteous' is being used by Matthew, verses like 5:20 become much clearer. Jesus tells the disciples that unless their righteousness surpasses that of the Pharisees and the teachers of the law, they will certainly not enter the kingdom of heaven. But we don't have to read on very far in the Gospel to realise that of course this must be the case. Given how opposed the Pharisees are to Jesus and how shallow their visible righteousness really is, it should be no surprise that the disciple of Jesus is expected to be very different.

---

[12] Pennington, *Sermon on the Mount*, 91 (his emphasis).

The opposition of the Pharisees to Jesus will become apparent very quickly. In 9:34 and 12:24 they attribute his power to exorcise to the power of Beelzebul, the prince of demons, thereby blaspheming the Holy Spirit at work in him. The teachers of the law are likewise presented as generally hostile to Jesus, who (as we noted in the Introduction) he frequently links closely with the Pharisees. In 16:21, 20:18 and 26:57 they are shown among those conspiring to bring about his execution and death. It will become very clear that rejecting Jesus is to reject the one who sent him (compare 10:40). So the Pharisees and teachers of the law are fundamentally misaligned with the will of God to bring about his saving purposes in salvation.

In 5:20, the context suggests that Jesus's focus is on righteousness as an alignment with the moral will of God, expressed in visible day-to-day behaviour. But even though both Pharisees and teachers of the law would think about themselves as doers as well as teachers of the law, there is a severe mismatch with God's will at this level too. Their understanding and interpretation of the law is frequently at fault. Jesus will expose the superficial, merely external nature of their 'righteousness' in 5:21–48, 15:1–20 and Matthew 23.

So although 5:20 would initially have shocked the first disciples (because of the reputation of the Pharisees and teachers of the law for 'righteousness'), just as it also shocks us, in the end we should also be able to read the verse and say, 'Well, yes, of course.'

At the other end of the Sermon, 7:21–3 shows a similar principle at work on the Day of Judgment. Even someone who calls Jesus 'Lord' and does and says many things in his name, if they are 'lawless' and misaligned with the will of God, then Jesus's chilling verdict will be, 'I never knew you' (7:23).

This also helps us understand 5:20 more clearly. If someone fails to enter the kingdom of the heavens because their righteousness did not surpass that of the Pharisees and teachers of the law, it will not be because entry comes directly by surpassing certain standards of behaviour, but because the absence of good fruit in their lives will have shown Jesus never knew them. Entry to the kingdom is through Jesus, through faith in Jesus, following him as one of his disciples. The person identified in 7:21–3 shows through their fruitlessness that they never were a true disciple of Jesus.

3. How to be 'light' • Matthew 5:21–48

Jesus is teaching his disciples in the sight and hearing of a crowd, as part of his proclamation in Galilee of the gospel of the kingdom (4:23–5:2). In the teaching so far, we have heard Jesus talk about the nature and identity of true disciples (5:3–6, poor in spirit etc.; 5:13, the salt of the earth), and the function and vocation of true disciples (5:7–10, merciful etc.; 5:14–16, the light of the world). In 5:17–20, Jesus has claimed that he and his teaching will fulfil the Law and the Prophets. As the disciples follow this teaching (with real-life responsiveness and a 'righteousness' greater than that of the teachers of the law and the Pharisees), they will fulfil their vocation to be the light of the world, doing good works to the glory of their Father. In 5:21–48 we get a representative sample of Jesus's teaching, addressing a number of key ethical areas.

Murder

21 'You have heard that it was said to the people long ago, "You shall not murder,[a] and anyone who murders will be subject to judgment." **22** But I tell you that anyone who is angry with a brother or sister[b,c] will be subject to judgment. Again, anyone who says to a brother or sister, "Raca,"[d] is answerable to the court. And anyone who says, "You fool!" will be in danger of the fire of hell.

23 'Therefore, if you are offering your gift at the altar and there remember that your brother or sister has something against you, **24** leave your gift there in front of the altar. First go and be reconciled to them; then come and offer your gift.

25 'Settle matters quickly with your adversary who is taking you to court. Do it while you are still together on the way, or your adversary may hand you over to the judge, and the judge may hand you over to the officer, and you may be thrown into prison. **26** Truly I tell you, you will not get out until you have paid the last penny.

Adultery

27 'You have heard that it was said, "You shall not commit adultery."[e] **28** But I tell you that anyone who looks at a woman lustfully has already committed adultery with her in his heart. **29** If your right eye causes you to stumble, gouge it out and throw it away. It is better for you to lose one part of your body than for your whole body to be thrown into hell. **30** And if your right hand causes you to stumble, cut it off and throw it away. It is better for you to lose one part of your body than for your whole body to go into hell.

Divorce

31 'It has been said, "Anyone who divorces his wife must give her a certificate of divorce."[f] **32** But I tell you that anyone who divorces his wife, except for sexual immorality, makes her the victim of adultery, and anyone who marries a divorced woman commits adultery.

Oaths

33 'Again, you have heard that it was said to the people long ago, "Do not break your oath, but fulfil to the Lord the oaths you have made." 34 But I tell you, do not swear an oath at all: either by heaven, for it is God's throne; 35 or by the earth, for it is his footstool; or by Jerusalem, for it is the city of the Great King. 36 And do not swear by your head, for you cannot make even one hair white or black. 37 All you need to say is simply "Yes," or "No"; anything beyond this comes from the evil one.g

Eye for eye

38 'You have heard that it was said, "Eye for eye, and tooth for tooth."h 39 But I tell you, do not resist an evil person. If anyone slaps you on the right cheek, turn to them the other cheek also. 40 And if anyone wants to sue you and take your shirt, hand over your coat as well. 41 If anyone forces you to go one mile, go with them two miles. 42 Give to the one who asks you, and do not turn away from the one who wants to borrow from you.

Love for enemies

43 'You have heard that it was said, "Love your neighbouri and hate your enemy." 44 But I tell you, love your enemies and pray for those who persecute you, 45 that you may be children of your Father in heaven. He causes his sun to rise on the evil and the good, and sends rain on the righteous and the unrighteous. 46 If you love those who love you, what reward will you get? Are not even the tax collectors doing that? 47 And if you greet only your own people, what are you doing more than others? Do not even pagans do that? 48 Be perfect, therefore, as your heavenly Father is perfect.

a 21 Exodus 20:13
b 22 The Greek word for *brother or sister* (*adelphos*) refers here to a fellow disciple, whether man or woman; also in verse 23.
c 22 Some manuscripts *brother or sister without cause*
d 22 An Aramaic term of contempt
e 27 Exodus 20:14
f 31 Deut. 24:1
g 37 Or *from evil*
h 38 Exodus 21:24; Lev. 24:20; Deut. 19:21
i 43 Lev. 19:18

There are some obvious and striking repeating patterns in these verses, dividing them into two blocks of three sayings. (We shall see that, like elsewhere in the Gospel, Matthew does like at least microstructure to be arranged into groups of three.[13]) The first block deals with the issues of anger, lust and casual divorce:

[13] As noted by Dale C. Allison, Jr., 'The Structure of the Sermon on the Mount', *Journal of Biblical Literature* 106 (1987): 423–45.

5:21–6 Anger	5:27–30 Lust	5:31–2 Casual divorce
You have heard that it was said to the people long ago . . .	You have heard that it was said . . .	It has been said . . .
I tell you . . .	I tell you . . .	. . . I tell you . . .
(Two examples)	If your right eye . . .	

Table 6

The second block deals with ungodly oath-making, retaliation and conditional love:

5:33–7 Ungodly oath-making	5:38–42 Retaliation	5:43–8 Conditional love
Again, you have heard that it was said to the people long ago . . .	You have heard that it was said . . .	You have heard that it was said . . .
. . . I tell you . . .	. . . I tell you . . .	. . . I tell you . . .
All you need to say is simply 'Yes,' or 'No'. . . .	If anyone slaps you on the right cheek . . .	

Table 7

The section ends in 5:43–8, where Jesus shows his desire for the disciples to 'be children [sons] of your Father in heaven' (5:45). That is, Jesus's aim in all this is that those observing the disciples' behaviour should see something of the character of the Father. This is similar to the idea in 5:16, but also shows the restoration of their human identity as those made in the image of God (Genesis 1:26–7).

The obvious repeated pattern in these verses is Jesus saying, 'You have heard that it was said,' or, 'It has been said,' followed by a quote. In the context (especially following 5:20), it makes sense to take this as, 'You have heard it said from the Pharisees and teachers of the law in their teaching on the law of Moses . . .'[14] When Jesus then says, 'But I tell you . . .', he is correcting the teaching from these people. As he does so, he is fulfilling the Law and the Prophets (5:17). There are two aspects to this:

First, he is fulfilling what the Law and the Prophets said on each issue

---

[14] That is, Jesus is correcting (and expanding, in the light of his coming) the *teaching* of the Law, not the Law itself. As Pennington puts it, 'the wisdom, ethics, and vision of his teaching are *not* new or antithetical to what God has said'. Pennington, *Sermon on the Mount*, 20.

by bringing out its true meaning and application. This is in contrast to the teaching of the Pharisees and scribes. He is teaching with true authority (as the crowd listening in will recognise in 7:28–9).

Second, Jesus is fulfilling what the Law and the Prophets said on each issue by fully 'interiorising' what they said, emphasising that merely external conformity is not enough. Jesus has already said, 'Blessed are the pure in heart' (5:8), and his teaching here applies this principle across a range of issues. We need to be careful how we put this. It is not that the Law was unconcerned with obedience from the heart (as the tenth commandment shows very clearly and explicitly). Likewise, the ethical instruction of the Wisdom literature was very much concerned with the heart (e.g., Proverbs 3:1). But the Law was not powerful to bring about obedience from the heart, and in Jesus's day the Pharisees and teachers of the law were approaching (and teaching) the Law with a concern for not much more than surface behaviour. What's more, some laws (the 'case laws' on issues like oaths and divorce) were concerned with limiting the damage done from the hardness of the people's hearts, as Jesus will explain in 19:8. In addressing the heart, Jesus will be encouraging his disciples not to use such laws to excuse bad behaviour, as the Pharisees and teachers of the law were doing.

The crowds, though no doubt impressed by Jesus's expression of authority, would be listening to this with incredulity. Jesus seems to be describing impossible behaviour. Who can control their passions in this way (5:21–6)? Who can meet these standards of faithfulness and honesty (5:31–7)? Who can endure such shame or show such love (5:38–47)? Only as humbled disciples, brought into what Jesus has done (to forgive sins and wipe away shame) and is doing (to bring light to the world), can we make sense of this. Even then, it is very demanding! (If too overwhelming, it should humble us still further, taking us back to the reassurances of 5:3–6.)

In the wider structure of the Sermon, this teaching expands what Jesus has said about the disciples' function in the world (5:7–10, 14–16). This is what it means in practice to be merciful, pure in heart, peacemakers, doing good because of Jesus – even in the face of hostility and hatred. Jesus is teaching what it means in practice to shine light in the world to the glory of the Father.

Murder, adultery and divorce (5:21–32)

Jesus quotes the commandments on murder and adultery (Exodus 20:13–14) and refers to the case law on divorce (Deuteronomy 24:1–4). But while the teachers of the law might be satisfied with a degree of surface conformity, Jesus is concerned with the heart.

The physical act of murder, or words of hatred and insult (5:22b), are external symptoms, visible evidences, of a deeper problem – an unrighteous hostility towards someone. This inner hostility will be judged (5:22a) – even if unseen and unheard. If it is made audible in offensive and hostile words, it will be subject to legal sanction or the fire of hell (5:22b). ('Hell' or 'Gehenna' here was originally just the place name of a valley south of Jerusalem, the valley of Hinnom, but by the first century it was used as a name for the place of fiery judgment reserved for extreme wickedness – such as that described in Jeremiah 7:31–2.[15])

Jesus is not saying that anger is equivalent to murder. Under the Law (and indeed any other legal system one could point to), murder is a serious crime with serious penalties attached to it, while anger is not. The penalties are related to the actual external damage done. But Jesus is saying that anger and violent acts like murder *are* strongly connected, and that the anger is the root or source of the problem. Jesus's teaching here is pastorally practical. If anyone is serious about obeying the commandment not to murder (and of course they should be!), then they will want to deal with the issue at its source. They will want to deal with the anger and hostility at the root of the problem.

Jesus then gives two examples of how to do this in practice. The first is in verses 23–4. If in the act of relating to God ('offering your gift at the altar') they remember they have broken relationship with another (in anger), they are to act first to bring about reconciliation. Unresolved hostility to a neighbour would be a symptom of a heart still full of ungodly anger and therefore incompatible with humility and peace towards God. Likewise, in verses 25–6, those who unreasonably refuse to settle with an adversary (one who stands in the right) imply an anger towards them just like those Jesus warns in 5:22, and they are therefore just as much subject to judgment.

Anger is seen as a 'respectable' or 'semi-respectable' sin in the world around us, or even perfectly acceptable on some occasions. Disciples of Jesus too easily fall into the same error, but here is an opportunity to stand out as different, to the glory of the Father. Not that this is easy in some circumstances. It is frequently costly – and that is the point! When control of anger fails, Jesus teaches his followers what to do. If it spills out and damages a relationship, then it is not enough simply to

---

[15] BDAG, *'Gehenna'*.

ask God for forgiveness. Part of seeking forgiveness from God is to seek reconciliation with those who have been hurt (5:23–6). This, too, may be personally costly, but once again gives glory to God.

Similar to murder and anger, in verses 27–30 the physical act of adultery is an external symptom, a visible evidence, of a deeper problem – of distorted and misapplied sexual desire. Relational–sexual coveting (lust) is strongly related to, and a root cause of, relational–sexual theft (adultery). Anyone who looks at a woman, says Jesus, with the intent of desiring to have her in the sexual act of adultery, 'has already committed adultery with her in his heart' (5:28). The determination the disciples should show in putting such ungodly passions to death is described in 5:29–30.

There are obvious applications from Jesus's teaching here to lechery and pornography use today, but we shouldn't forget other related applications such as sexual banter or flirting. These also incite lust in others and can easily lead to more physical expressions of sexual immorality. So what should we do? Again, Jesus's teaching here is pastorally practical – so long as we realise that 5:29–30 should be taken metaphorically rather than literally. This is not because the actions Jesus describes are too severe. Rather, it should be clear that getting rid of eyes or hands wouldn't actually deal with the problem of twisted sexual desire, which lies in the heart (5:28). The point of the metaphor is to show just how uncompromising we should be in putting lust to death. As before, if anyone is serious about obeying the commandment not to commit adultery (and of course they should be!), then they will want to deal with the issue at its source. Note carefully that Jesus isn't saying the issue lies simply with acting on (or inflaming) desires we might experience; the problem lies with the desires themselves, which need to be cut out at the root. We still might be thinking, 'Yes, for sure, but how?' The logic of the Sermon suggests by humbling ourselves, seeking to follow Jesus, remembering who we are and what we're here for, focusing on the kingdom and our Father in the heavens, and seeing just how worthy of judgment the lust is in the light of all this (as in 5:29–30). View the false desires rightly, though God's eyes, and we should lose our appetite. More positively, how wonderful it is when church families become safe places for both sexes, free from the sexual threat and danger of the world around us. (Conversely, of course, how terrible it is when they are not.)

In 5:31, Jesus is quoting the contemporary teaching about divorce ('Anyone who divorces [releases/sends away] his wife must give her a certificate of divorce'), rather than the law, since Deuteronomy 24:1 actually says something quite different. Jesus will have more to say on this in

19:1–12, and this is undoubtedly a complex and contentious issue. But here it's clear that 'sending away' a wife without good reason doesn't dissolve a marriage, irrespective of whether a certificate has been given or not. 'Sending away' – essentially, discarding – a wife on a whim was common practice at the time – very much in Gentile culture, but increasingly so in Jewish culture too. Jesus says that it just generates more sin: any future 'marriage' involves adultery, since the original marriage still stands. (By implication, the same would apply if the first husband married another, as Jesus makes explicit in Matthew 19:9.)

Divorce (5:31–2) is another area where disciples of Jesus should be able to stand out as visibly different from the world around them. In western culture, there is something like a pandemic of casual divorce, and other parts of the world are either catching up or not so different. Matthew considers it such an important issue that he will have Jesus return to it at greater length in 19:1–12.

Oaths, retaliation and love (5:33–48)

In the second part of Jesus's teaching on how to be light in 5:21–48, he quotes from teaching on the issue of oaths, mentioned in the case law of Leviticus 19:12 and elsewhere, the 'eye for eye . . .' in Exodus 21:24 and the command to love neighbours in Leviticus 19:18. The teachers of the law seem to be satisfied with working around or manipulating these regulations to defend their own interests and practice, unconcerned by the corruption of their hearts, draining the regulations of love and God-glorifying purpose. Jesus is concerned with refilling the hearts of his disciples with a Godlike love that becomes visible to his glory across all these areas.

Oath-making was assumed in the OT, but only in the sense that if an oath is taken it should be honoured. Oaths helped a society of habitual liars to function a little more smoothly, but were never meant as a substitute for simply telling the truth. What's more, by Jesus's day oath-making was being wildly abused to an absurd degree (see also 23:16–22). Better, then, just to let your yes be yes and your no be no.

In other words, this is another area where disciples of Jesus should be able to stand out as visibly different from the world around them. We live in a world where – across many cultures – vast sums of money are spent on small print and litigation. Talking straight with others is costly, especially when we feel it puts us at a disadvantage compared to those who don't. Jesus will have more to say on oaths in 23:16–22, but here the basic idea should be clear. Faithfulness and truthfulness are characteristics of our Father in the heavens, and when his children embrace the cost and follow suit, it's to his glory.

The command 'eye for eye . . .', which Jesus quotes in 5:38, was intended to inform judicial decisions, keeping punishment proportional to the crime. The teachers of the law seem to be misapplying this to defend personal retaliation against aggression.

In the twenty-first century world, they would have many agreeing with them. There is an almost universal consensus that 'tit-for-tat' is reasonable justice in personal relations. Responding strongly and even violently when one is shamed or dishonoured is not just considered acceptable, but is encouraged, even in the West. (Western culture is far more driven by personal honour than we might imagine.) So when Jesus says, 'Do not resist,' he is again proposing something radically countercultural. We get the general idea, but at first glance the examples in these verses seem extreme. Most of us would instinctively want to retaliate in such cases. But if we remember what we believe, who we are and what we're here for, and whose children we are, then there can be almost something rewarding about acting so far from expectation. It can often expose how unreasonable an aggressor is being, shaming them even as they attempt to shame us. The principle in 5:42 is similar: with the kingdom before us and our Father protecting us, we can easily afford to sit loose to our possessions. (Although we may still need to take care in many contexts that whatever we give away truly has at heart the best interests of those we are giving to.)

As Jesus notes in 5:43–8, we also tend to be 'tit-for-tat' people with regard to love, only responding with love when we have been loved (conditional love). Notice how Jesus draws in the Gentiles here, as a further point of comparison. This tends to be how secular society works. To love enemies, even to pray for them, in such a context is the ultimate 'crazy kingdom behaviour' in Matthew 5 that stands out as different, showing our likeness to our Father (5:48).

In verse 43, the teachers of the law have added 'and hate your enemy' to the command to love our neighbours, but there is no such direct command in the Old Testament. There is a yearning across the Bible (in the Psalms, for example) for God to act in justice and judgment against the wicked. But the teachers are twisting this lament to excuse them for being selective (for self-centred reasons) about which neighbours they love. Rather, entrusting final justice to God frees us to love all our neighbours without exception, even those who hate us.

The final verse of Matthew 5 returns to the principle raised earlier

(5:16), to do things in the likeness of our Father – in this case, showing love towards both the righteous and the unrighteous (5:45). This is another verse that has led people to the (unhelpful) second approach outlined in the introduction to the Sermon on the Mount above. Like the word usually translated as 'blessed' in 5:3–12, the word translated as 'perfect' here is yet another word that's very hard to translate accurately. But the one thing we can be sure it doesn't mean in this context is 'perfect'![16] So, yes, our heavenly Father is perfect in every respect, but that's not what Jesus is talking about here. He is talking about the consistency and integrity of the Father. The Father is consistent in his love to both the wicked and the good, the righteous and the unrighteous (5:45). Jesus expects his disciples to imitate this, loving their enemies as well as those who love them back (5:44, 46–7).

Jesus uses the same word in 19:21 of the man who asks him about eternal life: 'If you want to be perfect, go, sell your possessions and give to the poor, and you will have treasure in heaven. Then come, follow me.' This is a man who has shown some external conformity to the Law (19:18–20) but internally has a divided heart, devoted to his possessions where he should be devoted to God. Letting go of this false devotion by selling his possessions and giving to the poor would not make him 'perfect' as we understand the word, but it would deal with this inconsistency. Jesus is looking for a wholehearted devotion to God in those who would become his disciples and follow him (and thereby find eternal life).

This theme of consistency between the inner and outer person runs all the way through the Sermon on the Mount and on throughout the whole Gospel, not just 19:16–22. It is what the Pharisees and teachers of the law, in particular, do not have. It is what Jesus sums up in 5:8 – the wise person living the good life is 'pure in heart'. There is a purity and consistency in their devotion to God that spills out into behaviour to his glory – such as showing mercy (5:7) and bringing peace (5:9). In 5:21–48, Jesus internalises for his disciples what they might before have seen as merely external, bringing them to care about the heart attitudes behind their behaviour. In 6:1–18, he will take their attention off external approval and onto the inner, secret life seen only by their Father in heaven. In 6:19–24, he teaches his disciples to avoid the divided loyalty he later exposes in the rich man of 19:16–22.

---

[16] Which does make this one of the most unhelpful translation mistakes ever made, cascading down from the very earliest English versions to today, with seemingly no one brave enough to challenge the status quo.

SUMMARY AND PURPOSE

The overall purpose of the Sermon on the Mount for a disciple is a deep, humble, heart-based, exclusive dependence on God as Father, flowing out into radical behaviour that brings others to praise him, setting the foundations for a disciple-making discipleship. (It functions in a different way for the crowd looking on and listening in – see the introductory comments above.)

Jesus's purpose in 5:21–48 is to equip the disciples to let their 'light shine before others', to the glory of their Father (5:16), teaching them to show visibly their relationship with him and their sure belief in the coming kingdom. The changed behaviour flows from changed hearts – contrasting with a world where uncontrolled passions and selfishness are the driving forces.

Part of Jesus's purpose here is a change of thinking on why we should do 'good deeds'. Our natural sinful tendency is to have an individualistic, selfish approach – we do these things if there's some hope of a 'good' return on what it has cost us. In contrast to this, Matthew 5 is all about developing a God-centred, Father-centred approach. Followers of Jesus do the things described here (and things like them) for the glory of the Father (5:16), not their own glory. The cost they undertake demonstrates that they believe 100 per cent in the kingdom he is bringing about, 100 per cent in the justice he will finally exercise, and that they trust him 100 per cent to look after them as his children.

4. How to be 'salt' part 1 • Matthew 6:1–18

Jesus is teaching his disciples in the sight and hearing of a crowd, as part of his proclamation in Galilee of the gospel of the kingdom (Matthew 4:23–5:2). In the teaching so far, we have heard Jesus talk about the nature and identity of true disciples (5:3–6, poor in spirit, etc.; 5:13, the salt of the earth) and the function and vocation of true disciples (5:7–10, merciful, etc.; 5:14–16, the light of the world). I argued above that for the disciples to be 'the salt of the earth' means that they are those on earth with whom God has made a 'covenant of salt' through their relationship to him as disciples of Jesus. This is why the disciples are able to relate to him and address him as 'Father'. The teaching in 6:1–7:11 focuses closely on this, encouraging the disciples to pursue an authentic, exclusive and fully dependent relationship with their Father in heaven. It is, so to speak, teaching on 'how to keep salty'.

Giving to the needy

6 'Be careful not to practise your righteousness in front of others to be seen by them. If you do, you will have no reward from your Father in heaven.

2 'So when you give to the needy, do not announce it with trumpets, as the hypocrites do in the synagogues and on the streets, to be honoured by others. Truly I tell you, they have received their reward in full. 3 But when you give to the needy, do not let your left hand know what your right hand is doing, 4 so that your giving may be in secret. Then your Father, who sees what is done in secret, will reward you.

Prayer

5 'And when you pray, do not be like the hypocrites, for they love to pray standing in the synagogues and on the street corners to be seen by others. Truly I tell you, they have received their reward in full. 6 But when you pray, go into your room, close the door and pray to your Father, who is unseen. Then your Father, who sees what is done in secret, will reward you. 7 And when you pray, do not keep on babbling like pagans, for they think they will be heard because of their many words. 8 Do not be like them, for your Father knows what you need before you ask him.

9 'This, then, is how you should pray:

' "Our Father in heaven,
 hallowed be your name,
10 your kingdom come,
 your will be done,
 on earth as it is in heaven.
11 Give us today our daily bread.
12 And forgive us our debts,
 as we also have forgiven our
 debtors.
13 And lead us not into temptation,[a]
 but deliver us from the evil
 one.[b] "

14 For if you forgive other people when they sin against you, your heavenly Father will also forgive you. 15 But if you do not forgive others their sins, your Father will not forgive your sins.

Fasting

16 'When you fast, do not look sombre as the hypocrites do, for they disfigure their faces to show others they are fasting. Truly I tell you, they have received their reward in full. 17 But when you fast, put oil on your head and wash your face, 18 so that it will not be obvious to others that you are fasting, but only to your Father, who is unseen; and your Father, who sees what is done in secret, will reward you.

---

a 13 The Greek for *temptation* can also mean *testing*.
b 13 Or *from evil*; some late manuscripts *one, / for yours is the kingdom and the power and the glory for ever. Amen.*

Jesus uses two reference groups for comparison in this second part of the main body of the Sermon. The first are the 'hypocrites' (6:2, 5, 16;

also 7:5). Later in the Gospel, Jesus will use this word of both Pharisees and the teachers of the law (15:7; 22:18; 23:13, 15, 23, 25, 27, 29). In other words, they are those who will not enter the kingdom to enjoy the benefits described in 5:3–12. The other group are the 'pagans' or Gentiles (6:7; 32), who do not know God or what he is like. About both groups, Jesus says to his disciples, 'Don't be like them.' Instead, in secret, seek your Father's 'reward' (6:4, 6, 18), store up treasures in heaven (6:20) and seek his kingdom and his righteousness (6:33). In other words, they should have their relationship with him at the centre, focused on where he is (in the heavens rather than on the earth), aligned with his will and purpose, secure in his responsiveness to prayer and confident in the future kingdom. This is the kingdom that will come from the heavens, bringing all the benefits described in 5:3–12, central to which are seeing and knowing God himself. These are good things to pursue. Jonathan T. Pennington is right when he comments that desiring such rewards 'is nothing to be ashamed of or any diminishing of virtue'.[17]

Like in Matthew 5:21–48, there are two blocks of teaching here, 6:1–18 and 6:19–7:12, each divided into three parts. Following a general, summary warning about performing acts of 'righteousness' in front of others (6:1), the first block has some obvious and striking repeating patterns that divide the verses into three parts:

6:2–4 **When you give out of mercy . . .**	6:5–15 **When you pray . . .**	6:16–18 **When you fast . . .**
Do not be like the hypocrites . . . Amen I say to you they have received their reward in full . . . But rather . . . And your Father, who sees what is done in secret, will reward you	Do not be like the hypocrites . . . Amen I say to you they have received their reward in full . . . But rather . . . And your Father, who sees what is done in secret, will reward you And don't be like the pagans . . . Pray like this	Do not be like the hypocrites . . . Amen I say to you they have received their reward in full . . . But rather . . . And your Father, who sees what is done in secret, will reward you

Table 8

The main pattern is broken in 6:7–15 with some extended teaching on prayer, including what has become known as the Lord's Prayer.

---

[17] Pennington, *Sermon on the Mount*, 233.

In the wider structure of the Sermon, this teaching expands what Jesus has said about the disciples' identity and nature (5:3–6, 13). This is what it means in practice to be humble and dependent upon God as Father, maintaining the 'saltiness' of our enduring covenant relationship with him.

The crowds would perhaps have smirked as Jesus exposed and lampooned the 'hypocrites' (6:2, 5, 16 – linked to the Pharisees and teachers in 15:1 and chapter 23) and the babbling Gentiles (6:7). However, they should also have been convicted that they don't have the secret relationship with the Father, under his approval (6:4, 6, 18), that Jesus talks about. Only as humbled disciples, brought into what Jesus has done (to forgive sins), adopted into God's (missionary) family, does it make sense to pursue such a secret relationship.

The main principle: it is not about you! (6:1)

Back in Matthew 5:16, Jesus encouraged his disciples to let their light shine before others, 'that they may see your good deeds and glorify your Father in [the heavens]'. We can relate this to the 'righteousness' that should surpass that of the Pharisees and scribes (Matthew 5:20). If we want to know what kind of behaviours Jesus is referring to, then there are plenty of examples in Matthew 5:21–48.

Here in Matthew 6:1, Jesus tells us there are kinds of behaviour that, even though they go under the label 'righteousness', should not be done to be seen by others. The three examples Jesus gives (verses 2–4, giving to the poor; verses 5–15, prayer; and verses 16–18, fasting) are all stereo-typical 'righteous' behaviours which have been so abused by religious people that if they are done in public no longer give glory to God. Jesus teaches that they are therefore a test of someone's personal relationship with the Father. He warns that to do such things in order to be seen by others will mean no 'reward' from the Father. The word translated 'reward' often means simply 'payment' or 'wages', but more specifically can mean 'positive recognition' or 'approval'. This fits well here.[18] In the examples, the 'hypocrites' do things in the sight of others to gain their approval and admiration. Unlike the good works of 5:16, there is no concern for the glory of the Father, and therefore no approval from him.

---

[18] Although, as noted above, the approval goes along with all the other future kingdom benefits to the true disciple of Jesus described in 5:3–12. The 'hypocrites', if we take them not to be disciples, have neither the divine approval nor any of these benefits. In seeking the admiration of others, they have 'received their reward in full' (6:2, 5, 16). It is all they get.

Doing the costly and difficult things Jesus described in 5:21–48 demonstrates a belief in the reality of the coming kingdom and a trust in one's heavenly Father. Hence their value in giving him glory. But doing the things Jesus describes in 6:2–18 to be seen by others – that is, for the personal approval of others – demonstrates no such belief or trust. A personal relationship with the Father can only be demonstrated by doing such things in secret.

Giving out of mercy (6:2–4)

The first example is mercy-giving, or 'giving to the needy' (verse 2). Jesus begins by saying, as he will with all three examples, 'Whenever you do this . . .' These are all expected aspects of Jewish life, and Jesus expects them to continue to be so for his disciples. But they are not to be like 'the hypocrites', drawing others' attention to the giving as if sounding a trumpet. The word 'hypocrite' was originally used of theatrical actors, but Jesus is using it metaphorically of those who pretend to be devoted to God in a culture where such devotion was highly esteemed and approved of. Jesus says, that will be the only approval they will receive. They will receive no approval from the Father.

To receive the approval of the Father means giving in secret (verses 3 and 4). If even your left hand doesn't know what your right is doing when you give, let alone anyone else, then public acclaim becomes impossible!

Praying (6:5–15)

Jesus gives a similar warning against praying 'to be seen by others' (verse 5). The solution is again to do the activity in secret, where only the Father can see what you are doing (verse 6).

The negative examples in verse 5 are about doing private, individual prayer to God in public. Jesus is not talking about corporate prayer here; rather, he is saying, 'Do your private prayer in private.' That corporate prayer is a good thing is implied by the phrasing of the Lord's Prayer – 'Our Father in [the heavens] . . . Give us today, etc.' – which seems to suggest praying as part of a group.[19]

---

[19] We see this also in the frequency with which corporate prayer is described positively in the book of Acts – e.g., Acts 1:24; 4:31; 6:6; 8:15; 12:12; 13:3; 14:23; 16:25; 20:36; 21:5. Indeed, it seems to be assumed as good practice all across the New Testament.

Doing private, individual prayers in public 'to be seen by others' seems to have been common among some Jewish people in the first century, just as it is in Islam today. But even those in cultures where the temptation to pray private prayers in public is not especially strong can learn from these warnings. At the very least, Jesus is implying that private prayer should constitute the main bulk of his disciples' prayer life. It is therefore not to be neglected. We might also conclude that when we do pray with others, we need to take special care not to be doing so for the approval of those around us watching and listening (rather like not letting the left hand know what the right is doing in verse 3).

Jesus adds a further warning here – somewhat different from the others. His disciples are also not to be like the 'pagans' (verse 7) – that is, like the Gentiles. The Gentiles do not know God, even less know him as Father, and assume they need many words to get the attention of the gods. Don't be like them, says Jesus – the purpose of your praying is in any case not to inform God of something he already knows (verse 8). The solution is to pray simple, uncomplicated prayers like the example Jesus gives in verses 9–13.

The Lord's (example) Prayer

There is a good case for seeing the prayer as a sequence of seven petitions, with 'Give us today our daily bread' (verse 11) at the centre.[20] A further case can be made for grouping the first three together and the final three together, giving a 3+1+3 structure.

The first three petitions express a restored relationship with God, who can now be addressed as 'Father' (verse 9).[21] The petitions are aligned with his will and purposes. First, his ultimate purpose in all creation and redemption is that he would be known and glorified in all the cosmos (compare 5:16), his name 'hallowed' universally (verse 9). The second petition – 'your kingdom come' – is the desire of someone who has believed in the nearness of the kingdom (3:2; 4:17) and now yearns for this kingdom to come from the heavens and fill the cosmos (verse 10a). The third petition (verse 10b) expresses what this will entail: God's will done 'on earth as it is in heaven'. We have already noted that in Matthew's Gospel, God's will is closely linked to the language of 'righteousness'.

---

[20] David Wenham, 'The Sevenfold Form of the Lord's Prayer in Matthew's Gospel', *Expository Times* 121, no. 8 (2010).

[21] As Kapolyo, 'Matthew', 1148, notes, the expectation here is a combination of intimacy and reverence, much like that between African grandchildren and their grandparents.

In other words, this is the petition of someone who hungers and thirsts for righteousness (5:6).

The central petition – 'Give us today our daily bread' (verse 11) – perhaps also has some sense of wanting to hasten the arrival of what God has promised. This is because 'bread' in the Bible is often a way of talking about the life bread enables, and the word translated here as 'daily' can also be translated 'of tomorrow'. So we could read this as, 'Give us today the (eternal) life (you have promised) for tomorrow.' But it is more likely that the petition is straightforwardly about being provided for physically today. This might sound a little too ordinary and prosaic (especially given the prominent position of the petition in the prayer), but this kind of daily trust in the provision of the Father turns out to be really important, as Jesus will expand on in 6:19–34.

The final three petitions are cries for help in the face of ongoing sin and evil. The first petition is for forgiveness of 'debts' (verse 12a). We can see from verses 14 and 15 that this is a way of talking about sin or transgression. Most likely, Jesus uses the word 'debt' so that when we get to the parable of the unmerciful servant in 18:23–34 later in the Gospel we will make the connection. That parable uses financial debt as a metaphor for sin against someone, and explains how impossible it is for someone to be forgiven if they refuse to forgive others. (Jesus will soon make a similar point in 7:2: 'with the measure you use, it will be measured to you'.) Hence the second part of verse 12. A disciple cannot appeal for forgiveness and expect a positive answer without a willingness to forgive others – a point Jesus reinforces in verses 14 and 15.

The fact that this point about forgiveness surrounds the second and third petitions suggests all three are somehow related. The second and third petitions are related to one another with a prominent 'but'. Being kept from 'temptation' or 'testing' is (verse 13a) equivalent to being delivered from the evil one (verse 13b). This suggests the 'testing' is a very serious event – one where the evil one succeeds in causing someone to stumble or fall. In the context, as Jesus will expand on in Matthew 18, it seems Jesus has in mind the victory won by the evil one when one disciple fails to forgive another.

Putting this all together, Jesus is teaching that the purpose of praying like this is not to manipulate God like the pagans (verse 7), but for his disciples to align themselves with the will and purpose of God (verses 9–10), to depend on him for life today (verse 11) and to depend on him in the battle with sin and evil – especially for forgiveness and perseverance in forgiving others (verses 12–15).

Fasting (6:16–18)

The final warning is against being like those who fast 'to show others they are fasting' (verse 16). The solution is similar: to hide the fasting from others so that it can only be seen by your Father (verses 17–18).

Christian attitudes to fasting have varied enormously across history and different groups. Jesus seems to be assuming it will be a part of his disciples' lives one way or another, even if they were to be different from John's disciples and the Pharisees (Matthew 9:14–19 – see below, where there will be more to say on the subject). This is supported by other material in the New Testament that links fasting to earnest prayer at significant moments, such as commissioning for mission (Acts 13:2–3). But Jesus's teaching here suggests that if it is done rightly, most people shouldn't realise it is happening at all.[22]

SUMMARY AND PURPOSE

The purpose of the Sermon on the Mount for the disciples of Jesus is a deep, humble, heart-based, exclusive dependence on God as Father, flowing out into radical behaviour that brings others to praise him, setting the foundations for a disciple-making discipleship. The first half of the main body of the sermon (5:20–48) has focused on this radical behaviour to the glory of the Father. That is, it has focused on being 'the light of the world' (5:16). As we move into the second half of the main body of the sermon (6:1–7:11), Jesus warns of behaviour that fails to do this. These are 'righteous' activities that others might associate with someone's relationship to God, but if done wrongly do not give glory to him. Specifically, Jesus warns against so-called 'righteous' activity aimed at generating glory and approval from human observers. Instead, Jesus encourages his disciples to do these things secretly. They will then be expressing a deep, humble, heart-based dependence on God as Father, seeking his approval alone. I argued earlier that this is what Jesus means by being 'the salt of the earth' (5:13). This then becomes the dominant emphasis in the rest of 6:1–7:11.

The purpose of 6:1–18 is therefore for the disciples to shun seeking the glory and praise of human observers, but to seek instead the approval

---

[22] Brian Wintle comments that in South Asia fasting is more common among those of other faiths than it is among Christians. Brian Wintle, 'Matthew', in *South Asia Bible Commentary*, ed. Brian Wintle (Grand Rapids: Zondervan, 2015), 1233. There might therefore be a temptation to show an equivalent level of piety, but Jesus's teaching would strongly warn against this.

of their Father, expressing and pursuing their relationship with him in ways only he can see. Central to this is prayer (6:5–15). This should be private and secret at heart, simple and in tune with the character of a sovereign and loving Father. It should show an alignment with his will and purpose for the world, a dependency on his daily provision and a crying out for the protection needed to persevere – for forgiveness and a forgiving heart, and against sin and apostasy.

5. How to be 'salt' part 2 • Matthew 6:19–7:12

The teaching in 6:1–7:11 expands on what it means to be 'the salt of the earth' (5:13), encouraging the disciples to pursue an authentic, exclusive and fully dependent relationship with their Father in the heavens. The first part (6:1–18) has encouraged the disciples to put aside outward appearances to pursue a secret relationship with their Father, especially in prayer. This second part will encourage an undivided, humble and persevering relationship with the Father.

Treasures in heaven

19'Do not store up for yourselves treasures on earth, where moths and vermin destroy, and where thieves break in and steal. **20**But store up for yourselves treasures in heaven, where moths and vermin do not destroy, and where thieves do not break in and steal. **21**For where your treasure is, there your heart will be also.

22'The eye is the lamp of the body. If your eyes are healthy,**c** your whole body will be full of light. **23**But if your eyes are unhealthy,**d** your whole body will be full of darkness. If then the light within you is darkness, how great is that darkness!

24'No one can serve two masters. Either you will hate the one and love the other, or you will be devoted to the one and despise the other. You cannot serve both God and Money.

Do not worry

25'Therefore I tell you, do not worry about your life, what you will eat or drink; or about your body, what you will wear. Is not life more than food, and the body more than clothes? **26**Look at the birds of the air; they do not sow or reap or store away in barns, and yet your heavenly Father feeds them. Are you not much more valuable than they? **27**Can any one of you by worrying add a single hour to your life**e**?

28'And why do you worry about clothes? See how the flowers of the field grow. They do not labour or spin. **29**Yet I tell you that not even Solomon in all his splendour was dressed like one of these. **30** If that is how God clothes the grass of the field, which is here today and tomorrow is thrown into the fire, will he not much more clothe you – you of little faith? **31** So do not worry, saying, "What shall we eat?" or "What shall we drink?" or "What shall we wear?" **32** For the pagans run after all these things, and your heavenly Father knows that you need them. **33** But seek first his kingdom and his righteousness, and all these things will be given to you as well. **34** Therefore do not worry about tomorrow, for tomorrow will worry about itself. Each day has enough trouble of its own.

Judging others

7 'Do not judge, or you too will be judged. **2** For in the same way as you judge others, you will be judged, and with the measure you use, it will be measured to you.

3 'Why do you look at the speck of sawdust in your brother's eye and pay no attention to the plank in your own eye? **4** How can you say to your brother, "Let me take the speck out of your eye," when all the time there is a plank in your own eye? **5** You hypocrite, first take the plank out of your own eye,

and then you will see clearly to remove the speck from your brother's eye.

6 'Do not give dogs what is sacred; do not throw your pearls to pigs. If you do, they may trample them under their feet, and turn and tear you to pieces.

Ask, seek, knock

7 'Ask and it will be given to you; seek and you will find; knock and the door will be opened to you. **8** For everyone who asks receives; the one who seeks finds; and to the one who knocks, the door will be opened.

9 'Which of you, if your son asks for bread, will give him a stone? **10** Or if he asks for a fish, will give him a snake? **11** If you, then, though you are evil, know how to give good gifts to your children, how much more will your Father in heaven give good gifts to those who ask him! **12** So in everything, do to others what you would have them do to you, for this sums up the Law and the Prophets.

---

c 22 The Greek for *healthy* here implies *generous.*

d 23 The Greek for *unhealthy* here implies *stingy.*

e 27 Or *single cubit to your height*

The structure here is less obvious, and there is much less agreement on it. But a case can be made that it again divides into three. Each part begins with a negative prohibition and then moves on to teach the positive counterpart. As in 6:1–18, the basic pattern is broken by some extended teaching. This time it is on keeping ourselves away from certain kinds of worry and anxiety (6:25–34):

6:19 Do not treasure-store treasure on earth . . .	7:1–2 Do not play at being the Judge . . .	7:6 Do not give . . . neither . . .
6:20–21 . . . but in heaven 6:22–4 (Two reasons) Extended teaching: 6:25–34 Therefore I say to you do not worry . . .	7:3–5 . . . but examine yourself, then help your brother	7:7–11 . . . but cherish and depend upon your Father's love in prayer

Table 9

Matthew 7:12 serves a wider purpose in the structure of the Sermon. By referring again to 'the Law and the Prophets', it serves as a bookend to Jesus's teaching in 5:21–7:11, which has fulfilled the teaching of the Law and the Prophets (5:17–20). It also gives the summary principle behind everything Jesus has said about relating to others.

Do not treasure-store on earth (6:19–24)

More literally, Jesus says, 'Don't treasure-store for yourself treasure on earth, . . . But treasure-store for yourself treasure in heaven' (verses 19–20). We can understand 'treasure on earth' more or less (financial security), but what about 'treasure in heaven'? As we saw above, and as so often in the Sermon, the answer lies in the Beatitudes (5:3–12). To be the kind of disciple described there and to do the kinds of things described there is to 'invest' in heaven, with the 'reward' of our Father's approval both now and in the future, and all the benefits outlined in Jesus's promises.

The 'heart' (verse 21) is the seat of our decision-making. Those with treasure in heaven are those whose decisions (hearts) are focused on God's rule and his future, expressing a concern for his righteousness (his will to be done), and a confident belief in the reality and nearness of his kingdom. This is contrasted here with building treasure 'on earth', which we can take to be doubting God, his goodness, his future and his kingdom, and doing things with money and material possessions that express such doubt. Hoarding money and possessions (verse 19) would be an expression of such doubt; likewise, envy (verses 22–4) and material anxiety (verses 25–34). But hoarding money and possessions is also just plain foolish. Wealth is deceptive (compare 13:22), promising security without being able to deliver in a world of decay and evil (verse 19b). The truly wise person finds security with their Father in the heavens (verse 20b).

It is very hard to understand verses 22–4 without some background knowledge. In what way can an eye be a 'lamp'? On the whole, the ancient world thought about how we see differently from modern science, with rays coming out of the eye rather than going in.[23] The eye therefore (figuratively) revealed something about the inside of a person – about their heart. To have a 'healthy', 'single' or 'good' eye revealed a generosity inside. For example, the Hebrew for a generous person in Proverbs 22:9 is 'a person of good eye'. To have an 'unhealthy', 'bad' or 'evil' eye (verse 23) revealed an ungenerous spirit inside, seeing others as economic competitors or rivals for scarce resources. The phrase is used in Deuteronomy 15:9, Proverbs 23:6, 28:22 and, significantly, Matthew 20:15. Such a person has divided loyalties, holding back in generosity out of devotion to a different master; that is, to 'Money' (verse 24). The word Jesus uses is 'Mammon' – an Aramaic word for wealth, used for the Syrian god of riches.[24] To call upon this alternative master is functionally equivalent to depending upon an idol for material blessing or security. Instead, Jesus is encouraging the single-minded (single-eyed) financial generosity that flows from a heart devoted to our Father in the heavens, confident in his generous protection and provision, and his coming kingdom.

Do not worry (6:25–34)

To 'worry' is mentioned no fewer than six times in verses 25–34, and three of these are specifically an exhortation not to worry (verses 25, 31 and 34). What kind of worry? Jesus is not telling us to be carefree and unconcerned. There are some good and rational kinds of worry – such as the 'worry' Paul has for all the churches (2 Corinthians 11:28). Rather, this is specifically, 'Do not worry about your life' (verse 25) – about what you need to live and survive (such as food and clothing). In other words, it is very closely related to the storing of treasure on earth in verse 19, the 'unhealthy' eye of verse 23 and the devotion to money in verse 24.

Jesus deals with food first (verses 26–7). Worry about food reveals a misunderstanding or misrepresentation of the Father. He feeds the birds

---

[23] Some scholars do claim that it is possible to make sense of these verses using an 'intromission' model of sight (that is, rays of light going *into* the eye). See Charles Quarles, *Sermon on the Mount: Restoring Christ's Message to the Modern Church* (Nashville: B&H, 2011), 244–7. But it remains extremely hard to see how the eye could be in any way described as a 'lamp' under this understanding.

[24] Samson Uytanlet notes how many cultures likewise appeal to some kind of 'god of wealth'. For example, some Chinese people believe in 'the cái shén (財神) or the "god of wealth," the god who "specializes" in the giving of wealth and one that can be called alongside other gods'. Uytanlet and Kwa, *Matthew*, 104.

of the air, so how much more will he feed his own children (verse 26)? What is more, as with storing treasure on earth, such worry is foolish – it doesn't actually change anything (verse 27).

The pattern is similar as Jesus turns to deal with clothing (verses 28–30). Worry about clothing reveals 'little-faith' (verse 30). Your Father clothes the grass of the field with glory, so how much more will he clothe his own children? Indeed, all such material anxiety is pagan-like (verses 31–2), typical of those who do not know God and do not trust him to know what we need (compare verse 8).

So, as before (verse 8), the exhortation is essentially, 'Do not be like them.' Instead, be a consistently 'salty' disciple of Jesus. Verse 33 picks up on the language of the Beatitudes: seek as first priority the kingdom and 'his righteousness'. As with previous uses of this word in the Sermon (5:6, 10, 20; 6:1), Jesus is talking about 'the righteous conduct that God requires of his people'.[25] Strive to be such a disciple, and your Father will give you 'all these things' (verse 33).

In the context, from verse 31, 'all these things' are things to eat, drink and wear. The disciples have also been told that their Father 'knows that you need them' (verse 32). So we can take 'all these things' in verse 33 to be 'everything material you need to do what I have called you to do'. One implication of this is that if we cannot get it, we do not need it. Sometimes, of course, Christians cannot get food, water or clothing. And yet still they need not worry, knowing that their Father cares for them more than anything in his creation and the kingdom of heaven is theirs. Jesus will make a similar point in chapter 10: because they know God as Father, they need not be afraid of those who would persecute them – even to death (Matthew 10:26, 28, 31).

Verse 34 returns us to the daily focus that was at the heart of the Lord's Prayer (verse 11). The exhortations in 6:19–33 have been to make the right choices about material things facing us today. Doing this in the context of a faithful, 'salty' relationship with the Father means that we can entrust things outside our choices and control to him: not just for tomorrow, but for all the future.

This concludes Jesus's teaching on money and possessions in the Sermon. Many disciples reading this today will be materially rich people (whether they feel it or not). What is more, since the Industrial Revolution, the nature of poverty has changed. As Jesus was speaking, not to have enough food for physical survival was a possibility for a higher proportion

---

[25] Olmstead, *Matthew 1–14*, 139.

of people compared to today, even in the majority world. And yet still the world runs after security in further wealth, finds generosity difficult, ends up being controlled by money and is often anxious about finding material provision for the future. Joe Kapolyo comments that even places that are relatively poor in global terms are hardly free from such materialism. Indeed, 'this longing for material riches fuels the preaching of a prosperity gospel in many parts of Africa'.[26] As with other parts of the Sermon, the teaching of 6:19–34 should convict disciples in all kinds of economic circumstances of their 'little faith' – driving them back to the Beatitudes, seeking God's mercy as they let go of false and deceptive security.

Do not play at being Judge (7:1–5)

The teaching of 7:1–2 should remind us of the final part of the Lord's Prayer (6:12–15). If you don't forgive people, then you can't expect to be forgiven. Likewise, if you 'judge' people, then you can expect to be judged using the same measure (verse 2). Jesus is not talking about judgments in civil courts or church discipline,[27] and he is certainly not discouraging moral discernment. Instead, he is warning his disciples about taking on his Father's role as Judge of the earth. So don't judge people as if you were (a merciless) God, or you will be judged by God (without mercy). As we noted above, Jesus will later illustrate this principle at length in the parable of the unmerciful servant (18:21–35).

The 'plank' in verses 3–5 is a structural beam for a building, for holding up a floor or a roof, representing a serious sin. Jesus's illustration suggests that this serious sin (verses 3–4) needs to be dealt with (verse 5) before someone can help another person with a lesser sin. In the context, the serious sin Jesus has just mentioned is the sin of playing the Judge (verses 1–2). If we approach a struggling disciple as Judge, then we are dangerously forgetting and dismissing the mercy that has been shown to us. This is similar to the teaching in 6:12–15. The additional point here is that this attitude prevents us from helping others. On the other hand, if we approach someone not as Judge but as a humble brother or sister, as a forgiven sinner, then the good news is that we can help them.[28]

---

[26] Kapolyo, 'Matthew', 1148.

[27] As 1 Corinthians 5:12 should make clear.

[28] Compare John Newton: 'A man, truly illuminated, will no more despise others, than Bartimaeus, after his own eyes were opened, would take a stick, and beat

Do not throw it all away (7:6–11)

To be 'sacred' or 'holy' in verse 6 is to be dedicated or set apart for God's service, as Jesus's disciples have been – as the salt of the earth and the light of the world (5:13–16). A 'pearl' represented the most precious thing one could think of (compare 13:45–6). 'Dogs' and 'pigs' were stereotypically unclean and associated with the Gentiles and hostile pagan nations (compare 15:26–7). Throughout the Sermon, Jesus has been warning his disciples not to lose their distinctiveness by becoming like the pagan world around them (5:47; 6:8, 32).

It is very common to link verse 6 to the immediate previous verses and to take it as a warning against (gospel-centred) speech that will be rejected.[29] But these contextual considerations suggest it is much more likely to be a general warning. It is very similar, with some shared vocabulary, to the warning at the beginning of the main body of the Sermon: to not lose 'saltiness' and so be trampled underfoot (5:13). We could paraphrase it like this: Do not throw away what you have through your precious relationship with your Father, leaving yourself at the mercy of a hostile world.

The repeated word in verses 7–11 is 'ask'. The positive counterpart to throwing away a relationship with the Father is nurturing it through greater and bolder dependence in prayer. Jesus promises a response to those who seek and ask in dependence (verses 7–8). He then backs up the promise with a contrast: if we (though 'evil', verse 11) know how to give good gifts, how much more will our Father in the heavens (verses 9–10)! The call to radical and bold dependence on our loving Father here in many ways summarises the positive teaching since the beginning of chapter 6.

The positive counterpart to being a hypocrite in 6:1–18 was prayer. Likewise, the positive counterpart to being pagan-like or unhelpfully judgmental in 6:19–7:11 is also prayer. Perhaps if we fully understood the value of our relationship with our Father (verse 6), we would ask for more (verses 7–11). But the promise that 'everyone who asks receives' raises a number of issues. What about unanswered prayer? Given that our Father knows what we need (6:8, 32) and is perfectly loving (7:9–11), we should perhaps conclude that a genuinely unanswered prayer must be outside the will and promises of God and really would not have been good for us.[30] We might

---

every blind man he met.' Quoted in Tony Reinke, *Newton on the Christian Life: To Live Is Christ* (Wheaton: Crossway, 2015), 15.

[29] For example, Pennington, *Sermon on the Mount*, 259–62, among many.

[30] Compare John Piper, 'You Can Never Ask Too Much', 12 January 2013. www.

also wonder if we are asking for things that are too small or unimportant. Certainly, a good alternative to being like the pagans and to 'run after' the food and clothing we need is simply to ask for them. But perhaps the most valuable thing we could ask for, as suggested by Jesus's Sermon, would be to have whatever we need to put his teaching into practice.

So in everything . . . (7:12)

The 'So' beginning verse 12 may well be there in part to summarise all the teaching since the last time Jesus mentioned 'the Law and the Prophets' in 5:17. But it may also connect to what he has just said in 7:7–11. Jesus has come to fulfil the Law and the Prophets (5:17) but, amazingly, those who follow him, listen to him and prayerfully depend upon their Father can join in! The love for others that proved impossible before now becomes possible through knowing the Father and being free to ask him for whatever help is needed.[31]

SUMMARY AND PURPOSE

The purpose of this section of the Sermon (6:9–7:12) is to encourage an exclusive, humble and prayerful dependence upon the Father over and against a dependence on money and material wealth. Jesus is promoting a relationship that is so strong and undivided that his disciples do not worry about the future, knowing they are secure in his hands. The expectation is that this will also change their relations to those around them, showing itself in generosity (6:22) and humble help to those struggling with sin (7:3–5), fulfilling the Law and the Prophets in their love for others (7:12).

---

desiringgod.org/articles/you-can-never-ask-too-much: 'God ignores no prayers from his children. And he gives us what we ask for, or something better (not necessarily easier), if we trust him.' (Accessed 9 February 2024.)

[31] As is often noted, the so-called 'golden rule' in this verse is not dissimilar to maxims in other ethical systems. Samson Uytanlet notes that it effectively the same as a proverb attributed to Confucius, and not in itself a superior way of putting it (as is sometimes claimed). Uytanlet and Kwa, *Matthew*, 109. Jesus's point in the Sermon is that this behaviour, which everyone can agree is good behaviour (even across different ethical systems and cultures), *is now possible* in a new way for those who are his disciples.

6. Take the narrow path • Matthew 7:13–29

We have reached the end of the Sermon. And like many sermons, this one ends with a rousing final appeal. The Sermon began with a gentle, general, indirect sequence of sayings recommending a life of true wisdom (5:3–10). These sayings specified the positive advantages of adopting this life over all other lives – the things that make it the best possible life to be living, even though it may not appear so at first. The Sermon ends with much stronger, more direct exhortations to go the right way, exhortations that not only specify the advantages of doing so, but also spell out the catastrophic consequences of going the other way.

The narrow and wide gates

13 'Enter through the narrow gate. For wide is the gate and broad is the road that leads to destruction, and many enter through it. 14 But small is the gate and narrow the road that leads to life, and only a few find it.

True and false prophets

15 'Watch out for false prophets. They come to you in sheep's clothing, but inwardly they are ferocious wolves. 16 By their fruit you will recognise them. Do people pick grapes from thorn-bushes, or figs from thistles? 17 Likewise, every good tree bears good fruit, but a bad tree bears bad fruit. 18 A good tree cannot bear bad fruit, and a bad tree cannot bear good fruit. 19 Every tree that does not bear good fruit is cut down and thrown into the fire. 20 Thus, by their fruit you will recognise them.

True and false disciples

21 'Not everyone who says to me, "Lord, Lord," will enter the kingdom of heaven, but only the one who does the will of my Father who is in heaven. 22 Many will say to me on that day, "Lord, Lord, did we not prophesy in your name and in your name drive out demons and in your name perform many miracles?" 23 Then I will tell them plainly, "I never knew you. Away from me, you evildoers!"

The wise and foolish builders

24 'Therefore everyone who hears these words of mine and puts them into practice is like a wise man who built his house on the rock. 25 The rain came down, the streams rose, and the winds blew and beat against that house; yet it did not fall, because it had its foundation on the rock. 26 But everyone who hears these words of mine and does not put them into practice is like a foolish man who built his house on sand. 27 The rain came down, the streams rose, and the winds blew and beat against that house, and it fell with a great crash.'

28 When Jesus had finished saying

these things, the crowds were amazed at his teaching, **29** because he taught | as one who had authority, and not as their teachers of the law.

There are three parts to these final exhortations: verses 13–14, verses 15–23 and verses 24–7. The second is longer, and could be divided in two, but actually deals with the one subject of false prophets (even if what Jesus says has wider implications). As with other three-part structures in the Sermon, one of the parts is expanded – here it is the middle one, with more teaching on who does not qualify to enter the kingdom in verses 21–3.

So the structure is:

(13–14) Choose the narrow gate
    13b The wide gate and easy way
    14 The narrow gate and hard way
(15–23) Beware of false prophets
    16–20 Recognise them by their fruit
    21–3 They will be judged according to their fruit
(24–7) Hear these words and do them
    24–5 The wise man, building on rock
    26–7 The foolish man, building on sand

In each part, as Jonathan T. Pennington comments, there is a 'difference between external appearance and internal reality, a theme at the heart of the Sermon'.[32] Jesus is also mapping out the consequences that flow from each choice (choosing which way to go or where to build) or identity (what kind of 'tree' someone is, or whether they are known by Jesus):

---

[32] Pennington, *Sermon on the Mount*, 269.

Choose the narrow gate (13–14)

Narrow gate / hard way	➡	Life
Wide gate / easy way	➡	Destruction

Watch out for false prophets (15–20, testing their fruit)

Good tree	➡	Good fruit
Bad tree	➡	Bad fruit

The test for them (and everyone) on 'that day' will be based on having done the will of the Father (21–3)

Known by Jesus (and the Father)	➡	Doing his will
'I never knew you'	➡	'Lawlessness'

Hear my words and put them into practice (24–7)

Build on the rock	➡	House stands in storm
Build on the sand	➡	House falls in storm

Table 10

It may well be at this point that Jesus lifts his eyes from his disciples to address both disciples and crowd together. The call to enter in verse 13 is quite general, if a little enigmatic. Only in 11:28 will it become explicit that Jesus is calling people to come to him (that is, he is the 'narrow gate' in verse 13a).

Choose the narrow gate (7:13–14)

Although this is the exhortation section of the Sermon, there are actually only two explicit exhortations here: a call to enter (verse 13) and a call to watch out (verse 15). In the context, the first of these is about entering into the future life of the kingdom of the heavens (see 7:14, 21 and compare 5:20). The danger is of being deceived by appearances. The way and path to destruction is wide and broad – appearing to be easy. What is more, there are many travelling this way. Jesus has picked out Pharisees, teachers of the law, hypocrites, tax collectors and pagans (Gentiles). We instinctively feel safer following the herd. But if the herd is heading to destruction, this turns out not to be wisdom but foolishness.

Beware of false prophets (7:15–23)

The second exhortation is to watch out (verse 15). There are some claiming to be on the right path (they are in 'sheep's clothing') but whose aim is actually destruction (they are 'wolves' – enemies of the sheep). The repeated words in verses 16–20 are 'tree' and 'fruit.' The contrast between two types of tree bearing two kinds of fruit shows us how to beware of the wolves of verse 15. This is not an exhaustive test. In 1 John, which deals with very similar issues, John has three tests: the test of doctrine (that is, are they speaking the truth?), the test of obedience and the test of love. Jesus's test only covers the last two of those directly: obedience and love. This is consistent with the emphasis in the Sermon on humble dependence on God as Father leading to 'light' and love. If there is no 'light' and love (good fruit), then there may well be no humble dependence on God as Father (good tree). For what to look for in practice, we can look back over the detail of Jesus's teaching on the characteristic 'fruit' of a true disciple.

Verses 21–3 are the most challenging part of this section. They connect to the previous verses in that the wolves 'in sheep's clothing' of verse 15 may be professing Christians who have done spectacular signs, but may nonetheless be false prophets. Nevertheless, verse 21 stands as a general warning that mere profession of Jesus's name is not enough on its own to enter the kingdom of the heavens. It is necessary to show the authenticity of commitment to Jesus by doing the will of Jesus's Father. In this context, this means especially being 'salt' and 'light' in the world by listening to and doing what Jesus says in the Sermon. As in Paul's letters, life with God comes by faith alone. But faith is never alone: it is 'lively' – always expressed in practical ways. (There is a similar emphasis in the final section of the Sermon, verses 24–7 below.)

We should take careful note that those whom Jesus will declare to be 'evildoers' (literally, 'lawless ones', verse 23) on 'that day' (of Judgment) are not true disciples who become false disciples. They never were true disciples: Jesus also declares, 'I never knew you.'[33] Pennington may also be right to suggest the words of those before Jesus on that day are not words of surprise: 'their remonstrance in 7:22 (and 25:44) is not one of genuine surprise but self-justification'.[34]

These exhortations and warnings do seem designed to unsettle the

---

[33] Compare 1 John 2:19: 'They went out from us, but they did not really belong to us. For if they had belonged to us, they would have remained with us; but their going showed that none of them belonged to us.'
[34] Pennington, *Sermon on the Mount*, 278.

disciples to some extent. Are they being deceived to go down the wrong path – by outsiders? – by outsiders disguised as insiders? – by themselves? But, having said this, the basic exhortation beginning at verse 13 to 'enter through the narrow gate' is entirely free and open. The path to life in the kingdom of the heavens is there through Jesus, and anyone may take it.

Hear these words and do them (7:24–7)

Verse 24 begins with an important 'therefore'. This could be a way of introducing a concluding statement for the whole Sermon, but it may also link these verses closely with what Jesus has just been saying in verses 21–3. Jesus was warning against false prophets in verses 15–20, and in verses 21–3 warned that they remain false prophets even if they say and do spectacular things in his name – if they act against the will of his Father. Verses 24–7 explicitly generalise this principle and connect it to the teaching of Jesus. To be against the will of the Father is the same as listening to Jesus but not doing what he says, and anyone like that is in danger. The connection between these verses and verses 21–3 also suggests that the rain/streams/wind in verses 24–7 are not merely the 'storms of life', but the storm of final Judgment on the world.

Jesus makes his contrast by stating two responses to his teaching and connecting each with a short story about building a house. There are some repeated ideas. Both responses involve listening to Jesus. In both cases, the one listening 'is like' (literally, 'will be likened to' [i.e., at the Judgment]) a man building a house. Both stories involve the house facing a severe storm. The similarities highlight the differences. The first response involves doing what Jesus says; the second, not doing. The first man is 'wise' or 'prudent'; the second is 'foolish'. The first house is built on rock; the second on sand. The first house stands in the storm; the second falls 'with a great crash'. This is the final emphasis.

These verses therefore strongly encourage us to listen to Jesus and do what he says. But looking back at what Jesus has said shows this is not just about doing stuff – and even when it is, it's not so much about what I do, but what we do to bring light to the world and praise to the Father. Doing what Jesus says means first being humble (5:3–6), being the salt of the earth (5:13 – a dependence on God expanded in 6:1–7:11). Only then does it mean doing acts of mercy and love in his name (5:7–10), being the light of the world (5:14–16 – expanded in 5:21–48). Jesus is not *merely* saying, 'Build your life on me' (although he is saying this). He is not merely saying, 'Build your life on me by listening to me and doing the works I tell you to do' (although he is in part saying that). He is saying, 'Build your lives and your light-spreading mission in the world by listening to everything I have said and responding with humble dependence and commitment.' (Compare 16:17–18, also about building upon a 'rock'.)

This can be compared to the negative examples Jesus has given within the Sermon. The teachers of the law and the Pharisees have been teaching contrary to Jesus. The 'hypocrites' and the Gentile pagans have been doing things contrary to his teaching. If the disciples build a mission in the world that isn't founded on Jesus and his teaching (and doing his will, which is the will of the Father), then it will not stand in the coming Judgment and they may well fall with it. Again, appearances can be deceptive. Joe Kapolyo notes that in places like Africa where the growth in churches is so remarkable, 'If people are just hearing Jesus's words but not doing them, the church is built on sand.'[35]

The crowd's reaction (7:28–9)

In 7:28–9, the crowd correctly notes the astonishing authority with which Jesus has spoken – he has spoken as the Lord. The question is: will they come and submit to him as Lord? The question for Jesus's disciples is: are they properly recognising and respecting the authority of their teacher?

SUMMARY AND PURPOSE
The purpose of this final section of the Sermon is to exhort the disciples to follow Jesus on the countercultural path he has laid out for them and to warn them of the path to destruction down which many will go – and down which some even from within their own ranks will try to pull them. Jesus wants the disciples to build their mission in the world upon his teaching, faithfully put into action – promising them that if they do so, their work will survive the coming Judgment, but also warning them of the consequences if they do not.

---

[35] Kapolyo, 'Matthew', 1151.

6

Proclaiming in Deed

MATTHEW 8–9

1. Proclaiming in deed part 1 • Matthew 8:1–22

The overall context of 4:12–10:42 is that, building on the proclamation of John, Jesus is now proclaiming the nearness of the kingdom of the heavens (4:17). He has called his first disciples to follow him, promising to make them 'fishers of people' (4:18–22). He has begun a ministry in Galilee: of teaching in the synagogues, proclaiming the gospel of the kingdom and healing every disease and affliction (4:23). This has been attracting great crowds of people from all the surrounding regions (4:23–5). In other words, he has been proclaiming the kingdom in word and deed. Matthew has not yet given us an example of Jesus's synagogue teaching, but he has given us an extended example of Jesus teaching his disciples in the sight and hearing of the crowds (Matthew 5–7, the Sermon on the Mount). In chapters 8–9, he then turns to the proclamation of the kingdom in deed – a compressed, quick-fire overview of Jesus's healing and exorcism ministry.

Jesus heals a man with leprosy

8 When Jesus came down from the mountainside, large crowds followed him. **2** A man with leprosy[a] came and knelt before him and said, 'Lord, if you are willing, you can make me clean.'

3 Jesus reached out his hand and touched the man. 'I am willing,' he said. 'Be clean!' Immediately he was cleansed of his leprosy. **4** Then Jesus said to him, 'See that you don't tell anyone. But go, show yourself to the priest and offer the gift Moses commanded, as a testimony to them.'

The faith of the centurion

5 When Jesus had entered Capernaum, a centurion came to him, asking for help. **6** 'Lord,' he said, 'my servant lies at home paralysed, suffering terribly.'

7 Jesus said to him, 'Shall I come and heal him?'

8 The centurion replied, 'Lord, I do not deserve to have you come under my roof. But just say the word, and my servant will be healed. **9** For I myself am a man under authority, with soldiers under me. I tell this one, "Go," and he goes; and that one, "Come," and he comes. I say to my servant, "Do this," and he does it.'

10 When Jesus heard this, he was amazed and said to those following him, 'Truly I tell you, I have not found anyone in Israel with such great faith. **11** I say to you that many will come from the east and the west, and will take their places at the feast with Abraham, Isaac and Jacob in the kingdom of heaven. **12** But the subjects of the kingdom will be thrown outside, into the darkness, where there will be weeping and gnashing of teeth.'

13 Then Jesus said to the centurion, 'Go! Let it be done just as you believed it would.' And his servant was healed at that moment.

Jesus heals many

14 When Jesus came into Peter's house, he saw Peter's mother-in-law lying in bed with a fever. **15** He touched her hand and the fever left her, and she got up and began to wait on him.

16 When evening came, many who were demon-possessed were brought to him, and he drove out the spirits with a word and healed all who were ill. **17** This was to fulfil what was spoken through the prophet Isaiah:

> 'He took up our infirmities
> and bore our diseases.'**b**

The cost of following Jesus

18 When Jesus saw the crowd around him, he gave orders to cross to the other side of the lake. **19** Then a teacher of the law came to him and said, 'Teacher, I will follow you wherever you go.'

20 Jesus replied, 'Foxes have dens and birds have nests, but the Son of Man has nowhere to lay his head.'

21 Another disciple said to him, 'Lord, first let me go and bury my father.'

22 But Jesus told him, 'Follow me, and let the dead bury their own dead.'

---

a 2 The Greek word traditionally translated leprosy was used for various diseases affecting the skin.

b 17 Isaiah 53:4 (see Septuagint)

We need to be clear that the miracles here are supportive proclamation. On their own, the deeds are frequently misunderstood and misinterpreted.[1] Jesus works hard to bring about a true interpretation – e.g., by sending the man cleared of skin disease to the priests in 8:4, or by explicitly linking the healing of a paralytic to his authority to forgive sins in 9:6. But although there is much amazement spreading as a result of the deeds (9:8, 26, 31, 33), there is little evidence that many were able to see their

---

[1] This will be one of the key themes of Matthew 11–12.

true significance, and for some they simply generated hostility (e.g., the herdsmen in 8:34; the Pharisees in 9:11, 34). Even Jesus's own disciples are slow to get the point (8:26).

The common feature of all those who are healed or restored in Matthew 8–9 is that they were previously all obviously and visibly struggling under the shadow of death. The healings and exorcisms therefore all prefigure resurrection: lifting or raising people back to life, rescuing them from the present evil age. For those with eyes to see, they are a window into the coming kingdom, where the shadow of death will be lifted entirely. Rightly understood, they illustrate what the kingdom will be like. There is explicit confirmation that this is what Jesus is doing in 8:29. The demons in the two men ask Jesus, 'Have you come here to torture us before the appointed time?' The future destruction of evil is brought into the present. The same principle can be seen across all the miracles. They signify that Jesus has come 'before the appointed time' to save people from the shadow of death. In the middle of Matthew 8–9, in 9:1–8 and 9:9–13, we shall learn that this means dealing with their sins.

(See also the Introduction, on the closeness of death in the first century Mediterranean world.)

We see Matthew's liking of triadic structures working overtime here. There are three main sections (8:1–22, 8:23–9:17 and 9:18–38). Each of these further splits into three: miracles, followed by a summary of some sort, followed by an episode not involving a miracle but emphasising something Jesus says. The miracles section of each part is also divided into three sets of miracles:

8:1–22 The radical authority of Jesus to rescue people from the shadow of death	8:23–9:17 The radical authority of Jesus to defeat evil and forgive sins	9:18–38 The radical compassion of Jesus for the harassed and helpless
Three sets of miracles: 8:2–4 A man with skin disease 8:5–13 A centurion's servant 8:14–15 Peter's mother-in-law	Three sets of miracles: 8:23–7 The rebuking of the storm 8:28–34 Two demoniacs 9:1–8 A paralytic	Three sets of miracles: 9:18–26 Two daughters 9:27–31 Two blind men 9:32–4 A mute demoniac
8:16–17 A summary and Matthew's comment.	9:9–13 The call of Matthew and its aftermath	9:35 A summary

8:18–22 Jesus's words: A serious call	9:14–17 Jesus's words: Don't miss the bridegroom	9:36–8 Jesus's words: Pray earnestly

Table 11

This leaves multiple ways of splitting up these chapters. I shall take each of the three main sections in turn, beginning with 8:1–22.

A man with skin disease (8:1–4)

Jesus has come 'before the appointed time' to give an advance demonstration of the kingdom, and the defeat of death, sickness, evil and sin. The opening miracle in this section introduces the two big themes we shall see across Matthew 8–9. The first of these, seen across every miracle here, is a visual demonstration of Jesus's ability and authority to take someone out of the realm of corruption and death and bring them back to a state of holiness and life. This is seen by the vast crowd that has followed Jesus down the mountain (verse 1). But Jesus is concerned for this to be witnessed carefully by a priest (verse 4). The second theme, seen in some but not all the miracles, is the attitude of those interacting with Jesus, all of whom recognise his authority and ability to take someone out from under the shadow of death.

The word 'leprosy' Matthew uses in verses 2 and 3 had a wider range of application than its usage today (to Hansen's disease), being used of any kind of 'serious skin disorder'.[2] Whatever the strict medical reality, it would have been covered by the laws on defilement and purification in Leviticus 11–15 (especially chapters 13–14) that are in the background here. These laws were a practical and visual illustration for God's people of the deadly dynamic of sin and infirmity profaning what is holy, polluting all things and bringing death. The pollution is infectious and inescapable: even if someone does not directly cause it, it can still corrupt them. Once this has happened, the laws articulate the extreme difficulty of cleansing and sanctification through sacrifice. For the man with skin disease here, the prospects of finding cleansing would be slim indeed. The whiteness of the skin means he would look like a walking corpse. He is like the living dead – a tragic visual illustration of the condition of humanity: helplessly trapped under the shadow of death.

The ability of Jesus to deal with this condition is shown here to be

---

[2] BDAG, 'lepros', 'lepra'.

exceptional. Touch, under the law, spreads pollution, not cleansing. Here the dynamic is reversed. Jesus willingly and deliberately reaches out and touches the man, and Matthew tells us the skin disease (and all the associated uncleanliness) is removed 'immediately' (verse 3). Jesus instructs him to go to a priest and to offer the appropriate thanksgiving gift for the cleansing. Whether he does so or not, this is a testimony to us that something beyond what the Law could bring about has happened: something foreseen by the prophets (e.g., Isaiah 35:5–6) is now taking place.

The cleansing has taken the man from under the shadow of death and brought him back into the realm of life. Like the other miracles concerning individuals in Matthew, this is therefore a picture of resurrection.[3] We shall see this even more clearly as these next two chapters of the Gospel unfold.

Matthew shows us only the positive aspects of the man's interaction with Jesus here. The man kneels before Jesus (verse 2). This word was last used by Matthew to describe the worship of the Magi before the infant Jesus in 2:11. As John Nolland puts it, 'all such responses to Jesus are on the way towards the Christian recognition of Jesus as worthy of divine worship'.[4] Hence the man's strong belief that Jesus is able to cleanse him.

A centurion's servant (8:5–13)

We get similar elements in the second miracle. We are told the centurion's servant is lying paralysed (verse 6).[5] In other words, he looks like a corpse. He is also 'suffering terribly' (or, better, 'tormented terribly'). The centurion's anguish and urgency suggests the servant is perhaps not expected to live much longer. Again, Jesus's ability to deal with the servant's condition is shown to be extraordinary. When Jesus sends the centurion away in verse 13, we are told the servant is healed at a distance 'at that moment'.

But the emphasis here is on the centurion's interaction with Jesus on behalf of his servant. The centurion shows the deference and humility

---

[3] As argued persuasively for the miracles in Mark's Gospel by Peter Bolt, *Jesus's Defeat of Death: Persuading Mark's Early Readers* (Cambridge: Cambridge University Press, 2003).

[4] Nolland, *Matthew*, 349.

[5] The phrase used here for the paralysed man is *'pais mou'*, which in the LXX consistently means 'my servant' (Nolland, *Matthew*, 354). There is really no warrant at all for suggesting a more intimate relationship between the two men, as is sometimes claimed.

appropriate to a Gentile approaching someone with divine authority (verse 8a).[6] He expresses a strong belief that Jesus is able to heal his servant with just a word (verse 8b). He understands Jesus's authority in the light of his own authority and sees it as far greater (verse 9). Such faith is strongly commended by Jesus (verse 10). But Matthew's purpose goes beyond merely encouraging a faith like this. Building on his portrayal of the Magi in 2:1–12, Matthew is preparing his Jewish readers for the blessings of the kingdom to spread out into the nations to some very unexpected people, while warning them that (at least some of) 'the subjects of the kingdom' will be thrown outside in judgment. In that place 'there will be weeping and gnashing of teeth', which is a warning Jesus will use a number of times again in Matthew's Gospel (13:42, 50; 22:13; 24:51; 25:30). 'Gnashing of teeth' is a way to talk about anger, so it seems likely that the weeping here is weeping with tears of anger – or perhaps also regret. The 'subjects of the kingdom' would have felt entitled to be part of the kingdom; Jesus is warning them how angry and regretful they will be when they are denied entry.

As his Gospel becomes more widely read and heard among the nations, these episodes will become an encouragement for Gentiles to approach Jesus with faith, no matter how unworthy they are or feel.

Peter's mother-in-law (8:14–15)

Peter's mother-in-law is 'lying in bed with a fever', but a 'fever' in the ancient world was more than a bad headache. It was one of the greatest killers.[7] The fact that she is lying in bed also means she probably isn't expected to live. Jesus's ability to deal with her condition is again shown to be extraordinary, as he touches her and the fever leaves (verse 15). Verse 15 ends more literally, 'And she was raised up and began to wait on him.' Her attitude and response is one of willing service.

A summary and Matthew's comment (8:16–17)

Matthew's summary (verse 16) shows that the two incidents so far are, as examples of Jesus's ministry at the time, just the tip of the iceberg. Even on one evening, Jesus restores many people through exorcism and healing.

---

[6] There are similarities to the faith of the Canaanite woman in Matthew 15:21–8.
[7] Bolt, *Jesus's Defeat of Death*, 76–87.

We should still see this as a picture of the future kingdom victory over evil, death and illness brought forward 'before the appointed time'. The rolling back of the shadow of death is limited to a single geographic location and it isn't permanent or eternal. Nonetheless, it is an impressive demonstration! As hinted in 4:23, Matthew considers the driving out of spirits as very similar to the activity of healing from illness. This is probably because 'demons' and 'unclean spirits' were considered to be connected to the dead, even beings of the under-world – the place of the dead, otherwise known as Hades or Sheol.[8] (The connections between demons, death, evil, destruction and the place of the dead will be confirmed later in the chapter, in 8:28–34.) To cast out a demon was therefore just as much a demonstration of taking someone out from under the shadow of death as restoring them through healing.

Matthew's further comment is that all this fulfils what was spoken through the prophet Isaiah, words spoken of the Servant of the Lord in Isaiah 53:4. Matthew's purpose in doing this is to strengthen our understanding of who Jesus is. He is the Servant figure of Isaiah 52:13–53:12. Matthew understands Isaiah to be saying that the Servant will carry away our infirmities and diseases. But he also knows that such physical ailments are related to spiritual distress and are ultimately caused by the sin and rebellion of all humanity.[9] Matthew will say more about the relation between physical healing and the forgiveness of sins in 9:1–13. Later in the Gospel, he will explain how such things can happen, as he shows Jesus fulfilling Isaiah 53:12, dying as a curse-bearer and sin-bearer.

Jesus's words: a serious call (8:18–22)

The gravity of Jesus's true identity revealed in Matthew 8 so far, as the Servant of the Lord, deserving of divine worship, exhibiting divine authority, helps to explain the otherwise difficult exchanges in verses 18–22. What we have here is a contrast between a teacher of the law, verse 19, and a disciple, verse 21. The teacher of the law gets a negative response. Jesus seems to be saying, 'You don't know who I am, what I have come to do or what you are promising.' The disciple gets a response

---

[8] Bolt, *Jesus's Defeat of Death*, 54–64.
[9] Remembering, of course, that there may be no relation at all between the particular sins of an individual and their particular condition, as we see from John 9:2–3.

which, although almost offensively challenging, is nonetheless positive. It is a call to leave death behind and follow him urgently.

Once again there is a crowd around Jesus (verse 18). They are no doubt amazed by what they have seen and heard from Jesus, but do not yet recognise him as Lord. The question is: who will truly recognise Jesus, leave the crowd and follow him across the lake?

The first contender is a teacher of the law who addresses Jesus as a fellow 'Teacher' and makes a commitment to follow him wherever he may go (verse 19). Jesus's reply is a rebuke: you cannot follow him unless you know who he is and what he has come to face. This is the first time Jesus uses the title 'Son of Man' of himself in Matthew's Gospel. As discussed in the Introduction, this almost certainly links to the vision in Daniel 7. What Jesus says here suggests he is referring to the tribulation under the 'beasts' experienced by the one like a son of man before his vindication and victory.[10] He has no rest, 'nowhere to lay his head'. The teacher of the law does not understand what he is committing to.

The second contender looks more promising, and is described as a 'disciple' (verse 21). He addresses Jesus as 'Lord'. But he is also holding back, asking, 'First let me go and bury my father.' Most likely, this is a request to stay with an alive father until his death, rather than a request to bury an already dead father. But either way, Jesus's response is challenging and provocative. There is an urgency to being a disciple and follower of Jesus that means leaving the realm of death behind.

SUMMARY AND PURPOSE

Matthew is teaching us about Jesus's ability and authority to take someone out from the realm of corruption and death and bring them back to a state of holiness and life. He can do this with a touch (even when touch would normally corrupt the toucher), and he can do this at a distance. Such things suggest a divine authority, but we also learn that Jesus wants to be understood as the 'one like a son of man' engaged in restless suffering on the earth (8:20).

The purpose of Matthew 8–9 is to respond to Jesus's demonstrations of the kingdom made 'before the appointed time'. In 8:1–22, this includes an attitude towards Jesus of worship, humble faith in his authority and an eagerness to serve, while following him in restless suffering and with urgency.

---

[10] This tribulation is parallel to the suffering of Isaiah's Servant figure.

2. Proclaiming in deed part 2 • Matthew 8:23–9:17

In chapters 8–9, Matthew has turned from the proclamation of the kingdom in word (Matthew 5–7, teaching his disciples to live in the light of the coming kingdom) to proclaiming it in deed – a compressed, quick-fire overview of Jesus's healing and exorcism ministry.

Jesus calms the storm

23 Then he got into the boat and his disciples followed him. **24** Suddenly a furious storm came up on the lake, so that the waves swept over the boat. But Jesus was sleeping. **25** The disciples went and woke him, saying, 'Lord, save us! We're going to drown!'

26 He replied, 'You of little faith, why are you so afraid?' Then he got up and rebuked the winds and the waves, and it was completely calm.

27 The men were amazed and asked, 'What kind of man is this? Even the winds and the waves obey him!'

Jesus restores two demon-possessed men

28 When he arrived at the other side in the region of the Gadarenes,^c two demon-possessed men coming from the tombs met him. They were so violent that no one could pass that way. **29** 'What do you want with us, Son of God?' they shouted. 'Have you come here to torture us before the appointed time?'

30 Some distance from them a large herd of pigs was feeding. **31** The demons begged Jesus, 'If you drive us out, send us into the herd of pigs.'

32 He said to them, 'Go!' So they came out and went into the pigs, and the whole herd rushed down the steep bank into the lake and died in the water. **33** Those tending the pigs ran off, went into the town and reported all this, including what had happened to the demon-possessed men. **34** Then the whole town went out to meet Jesus. And when they saw him, they pleaded with him to leave their region.

Jesus forgives and heals a paralysed man

9 Jesus stepped into a boat, crossed over and came to his own town. **2** Some men brought to him a paralysed man, lying on a mat. When Jesus saw their faith, he said to the man, 'Take heart, son; your sins are forgiven.'

3 At this, some of the teachers of the law said to themselves, 'This fellow is blaspheming!'

4 Knowing their thoughts, Jesus said, 'Why do you entertain evil thoughts in your hearts? **5** Which is easier: to say, "Your sins are forgiven," or to say, "Get up and walk"? **6** But I want you to know that the Son of Man has authority on earth to forgive sins.' So he said to the paralysed man, 'Get up, take your mat and go home.' **7** Then the man got up and went home. **8** When the crowd saw this, they were filled with awe; and they praised God, who had given such authority to man.

The calling of Matthew

9 As Jesus went on from there, he saw a man named Matthew sitting at the tax collector's booth. 'Follow me,' he told him, and Matthew got up and followed him.

10 While Jesus was having dinner at Matthew's house, many tax collectors and sinners came and ate with him and his disciples. **11** When the Pharisees saw this, they asked his disciples, 'Why does your teacher eat with tax collectors and sinners?'

12 On hearing this, Jesus said, 'It is not the healthy who need a doctor, but those who are ill. **13** But go and learn what this means: "I desire mercy, not sacrifice."**a** For I have not come to call the righteous, but sinners.'

Jesus questioned about fasting

14 Then John's disciples came and asked him, 'How is it that we and the Pharisees fast often, but your disciples do not fast?'

15 Jesus answered, 'How can the guests of the bridegroom mourn while he is with them? The time will come when the bridegroom will be taken from them; then they will fast.

16 'No one sews a patch of unshrunk cloth on an old garment, for the patch will pull away from the garment, making the tear worse. **17** Neither do people pour new wine into old wineskins. If they do, the skins will burst; the wine will run out, and the wineskins will be ruined. No, they pour new wine into new wineskins, and both are preserved.'

----
c 28 Some manuscripts *Gergesenes*; other manuscripts *Gerasenes*
a 13 Hosea 6:6

Like the first section, the second section divides into three parts:

8:23–9:8 Three miracles:
    8:23–7 Rebuking the storm
    8:28–34 Two demoniacs healed
    9:1–8 A paralytic forgiven (and healed)
9:9–13 The call of Matthew and its aftermath
9:14–17 A dispute about fasting. Jesus's words: Don't miss the bridegroom

(See also the Introduction on the closeness of death in the first century Mediterranean world.)

We shall again here see that the people being healed all represent people obviously and visibly under the shadow of death. They are a window into the coming kingdom, where the shadow of death will be lifted entirely. They illustrate the kingdom. In this section we have confirmed that Jesus has come 'before the appointed time' (8:29) to save people from the shadow of death. In 9:1–8 and 9:9–13, we shall learn that this means dealing with their sins.

Rebuking the storm (8:23–7)

By having Jesus use the title 'Son of Man' in verse 20 above, Matthew has raised a connection with the vision in Daniel 7 that will be helpful as we process this episode on the sea. (Indeed, this episode expands on verses 19–22 by showing us the kinds of places Jesus does 'lay his head' – in the midst of a stormy tribulation! – and, verse 23, the expectation that his disciples will follow him to such places.) In Daniel 7, the 'beasts' – which bring death and destruction to God's people – come out of the sea, which in the ancient world was considered a place of fear and the peril of death, even a portal to the underworld, the place of the dead.[11] One way of portraying people in a world under the shadow of death is therefore to show them in the midst of a life-threatening sea-storm, which is what we have here in verses 24–5.

In this setting, Matthew shows Jesus both unafraid (able to sleep) and with an extraordinary authority. This is the kind of authority over sea-storms associated only with God himself (Psalms 104:7; 106:9).

The disciples are depicted negatively: scared for their lives (verse 25), showing 'little faith' (verse 26) and not yet answering their own question about Jesus's identity (verse 27).

Two demoniacs restored (8:28–34)

The shadow of death is very obvious on the other side of the lake, in the (mostly) Gentile region of the Gadarenes (verse 28): two demon-possessed men come from the tombs.[12] What is more, the demons are

---

[11] Bolt, *Jesus's Defeat of Death*, 136–43, 151–3. See also Revelation 20:13.

[12] That there are two of them is a surprise, given that Mark and Luke only mention one (Mark 5:2; Luke 8:27). The best explanation is that there were indeed two men. Matthew likes mentioning pairs of people being healed or helped by Jesus whenever he can (as in 9:27 and 20:30), and in his shorter episode there is no reason not to. In their longer accounts, Mark and Luke choose to focus on the man about whom there is a helpful follow-up story to tell (Mark 5:14–20; Luke 8:34–9). See also D. A. Carson, *Matthew, Chapters 1 through 12* (Grand Rapids: Zondervan, 1995), 217.

causing the men to be violent (verse 28), and after being cast out of them, exercise powerful destructive violence on a herd of pigs (verse 32). They show a prevalence for pigs, for that which is 'unclean' (Leviticus 11:7) and therefore associated with death and corruption, and for the sea (associated with the place of the dead, as in the previous episode).

As before, Jesus's authority over the forces of death, here represented by the demons, is unchallenged.[13] They recognise it immediately – and are just a little surprised (and no doubt annoyed!) that their destruction is happening early (verse 29). Matthew does not tell us explicitly why Jesus agrees to their request in verse 31. But being cast into the pigs (rather than simply destroyed instantly) does expose the unclean, destructive nature of the demons and demonstrates the scale of the forces the two men are saved from. It also provokes the local population to respond to Jesus and what he has done.

As with the disciples in the previous episode, the response is depicted negatively. Despite the extraordinary faith of the centurion in verses 5–13, being Gentile certainly doesn't guarantee a good attitude to Jesus. The request to leave the region in verse 34 may simply be because they are scared of someone more powerful than the demons (although Matthew says nothing about their fear), or because their hatred of the (previously) demon-possessed men cannot accommodate their restoration. More likely, by drawing attention to the herdsmen in verse 33, Matthew is implying the townspeople associate Jesus with the loss of livelihood owing to the death of the pigs. If so, then he is highlighting another feature of true faith: that it is able to look beyond immediate losses to the (incomparable) future gains of the kingdom.

A paralytic forgiven – and healed (9:1–8)

Like the centurion's servant in 8:6 and Peter's mother-in-law in 8:14, the shadow of death shows itself here in a person unable to move – stretched out horizontally like a corpse. The new thing here is that Matthew wants us to link the reality of the shadow of death to the deeper reality of sin.

The default belief in many cultures is that disability is seen as a

---

[13] Western readers tend to be very dismissive of the Gospel accounts of demon possession. But as Joe Kapolyo notes, 'We in Africa do not have any such difficulties with the idea, and neither did Jesus and his disciples.' Kapolyo, 'Matthew', 1154. Likewise in South Asia: Wintle, 'Matthew', 1238.

punishment for past sins.[14] But Matthew doesn't indicate that he wants us as readers to link the man's condition to individual sins peculiar just to him.[15] Rather, in the background is the fundamental biblical conviction that the ultimate cause of the shadow of death is the human sin against God that began with Adam. Jesus's ministry to save people from the shadow of death is therefore necessarily connected to his ministry to save his people from their sins (1:21). Indeed, it depends upon it.

Jesus shows here his willingness to forgive sins (verse 2). He then goes on to show his authority to forgive sins by healing the man (verses 4–7). The argument is not complicated here. The answer to the question in verse 5 is, 'Both are impossible.' Forgiving sins, at the fundamental level of removing them completely, and the kind of instant healing Jesus does in verse 6 are equally impossible from a human point of view. Both depend upon a divine authority (or a divinely given authority). Doing one proves that you have a divine authority and therefore the authority to do the other. Forgiving sins is an invisible activity, so Jesus shows his authority to do this by doing something visible, by healing the man.

There are multiple attitudes and responses to Jesus shown here. First, there are the friends of the paralysed man. Jesus responds to their expression of faith, their trust that he will do the best for the man. And he does do the best for him – by forgiving him. Matthew's purpose here seems to be to stretch our awareness of what is 'best' for someone beyond the obvious, external and short term.

The teachers of the law in verse 3 respond to the declaration of forgiveness with an internal accusation of blasphemy. This is (miraculously) brought out into the open by Jesus. The accusation is false, given who Jesus is and therefore the kind of authority he has. By describing their thinking as 'evil' (verse 4), Jesus discourages those around him (and us reading about it) from thinking as they do.

The final response is from the crowd in verse 8. As previously, they respond to the healing miracle with awe and amazement, but here do seem to draw the kinds of conclusions about Jesus's authority he wants them to make – at least to some extent. However deep this recognition goes, it does encourage us to be making conclusions about Jesus along the same lines.

---

[14] Joe Kapolyo suggests this is certainly true in Buddhist cultures and some African cultures. Kapolyo, 'Matthew', 1151. Likewise Uytanlet and Kwa, *Matthew*, 168.

[15] Had this been the case, we would expect the forgiveness of sins to result in an instant healing, but it doesn't.

The call of Matthew and its aftermath (9:9–13)

In the forgiving and healing of the paralysed man in verses 1–8, Matthew has expanded and deepened his portrait of the kind of world we live in to encompass not just the shadow of death (as in 8:1–22) and the presence of chaos and evil (as in 8:23–34), but also the all-pervasive underlying problem of *sin*. The most visible manifestation of human sin at the time were the 'tax collectors' and 'sinners' (verses 9 and 10–11). The 'tax collectors' had sided with the Romans, were often coercive and frequently took more than they should.[16] Here they are here classed alongside 'sinners', which is probably referring to notorious *sexual* sinners (compare 21:31).

What Jesus does with such people in verses 9–13 is to call them to follow him (verses 9 and 13), just as he called Peter, Andrew, James and John in 4:18–22. He also eats with them (verse 10). This is either with people he has already called and who have followed (like Matthew), or perhaps in order to call them.

The response of the Pharisees is to ask *why* Jesus eats with such people. This could be a reasonable question. After all, the Psalms and Proverbs, for example, strongly discourage associating or eating with wicked people (e.g., Psalm 1:1; Proverbs 23:6–7). We also find the same concern to dissociate from wicked people elsewhere in the New Testament.[17] But Jesus's response in verses 12 and 13 suggests that the motivation behind the question is not a true desire to maintain holiness but a distaste for showing mercy. They don't want to show mercy, and by not showing mercy and distancing themselves from notorious sinners they are attempting to give the illusion of holiness and righteousness. The question is aggressive, implying that Jesus's holiness is compromised, and that of his disciples.

The first part of Jesus's answer (verse 12) builds on the connection between illness and sin we have seen since the start of the chapter. If sinners are like sick people, then Jesus is not like someone eating with them as a fellow sick person, but like a *doctor*, coming among them and acting with mercy to heal them. In verse 13, Jesus then quotes from Hosea

---

[16] France, *The Gospel of Matthew*, 351–2.

[17] Compare Paul in 1 Corinthians 5:11: 'you must not associate with anyone who claims to be a brother or sister but is sexually immoral or greedy, an idolater or slanderer, a drunkard or swindler. Do not even eat with such people.' (Note that in the previous verse Paul also clarifies that the Corinthians will necessarily have to associate with the immoral people 'of this world', unless they were to leave this world.)

6:6. The Lord requires the same compassionate attitude from his people to others that he shows to them, over and above religious observance through sacrifice. This is the compassion Jesus is showing to sinners by calling them.

Jesus doesn't say here precisely who he means by the group 'the righteous' – or indeed whether this group has any members in it! He just says he has not come to call them. The irony is that because of their harsh attitude to fellow Israelites (and Jesus and his disciples), the Pharisees show themselves outside this group. In other words, they need Jesus just as much as more notorious sinners. But because they also distance themselves from the 'sinners' here, they exclude themselves from the salvation, restoration and forgiveness for sinners Jesus has come to bring.[18]

The connection between healing and forgiveness we saw in the forgiveness and healing of the paralytic in verses 1–8 is now confirmed. Jesus heals like a perfect physician; he also calls sinners. The two go together. In demonstrating his authority to deal with death, and everything that may be associated with death, all the miracles across Matthew 8–9 confirm his authority to deal with sin – to forgive it.

A dispute about fasting (9:14–17)

In this section running from 8:23, Matthew has shown Jesus as a rebuker of storms, a destroyer of demons and a forgiver of sins – all activities someone familiar with the Hebrew Bible would associate with YHWH himself. Here in verse 15, at the end of the section, Jesus describes himself as 'the bridegroom' at a wedding. (He also ascribed a title to himself at the end of the last section, where he called himself 'Son of Man', 8:20.) This is also a very suggestive way to talk about himself. In the Hebrew Bible, YHWH frequently describes the relation between himself and his people as like a marriage, and the longed-for re-establishment of the relationship as like a wedding feast, with himself as the bridegroom or husband (as in Isaiah 62:4–5 and Hosea 2:14–23).

The question that prompts Jesus to talk this way comes from John's disciples, who ask why Jesus's disciples do not join them and the Pharisees in frequent corporate acts of fasting. Jesus understands such fasting to be some kind of expression of collective and public mourning

---

[18] Compare 8:12. As Jesus will say to the chief priests and elders later in the Gospel, 'the tax collectors and the prostitutes are entering the kingdom of God ahead of you' (21:31).

in verse 15. This is not prescribed by the Law, but could well have been appropriate for those struggling under the shadow of death and waiting for YHWH to restore things. In other words, it is the kind of fasting appropriate at a funeral. But in his response, Jesus indicates they have misread the occasion and failed to recognise his identity. His disciples are guests at a wedding, not a funeral. Feasting is appropriate (as in verse 10), not fasting. In other words, Jesus has come to end the wait, fulfil the hopes of the prophets and joyfully re-establish the relationship between the Lord and his people.

Only when the bridegroom is taken from them should his disciples fast (verse 15b) – that is, mourn. This is a first hint in Matthew's Gospel that Jesus is fully aware he is heading towards his death.[19]

Matthew ended the last section (8:1–22) with two wisdom sayings from Jesus (8:20, 22). He does likewise here in verses 16–17. What Jesus says is puzzling if we try to read these as mini allegories. It is more helpful to pick out the proverbial principle from the sayings, which here is, 'If you fail to recognise the newness of something, it will ruin what you have.' A patch, if it is new cloth, will tear the piece you are mending. Fail to recognise that wine is new, and you will ruin your old wineskins. This fits the context here, where John's disciples and the Pharisees have failed to recognise Jesus and the new thing he is doing as a 'bridegroom', in fulfilment of the old.

SUMMARY AND PURPOSE
Matthew is teaching us here about Jesus's authority over the forces that ultimately bring or desire death: the sea-storm, the demonic and sin itself. We learn of Jesus's willingness to rescue sinners from these forces: this is what he has come to do. He has come to restore them and to feast with them. Knowing him as a disciple is like being at a wedding, where he is the bridegroom.

The purpose of Matthew 8–9 is to respond to Jesus's demonstrations of the kingdom made 'before the appointed time'. In 8:23–9:17, this includes an attitude towards Jesus of faith in his power and authority, and

---

[19] This does not imply that corporate fasting like the disciples of John and the Pharisees should now return as a permanent norm for Jesus's disciples. Matthew is keen to emphasise at the end of the Gospel the close ongoing presence of Jesus with his disciples (28:20). He may have been taken away in death, but he came back! On the other hand, this does not mean fasting has no place in the Christian life, as Jesus himself has hinted in 6:16–18. It still may be appropriate for individual, personal reasons – or even corporately, alongside prayer for mission (Acts 13:1–3).

a humble willingness to come to him for the forgiveness of sins. Finally, Matthew warns his readers of the foolishness of missing out on all of this – of missing the party, as it were.

3. Proclaiming in deed part 3 • Matthew 9:18–38

In chapters 8–9, Matthew has turned from the proclamation of the kingdom in word (Matthew 5–7, teaching his disciples to live in the light of the coming kingdom) to proclaiming it in deed – a compressed, quick-fire overview of Jesus's healing and exorcism ministry. This is the third and final section of these chapters.

Jesus raises a dead girl and heals a sick woman

18 While he was saying this, a synagogue leader came and knelt before him and said, 'My daughter has just died. But come and put your hand on her, and she will live.' **19** Jesus got up and went with him, and so did his disciples.

20 Just then a woman who had been subject to bleeding for twelve years came up behind him and touched the edge of his cloak. **21** She said to herself, 'If I only touch his cloak, I will be healed.'

22 Jesus turned and saw her. 'Take heart, daughter,' he said, 'your faith has healed you.' And the woman was healed at that moment.

23 When Jesus entered the synagogue leader's house and saw the noisy crowd and the people playing pipes, **24** he said, 'Go away. The girl is not dead but asleep.' But they laughed at him. **25** After the crowd had been put outside, he went in and took the girl by the hand, and she got up. **26** News of this spread through all that region.

Jesus heals the blind and the mute

27 As Jesus went on from there, two blind men followed him, calling out, 'Have mercy on us, Son of David!'

28 When he had gone indoors, the blind men came to him, and he asked them, 'Do you believe that I am able to do this?'

'Yes, Lord,' they replied.

29 Then he touched their eyes and said, 'According to your faith let it be done to you'; **30** and their sight was restored. Jesus warned them sternly, 'See that no one knows about this.' **31** But they went out and spread the news about him all over that region.

32 While they were going out, a man who was demon-possessed and could not talk was brought to Jesus. **33** And when the demon was driven out, the man who had been mute spoke. The crowd was amazed and said, 'Nothing like this has ever been seen in Israel.'

34 But the Pharisees said, 'It is by the prince of demons that he drives out demons.'

The workers are few

35 Jesus went through all the towns and villages, teaching in their synagogues, proclaiming the good news of the kingdom and healing every disease and illness. **36** When he saw the crowds, he had compassion on them, because they were harassed and helpless, like sheep without a shepherd. **37** Then he said to his disciples, 'The harvest is plentiful but the workers are few. **38** Ask the Lord of the harvest, therefore, to send out workers into his harvest field.'

Like the first and second sections, the third section divides into three parts:

> 9:18–34 Three miracles:
> > 9:18–26 Two daughters
> > 9:27–31 Two blind men
> > 9:32–4 A mute demoniac
> 9:35 A summary
> 9:36–38 Jesus's words: Pray earnestly

Again, we shall see that the people being healed all represent people obviously and visibly under the shadow of death. Their healings are like a window into the coming kingdom, where the shadow of death will be lifted entirely. They show that Jesus has come 'before the appointed time' to rescue people for the kingdom.

The examples show Jesus dealing with intense grief, long-suffering shame, ignorance and false speech. The responses in this final round of miracles are more hostile: derision, disobedience and slander.

Two daughters (9:18–26)

These verses interleave the stories of two 'daughters': one who definitively demonstrates Jesus's power to raise from death to life; the other who demonstrates the lifting of uncleanliness and shame, and the nature of true faith – a desperate dependence on Jesus.

If we have not yet grasped that the miracles in Matthew 8–9 are mini-demonstrations of resurrection, displays of the future kingdom (brought forward in time for us to see in advance), then the daughter of the synagogue leader in verses 18 and 23–5 should make this crystal clear. She 'has just died' (verse 18). At the house (verse 23) there is a crowd of people already mourning, who laugh when Jesus suggests her death is not permanent – more like being asleep.

The woman in verse 20 is alive, but like the other characters in this section of Matthew, very much under the shadow of death. Throughout the Bible, blood (or other fluids) outside a body consistently represents death and uncleanliness (as in Leviticus 15:33). She is no doubt also suffering under the shame associated with her condition, and Matthew specifically mentions her twelve years of desperate struggle.

We have already seen Jesus's power to heal by touch (8:3) and at a distance (8:8, 13). Here, the woman with bleeding is healed by a touch of the hem of his cloak (verses 20–21). As with the man with skin disease (8:3), she is made clean rather than Jesus made unclean.

The synagogue leader's daughter is also healed by touch, by Jesus taking her hand (verse 25). The end of verse 25 is better translated 'the girl was raised up'. As with Peter's mother-in-law in 8:15, this is the same word Matthew uses for the resurrection of Jesus in 28:6. Her 'resurrection' is a picture, pointing forward to Jesus's resurrection and the final resurrection. (But only a picture: she will go on to die again, while Jesus will not.)

Like the man with skin disease in 8:2, the centurion in 8:5–13 and the friends of the paralytic in 9:1–8, the synagogue leader believes Jesus is able to restore his daughter's life (verse 18) – even from death! Jesus responds to his faith by getting up and following him towards his house (verse 19). Likewise, the woman with bleeding is convinced in her desperation that Jesus can restore her (verse 21). Jesus responds by engaging with her personally and affectionately, encouraging her with the words, 'Take heart,' strongly commending her faith, and by healing her (verse 22). Even in situations of the greatest emotional distress and despair, Matthew is encouraging the imitation of such faith, portrayed here as a desperate, wholehearted, all-embracing dependence.

The news of the raising to life spreads (verse 26). But, as we shall see, this is no guarantee it is being interpreted rightly.

Two blind men (9:27–31)

Like the other conditions in these chapters, physical blindness would have been associated with death in the first century.[20] The dead do not see. 'Blindness' can also be used metaphorically, as in spiritual blindness, or ignorance. Jesus will use it this way later in the Gospel, in 13:10–17 and 15:14, for example. This could be why the two blind men are included here, as Matthew begins to focus on the spread of the news of Jesus's miracles, and the interpretation of what he has done (paving the way

---

[20] For extensive evidence on this, see Bolt, *Jesus's Defeat of Death*, 211–15.

for taking up this narrative in chapters 11–12). Spiritual blindness is the deeper, as yet unresolved problem at this point in the Gospel.

As before, Jesus is able to restore the men with just a touch. Here, it is a touch to the eyes (verse 29) – another hint that we are intended to take special note of their blindness.

The response of the men to Jesus is mixed. On the one hand, even when physically blind, they have sufficient 'sight' to identify him as 'Son of David' and to cry out for mercy (verse 27).[21] As others have done, they believe Jesus is able to restore them (verse 28) and are commended for their belief (verse 29). On the other hand, their 'sight' is not so strong that they are able to 'see' that news of the healing is kept secret (verse 30), and they explicitly disobey Jesus's strong command.

Why does Jesus tell the men to keep it secret, and with such strong language? Surely, if the miracles are displays of the future kingdom, then people need to know about them? Yes, but only if the news is communicated and processed rightly. Hence Jesus's command to spread the news via the priest in 8:4. As we shall see in verse 34, news of the miracles at the time was frequently interpreted wrongly.

If the men had kept their healing secret, this would not have rendered it pointless as a witness to Jesus. As recorded eyewitness testimony in the Gospel accounts, the news of the miracles is communicated rightly (and continues to be) – to a later, post-resurrection readership. For us as readers, we have Jesus's response in 11:5, where Jesus alludes to Isaiah 35:5,[22] which specifically mentions the eyes of the blind being opened. 'The time for the fulfilment of the Isaianic promises has dawned.'[23] And we are further helped to process and interpret the news as the Gospel narrative unfolds, culminating in the sin-bearing and curse-bearing death of Jesus for the forgiveness of sins.

A mute demoniac (9:32–4)

We have already noted the connection between demon-possession and death (especially in 8:28). Muteness was also associated with death in the first century.[24] The dead do not speak. Even today, we sometimes

---

[21] Like one of the psalmists crying out to YHWH: e.g., Psalms 6:3; 9:13; 25:4; 25:11; 26:6; 30:10; 40:11; 50:3; 55:2; 56:1–2; 85:7; 118:5, 25; 123:3.

[22] And possibly also Isaiah 26:19; 29:18; 61:1.

[23] Nolland, *Matthew*, 451.

[24] Bolt, *Jesus's Defeat of Death*, 204–8.

use the phrase, 'the silence of the grave'. As with the blindness in verses 27–31, the choice of condition here, and the positioning of this event so prominently as the last of the miracles in Matthew 8–9, is likely to be deliberate and significant. The man is suffering under the shadow of death in such a way that he is unable to speak.

As before, Jesus is fully able to restore the man, by casting out the demon. Matthew draws attention to the consequence: that the man is now able to speak (verse 33a; compare Isaiah 35:6).

The emphasis in these verses is on the responses to the miracle. The crowd is amazed (verse 33b) – although there is still no indication that they are inferring what they should about Jesus and the kingdom. The Pharisees respond with hostility (verse 34). They accuse him of being just another magician. We encountered a positive example of Magi, or magicians, in 2:1–10. But, more typically, Magi in the first-century Mediterranean world were those claiming to be able to heal, curse or exorcise demons through the occult manipulation of the underworld. Hence the reference to casting out demons by the prince of demons. (This negative reaction to the miracles will be resumed and expanded in the narrative in 12:22–32.)

This is the final miracle detailed in Matthew 8–9. The next chapter will relate Jesus's teaching on mission, as he sends out the Twelve, a key component of which is a command to speak words proclaiming the nearness of the kingdom (10:7). A major theme of 11:1–16:20 will be the words spoken by Jesus and their reception and interpretation. It seems likely we are expected to conclude from Matthew 8–9 that rescue from evil and the shadow of death frees people to speak, and is an encouragement to speak of Jesus and the kingdom. But verses 32–4 also begin the warning, expanded in the narrative to come, that reactions to this news are likely to be mixed.

A summary and an exhortation (9:35–8)

Verse 35 is almost word-for-word identical to 4:23. These verses bracket the section, summarising everything that happens in between: teaching, preaching or proclaiming the gospel of the kingdom, and healing and exorcism. Matthew leaves us in no doubt that Jesus's ministry of proclaiming the nearness of the kingdom has been astonishing (7:28; 8:10, 27). However, what he has done is not enough, given the scale of the problem.

As in 4:23–5, we are reminded of the crowds following Jesus (verse 36). In 5:1, the surprise was that in response to seeing the crowds, Jesus addressed not them but his disciples. Here, when he sees the crowds (the wording is identical to 5:1), Jesus instead expresses compassion towards them. That is, having taught and shown the disciples what ministry in light of the coming kingdom looks like (4:23–9:35), Jesus now directs the attention of the disciples towards those they will be serving, encouraging them to have the same attitude towards them. As John Nolland comments, 'Compassion involves so identifying with the situation of others that one is prepared to act for their benefit.'[25] The situation that evokes this compassion is seeing the crowd 'harassed and helpless' (as if thrown to the ground and unable to get back up),' like sheep without a shepherd' (verse 36). This issue of an absence or failure of (human) leadership for God's people has echoed down the Scriptures (Numbers 27:17; 1 Kings 22:17; Ezekiel 34:5–6; Zechariah 10:2). Matthew has already highlighted similar deficiencies with the leadership in Jesus's day (2:1–10, 16–18, 22; 3:7–12; 5:20; 7:15–23, 29; 9:4, 11–13, 34). But the Lord (YHWH) has already promised to deal with his people's leadership problem and shepherd them himself (Ezekiel 34:11–16), a promise somehow associated with a leader born in Bethlehem (Micah 5:2). Matthew has strongly implied that this leader and shepherd is Jesus (2:6).

Still, although Jesus has come as shepherd, more help is needed (verses 37–8). The metaphor changes from shepherding to harvesting, with a field ripe for harvest representing the needy crowd. There are currently insufficient resources for the harvest. So the first thing is to ask 'the Lord of the harvest' for more workers in the fields. The word is a strong one, meaning 'ask for something pleadingly'.[26] Jesus doesn't instruct his disciples to ask for God to 'raise up leaders' for the harvest, despite the modern evangelical tendency to hear him that way. The leadership problem is solved by Jesus, as we saw above. What is needed are workers, and they are not raised up but 'cast out' – a horizontal movement, not a vertical one.

The immediate solution to the lack of 'workers' in the unfolding narrative is for Jesus to multiply his ministry twelvefold by sending out his closest disciples in chapter 10 to proclaim the kingdom to the lost sheep of the house of Israel. But given the scale of the problem of the shadow of death in the world, this, too, will be sorely inadequate. The ultimate solution in the Gospel to that problem will be the Great Commission (28:16–20). In other words, every disciple will be involved in the 'harvesting' work one way or another, not just leaders or specialists.

---

[25] Nolland, *Matthew*, 407.
[26] BDAG, '*deomai*'.

SUMMARY AND PURPOSE

Matthew is teaching us here about Jesus as the one who raises from the dead, opens blind eyes and frees people to speak. He strongly hints that these are metaphors of opening eyes to see the nearness of the kingdom and freeing people to speak of the kingdom. But we are also being taught about a resistance to true understanding and a lack of resources to deal with the needs of a multitude harassed, helpless and leaderless under the shadow of death. This sets the stage for the next part of Matthew's narrative.

The purpose of Matthew 8–9 is to respond to Jesus's demonstrations of the kingdom made 'before the appointed time'. In 9:18–38, this includes desperately turning to him at times of grief or distress, seeking to 'see' and understand the kingdom rightly, a desire to speak of the kingdom rightly and pleading in prayer for workers to proclaim the kingdom. Matthew is also beginning to warn his readers to expect mixed and often hostile responses.

7

Sending

MATTHEW 10

The section running from 4:23 to 9:38 (bracketed by almost identical summaries at 4:23 and 9:35) has outlined a representative sample of Jesus's proclamation of the gospel of the kingdom. This was immediately preceded by Jesus calling his first disciples to follow him, promising to make them 'fish for people' (4:18–22). Matthew 9 ended with Jesus encouraging his disciples to share his compassion for the crowds and to pray for workers to be cast out into the harvest field (9:36–8). These threads come back together in Matthew 10. Jesus has been proclaiming the gospel of the kingdom; now, having taught them and shown them what this means, he acts to multiply the proclamation – multiply it twelvefold, in fact. In Matthew 10 they start to 'fish for people'.

1. The Twelve sent out • Matthew 10

Jesus sends out the Twelve

10 Jesus called his twelve disciples to him and gave them authority to drive out impure spirits and to heal every disease and illness.

2 These are the names of the twelve apostles: first, Simon (who is called Peter) and his brother Andrew; James son of Zebedee, and his brother John; **3** Philip and Bartholomew; Thomas and Matthew the tax collector; James son of Alphaeus, and Thaddaeus; **4** Simon the Zealot and Judas Iscariot, who betrayed him.

5 These twelve Jesus sent out with the following instructions: 'Do not go among the Gentiles or enter any town of the Samaritans. **6** Go rather to the lost sheep of Israel. **7** As you go, proclaim this message: "The kingdom of heaven has come near." **8** Heal those who are ill, raise the dead, cleanse those who have leprosy,[a] drive out demons. Freely you have received; freely give.

9 'Do not get any gold or silver or copper to take with you in your belts – **10** no bag for the journey or extra shirt or sandals or a staff, for the worker is worth his keep. **11** Whatever town or village you enter, search there for some worthy person and stay at their house until you leave. **12** As you enter the home, give it your greeting. **13** If the home is deserving, let your peace rest on it; if it is not, let your peace return to you. **14** If anyone will not welcome you or listen to your words, leave that home or town and shake the dust off your feet. **15** Truly I tell you, it will be more bearable for Sodom and Gomorrah on the day of judgment than for that town.

16 'I am sending you out like sheep among wolves. Therefore be as shrewd as snakes and as innocent as doves. **17** Be on your guard; you will be handed over to the local councils and be flogged in the synagogues. **18** On my account you will be brought before governors and kings as witnesses to them and to the Gentiles. **19** But when they arrest you, do not worry about what to say or how to say it. At that time you will be given what to say, **20** for it will not be you speaking, but the Spirit of your Father speaking through you.

21 'Brother will betray brother to death, and a father his child; children will rebel against their parents and have them put to death. **22** You will be hated by everyone because of me, but the one who stands firm to the end will be saved. **23** When you are persecuted in one place, flee to another. Truly I tell you, you will not finish going through the towns of Israel before the Son of Man comes.

24 'The student is not above the teacher, nor a servant above his master. **25** It is enough for students to be like their teachers, and servants like their masters. If the head of the house has been called Beelzebul, how much more the members of his household!

26 'So do not be afraid of them, for there is nothing concealed that will not be disclosed, or hidden that will not be made known. **27** What I tell you in the dark, speak in the daylight; what is whispered in your ear, proclaim from the roofs. **28** Do not be afraid of those who kill the body but cannot kill the soul. Rather, be afraid of the One who can destroy both soul and body in hell. **29** Are not two sparrows sold for a penny? Yet not one of them will fall to the ground outside your Father's care. **b 30** And even the very hairs of your head are all numbered. **31** So don't be afraid; you are worth more than many sparrows.

32 'Whoever acknowledges me before others, I will also acknowledge before my Father in heaven. **33** But whoever disowns me before others, I will disown before my Father in heaven.

34 'Do not suppose that I have come to bring peace to the earth. I did not come to bring peace, but a sword. **35** For I have come to turn

> ' "a man against his father,
>   a daughter against her mother,
>   a daughter-in-law against her
>   mother-in-law –
> **36** a man's enemies will be the
>   members of his own
>   household." **c**

37 'Anyone who loves their father or mother more than me is not worthy of me; anyone who loves their son or daughter more than me is not worthy of me. **38** Whoever does not take up their cross and follow me is not worthy of me. **39** Whoever finds their life will lose it, and whoever loses their life for my sake will find it.

40 'Anyone who welcomes you welcomes me, and anyone who welcomes me welcomes the one who sent me. **41** Whoever welcomes a prophet as a prophet will receive a prophet's reward, and whoever welcomes a righteous person as a righteous person will receive a righteous person's reward. **42** And if anyone gives even a cup of cold water to one of these little ones who is my disciple, truly I tell you, that person will certainly not lose their reward.'

----

a 8 The Greek word traditionally translated *leprosy* was used for various diseases affecting the skin.
b 29 Or *will*; or *knowledge*
c 36 Micah 7:6

We have seen that Matthew often likes to arrange his material into groups of three. But, after the calling of the disciples in 10:1–4, this is one of the very few places in Matthew where there does seem to be a concentric structure:[1]

> A 10:5–15. The test of worthiness applied to Israel, anticipating Judgment.
>> B 10:16–23. Warnings about tribulation and family conflict.
>>> C 10:24–5. A warning that Jesus's followers will experience what he experiences.
>>>> D 10:26–31. The comfort of the sovereign, providential care of the Father.
>>> C' 10:32–33. A warning to follow Jesus and not to deny him.
>> B' 10:34–39. A warning not to avoid tribulation and family conflict.
> A' 10:40–42. The test of worthiness applied generally, anticipating reward.

The important thing to note here is the movement from specific to general. Jesus's teaching begins with named individuals (verses 1–4), a carefully restricted mission (verses 5–6) and some instructions in verses 7–15 (we can argue) that are specific to that time. It ends with similar principles but expressed in much more general terms – using words like 'whoever' and 'anyone' (verses 37–42). This suggests that although we

----

[1] It is also quite similar to the 3+1+3 structure of the Lord's Prayer in 6:9–13.

are intended to listen first and foremost to what Jesus is saying from the point of view of the Twelve and that first mission, the teaching is also meant to be relevant to the situation at the end of Matthew's Gospel, to disciples engaged with disciple-making in the nations (28:16–20).[2] All the warnings and words of comfort in verses 16–39, for example, apply just as much to the later setting – and in many ways fit a later setting more closely. The Twelve may in principle have been brought before 'governors and kings as a witness to them and the Gentiles' (verse 18, although we have no record of this happening), but the warning applies much more obviously and straightforwardly to disciples under the Great Commission.

Proclaiming the kingdom multiplied twelvefold (10:1–15)

Matthew 8–9 has outlined Jesus's ministry of exorcism and healing, part of his proclamation of the good news of the kingdom, and ended with a recognition that more was needed to deal with the crowds of harassed and helpless people (mostly Israelites) still struggling under the shadow of death. Matthew 10 begins with Jesus calling twelve disciples and giving them authority to do what he has been doing (verse 1), thus multiplying his ministry twelvefold.

The twelve disciples are then called 'apostles' (verse 2) – that is, those who are specially commissioned and sent out (as in verse 5). The list begins with Peter (in common with the other lists of apostles in the Gospels), who is also emphasised with the label 'first'. This alerts us that Matthew wants his readers to pay special attention to Peter as representative disciple in what follows. The first four names should remind us of 4:18–22 and Jesus's promise to make these disciples 'fish for people'. The mention of 'Matthew the tax collector' in verse 3 should remind us of 9:9–13 and Jesus's priority to call sinners. The addition of 'who betrayed him' to Judas's name in verse 4 warns us of the suffering and tribulation to come for Jesus.

Jesus's detailed instruction to the twelve disciples should first and foremost be understood as special and specific for the particular task he sets them in verses 5–6. This is explicitly more restricted than the ultimate task in Matthew's Gospel, which is the Great Commission in 28:16–20. The task here excludes the nations or Gentiles, and even the Samaritans, and is focused on the 'lost sheep of Israel' (verse 6).

---

[2] As also argued by Robert Morosco, 'Matthew's Formation of a Commissioning Type-Scene out of the Story of Jesus's, *Journal of Biblical Literature* 103, no. 4 (1984): 53–5, among others.

Verses 7 and 8 summarise the ministry Jesus has been doing from 4:23–9:35. The twelve disciples are to go and do likewise (and now have the authority to do so, verse 1). What he has been doing is multiplied twelvefold.[3]

In verses 9 and 10, Jesus restricts what the twelve disciples should take with them. These seem strange requirements, but we can argue they are designed to maximise the chances of a positive response from those of 'the lost sheep of Israel'. The disciples' appearance would have been recognisably like an Israelite in the middle of the Exodus (Exodus 12:11), evoking a sense of urgency and utter dependence on God, and prompting those they meet to remember their history. To turn up at the house of a fellow Israelite with no visible means of support should be a prompt for hospitality (compare Genesis 18:1–8). Certainly, to turn an Israelite away in such circumstances would have been a very strong rejection of both them and their message.

On the other hand, in verses 11–15, Jesus prepares the disciples for the real possibility of their message being rejected. The disciples are testing the worthiness of a household they visit (whether it is 'deserving', verse 13). The book of Genesis is very much in the background here. When the three angels or messengers in Genesis 18:1–8 visit Abraham and Sarah, they are warmly welcomed. In contrast, when two of the angels visit Sodom, the welcome they receive is shockingly dishonourable (Genesis 19:1–16). But the revelation and hope the disciples are able to proclaim to the lost sheep of Israel is so profoundly greater than anything spoken to Sodom (or its sister town Gomorrah), that rejection will make them far more culpable and deserving of judgment when it comes (verse 15).

Don't be surprised; be prepared (10:16–25)

Jesus begins here with a general warning to the disciples about what to expect when they are sent out: it will be like being sheep sent out among wolves (verse 16a). In other words, there is a high risk of harm or violent

---

[3] This includes healing, raising the dead, cleansing and exorcism, just like Jesus. I have been arguing above that these are mini-demonstrations of resurrection, a foretaste of the kingdom, where the shadow of death will be rolled away. They support the proclamation of the gospel of the kingdom. Following the greater miracle of Jesus's permanent resurrection, they become less necessary. The supportive role can now be taken by proclaiming the gospel of Jesus's resurrection. (Which is not to say they play *no* role in the mission to the nations, as we see in the book of Acts – just that they play a far lesser, and more occasional, role.)

death! The warning is accompanied by some general survival advice: to be as crafty as snakes and innocent as doves (verse 16b). This would have been provocative teaching, to say the least, evoking the 'crafty' serpent of Genesis 3:1. To survive the wolves, what Jesus wants from the Twelve is that sort of shrewdness – but without any hint of the evil. Hence, 'innocent as doves'. Earlier in the Gospel, a dove was associated with the Holy Spirit descending from the heavens to equip Jesus for the Servant ministry task he was publicly taking on from his Father (3:16). So Jesus wants them to be as smart about being compassionate servants of the Lord, equipped by the Spirit, as the serpent was smart about being evil.

Jesus then goes on to address three scenarios or situations that are more specific. The first is the danger of being accused of wrongdoing and brought before courts, both Jewish and Gentile (verses 17–20). Jesus warns the disciples to be on their guard – to be ready for it (verse 17). He assures them that they will be equipped by the Spirit to say the right thing (verses 19–20). Just as Jesus is equipped by the Spirit to do what he is doing as the Servant of the Lord, so are his disciples.

The second situation is having close relatives, and others, who want to kill them (verses 21–2). Again, Jesus warns the Twelve about the possibility of facing such hatred. The implicit instruction this time is to keep going, because, verse 22, 'the one who stands firm to the end will be saved'.

The third scenario is facing especially intense persecution in a town (verse 23a). The instruction is to flee to the next town. This might surprise us. Surely the right thing would be to stand firm? But the second part of the verse reminds the Twelve that they have limited time to go through the towns of Israel. The urgency of the situation demands that if one town is hostile in its response, the best thing is to move on and try somewhere else.

What event is Jesus referring to when he talks about 'before the Son of Man comes' (verse 23b)? We have already begun to see that when Jesus uses 'Son of Man' and 'coming of the Son of Man' language, he is drawing on the vision in Daniel 7 to talk about persevering through tribulation to find future vindication – either for himself or for his followers. We shall see that the moment of vindication that fits verse 23 is his own vindication in resurrection, following the tribulation and suffering of the cross. Jesus may have in mind the moment in 28:18 when, following his resurrection, he will declare to the remaining Eleven, 'All authority in heaven and on earth has been given to me.' This will also be the moment when the geographical restrictions of Matthew 10 come to an end, and the disciples will be sent to make further disciples in all the nations (28:19).

In verses 24–5 we learn why things will be as bad as this for the disciples. It is because of their connection to Jesus. They are doing these things for his sake (verses 18, 22). As his students, as his servants, they cannot expect to be treated better than their teacher and master (verse 24). If others blaspheme him with the name 'Beelzebul', they will surely do the same to them (verse 25). Beelzebul is probably a name used of a Canaanite god, but by this stage was considered a powerful demon and interchangeable with 'Satan'.[4]

Matthew will give us an example of Jesus being called Beelzebul (that is, the Spirit by which he casts out demons is dismissed as Beelzebul) in 12:24. Indeed, reading on in the Gospel, we shall find Jesus personally facing many other examples of the kinds of things he is warning his disciples about here. We shall find him more and more like a sheep among wolves, having to act shrewdly and yet with innocence, just as in verse 16. We shall see him constantly flexible, on the move, searching for opportunities for compassion. In the end, we shall see him arrested and unjustly put on trial. The pattern will be as in verses 17 and 18: first before the Jewish council, then before the Gentile governor, Pilate. We shall see him divided from his blood family, as in verse 21. And as the story proceeds, we see him more and more hated, culminating in his unjust execution on a cross. But he will stand firm and be vindicated in the end: his Father will save him and raise him. This will prove to be a great encouragement to the disciples following in his footsteps. The fact that he did take all this on and was proved right in the end as his Father raised him to life will demonstrate to them (and us, as readers of the Gospel) the veracity of verse 22. Those who stand firm to the end, trusting their Father in the heavens, will most definitely be saved!

Don't be afraid; be trusting (10:26–31)

Even before we see the outworking of Jesus's ministry and his vindication, Jesus gives here – right at the centre of his teaching in the chapter – three reasons why the disciples can face the dangers he has been warning them about without fear. The first two are related to specific dangers; the third is more general.

In verses 26–7, the encouragement is not to be afraid of the people back in verse 25 who maliciously slander Jesus and will do the same to those who follow him. Why not? Because 'there is nothing concealed that

---

[4] John Nolland, *Luke 9:21–18:34* (Dallas: Word Books, 1993), 637.

will not be disclosed, or hidden that will not be made known'. That is, anyone who lies against Jesus will be exposed in the end as a liar; likewise, anyone who lies against his followers. Jesus is promising that, eventually, at the coming Judgment, God will see to it that that the truth will be victorious. All lies will be publicly exposed. Therefore, those on the side of the truth need not be afraid to speak it boldly now (verse 27).

In verse 28, the threat is death, as Jesus has already warned in verse 21. The encouragement is not to fear those 'who kill the body but cannot kill the soul'. Jesus is probably not using 'soul' here to talk about some non-bodily component of a person, separable from the body and perhaps even immortal, as in some (but not all) Greek thought. Rather, in common with much of the language of the soul in the Old Testament, he means what is essential to a body being a living person. This only God can give or take away. He, then, is the one to fear, not the one who threatens physical harm.

The encouragement of verses 28–31 is more general, but still with the threat of death in view. Jesus has just told the disciples not to fear, but to fear; not to fear violent men, but to fear God. These verses help us see the kind of fear he has in mind: a fear that is not cowering but full of awe and respect towards the one with an intimate sovereignty over all things. In particular, an intimate sovereignty over death – even of the smallest, least valued bird (verse 29). He is even sovereign over the 'life and death' of the hairs on their heads (verse 30)! 'So don't be afraid' (of death, verse 31). If their Father cares about the life and death of the smallest creatures like sparrows, then how much more will he care for those who call him 'Father' – that is, his very own children.

Don't be disloyal; be faithful (10:32–9)

Back in verses 24–5, Jesus warned the Twelve that as his disciples and followers, they could expect to be treated in the same way he has been treated. Here he encourages and warns them not to seek to avoid this by dissociating from him. The encouragement is that those who publicly acknowledge their relationship with him can be assured of being acknowledged before the Father (verse 32). The warning is that denial of Jesus will result in a denial before the Father (verse 33).[5]

---

[5] These verses provide the background to what happens to Peter in Matthew 26–8. Peter boldly claims he will never deny Jesus (26:35), but then does so three times – the last especially emphatic (26:69–75). He weeps bitterly in expectation

Back in verses 21–3, Jesus warned them that even their own close family might betray them to death. Now he repeats the warning: what he has come to do may well not bring family peace – quite often family division (verses 34–6). He then gives the even greater warning that if the disciples try to avoid these divisions, placing peace in their families above loyalty to his family, then they are not worthy to be a part of it (verse 37). Jesus is not asking them to abandon family love. He is asking them to see the priority of a greater family love: the family love for God their Father and Jesus his Son, from which flow all other kinds of love. Experiencing family division is costly, of course. But this is what following Jesus entails: following him in the way of the cross, the way of suffering and loss (verse 38). Some of this would not make much sense at the time, especially the idea of taking up a cross. Would the disciples hear it as 'take up your yoke' – as in the command Jesus will issue in chapter 11? Would they hear an allusion to Isaac, who took wood upon his shoulders on the way to being sacrificed (Genesis 22)? It is possible they would make the connection to crucifixion, the ultimate and most horrific form of Roman execution, to which prisoners were forced to carry their crosses. But what they would make of this connection is hard to say. All we can say for certain is that after Jesus's crucifixion, all would become clear. To talk about 'taking up one's cross' would not have made much sense to the disciples until they had witnessed his manner of death.

This is another indication that Jesus has his sights chiefly on a post-resurrection setting as he delivers this instruction. It is a theme Jesus will pick up again in 16:24–5. As there, Jesus gives both warning and encouragement. Seeking an easy life now will result in loss later (verse 39a). Following a costly life now will result in reward later (verse 39b).

The test of worthiness generalised (10:40–42)

When Jesus first talked about sending the Twelve to the lost sheep of Israel in verses 11–15, he linked the 'worthiness' of a house they enter to the welcome they (and their message of the kingdom) receive. In verses 40–42, at the end of his teaching in Matthew 10, he returns to this principle. Now the principle is generalised. It applies not just to Israelite

---

of Jesus now denying him, as per verse 33 here. Nonetheless, remarkably, he is restored. (This is in contrast to Judas, who shows that Jesus's warning here is not hollow.) Peter's example adds to the encouragement to be resolutely Jesus-focused, even through serious failure.

households but to anyone who welcomes or receives the disciples. Such a person is welcoming not merely a disciple, but also Jesus and the Father who sent him (verse 40).

Welcoming a messenger and embracing who they are and the good thing they have come to share with you means sharing in the benefits of that good thing. A prophet has an intimacy with God because he has been given the very words of God by God. Those who welcome him as a prophet (and accept his words) come to share in this intimacy and all its benefits (verse 41a). Likewise for welcoming a 'righteous person' – that is, someone aligned with the will and purpose of God (verse 41b). And likewise for welcoming any of the 'little ones' who are Jesus's disciples (verse 42). And it does not have to be welcoming with a lavish feast (like Abraham in Genesis 18). Even a cup of water is enough to indicate a welcome.

SUMMARY AND PURPOSE

The overall purpose of Matthew is to make its readers who aren't disciples of Jesus into disciples of Jesus, and to motivate and equip its readers who are disciples of Jesus to be disciple-makers. The overall purpose of 4:12–10:42 is to respond to Jesus's proclamation, in word and deed, of the gospel of the kingdom of the heavens: following him, trusting him and being instructed by him to go and proclaim the gospel in our turn.

The purpose of Matthew 10, using a limited mission to Israel as a model and pattern for the mission to the nations, is to encourage and equip disciples to become gospel multipliers, motivated by compassion, caught up in earnest prayer, ready and willing to test people with news of the kingdom – following Jesus faithfully and trusting the Father loyally in the face of extreme opposition.

PART FIVE

....

JESUS'S MINISTRY IN GALILEE

MATTHEW 11:1–16:20

8

Spreading the Word in Galilee

MATTHEW 11–12

The main body of Matthew's Gospel began in Matthew 3–4 with the commissioning of Jesus for the task given to him by the Father. I argued above that at his baptism Jesus took on a mandate from his Father as the Servant of the Lord spoken of by Isaiah. (Matthew will confirm this in 12:15–21.) As he works towards completing this mandate, Jesus has begun by proclaiming the nearness of the kingdom (4:17). In 4:12–9:38, we saw a pattern of kingdom proclamation set out – a pattern Jesus expected his disciples to repeat and multiply in Matthew 10. In the remainder of the Gospel we shall see this pattern worked out in the personal narrative of Jesus. This begins with ministry and proclamation in Galilee. But to complete his mandate, Jesus must go to Jerusalem to be given over, to die and then to be raised to life. He will then return to Galilee to commission the disciples to make disciples in the nations.

This long section is divided into seven in the presentation below:

11:1–12:50 Spreading the word in Galilee (three parts).

13:1–52 The word in Galilee: parables (three parts). This is the third of Jesus's main blocks of teaching in Matthew, mostly given through parables.

13:53–16:20 The Word in Galilee: faith (three parts). This is a section dealing with the 'little faith' of the disciples and encouraging faith.

    16:21–20:34 Taking up his cross (three parts). This is a section structured around the three times Jesus predicts his suffering, death and resurrection (16:21; 17:22–3; 20:17–19) and encompasses the fourth of Jesus's main blocks of teaching (17:24–18:35).

21:1–23:39 Coming to Jerusalem (three parts).

24:1–25:46 The final briefing (two parts). This is the fifth and final of Jesus's main blocks of teaching.

26:1–28:20 Mission completed (and commissioned, three parts).

This is a 3+1+3 structure. The first three go together and take place in Galilee. The middle section (16:21–20:34) takes place on the way to Jerusalem. The final three (mostly) take place in Jerusalem , with a brief return to Galilee at the end.

1. Spreading the word in Galilee part 1 • Matthew 11

Jesus is still in Galilee, proclaiming the kingdom according to the pattern we have seen him establish in 4:12–10:42, but the responses now are quite mixed and often negative. As many scholars have observed, these rejections evoke a sense of crisis, and their beginning in Matthew 11 seems to be a major plot development in Matthew's narrative. In reply, Jesus either calls people to withdraw from the unrepentant to come to him, or withdraws himself to another place to proclaim elsewhere.

Jesus and John the Baptist

11 After Jesus had finished instructing his twelve disciples, he went on from there to teach and preach in the towns of Galilee.[a]

2 When John, who was in prison, heard about the deeds of the Messiah, he sent his disciples 3 to ask him, 'Are you the one who is to come, or should we expect someone else?'

4 Jesus replied, 'Go back and report to John what you hear and see: 5 the blind receive sight, the lame walk, those who have leprosy[b] are cleansed, the deaf hear, the dead are raised, and the good news is proclaimed to the poor. 6 Blessed is anyone who does not stumble on account of me.'

7 As John's disciples were leaving, Jesus began to speak to the crowd about John: 'What did you go out into the wilderness to see? A reed swayed by the wind? 8 If not, what did you go out to see? A man dressed in fine clothes?

No, those who wear fine clothes are in kings' palaces. 9 Then what did you go out to see? A prophet? Yes, I tell you, and more than a prophet. 10 This is the one about whom it is written:

' "I will send my messenger
    ahead of you,
  who will prepare your way
    before you."[c]

11 Truly I tell you, among those born of women there has not risen anyone greater than John the Baptist; yet whoever is least in the kingdom of heaven is greater than he. 12 From the days of John the Baptist until now, the kingdom of heaven has been subjected to violence,[d] and violent people have been raiding it. 13 For all the Prophets and the Law prophesied until John. 14 And if you are willing to accept it, he is the Elijah who was to come. 15 Whoever has ears, let them hear.

16 'To what can I compare this generation? They are like children sitting in the market-places and calling out to others:

17 ' "We played the pipe for you,
and you did not dance;
we sang a dirge,
and you did not mourn."

18 For John came neither eating nor drinking, and they say, "He has a demon." 19 The Son of Man came eating and drinking, and they say, "Here is a glutton and a drunkard, a friend of tax collectors and sinners." But wisdom is proved right by her deeds.'

Woe on unrepentant towns

20 Then Jesus began to denounce the towns in which most of his miracles had been performed, because they did not repent. 21 'Woe to you, Chorazin! Woe to you, Bethsaida! For if the miracles that were performed in you had been performed in Tyre and Sidon, they would have repented long ago in sackcloth and ashes. 22 But I tell you, it will be more bearable for Tyre and Sidon on the day of judgment than for you. 23 And you, Capernaum, will you be lifted to the heavens? No, you will go down to Hades.e For if the miracles that were performed in you had been

performed in Sodom, it would have remained to this day. 24 But I tell you that it will be more bearable for Sodom on the day of judgment than for you.'

The Father revealed in the Son

25 At that time Jesus said, 'I praise you, Father, Lord of heaven and earth, because you have hidden these things from the wise and learned, and revealed them to little children. 26 Yes, Father, for this is what you were pleased to do.

27 'All things have been committed to me by my Father. No one knows the Son except the Father, and no one knows the Father except the Son and those to whom the Son chooses to reveal him.

28 'Come to me, all you who are weary and burdened, and I will give you rest. 29 Take my yoke upon you and learn from me, for I am gentle and humble in heart, and you will find rest for your souls. 30 For my yoke is easy and my burden is light.'

---

a 1 Greek *in their towns*

b 5 The Greek word traditionally translated *leprosy* was used for various diseases affecting the skin.

c 10 Mal. 3:1

d 12 *Or been forcefully advancing*

e 23 That is, the realm of the dead

We shall see that the overall structure of Matthew 11–12 and Matthew 13:53–16:20 (either side of Jesus teaching in parables in 13:1–43) is quite similar. In Matthew 11–12, we find a 3x3 structure like this:

	Focus: Jesus's identity and his call to repent	Focus: Jesus's authority	Focus: Jesus as divine life-giver
Question, opposition, accusation or challenge	11:2–19 John the Baptist	12:1–8 Eating grain on the Sabbath	12:22–37 Jesus accused of devilry
	11:20–24 Unrepentant cities	12:9–14 Healing on the Sabbath	12:38–45 The teachers of the law and the Pharisees ask for a sign
The call to withdraw to be with Jesus (explicit or implied)	11:25–30	12:15–21 Confirmation of Jesus as Servant of the Lord	12:46–50

Table 12

The hesitant, lukewarm or negative responses begin with a question from John's disciples in 11:3 and rapidly escalate into negative accusations from the Pharisees and the teachers of the law. In 11:25–30, Jesus calls people to himself. In 12:15, he withdraws to a new place. In 12:46–50, he separates those on the inside from those on the outside.

Matthew 11 establishes this pattern. Jesus exposes not just poor responses to his own ministry, but also poor responses to John and his ministry (verses 2–19). He then exposes the poor responses of Chorazin, Bethsaida and Capernaum (verses 20–24). The chapter ends with and explanation and a gracious call to find true rest (verses 25–30).

John and Jesus (11:1–19)

The common characters in verses 1–19 are John the Baptist and Jesus himself. The people know John and have come to listen to John – Jesus takes this as given. From this starting point, Matthew then uses three sets of questions to move his readers to a deeper appreciation of both the kingdom John proclaimed, and Jesus himself:

- Question 1 (John asking Jesus about himself): 'Are you the one who is to come?' (verse 3).

- Question 2 (Jesus asking the crowd about John – given as three questions, but essentially asking one thing): What did you go out into the wilderness to see? (verses 7–9).

188

- Question 3 (Jesus asking the crowd about themselves): 'To what can I compare this generation?' (verse 16).

John the Baptist's question in verse 3 is very similar to questions anyone might ask about Jesus at this stage in Matthew's Gospel. This is despite five chapters of the clearest proclamation of the gospel of the kingdom ever given, expressed in teaching of astonishing authority and confirmed by accounts of deeds of extraordinary power, never seen before in Israel. And Jesus has just been teaching his disciples to multiply all this twelvefold. It is hard to see how he could have said or done anything more.

Whether John asks his question because he wants to provide an opportunity for Jesus to clarify to the crowd who he is, or whether he has real doubts that need addressing, is hard to say for sure. In John's situation, real doubts would be understandable. We know that back in chapter 3, John was saying that the one coming after him would come with the fire of judgment: his winnowing shovel in his hand, clearing the threshing floor, gathering his wheat and burning up the chaff with unquenchable fire. Now we can see from verse 2 that John is in prison. If the question expresses a real doubt, we can understand why! Either way, Matthew anticipates that many of his readers will still be unsure, and so he includes John's question.

The answer lies in verse 5: 'The blind receive sight, the lame walk, those who have leprosy are cleansed, the deaf hear, the dead are raised, and the good news is proclaimed to the poor.' This is a good summary of what Jesus has been doing in chapters 5 to 10 of Matthew's Gospel. People have been pulled from under the shadow of death and needy people have the good news of the kingdom preached to them. But it also summarises the expectations of the prophets about the one to come. John would know this instantly. Jesus has gathered together from up to five places in Isaiah the hopes of the prophets (Isaiah 26:19; 29:18; 35:5–6; 42:7, 18; 61:1). This is what they hoped for, and this is what he's done.

In other words: Yes, he is the one who is to come. No, they should not look for another. And in verse 6 Jesus says, 'Blessed is anyone who does not stumble on account of me.' Be assured, says Jesus, the one who accepts this and does not reject it really is on the best possible path in life.

Jesus then turns to speak to the crowd about John, asking them three rapid-fire rhetorical questions. What did they go out into the wilderness to see? Not the wilderness landscape, with its reeds. (Possibly Jesus is also hinting: not a leader like Herod Antipas, who imprisoned John, whose emblem is a reed but who leads and acts without principle, blown to and fro by political needs.) Not someone in the fine clothing. (Possibly Jesus is also hinting: not someone who dresses in the soft, even effeminate clothing of the urban political elite like Herod.) Rather, they went out to see a prophet, solid in conviction, and dressed to show it (that is, John, whom Herod has now imprisoned).

From this starting point – the crowd acknowledging that they went out because they believed John was a true prophet – Jesus probes the crowd further. Do they realise how great a prophet? He is nothing less than the messenger foretold by the prophet Malachi (verse 10, quoting loosely from Malachi 3:1). Indeed, he is greater than anyone (verse 11).[1] Verse 12 is hard to unpack, but probably Jesus is using the phrase 'the kingdom of heaven' (or 'of the heavens') to refer not just to the kingdom itself but also to the message and messengers of the kingdom. That is, the message of the kingdom has been under attack, has 'been subjected to violence', and the messenger has now been imprisoned by violent people. This is because, says Jesus (verses 13–14), he is the last and greatest of the prophets – nothing less than the one like Elijah also foretold by Malachi (Malachi 4:5), preparing for the visitation of the Lord (YHWH). He therefore attracts the greatest attention from the enemies of the kingdom.

In the middle of talking about John's greatness, Jesus adds that 'whoever is least in the kingdom of heaven is greater than he' (verse 11). The implication of what Jesus is saying is this: if you believed he was a prophet, why did you not listen and respond to his message of the kingdom? Now you have confirmed even more about his greatness, and the value of being part of the kingdom, is this not all the more the time to hear and respond? Hence verse 15: 'Whoever has ears, let them hear.'

The third key question in this section is again from Jesus to the crowd, in verse 16: 'To what can I compare this generation?' Jesus says they are like children sitting in the marketplaces and calling out to others:

> We played the pipe for you,
>   and you did not dance;
> we sang a dirge
>   and you did not mourn.

In this image, one group of children is trying to attract the attention of another. But a happy tune evokes no response, and a sad song evokes no

---

[1] It is not helpful to be too pedantic here. Jesus does not want his hearers to infer that John is greater than he is.

response. No matter what is said – whether upbeat or downbeat – the result is the same.

It has been the same with John the Baptist and Jesus. John the Baptist came with a message of austere conviction, but by some he was shamefully accused of being demonic. The Son of Man (that is, Jesus) came with a message of joy and compassion, and was similarly accused, this time of partying with sinners. Both accusations were untrue. In fact, John and Jesus and their respective messages were representatives of true wisdom, and this will indeed prove to be the case as their wisdom takes root in those with ears to hear it. Hence Jesus's use of the saying, 'Wisdom is proved right by her deeds' (verse 19).

Jesus on Chorazin, Bethsaida and Capernaum (11:20–24)

In the hearing of the crowd, Jesus then denounces the other places where the people have been unresponsive to his message and his miraculous demonstrations of the kingdom. Chorazin and Bethsaida are not otherwise mentioned in Matthew, but they are not far from places that are mentioned, and it is easy to see them within the extensive ministry summarised in 4:23 and 9:35. Here Jesus compares them to Tyre and Sidon, Gentile city ports associated with notorious wickedness by the prophets (see especially Ezekiel 28:2–23). Like the prophets, Jesus pronounces a 'Woe' against them. Here, the tone is something like a grieving lament that these towns are in such a miserable state because of the judgment coming their way. The shock is that Jesus rates the Galilean towns as worse than Tyre and Sidon. They have received a degree of clear revelation and warning never enjoyed by those other cities, and still have not repented. At the very least, they should have believed Jesus about the coming kingdom, changing their minds about the future, and thereby become convicted of their unsuitability for what is coming. Jesus's claim is that if the same message with the same signs had been preached in the notoriously wicked cities of Tyre and Sidon, they would have expressed their repentance with traditional Jewish signs of contrition and mourning by wearing sackcloth among ashes (verse 21) , as did the king of Nineveh in response to Jonah's preaching (Jonah 3:6). Jesus implies that this increases the culpability of the Galilean cities, and therefore the severity of the verdict they will receive on the future Day of Judgment.

Likewise for Capernaum, the centre of his Galilean ministry. This time the comparison is with Sodom, likewise a byword for wickedness. The lament against Capernaum is very similar to that against Chorazin and

Bethsaida (verses 23–4). Doubling up the laments like this communicates that the first example of unresponsiveness was not isolated, and perhaps suggests there were other unmentioned places whose inhabitants likewise did not repent. Had Capernaum responded rightly, it would have been 'lifted to the heavens' (verse 23). That is, figuratively, it would have become connected to the source of the coming kingdom and the new life signified by Jesus's kingdom-revealing miracles. As it is, it will 'go down to Hades'. That is, its future is now associated with Hades, the place of the dead.

Matthew is encouraging his readers to step back to see the irrationality of all the negative responses mentioned in 11:2–24. If they can be seen as slow, unreasonable or even wicked, then this encourages any reader to dissociate from them, opening the way to hear Jesus's personal call in verses 25–8 at the end of the chapter.

'Come to me' (11:25–30)

In verses 25–6, Jesus addresses the Father with praise. Given the open and general invitation he is just about to make (verses 28–30), we can take it he does so in the hearing of both his disciples and a more general crowd. What Jesus praises his Father for may seem strange at first, but we can quickly see it addresses the key issues raised earlier in the chapter. Many of the 'wise and learned' have not seen and recognised Jesus, have not properly heard his message concerning the kingdom and have not responded. We have seen this from the very beginning of Matthew's Gospel, when the teachers of the law in Jerusalem just sat in the city pontificating but did doing nothing to seek out the Messiah (2:4–6). And the unresponsiveness has now become very obvious, particularly in the towns Jesus has just mentioned in verses 20–24. And yet it is not as if there has been no response. Some have seen and recognised Jesus. This includes the disciples who have responded to his call to follow (4:16–22; 9:9) and the people in Matthew 8–9 who in their desperation have turned to him with faith. Jesus calls such people 'little children' in verse 25. His mission to Israel might in some ways look like a failure, but look beneath the surface and there is real life.

Here, there is no suggestion that the 'little children' are somehow naturally more responsive than the 'wise and learned'. Instead, Jesus locates the reason behind the different responses firmly in the control of the Father. Jesus tells us quite clearly that his Father has hidden these things from one group and revealed them to another (verse 25). He adds, 'for this is what you were pleased to do' (verse 26).

At first glance, these verses look like they have been lifted from one of Jesus's speeches in the Gospel of John. They should also remind us of the intimacy between Father and Son at Jesus's baptism. The Father set the Son a task to do the start of Matthew's Gospel – to save his people from their sins. And when he was baptised, Jesus gladly accepted that task and was formally empowered by the Spirit to do it – and his father was 'well pleased'. They are working together, in other words, under a divine sovereignty.

For the disciple dismayed by the unresponsiveness of 'this generation' to the message of the kingdom, what Jesus says here is at least partially reassuring. The mission to Israel may not look like it is going well, but if it is under the control of the Father (verses 25–6), then this should change how they feel about it. Likewise, if Father and Son are in inti-mate partnership when it comes to revealing the Son (verse 27), faithful disciples can simply trust that Father and Son know best (even if they cannot see how it is best), and get on with gospel proclamation.

But the verses also prepare someone reading or hearing Matthew's Gospel who has not yet become a disciple for the call Jesus is about to make in verses 28–30. They should evoke a desire to be one of those to whom the Father reveals 'these things' (verse 25; i.e., profound truths such as the kingdom) and a desire to know the Father, revealed by the Son (verse 27). So when Jesus opens up the opportunity to be a part of this in verse 28, such a reader should jump at the chance. In other words, the divine sovereignty implied in verses 25–7 by no means implies any kind of debilitating fatalism. It is compatible with the open moral responsibility to respond to Jesus's call.

The main invitation is in verse 28: 'Come to me.' This is very similar to the 'Come, follow me' with which Jesus called Simon and Andrew in 4:18. Here, the call is generalised to 'all you who are weary and burdened'. What is the burden? Jesus doesn't say here explicitly what it is. He has left it quite open and general. But we do know from chapters 1 and 2 of the Gospel that these are people weighed down by the failure of their nation and by their sin – this is why they were going out to John the Baptist to be baptised, for example. We have also begun to see that these are people whose leaders have failed them. They are 'harassed and helpless, like sheep without a shepherd' (9:36). More specifically, we do know that these are people weighed down by the shadow of death – which is why they've been coming to Jesus in such crowds to be healed. The promise Jesus makes to such people is, 'and I will give you rest' (repeated and expanded in verse 29 as 'you will find rest for your souls').

The invitation is broken into two parts in verse 29. First, there is, 'Take my yoke upon you.' There are consequences to becoming a disciple. As Jesus will go on to teach, there will be tribulation and difficulty before vindication and victory. Then, building on this, there is, 'Learn from me.' This is the invitation to be a *disciple*, one who is taught and instructed by Jesus how to live rightly. Jesus ends the invitation with two motivations. The first is focused on his character and nature. He is 'gentle and humble in heart' (verse 29). To be able to respond to an offer or invitation from someone, we need to be able to trust that they are on our side. The second motivation is focused on the outcome. Jesus promises again, 'You will find rest for your souls.' How so? Because his yoke is easy and his burden is light (verse 30). There may be some short-term costs of discipleship, but these will be bearable, and future life and vindication is secure.

SUMMARY AND PURPOSE

Jesus's proclamation ministry, backed up by the demonstration and illustration of the miracles he has done, has been more than enough to show that the kingdom is near. The principal purpose of this proclamation has been to change peoples' minds – to bring them to repent – so that they fully believe in the nearness of the kingdom and respond appropriately: with remorse for sin and a desperation to seek the one who can save them and cleanse them.

The purpose of Matthew's Gospel as a whole is to make disciples of Jesus who are in turn disciple-makers. The narrative in 11:1–16:20 describes Jesus's Galilean ministry with sobering realism: the message could not be clearer, but the responses are decidedly mixed. Nonetheless, this can still serve to help make Matthew's readers into disciples. As they see the irrationality of the responses clearly exposed by Jesus, they should dissociate themselves from them. The evidence of the miracles is clear (verses 5, 20–24), leaving no room for doubt. It does not make sense to recognise John as a prophet but then not to see how great a prophet he is – and it then makes even less sense not to listen to him (verses 7–15). It does not make sense to be immune to a message, whatever it is (verses 16–17), and is actually quite wicked to avoid a message through slander and blasphemy (verses 18–19). This should leave a reasonable listener open to hearing the gracious call of verses 25–30.

Jesus is also, however, doing all this with his disciples beside him, setting them a pattern to follow. Matthew is then using this to turn disciples of Jesus into disciple-makers. The disciples are encouraged to patient repetition of the gospel message of the kingdom, and not to get frustrated by slow responses (verses 2–6). They are shown here how to expose irrationality in peoples' responses, and to do so gently but firmly (verses 7–19). And they have Jesus's words to use in calling people to come to him (verses 25–30).

2. Spreading the word in Galilee part 2 • Matthew 12:1–21

Like Matthew 11, this section also has three subsections (12:1–8, 9–14, 15–21) and a movement from Jesus facing opposition and challenge in the first two subsections to him withdrawing in the final one. The first two recount episodes taking place on the Sabbath, interpreted as Sabbath-breaking by his opponents. Jesus then withdraws (12:15), an act Matthew presents as a fulfilment of Isaiah 42:1–4 in the seventh and longest of his ten fulfilment quotations.

Jesus is Lord of the Sabbath

12 At that time Jesus went through the cornfields on the Sabbath. His disciples were hungry and began to pick some ears of corn and eat them. **2** When the Pharisees saw this, they said to him, 'Look! Your disciples are doing what is unlawful on the Sabbath.'

3 He answered, 'Haven't you read what David did when he and his companions were hungry? **4** He entered the house of God, and he and his companions ate the consecrated bread – which was not lawful for them to do, but only for the priests. **5** Or haven't you read in the Law that the priests on Sabbath duty in the temple desecrate the Sabbath and yet are innocent? **6** I tell you that something greater than the temple is here. **7** If you had known what these words mean, "I desire mercy, not sacrifice,"[a] you would not have condemned the innocent. **8** For the Son of Man is Lord of the Sabbath.'

9 Going on from that place, he went into their synagogue, **10** and a man with a shrivelled hand was there. Looking for a reason to bring charges against Jesus, they asked him, 'Is it lawful to heal on the Sabbath?'

11 He said to them, 'If any of you has a sheep and it falls into a pit on the Sabbath, will you not take hold of it and lift it out? **12** How much more valuable is a person than a sheep! Therefore it is lawful to do good on the Sabbath.'

13 Then he said to the man, 'Stretch out your hand.' So he stretched it out and it was completely restored, just as sound as the other. **14** But the Pharisees went out and plotted how they might kill Jesus.

God's chosen servant

15 Aware of this, Jesus withdrew from that place. A large crowd followed him, and he healed all who were ill. **16** He warned them not to tell others about him. **17** This was to fulfil what was spoken through the prophet Isaiah:

18 'Here is my servant whom I have chosen,
    the one I love, in whom I delight;
  I will put my Spirit on him,
    and he will proclaim justice to the nations.
19 He will not quarrel or cry out;
  no one will hear his voice in the streets.
20 A bruised reed he will not break,
  and a smouldering wick he will not snuff out,
    till he has brought justice through to victory.
21 In his name the nations will put their hope.'**b**

---

a 7 Hosea 6:6
b 21 Isaiah 42:1-4

Eating grain on the Sabbath (12:1–8)

The situation here is that Jesus's disciples are seen picking heads of grain in a grainfield and eating them (that is, the kernels – as in Luke 6:1), and doing this on a Sabbath. There is no prohibition in the Law against eating on the Sabbath; the question is whether plucking heads of grain counts as work or harvesting, which are prohibited by the Law on the Sabbath (for example, in Exodus 34:21). The Pharisees have concluded that it does count as work or harvesting, hence the accusation that what the disciples are doing is 'unlawful' (or 'not permitted', verse 2).

The Pharisees would have acknowledged that it was permitted to overrule even quite precise commandments in certain circumstances, such as danger to life.[2] In such cases, human need can take precedence. But they are not taking *this* situation as a valid exception. (For example, the disciples could have stayed at home and eaten bread saved from the day before like everyone else.)

In Matthew's account, there are four stages to Jesus's response, effectively giving his interpretation of the Sabbath regulations as they apply to his disciples in this situation. First, he confirms that is indeed permitted to overrule commandments in certain circumstances, and argues that this is such a situation (verses 3–4). Here, Jesus appeals to David as a wise interpreter of the Law. David saw it was right in a situation of pressing need

---

[2] Compare John Nolland, appealing to 1 Maccabees 2:29–41: 'Danger to life was believed to override the requirements of the sabbath already from the Maccabean period.' Nolland, *Matthew*, 484.

for him and his companions to put to one side a specific commandment concerning the bread of the presence in Leviticus 24:5–9 and to accept the bread given to them by Ahimelech the priest (1 Samuel 21:1–6). For his men, this pressing need was caused by their allegiance to David, following him as the true Messiah. Jesus implicitly aligns himself with David. He, the true Messiah, is the good reason his disciples are not at home eating bread saved from the day before. Following him takes precedence.

Second, the Law itself accepts that there are situations where there is a higher priority at work than the prohibition against work on the Sabbath (verse 5). For example, the sacrifices made by the priests in the Temple on the Sabbath (Numbers 28:9–10) are a higher priority than applying the Sabbath prohibitions to the priests. This principle applies to the current situation, Jesus says, because he is present with his disciples, and he is 'greater than the temple' (verse 6).

Third, the prophets testify that mercy should always take priority, even over sacrifice (verse 7, quoting from Hosea 6:6, as in 9:13). So mercy takes precedence over sacrifice, which takes place in the Temple, which takes precedence over the Sabbath.

Finally, Jesus says, 'the Son of Man is Lord of the Sabbath' (verse 8). As we have seen before, Jesus uses the 'Son of Man' title for himself to allude to the vision in Daniel 7. He is the one who, even if he suffers tribulation and opposition now, will receive vindication, authority and the kingdom in the end. This explanation trumps all the others. That *Jesus* has allowed his disciples to pick grain is sufficient. He stands as the authority over, above and behind the Sabbath regulations. As Lord of the Sabbath he takes priority over the Sabbath itself, and it is his verdict that will be vindicated. As at 9:6 ('I want you to know that the Son of Man has authority on earth to forgive sins'), Jesus is ascribing to himself an authority way beyond any human authority.[3]

Jesus does not spell out here the *full* reasons why one thing takes precedence over another (such as the discipsles' needs over the holiness of the Sabbath). But a good understanding of the Law should realise that all laws have goals or purposes. The Sabbath regulations were a way to align the people to God's ultimate goal of rest in the cosmos. The Temple and sacrificial system were a (temporary) means to make this alignment possible. Ultimately, what was needed was mercy for God's people. And

---

[3] Indeed, the use of 'Lord' here does imply the divine name YHWH. The Sabbath is a Sabbath to/for YHWH (Exodus 16:23; 20:10; 35:2). France, *The Gospel of Matthew*, 463.

Jesus has come as Son of Man to fulfil all these goals and purposes. The truly righteous person – aligned with God's will, goals and purpose – would have been *with* the disciples following Jesus, not accusing them of wrongdoing from the sidelines.

Healing on the Sabbath (12:9–14)

The situation now would seem to be on the same day, in a synagogue attended by the Pharisees, and begins with the sudden appearance of a man with a shrivelled hand. Matthew perhaps implies that he has been brought in by the Pharisees so that they can ask (verse 10), 'Is it lawful to heal on the Sabbath?' and provoke him to do something they consider unlawful or not permitted.

The question is now whether healing a man on the Sabbath counts as 'work', and whether there are pressing urgent needs that might override the Sabbath requirements. The Pharisees think that it *is* work and (as they also concluded with the disciples eating grain in verses 1–12) that there is no pressing, urgent need to put the commandment to one side. The man is not about to die.

The response from Jesus is that healing the man would be entirely appropriate on the Sabbath. He knows that the Pharisees would rescue a trapped sheep on the Sabbath. This is even if the sheep is not at immediate risk of death and merely distressed. That is, they already know that doing good like this in response to a present need does not go against the Sabbath. It does not count as work. If this is true for a sheep, then how much more so for a person (verse 12)? Jesus then follows through on this argument and heals the man completely (verse 13). Good rules – such as the Sabbath regulations – cannot be in conflict with doing good.

The Pharisees' trap seems to have failed. They are the ones shown to be ethically inconsistent and against that which is good. This then prompts them to go out and plot how they might kill Jesus (verse 14). Their motive in setting up the situation was to accuse Jesus ('bring charges', verse 10). Now it seems they want to destroy him. Shedding innocent blood is one of the worst crimes in the sight of God, and was key to triggering the covenant curses under the Law (e.g., Manasseh in 2 Kings 21:16; 24:3–4), so the Pharisees are showing their fundamental lawlessness here. Their response to Jesus should indeed strike us as extreme, but not necessarily unexpected or unusual. We know from experience that people often behave in extreme ways when they feel their honour, authority or reputation (e.g., to interpret and police moral codes) is under threat.

Confirmation of Jesus as the Servant of the Lord (12:15–21)

Jesus now demonstrates what he taught his disciples to do when persecuted (in 10:23). He withdraws from the threat of death, and then continues his ministry in a more receptive place, keeping relatively hidden from sight (verses 15–16).

In the seventh of his 'fulfilment formulae', Matthew interprets this for us in the light of Isaiah 42:1–4. This is the longest of his quotations in the Gospel, and confirms that he wants us to see Jesus as Isaiah's Servant figure, the fulfilment of all his servant Israel should have been. Matthew's translation of these verses is his own, and matches the wording of 3:17 – confirmation, if we need it, that the understanding of the Father was that Jesus at his baptism was publicly taking on the Servant role. The fuller quotation here in Matthew 12 provides a commentary on what has happened since then.

The expectation given through the prophet in Isaiah 42:1, 3–4 (verses 18 and 20 here) and was that the Servant would bring forth or proclaim justice. Since 4:17, Jesus has been proclaiming the kingdom. We know, from the prayer in 6:9–13, that the coming of the kingdom is linked to God's will being done on earth as it is in heaven. In other words, the kingdom will be a place where justice has been done and where righteousness reigns.

The expected justice in Isaiah was for 'the nations' (Isaiah 42:1; verse 18 here), for the far reaches of the earth (Isaiah 42:4). Matthew has indicated the involvement of the nations or the whole earth/world a number of times already (e.g., 2:1–12; 4:15; 5:16; 8:5–13). Here in Matthew 12, the persecution he has faced has taken him to a more receptive area (12:15). The news of the kingdom is spreading outwards from its Galilean starting point: a dynamic that by the end of the Gospel will explicitly take it out to the nations.

The expectation in Isaiah 42:2–3 was that the Servant would faithfully bring about this justice in a quiet and gentle fashion, with compassion towards the 'bruised reed' and 'smouldering wick'. In Matthew 3:13–17, we noted the surprise (given John's expectation in 3:1–12) that Jesus did not come with an axe or with the fire of judgment. Rather, before the coming Judgment, something must happen first: the Servant work of dealing with the sin of the people.[4] His disposition towards the crowds

---

[4] See above on Matthew 3:13–17.

has been one of compassion (9:36). He has sent out the Twelve to imitate and multiply his own ministry: proclaiming the kingdom but moving on in the face of persecution to proclaim it elsewhere while there is time for people to respond (10:23). Jesus has called to himself those who are 'weary and burdened' (11:28). He then described himself as 'gentle and humble in heart', able to provide 'rest' for those who come to him (11:29). In all these things, Matthew has shown him very clearly fulfilling the expectations of Isaiah 42:1–4.

SUMMARY AND PURPOSE

As we have already noted, the narrative in 11:1–16:20 describes Jesus's Galilean ministry with sobering realism: a clear message, but with mixed responses; and here in 12:1–21, hostile to the point of plotting violence. Nonetheless, this can again serve to help make Matthew's readers into disciples. As they see the irrationality of the responses clearly exposed by Jesus, they should dissociate themselves from them. The Pharisees have shown themselves as petty and uncaring in the two episodes in verses 1–8 and 9–14. Their desire to kill Jesus in verse 14 is also very clearly not a godly one. On the other hand, Jesus has shown himself attractively on the side of the hungry, needy and broken throughout. What is more, he is bringing about the Lord's will in all these things, fulfilling his promises (verses 15–21). For those who have not yet responded to his call to come to him (11:28–30), this is further motivation to do so.

Once again Jesus is also doing all this with his disciples beside him, setting them a pattern to follow. Matthew is then using this to turn disciples of Jesus into disciple-makers. The disciples are shown by example here what they were warned about in Matthew 10: that they can expect a hostile response from those who consider themselves the gatekeepers of the contemporary moral code. (This is just as much an issue for disciple-makers today as it was in the first century.) The example Jesus sets here is one of withdrawing from conflict to continue with ministry. That is, rather than retaliating to hostility with hostility, Jesus encourages gentleness and compassion for the otherwise lost.

3. Spreading the word in Galilee part 3 • Matthew 12:22–50

Like Matthew 11 and 12:1–21, this section also has three subsections (12:22–37, 38–45, 46–50) and a movement from Jesus facing opposition and challenge in the first two subsections to him gathering people to himself in the final one. The first two recount episodes where Jesus is accused or challenged by the Pharisees and teachers of the law. Jesus is then shown with his true family gathered around him in verses 46–50.

Jesus and Beelzebul

22 Then they brought him a demon-possessed man who was blind and mute, and Jesus healed him, so that he could both talk and see. **23** All the people were astonished and said, 'Could this be the Son of David?'

24 But when the Pharisees heard this, they said, 'It is only by Beelzebul, the prince of demons, that this fellow drives out demons.'

25 Jesus knew their thoughts and said to them, 'Every kingdom divided against itself will be ruined, and every city or household divided against itself will not stand. **26** If Satan drives out Satan, he is divided against himself. How then can his kingdom stand? **27** And if I drive out demons by Beelzebul, by whom do your people drive them out? So then, they will be your judges. **28** But if it is by the Spirit of God that I drive out demons, then the kingdom of God has come upon you.

29 'Or again, how can anyone enter a strong man's house and carry off his possessions unless he first ties up the strong man? Then he can plunder his house.

30 'Whoever is not with me is against me, and whoever does not gather with me scatters. **31** And so I tell you, every kind of sin and slander can be forgiven, but blasphemy against the Spirit will not be forgiven. **32** Anyone who speaks a word against the Son of Man will be forgiven, but anyone who speaks against the Holy Spirit will not be forgiven, either in this age or in the age to come.

33 'Make a tree good and its fruit will be good, or make a tree bad and its fruit will be bad, for a tree is recognised by its fruit. **34** You brood of vipers, how can you who are evil say anything good? For the mouth speaks what the heart is full of. **35** A good man brings good things out of the good stored up in him, and an evil man brings evil things out of the evil stored up in him. **36** But I tell you that everyone will have to give account on the day of judgment for every empty word they have spoken. **37** For by your words you will be acquitted, and by your words you will be condemned.'

The sign of Jonah

38 Then some of the Pharisees and teachers of the law said to him, 'Teacher, we want to see a sign from you.'

39 He answered, 'A wicked and adulterous generation asks for a sign! But none will be given it except the sign of the prophet Jonah. **40** For as Jonah was three days and three nights in the belly of a huge fish, so the Son of Man will be three days and three nights in the heart of the earth. **41** The men of Nineveh will stand up at the judgment with this generation and condemn it; for they repented at the preaching of

Jonah, and now something greater than Jonah is here. **42** The Queen of the South will rise at the judgment with this generation and condemn it; for she came from the ends of the earth to listen to Solomon's wisdom, and now something greater than Solomon is here.

43 'When an impure spirit comes out of a person, it goes through arid places seeking rest and does not find it. **44** Then it says, "I will return to the house I left." When it arrives, it finds the house unoccupied, swept clean and put in order. **45** Then it goes and takes with it seven other spirits more wicked than itself, and they go in and live there. And the final condition of that person is worse than the first. That is how it will be with this wicked generation.'

Jesus's mother and brothers

46 While Jesus was still talking to the crowd, his mother and brothers stood outside, wanting to speak to him. **47** Someone told him, 'Your mother and brothers are standing outside, wanting to speak to you.'

48 He replied to him, 'Who is my mother, and who are my brothers?' **49** Pointing to his disciples, he said, 'Here are my mother and my brothers. **50** For whoever does the will of my Father in heaven is my brother and sister and mother.'

Jesus accused of devilry (12:22–37)

The background to Jesus's further confrontation with the Pharisees is the healing of a blind and mute demon-possessed man (verse 22). That he can now see and speak is evidence that the demon has been driven out. This provokes a divided response.

The first response comes from the crowd, who are astonished and openly wonder if Jesus could be the 'Son of David'. Matthew has already made it clear that Jesus is indeed the Son of David, the Christ or Messiah, right at the start of his Gospel (1:1, 16–17). Here, the people are connecting Jesus's power over demons and his victories against the kingdom of demons with what they would expect from the Davidic Messiah. Although they are only at this stage asking the question, Matthew is making it clear their response is in the right direction.

Back in 9:27, two blind men also called out to Jesus as 'Son of David'. Soon after this, the Pharisees made the claim, 'It is by the prince of demons that he drives out demons' (9:34). They make a similar claim here in Matthew 12, objecting to the suggestion that Jesus could be 'Son of David'. Now they claim he is driving out the demon by the power of 'Beelzebul', the prince of demons (verse 24). As we noted in Matthew 9, the Pharisees are essentially accusing Jesus of being a magus or magician.

Magi in the first-century Mediterranean world were those claiming to be able to heal, curse or exorcise demons through the occult manipulation of the underworld.[5] Hence the reference to casting out demons by the prince of demons, here given the name 'Beelzebul', as in 10:25

Matthew did not show us Jesus replying to the Pharisees in Matthew 9, but here we get an extensive response. It comes in two parts: an objection that the Pharisees' claim does not make sense (verses 25–7) and then a warning that their words place them at odds with the work of God against evil, cut them off from the forgiveness God is bringing, and will condemn them on the Day of Judgment (verses 28–37).

The Pharisees' words do not make sense because they are suggesting that the prince of the demons, the foremost among those who come from the place of the dead, is the power behind Jesus's life-giving healing and exorcism miracles. Jesus uses the name 'Satan' for him. He is the figure associated with accusation and deception, otherwise described as the 'devil', the slanderer, as Jesus himself experienced in 4:1–11. The devil is in turn associated with bringing death into the world (compare John 8:44). If the one who desires death, and who is prince among those who desire death, were to empower Jesus as he defeats death (as the Pharisees are claiming), then Satan's 'household' and 'kingdom' could not stand. He would be attacking himself (verses 25–6).

What is more, some of the Pharisees are involved with driving out demons (verse 27). If they were consistent, they should also then accuse their own of driving out demons by Beelzebul.

Jesus then moves to a new development in his response in verse 28, turning from a critique of their inconsistency to a warning. (It would be better not to have a 'But' at the beginning the translation of this verse, linking it to the previous verses, but rather 'Now, if it is by the Spirit of God that I drive out demons . . .') The Pharisees need to consider the severe consequences of being wrong in what they say. If they are wrong (and they are!) and it is by the Spirit of God that Jesus drives out demons, then God's rule and kingdom is being shown to them. Far from using Satan or appealing to Satan, Jesus is in fact binding Satan, the 'strong man', to 'plunder his house' and rescue people from the shadow of death (verses 28–9).

---

[5] Compare Uytanlet and Kwa, *Matthew*, 173. They comment that in the Philippines even today, 'The *mangkukulam* or *mambabarang* are persons who are believed to have the capacity to use demonic powers to pronounce curses on a person causing various forms of sicknesses or sometimes death.'

If this were the case (and it is the case!), then the Pharisees would then with their words be setting themselves against everything Jesus has come to do. They would not be 'with' him but 'against' him (verse 30a). That is, they would not be with him as he gathers, saves and forgives sinners, pulling them out from under the shadow of death, but rather with the demons as they scatter and destroy (verse 30b). We know at this stage of the Gospel that what Jesus has come to do by the Spirit is to save people from their sins, and to bring forgiveness. If the Pharisees blasphemously equate the Spirit to Beelzebul, then they place themselves against this work and outside its scope. This helps us to understand verses 31–2. By the Spirit, Jesus has come to forgive all kinds of sins (verse 31a), even the sin of speaking against himself, the one who has come as the 'Son of Man' (verse 32a). But to speak blasphemously against the Spirit is to reject the one who enables forgiveness, placing oneself permanently beyond the reach of forgiveness (verses 31b and 32b).

As in 7:16–20, Jesus now uses the metaphor of a tree and its fruit. Good trees produce good fruit; bad trees produce bad fruit. The fruit reveals what kind of tree it is (verse 33). The fruit Jesus has in mind this time is speech. Behind the evil words the Pharisees have spoken in blasphemy against the Spirit lie hearts that are full of evil and devoid of good (verses 34–5). Because words spoken reveal the heart, they will be used as evidence on the Day of Judgment (verses 36–7). Jesus strongly implies that the words the Pharisees have spoken against the Spirit – unless they recant of them and ask for mercy – will condemn them on that day.[6]

Jesus asked for a sign (12:38–45)

The next confrontation is prompted by the Pharisees – now joined by the teachers of the law – asking for a sign (verse 38). The request comes in response to Jesus's ministry of proclaiming the kingdom in Galilee, backed up by his wise teaching and his ministry of healing and exorcism (as summarised in 4:23 and 9:35). Each one of these death-to-life miracles has been a sufficient sign of the nearness of the kingdom. Given this, the Pharisees and teachers of the law are not asking for help to deal with

---

[6] To be clear: by blaspheming the Spirit, the Pharisees have offensively rejected the *means* of forgiveness, and it's for *this* reason they remain unforgiven. A sensitive disciple of Jesus who feels they may have committed this sin but who is constantly seeking forgiveness and not rejecting it cannot be in the same category. As Craig Blomberg puts it, 'in this text, only Jesus's enemies are in any danger'; Blomberg, *Matthew*, 204.

doubt. Their question is a negative response to Jesus – whom they take to be no more than a fellow 'teacher' – effectively saying what he has said and done is not enough for them to change their minds, believe in the reality of the coming kingdom, be convicted of their sins and come to him for salvation and forgiveness. This is what makes them part of a 'wicked and adulterous generation' (verse 39a), much like the unresponsive cities of 11:20–24. They thus deserve no further sign.

But Jesus adds an exception: no sign except the sign of the prophet Jonah (verse 39b). Jonah was three days and nights in the belly of a huge fish. This was a sign of the Lord's intent and determination to use Jonah as his prophet (whatever Jonah himself may have wished!). That Jonah was preserved through death in the fish and then cast out onto the land and sent to Nineveh by the Lord confirms and guarantees that the words he preached there were indeed the words of the Lord. Likewise with Jesus as Son of Man. He will be taken through death to a vindication that will confirm his deeds and words as truly the deeds and words of God himself. By the end of the Gospel we shall see this will correspond to three days in the tomb, followed by the vindication of his resurrection. This will be the ultimate sign of the truth about what Jesus has been saying about the nearness of the kingdom, surpassing and subsuming all the others. The reader of Matthew's Gospel will by this stage in chapter 12 already be repulsed by the sinful unresponsiveness of the Pharisees and teachers of the law. The reader may already have heard of Jesus's resurrection. They therefore have much more than enough to believe Jesus's preaching is true – if they are willing to listen.

But in their unresponsiveness, 'this generation', characterised by these Pharisees and teachers of the law, stand condemned. Jesus outlines how they stand condemned in relation to the three aspects of his ministry:

They stand condemned relative to his preaching (verse 41). This builds on what Jesus has said about Jonah in the previous verses. The 'men of Nineveh' responded to the preaching of Jonah. But Jesus is greater than Jonah and the content of his preaching is greater too, but 'this generation' have not responded. The men of Nineveh will therefore condemn them at the Judgment.

They stand condemned relative to his wise teaching (verse 42). The 'Queen of the South' is the Queen of Sheba who appears in 1 Kings 10:1–13 and 2 Chronicles 9:1–12, travelling to Jerusalem to hear and respond to the wise teaching of Solomon. But Jesus is greater than Solomon, as is the wisdom of his teaching, but 'this generation' have not responded. She will therefore condemn them at the Judgment.

They stand condemned relative to his exorcism ministry (verses 43–5). This has swept Galilee clean of impure spirits. The generation Jesus has been doing this among is like a person rescued from the grip of such a spirit. It has been a sign and foretaste of the cleansing and victory Jesus will bring to the whole world under the shadow of death and influence of evil. But those who reject him and what he is doing exclude themselves from this future. The evil will return – and Jesus warns it will be even worse than before. This will be the condition, he warns, of 'this wicked generation' (verse 45).

Jesus's true family (12:46–50)

Previously across Matthew 11–12, in the midst of much sinful unresponsiveness, Jesus has issued a general call to come to him to find rest from a world under the shadow of death (11:28–30) and has withdrawn from those who are unresponsive to the point of hostility to minister to others (12:15–21). Here at the end of the section we get another call, implicit this time, for the reader to distance themselves from the attitude of the Pharisees and teachers of the law and to become a full participant in what Jesus is doing – depicted here as being a part of his true family. Jesus is speaking in a culture that puts the highest value on family ties, family loyalty and family honour. What he says here is therefore deliberately provocative, marginalising the ties with his genetic mother and brothers (verses 46–8), and putting the emphasis instead on his disciples (verses 49–50). As in 8:21–2 and 10:34–7, Jesus does not want family ties to be impediments to following him.

The one criterion Jesus gives here for being one of his true family members is doing 'the will of my Father in [the heavens]' (verse 50). This is the same criterion he gave for entry into the kingdom on the Day of Judgment in 7:21. As there, we should not take this too narrowly, as merely obedience to a set of ethical commands, for example (although it does encompass obedience). To do the will of the Father in Matthew's Gospel is first and foremost about coming to Jesus in faith to find forgiveness of sins, and then to follow him.

These verses are similar to the section in 13:53–8, which is also about those who should be close to Jesus (because they live in his home town) not knowing him. The two sections form brackets around Jesus's teaching in parables in 13:1–52. This helps reinforce that the parables are a commentary on the proclamation of the kingdom in the midst of unresponsiveness and apparent failure.

SUMMARY AND PURPOSE

Jesus's Galilean ministry continues to provoke mixed responses. But this can again serve to help make Matthew's readers into disciples. Anyone from a Pharisaic or scribal background reading or hearing this material should feel exposed and convicted by these accounts – and indeed warned about the implications of their unbelief and the dangers of blaspheming what God is doing. Any other reader or hearer should see again the irrationality of the responses clearly exposed by Jesus. The warning here about missing out on what God is doing as he brings life and forgiveness from sins is especially strong.

Jesus is again doing all this with his disciples beside him, showing them what will face them as disciple-makers in the future. Like him, they will have their motives and methods questioned. Like him, they will have their message dismissed as inadequate. But the section ends with a strong encouragement that it is those following Jesus and listening to him as his disciples who are those doing the will of God.

9

The Word in Galilee: Parables

MATTHEW 13:1–52

1. Spreading the word in Galilee: parables
part 1 • Matthew 13:1–23

The context of Matthew 13 highlights that the experience of mission is often a mixed one, with many disappointments. Back in chapter 10, as he sent them out with the message of the kingdom, Jesus warned the Twelve that they should expect negative responses. Since then, this has been his own experience. Even John the Baptist has expressed doubts. The message seems to have failed: the generation as a whole has not grasped the nearness of the kingdom, and the Pharisees have been explicitly hostile. What is more, topping and tailing Matthew 13 there are stories that highlight the depth of the problem. In the first, in 12:46–50, even Jesus's blood relatives are shown to be unresponsive. In the second, at the end of chapter 13, Jesus's home town is profoundly unresponsive.

The parable of the sower

13 That same day Jesus went out of the house and sat by the lake. **2** Such large crowds gathered round him that he got into a boat and sat in it, while all the people stood on the shore. **3** Then he told them many things in parables, saying: 'A farmer went out to sow his seed. **4** As he was scattering the seed, some fell along the path, and the birds came and ate it up. **5** Some fell on rocky places, where it did not have much soil. It sprang up quickly, because the soil was shallow. **6** But when the sun came up, the plants were scorched, and they withered because they had no root. **7** Other seed fell among thorns, which grew up and choked the plants. **8** Still other seed fell on good soil, where it produced a crop - a hundred, sixty or thirty times what was sown. **9** Whoever has ears, let them hear.'

10 The disciples came to him and asked, 'Why do you speak to the people in parables?'

11 He replied, 'Because the knowledge of the secrets of the kingdom of heaven has been given to you, but not to them. 12 Whoever has will be given more, and they will have an abundance. Whoever does not have, even what they have will be taken from them. 13 This is why I speak to them in parables:

'Though seeing, they do not see;
though hearing, they do not
hear or understand.

14 In them is fulfilled the prophecy of Isaiah:

' "You will be ever hearing but
never understanding;
you will be ever seeing but
never perceiving.
15 For this people's heart has become
calloused;
they hardly hear with their ears,
and they have closed their eyes.
Otherwise they might see with
their eyes,
hear with their ears,
understand with their hearts
and turn, and I would heal them." a

16 But blessed are your eyes because they see, and your ears because they hear. 17 For truly I tell you, many prophets and righteous people longed to see what you see but did not see it, and to hear what you hear but did not hear it.

18 'Listen then to what the parable of the sower means: 19 when anyone hears the message about the kingdom and does not understand it, the evil one comes and snatches away what was sown in their heart. This is the seed sown along the path. 20 The seed falling on rocky ground refers to someone who hears the word and at once receives it with joy. 21 But since they have no root, they last only a short time. When trouble or persecution comes because of the word, they quickly fall away. 22 The seed falling among the thorns refers to someone who hears the word, but the worries of this life and the deceitfulness of wealth choke the word, making it unfruitful. 23 But the seed falling on good soil refers to someone who hears the word and understands it. This is the one who produces a crop, yielding a hundred, sixty or thirty times what was sown.'

_____

a 15 Isaiah 6:9,10 (see Septuagint)

In a context of mixed and often hostile responses, Jesus chooses, when confronted with a huge crowd, to go out into the lake and speak to them from a boat, in parables (verse 2).

Each of the parables involves uncovering something that is hidden, obscured or misleading. The seed that falls on some of the soils in the first parable is apparently unproductive, and its long-term future remains hidden for a while. The good seed in the parable of the weeds is obscured or partially hidden by the weeds. The mustard seed in the next parable is, in the first place, effectively hidden in that it is so small. Yeast is invisible. Then we get to parables about hidden treasure and a pearl whose value is hidden to many. The good fish in the final parable are in some sense hidden among bad. But in most of the parables, the hidden thing or the misleading thing is finally uncovered. The seed on unsuitable soil fails but the seed on good soil succeeds. The wheat in the parable of the weeds is finally separated. We come to see that what was once a mustard seed becomes something huge. The tiny amount of yeast spreads through the whole batch. The treasure is uncovered; the pearl is bought. The good fish are selected and kept.

We can divide the parables into three like this:

	First group	Second group	Third group
Parables	13:1–9 Parable of the sower (or soils)	Three parables: 13:24–30 Parable of the weeds 13:32–3 Parable of the mustard seed 13:33 Parable of the yeast	Three parables: 13:44 Parable of the treasure 13:45–6 Parable of the pearl 13:47–8 Parable of the net
	↑Public	↑Public	↑Private
Purpose and interpretation	↓Private 13:10–17 Purpose of para- bles part 1 13:18–23 Interpretation of the sower	↓Private 13:33–5 Purpose of para- bles part 2 13:36–43 Interpretation of the weeds	↓Private 13:49–50 Interpretation of the net 13:51–2 Purpose of para- bles part 3

Table 13

The first section is concerned with the parable of the sower or soils (verses 1–23). It is given a prominent place, and it seems to be the parable that underlies all the other parables.

In the second section, we have three parables grouped together: the parable of the weeds, the parable of the mustard seed and the parable of the yeast. And then Matthew says something about why Jesus is speaking in parables. Then we have another private session with the disciples. And Jesus explains the parable of the weeds.

In the third section, we get three more parables grouped together: the parable of the hidden treasure, the parable of the pearl and the parable of the net. The parable of the net actually finishes at the end of verse 48. Then Jesus gives an explanation. He finishes the parables by saying something more about what happens when they are understood.

The other feature dividing the material is that most of the parables are given in public, before a crowd, although all the parables in the third group are given privately to his disciples in the house they are staying at (from verse 36). All of the explanations of the parables and why Jesus is speaking in parables are given privately. This distinction puts into practice what Jesus says in verses 11 and 12. To the disciples, secrets are revealed. To the one who has, more will be revealed.

Parable of the sower (13:1–9)

From the relatively intimate indoor setting of 12:46–50, Matthew takes us outside on the same day, with Jesus confronting a huge crowd by the side of the lake. The crowd is so large, he has to speak to it from a boat (verse 2). Far from being intimate or family-like, the water expresses a degree of distance between them, heightened by him then speaking in parables.

There are many questions raised by this first parable of a seed-sower scatting seed over various different terrains. Who exactly is the farmer or the sower? Jesus doesn't say. And what is the farmer doing? Is he sowing before ploughing the field? Or after? Why is he sowing apparently so carelessly? Again, Jesus doesn't say, and he doesn't seem that interested in the agricultural details. The emphasis is rather on the seed – and this will make most sense if we imagine this seed being spread or broadcast in huge volumes, spread generously as if there is an unlimited supply.

We are shown other details too. There is a path. There are birds flocking to the scene, eager for a quick meal. It is a varied landscape: as well as the path, there is thin, rocky ground; ground covered with weeds and thorns; and clear, well-tilled ground. The parable tells a simple story about the two outcomes for the seed.[1] The farmer sows (verse 3). Some seed comes to nothing: because of where it falls, it is snatched by the birds (verse 4), scorched by the sun (verses 5–6) or choked to death by thorns (verse 7). But, says Jesus, other seed fell on good soil, where it produced

---

[1] It is one that is readily understandable across many cultures. Joe Kapolyo shows how it can be easily retold 'in terms that would be more familiar in rural Zambia'; Kapolyo, 'Matthew', 1163.

a crop – 'a hundred, sixty or thirty times what was sown' (verse 8). Jesus finishes with an exhortation: 'Whoever has ears, let them hear' (verse 9).

The purpose of parables part 1 (13:10–17)

The disciples come to Jesus (verse 10a). It makes best sense to take it that this is not while Jesus is in the boat, but later, when they are alone with him and in private. They ask the question everyone should be asking at this point: 'Why do you speak to the people in parables?' (verse 10b).

What Jesus says in response is an expansion of 11:25–7, where he openly praised his Father for choosing to hide things (i.e., the reality of the coming kingdom) from the 'wise and learned' and revealing them instead to 'little children' (11:25). Jesus also said that it was his choice as Son to reveal the Father to some and not to others (11:27).

We find the same pattern here in verse 11. Jesus says that he is speaking in parables because the 'knowledge of the secrets of the kingdom of heaven has been given to you' (that is, his disciples), 'but not to them' (that is, the crowd). So speaking in parables is a means of revealing hidden knowledge to some and concealing it from others. Those who have some knowledge of the kingdom, because they are disciples of Jesus who know the Father, will be given more understanding (verse 12a). Those who have not responded to Jesus's proclamation of the kingdom or his call to come to him will have even what they have taken away (verse 12b). From what Jesus goes on to say in verses 13–15, it seems this means that even the opportunity to hear, see, understand and turn will be taken away.

Jesus does not explicitly explain how the speaking in parables will function to divide hearers, revealing knowledge to some, hiding it from others. Parables have real content in them (as we shall see), but they do require higher effort to process and interpret, and sometimes even further explanation. So it may well be that their difficulty will repel those who are not yet interested (who hear them as undecipherable riddles or even gibberish), but will draw in those who are already interested. In the narrative, this is illustrated through the disciples who, separated from the crowd, come to Jesus to ask for more understanding in verse 10.

Lest we think that concealing knowledge like this is unjust, Jesus goes on to explain that his speaking in parables is a judgment against unresponsive people. Knowledge is concealed from those who hardly hear with their ears and who have closed their eyes (verse 13). This fulfils what the Lord was doing through the prophet Isaiah. The death of Uzziah in Isaiah 6:1 marked a transition to a new era in the history of Judah under Ahaz, an era when both king and people quickly proved to be wickedly unresponsive to the word of the Lord. Into this era Isaiah was commissioned as a prophet whose words would not turn the people back to the Lord but rather reinforce an already very serious refusal to hear and understand (verse 14; Isaiah 6:9). These were people with hearts that had become 'calloused' (verse 15; Isaiah 6:10) – that is, thickly covered in fat and therefore diseased, dull and insensitive. The prophets like Isaiah needed to know this, because otherwise they would have understandably wondered what on earth was the point of passing on a message no one was listening to. Jesus quotes from Isaiah and applies the same principle to the Galilean crowd he has just been preaching to, because his disciples (and us as readers) also need to know that this is a possible effect and purpose of preaching. An absence of a response does not mean God's word has failed. God's word does not only call; it also hardens and judges.

Having said this, although speaking in parables is an act of judgment against the crowd, it is not as if Jesus is condemning everyone in the crowd fatalistically to permanent 'blindness' and 'deafness'. Just as he followed the unresponsiveness of 11:1–24 with a statement of God's sovereignty (11:25–7) and an invitation and exhortation (11:28–30), so we get something similar here. As in 11:25–7, Jesus is insistent here that God chooses to whom he reveals the kingdom. But we also need to remember that parable ended with an open invitation and exhortation: 'Whoever has ears, let them hear' (verse 9). As we saw in 11:28–30, the open invitation to come to him is always there.

On the other side of the division, the picture is more positive (verses 16–17). We have already heard from verse 11 that these are people who are given the secrets of the kingdom of the heavens. It is by no means that these people are in some way more deserving because of their responsiveness. Instead, Jesus encourages the disciples to recognise just how good it is that they have eyes that do what eyes are meant to do, and ears that do what ears are meant to do (verse 16). Then he emphasises the extraordinary grace that has privileged them with seeing the kingdom come near and hearing him proclaim it and teach on it. These things, those of old longed to see (verse 17).

The private explanation (13:18–23)

Finally, we come to the explanation of the parable. Verse 19 provides the key to making sense of it. The seed sown on the path represents the word or message of the kingdom coming to someone. The seed in

Jesus's farming story is the message, or word, of the kingdom. In other words, this is another picture of the divisive work of God's word. Jesus is uncovering for us another picture, a God's-eye view, of the division that happens when God speaks into the world.

In the parable, the seed sown on the path was eaten up by birds (verse 4). Now we see this represents someone hearing but not understanding. Or, to put it another way, the evil one comes and takes away what was sown in their heart.

In the parable, the seed that fell on rock had little root and was scorched and withered by the sun (verses 5 and 6). Now we see this represents someone who receives the word of the kingdom with joy, but who quickly fall away when things get difficult for them (verses 20–21).

In the parable, the seed that fell among the thorns was choked (verse 7). Now we see this represents someone who hears the word of the kingdom but is 'choked' by 'the worries of this life' and 'the deceitfulness of wealth' (verse 22). Jesus describes the plant springing from this seed as 'unfruitful' rather than explicitly calling it dead. But both John the Baptist (3:8) and he (in, for example, 7:15–23) have previously warned of the fatal dangers of fruitlessness. So it would be foolish to find a glimmer of hope for such people in verse 22. It is safer to see them on the wrong side of the basic divide between seed that fails (verses 3–7, 19–22) and seed that succeeds (verses 8 and 23).

In the parable, the seed that fell on good soil produced a crop of fruit many times what was sown (verse 8). Now we see this represents someone who hears the word and understands it (verse 23). In other words, the opposite of the first kind of soil in verse 19; and, unlike the soil-types two and three, the understanding endures under pressure. These are the responsive people who, unlike the blind and deaf of verse 15, have had their eyes and ears opened, have seen the reality of the kingdom, have heard and understood, have turned back to God and have been healed and forgiven.

Jesus doesn't say here what he means by 'producing a crop' – which could also be translated 'being fruitful'. Previously in Matthew, 'fruit' has been behavioural (3:8; 7:15–23). But verses 8 and 23 do suggest some kind of multiplication of fruit-bearing plants. Both kinds of 'fruit' are important in Matthew's Gospel. The Gospel ends with disciples sent out to be fruitful and to multiply disciples (28:19), disciples who will be fruitfully obedient to what Jesus has taught (28:20).

SUMMARY AND PURPOSE

The overall purpose of Matthew's Gospel is to make its readers who aren't disciples of Jesus into disciples of Jesus, and to motivate and equip its readers who are disciples of Jesus to be disciple-makers.

The narrative so far in 11:1–16:20 has been describing Jesus's Galilean ministry with sobering realism: a clear message, but with mixed responses. This basic pattern is uncovered and illustrated here in the parable of the sower. It is what we might call a 'God's-eye' view or reflection on what has been happening. For 'whoever has ears' (verse 9), this reveals a simple division between the unresponsive and the responsive. For those who see this, there is then every incentive to get oneself on the right side of the division, and to come to Jesus for further knowledge and understanding. The details in verses 21–2 also warn the disciple – especially the relatively young disciple – about the kinds of things that could throw them off-course.

But the main purpose of these verses fits within the main purpose of 11:1–16:20 as a whole (as we should expect). Jesus is helping his disciples process what is happening in such a way that will equip them to continue in the future what he has been doing. First appearances are deceptive. There is success, even if it doesn't always look that way. Finally, after ages and ages of unresponsiveness in the history of Israel, there is a fruitful result. In among contemporary continuing unresponsiveness, there is a result. There is seed that is productive. The incentive is therefore to spread more 'seed', not less.

2. The word in Galilee: parables part 2 • Matthew 13:24–43

Like the first part of Jesus's teaching in parables, this section divides into two, with Jesus speaking to a crowd in verses 24–35 and then privately to his disciples in verses 36–43. Like the parable of the sower, the parable of the weeds in the field (often known as the 'parable of the tares') is given as an unexplained story first (verses 24–30), but with further explanation later (verses 36–43). In the middle of the section we get an editorial comment from Matthew (verses 34–5) giving a further, more positive, reason why Jesus is speaking in parables.

The parable of the weeds

24 Jesus told them another parable: 'The kingdom of heaven is like a man who sowed good seed in his field. 25 But while everyone was sleeping, his enemy came and sowed weeds among

the wheat, and went away. **26** When the wheat sprouted and formed ears, then the weeds also appeared.

27 'The owner's servants came to him and said, "Sir, didn't you sow good seed in your field? Where then did the weeds come from?"

28 ' "An enemy did this," he replied.

'The servants asked him, "Do you want us to go and pull them up?"

29 ' "No," he answered, "because while you are pulling up the weeds, you may uproot the wheat with them. **30** Let both grow together until the harvest. At that time I will tell the harvesters: first collect the weeds and tie them in bundles to be burned; then gather the wheat and bring it into my barn." '

The parables of the mustard seed and the yeast

31 He told them another parable: 'The kingdom of heaven is like a mustard seed, which a man took and planted in his field. **32** Though it is the smallest of all seeds, yet when it grows, it is the largest of garden plants and becomes a tree, so that the birds come and perch in its branches.'

33 He told them still another parable: 'The kingdom of heaven is like yeast that a woman took and mixed into about thirty kilograms of flour until it worked all through the dough.'

34 Jesus spoke all these things to the crowd in parables; he did not say anything to them without using a parable. **35** So was fulfilled what was spoken through the prophet:

'I will open my mouth in
parables,
I will utter things hidden since
the creation of the world.'**b**

The parable of the weeds explained

36 Then he left the crowd and went into the house. His disciples came to him and said, 'Explain to us the parable of the weeds in the field.'

37 He answered, 'The one who sowed the good seed is the Son of Man. **38** The field is the world, and the good seed stands for the people of the kingdom. The weeds are the people of the evil one, **39** and the enemy who sows them is the devil. The harvest is the end of the age, and the harvesters are angels.

40 'As the weeds are pulled up and burned in the fire, so it will be at the end of the age. **41** The Son of Man will send out his angels, and they will weed out of his kingdom everything that causes sin and all who do evil. **42** They will throw them into the blazing furnace, where there will be weeping and gnashing of teeth. **43** Then the righteous will shine like the sun in the kingdom of their Father. Whoever has ears, let them hear.

---

b 35 Psalm 78:2

Each of the three parables beginning this section begins with Jesus saying, 'The kingdom of heaven is like . . .' (verses 24, 31, 33). We might be expecting a sequence of similes, illustrations or comparisons that build a picture of what the kingdom of heaven is like (or will be like). But this would be to misunderstand how parables work and does not in any case fit very well with what Jesus goes on to say. What Jesus has said back in verse 11 suggests that to 'whoever has ears' (verse 9) the parables will reveal otherwise hidden secrets about the kingdom of the heavens. It is generally the end point of the story that reveals most about what the kingdom of the heavens will be like. For those seeking the kingdom (6:33), looking forward to it, the stories will then tell them what they need to know in the present.

Three more parables (13:24–33)

In what has become known as the 'parable of the tares' (verses 24–30), Jesus tells another farming story. A man sows good seed in his field. His enemy sows weeds in the same field. These are called 'tares' in some older English translations. They could be a type of ryegrass, which looks like wheat in its early stages of growth. There is then a time when both wheat and weeds appear, growing together, and a decision needs to be made about what to do. The owner says: do nothing, because while you are pulling the weeds, you may root up the wheat with them (verse 29). Wait for the time of the harvest, he says. Then the tares can be collected first and tied in bundles to be burned, and then the wheat gathered and brought into the barn. Then Jesus starts another story.

We could perhaps work out that this is something to do with the persistence of evil in the present age, because the weeds are sown by an 'enemy'. The coming of the kingdom will be like a farmer sowing good seed in a field but an enemy sowing weeds. In other words, it won't come straight away. And while you wait, there will be plenty of evil all around, some of it disguised. But in the end, when the kingdom does come, the evil will be completely extracted and destroyed. Beyond this, it is hard to make sense of this story of the weeds on our own. (We get more, of course, in the private explanation Jesus gives to his disciples in verses 36–43.)

Jesus continues to help those seeking the kingdom in the parable of the mustard seed (verses 31–2). This is how the kingdom of the heavens works or comes about – looking under the surface and behind the scenes. We begin with a man planting a mustard seed, the smallest of all the seeds.[2]

---

[2] There is no need to be pedantic here. We only need to grasp that a mustard

In the end, we have the largest of garden plants, even a tree – where birds perch in the branches. There is no description of the process by which this happens: just a simple comparison between how things are now and how things will be. The tree in the dream referred to in Daniel 4:21 – in which birds also live among the branches – represented Nebuchadnezzar II's kingdom at its greatest. To 'whoever has ears', the story reveals that something presently barely visible will nonetheless become a kingdom greater than any other kingdom. Greater, even, than the Babylonian kingdom under Nebuchadnezzar, or the Roman kingdom/empire of the first century – one that will fill the whole earth (Daniel 2:35).

The parable of the yeast, or leaven, is very similar (verse 33). This is how the kingdom of the heavens works or comes about – looking under the surface and behind the scenes. At the beginning, there is a tiny piece of yeast or leaven and a very large quantity of flour – about 13 litres of it, weighing about 30kg. 'How on earth is that going to work?' we might wonder. But, in the end, we have a huge piece of dough that is all worked through – enough to make an awful lot of bread!

This image is a particularly subversive one, because leaven working through dough is often used in the Bible to illustrate something bad working through something good and spoiling it. But when it comes to the kingdom of the heavens, says Jesus, it is the other way round! The good spreads through the bad and in the end will take over completely. In the kingdom of the heavens, heaven and earth are reunited into one unified kingdom, filled completely with life and blessing.

The purpose of parables part 2 (13:34–5)

Jesus speaks nothing to the crowd apart from using parables (verse 34). We were seeing in verses 10–17 that this will divide the crowd. Those without 'ears to hear' will hear nothing. But Matthew's comment here points to a more positive purpose for speaking in parables. For those to whom the secrets of the kingdom of the heavens are given, Jesus is speaking wisdom, opening up secrets and explaining riddles from the past.

The prophet Matthew quotes from here is Asaph, author of Psalm 78. This suggests that at least part of the reason why Jesus is speaking in parables is to uncover the truth about the outworking of history, particularly the history of Israel. Psalm 78 is the central Psalm of the eleven Psalms of Asaph in Book III of the Psalms. It is an extended meditation on the

---

seed would have been among the smallest seeds known to the crowd at the time.

history of Israel. Asaph is uncovering the history of Israel for those who have hidden it away and forgotten it. In particular, he is recounting how Israel in sin forgot the Lord and then, under David, remembered the Lord and the power of the Most High. And he is implying that the people of God in their current crisis need to remember that all over again. What Asaph began, Jesus is completing.

Another private explanation (13:36–43)

In private, in the house where they are staying, and away from the crowd, Jesus explains more about the parable of the tares. The first part of the explanation (verses 37–9) links the details in the set-up of the story to figures and events the disciples have already seen something of in Jesus's Galilean ministry. The sower of verse 24 is the Son of Man (verse 37), which is how Jesus has been speaking of himself in 8:20; 9:6; 10:23; 11:19; 12:8, 32, 40 – with the 'man' of Daniel 7 who suffers but is then vindicated very much in the background. The field of verse 24 is the world (verse 38).[3] The good seed sown by the Son of Man (verse 24) represents the people of the kingdom (verse 38), such as the disciples. The weeds sown in verse 25 are the people of the evil one (verse 38). That is, the people of the enemy back in verse 25, who is the devil, the slanderer (verse 39).

Putting all this together, we can see that the story will help the disciples process what has been happening as Jesus has been proclaiming the kingdom, calling people to follow him and making disciples. Jesus is uncovering a hidden reality: there are other forces involved, spreading lies and building a people opposed to God. Like the parable of the sower, this one also helps the disciples process and not be thrown off course by the mixed responses to Jesus's ministry.

Jesus doesn't say anything further here about the middle part of the parable, when the owner's servants come to the man and ask about the weeds and what to do about them, and the owner tells them to leave the weeds until the harvest (verses 26–30a). But from what Jesus has said, we can conclude that there is a time when the sons of the kingdom, sown by the Son of Man, coexist in the world alongside the sons of the evil one, sown by the devil. This is consistent with what Matthew has already shown in the Gospel so far. Jesus has not yet come to bring the

---

[3] The field is not being set up to represent anything like a mixed church or Christian denomination. Nevertheless, we do know from Matthew 7:15–23 that 'wolves in sheep's clothing' will be coexisting alongside true disciples in the future.

fiery judgment expected by John the Baptist (3:7–12), but has come to stand alongside sinners for their salvation, preparing them for the Judgment (3:13–17). He has come as someone 'gentle' (11:29), who will not break a bruised reed or snuff out a smouldering wick (12:20).

Jesus's explanation in verses 36–43 moves straight to the end of the story, to the harvest (verse 39). This greatly expands on the description of the harvest in the parable (verse 30). We discover that the harvest in the parable represents 'the end of the age' and the harvesters represent angels (verse 39). In the parable, the weeds were collected and tied in bundles to be burned (verse 30). Now we learn much more. The angels will remove from the kingdom 'everything that causes sin and all who do evil' (verse 41). The fire will be a 'blazing furnace' into which those who do evil will be thrown, and there will be 'weeping and gnashing of teeth' (verse 42). In Daniel 3:6, a blazing furnace was set up by the enemies of God and his people for those who refused to worship a statue of the king. Jesus is saying that in the future all this will be reversed, with the enemies burnt up. As in 8:12, outside the kingdom, from those excluded, there will be permanent regret and anger.

The overall picture of the kingdom is of a place where all evil is removed completely and for ever. What is more: no weeping and no anger. This is what the disciples need to know as they coexist with evil people in the present. It encourages them further to seek the kingdom of their Father. Those from the 'good seed' (verse 24), the 'people of the kingdom' (verse 38), are described here as those who will be 'the right-eous', and they will be in a place where they can 'shine like the sun' (verse 43). Jesus ends by repeating the exhortation of verse 9: 'Whoever has ears, let them hear.'

SUMMARY AND PURPOSE

This middle section of the parables – like the others – will to some extent help readers who aren't disciples of Jesus to become disciples of Jesus. The teaching here reinforces the basic Gospel message that the kingdom of the heavens is near. The truth about the future is being uncovered: evil will be destroyed for ever in a kingdom that will fill everything. The warnings about being outside this in verses 40–43 are especially strong. It makes sense to change one's mind about the future, to repent.[4]

But the main purpose of these verses is again to help those who are already disciples to persevere. Disciples dismayed by ongoing evil all

---

[4] See the previous comments on 'repentance' in 3:2 and 4:17.

around them are assured there are good reasons for this, and that in the end the evil will be completely removed, for ever. Disciples struggling because they cannot yet see the kingdom are reassured that in the end it will be unmissable: bigger than they ever could have imagined and filling the entire cosmos.

3. The word in Galilee: parables part 3 • Matthew 13:44–52

This final section of Jesus's teaching in parables seems to take place in the same setting as verse 36: that is, in 'the house' [where Jesus is staying]. In other words, we don't get the same division into public teaching followed by private teaching as we did in the first two sections. Everything takes place in private. Nevertheless, in verses 44–8 Jesus is again teaching in parables – three of them, as in verses 24–33. And, as in the previous sections, Jesus finishes with teaching focused on explanation and purpose (verses 49–52).

The parables of the hidden treasure and the pearl

44 'The kingdom of heaven is like treasure hidden in a field. When a man found it, he hid it again, and then in his joy went and sold all he had and bought that field.

45 'Again, the kingdom of heaven is like a merchant looking for fine pearls. **46** When he found one of great value, he went away and sold everything he had and bought it.

The parable of the net

47 'Once again, the kingdom of heaven is like a net that was let down into the lake and caught all kinds of fish. **48** When it was full, the fishermen pulled it up on the shore. Then they sat down and collected the good fish in baskets, but threw the bad away. **49** This is how it will be at the end of the age. The angels will come and separate the wicked from the righteous **50** and throw them into the blazing furnace, where there will be weeping and gnashing of teeth.

51 'Have you understood all these things?' Jesus asked.

'Yes,' they replied.

52 He said to them, 'Therefore every teacher of the law who has become a disciple in the kingdom of heaven is like the owner of a house who brings out of his storeroom new treasures as well as old.'

Three final (private) parables (13:44–8)

The two parables in verses 44–6 are closely tied together, telling very similar stories (much like the two parables in verses 31–3). Jesus makes this especially clear by beginning the second one by saying, 'Again . . .' As before, when Jesus says, 'The kingdom of heaven is like . . .', he is indicating that the parables will reveal otherwise hidden secrets about the kingdom of the heavens. As before, the end point of the stories reveals most about what the kingdom of the heavens will be like (here, valuable beyond compare). For those seeking the kingdom (6:33), looking forward to it, the stories will tell them what they need to know in the present (here, that the kingdom is worth giving up everything for).

The stories are very simple. In the first of these parables (verse 44), a man finds treasure hidden in a field, hides it again and joyfully goes to sell everything he has. Having sold everything he has, the man buys the field and gains the treasure. In verse 45, a merchant is looking for fine pearls. He then finds a pearl of great value and goes away to sell everything he has (verse 46). Having sold everything he has, the merchant buys the pearl.

Who are the man in the first parable and the merchant in the second? The sower in the parable of verses 1–23 was sowing the word of the kingdom (verse 18). So far in the Gospel, this has been Jesus, or Jesus through the Twelve (as in Matthew 10). In the parable of the weeds, Jesus explicitly identified the man who sowed good seed (verse 24) with the Son of Man (verse 37) – that is, with himself. So should we take the man and the merchant in these parables also to represent Jesus? If we did, they would be stories revealing how much Jesus values the kingdom and the cost he is prepared to undergo to secure it. While this is a true thought, it is not one that fits the context very well and is something Jesus will express much more clearly later in the Gospel (in 20:28 for example, the Son of Man giving himself as a ransom for many). So it is unlikely Jesus intends us to read the stories this way, and while our conclusions from doing so would be broadly true, there would be little gain. When we allegorise a story a way the author never intended, we always get out somewhat less than whatever we put in. On the other hand, Jesus has already spoken of the importance of laying up treasure in heaven (using the same word for 'treasure' as here) for a future reward (6:19–24). We should therefore read these stories along similar lines. The man and the merchant represent one of Jesus's disciples, seeing the future reward in the kingdom and giving up everything in the present.

Some over-read these parables in other ways, getting sidetracked by the ethics of the stories, for example. Isn't the first man being deceptive, not telling the original owner of the field about the treasure? And are they not they both being a little greedy and materialistic? But that is to miss the point. The point is that we can readily understand from experience how someone who discovers something of great value might sell absolutely everything to get hold of it. Likewise, says Jesus, as you discover the value of being part of the kingdom, you will want to invest absolutely everything to be there.

The parable of the dragnet in verses 47–8 (with its explanation in verses 49–50) is obviously very similar to the parable of the weeds in verses 24–30. But there is an important difference in emphasis, with nothing corresponding to the sowing of the wheat and weeds in verses 24–9. Instead, we have much more on the gathering process at the end if the story. Here, a dragnet is run through the lake and picks up all kinds of fish. In the parable of the weeds we had a mixed field; now we have a mixed catch. There is some waiting: the fishermen wait until the net is full. But the story is mostly concerned with the fishermen pulling the mixed catch to the shore and sorting it. The bad fish go the same way as the weeds: thrown away. In this shorter parable, the act of throwing away gets more emphasis.

The parable of the net explained (13:49–50)

Jesus explains the parable immediately: this is how it will be the end of the age (verse 49). The angels will come to 'separate the wicked from the righteous and throw them into the blazing furnace, where there will be weeping and gnashing of teeth'. As in verse 42 and 8:12, outside the kingdom, from those excluded, there will be permanent regret and anger.

We can now see how the three parables in this section work together. All of them throw our focus on to the future. The first two reveal the value of being a part of the kingdom. The third is a final reminder in this chapter of the reality of the separating judgment to come with the kingdom, and the regret and anger that will accompany being excluded. The only rational course in the present is to invest everything in the kingdom, and to keep doing so until the end.

The purpose of parables part 3 (13:51–2)

Jesus asks the disciples whether they have understood all these parables and the rest of his teaching in Matthew 13 (verse 51). We might wonder if their answer of 'Yes' is entirely accurate, given their ongoing slowness to understand (look ahead to 16:8–12, for example). For the moment, we can take Jesus as introducing verse 52 by saying, 'Inasmuch as you have understood the parables, this is what you should do with what has been revealed to you . . .'

In the NIV of verse 52, Jesus speaks about a teacher of the law who has become 'a disciple in the kingdom of heaven'. But it makes better sense to translate like this:

> Therefore, every teacher of the law who has been made a disciple for the kingdom of the heavens is like a householder who brings out of his treasure store new and old.[5]

What, then, is Jesus saying here? We can start by remembering that what Jesus has been doing in this chapter is uncovering the secrets of the kingdom of heaven for his disciples. Verse 11, for example: 'the knowledge of the secrets of the kingdom of heaven has been given to you'. What he is now implying at the end of his teaching is that, inasmuch as they have understood what he has told them, they have received treasure of great value. We may well wonder quite how much the disciples have understood at this stage of the proceedings. But at some point they will understand, and that understanding will be of great value to them. In teaching these things Jesus has acted like a teacher of the law for the kingdom of the heavens. That is, he has acted like a teacher who serves, proclaims and promotes the kingdom of the heavens. Now he is saying that any person who is made a disciple, and who understands the kingdom of the heavens, may likewise serve, proclaim and promote the kingdom of the heavens. Just like Jesus in this chapter, such a person is uncovering things of great value for those they are teaching.

Indeed, they will be bringing out of the treasure store both new things and old things. New things: the gospel of the kingdom. All that Jesus has done and is doing to bring the kingdom of the heavens into reality. Old things: things that have been revealed before, things that God's people know about in principle, which have often been forgotten but are now being fulfilled through Jesus.

Jesus has therefore given three reasons for speaking in parables in this chapter. The first is to act as judgment against those unwilling to listen (verses 11–17). The second is to open up secrets and explain riddles from

---

[5] That is, the dative is a dative of advantage. Compare 2 Corinthians 5:13 or Revelation 21:2.

the past to the disciples, uncovering for them the truth about outworking of history, particularly the history of Israel (verses 34–5). And the third is to equip them to do the same for others.

SUMMARY AND PURPOSE

The overall purpose of Matthew is to make its readers who aren't disciples of Jesus into disciples of Jesus, and to motivate and equip its readers who are disciples of Jesus to be disciple-makers.

This final section of Jesus's teaching in parables serves both aspects of this purpose. Two future outcomes are highlighted: one is of great value for the one who finds it (verses 44, 46); the other involves catastrophic loss (verse 50). For the reader or hearer who is not yet a disciple, the encouragement is to drop everything, abandon every other priority in life, in order to be a part of the positive outcome and avoid the negative. Similarly, someone who is already a disciple is encouraged to persevere, whatever the ups and downs of discipleship in the present. What is more, the parables equip them to continue in the future what he has been doing. They, too, can uncover treasures new and old.

10

The Word in Galilee: Faith

MATTHEW 13:53–16:20

1. The word in Galilee: faith part 1 • Matthew 13:53–14:36

The episode in 13:53–8 corresponds to Jesus's response to his mother and brothers in 12:46–50, just before his teaching in parables (13:1–52). Both episodes show people who should know and respond to Jesus failing to do so. But having heard the parables and Jesus's teaching, if we have 'ears' to hear him, we should now know that the lack of response from Jesus's home town in 13:53–8 is unsurprising and does not mean his proclamation of the kingdom has failed, or that Jesus's claims about the kingdom are any less sure.

The episode in his home town also expresses the lack of response to Jesus as unbelief or a lack of faith (13:58). The section running from 14:1 to 16:12 picks up and develops the language and concepts of unbelief in those hostile to Jesus, 'little faith' and doubt in his own disciples, but also 'great faith' (expressed by the Canaanite woman in 15:22–8).

A prophet without honour

53 When Jesus had finished these parables, he moved on from there. **54** Coming to his home town, he began teaching the people in their synagogue, and they were amazed. 'Where did this man get this wisdom and these miraculous powers?' they asked. **55** 'Isn't this the carpenter's son? Isn't his mother's name Mary, and aren't his brothers James, Joseph, Simon and Judas? **56** Aren't all his sisters with us? Where then did this man get all these things?' **57** And they took offence at him.

But Jesus said to them, 'A prophet is not without honour except in his own town and in his own home.'

58 And he did not do many miracles there because of their lack of faith.

John the Baptist beheaded

14 At that time Herod the tetrarch heard the reports about Jesus, **2** and he said to his attendants, 'This is John the Baptist; he has risen from the dead! That is why miraculous powers are at work in him.'

3 Now Herod had arrested John and bound him and put him in prison because of Herodias, his brother Philip's wife, 4 for John had been saying to him: 'It is not lawful for you to have her.' 5 Herod wanted to kill John, but he was afraid of the people, because they considered John a prophet.

6 On Herod's birthday the daughter of Herodias danced for the guests and pleased Herod so much 7 that he promised with an oath to give her whatever she asked. 8 Prompted by her mother, she said, 'Give me here on a dish the head of John the Baptist.' 9 The king was distressed, but because of his oaths and his dinner guests, he ordered that her request be granted 10 and had John beheaded in the prison. 11 His head was brought in on a dish and given to the girl, who carried it to her mother. 12 John's disciples came and took his body and buried it. Then they went and told Jesus.

Jesus feeds the five thousand

13 When Jesus heard what had happened, he withdrew by boat privately to a solitary place. Hearing of this, the crowds followed him on foot from the towns. 14 When Jesus landed and saw a large crowd, he had compassion on them and healed those who were ill.

15 As evening approached, the disciples came to him and said, 'This is a remote place, and it's already getting late. Send the crowds away, so that they can go to the villages and buy themselves some food.'

16 Jesus replied, 'They do not need to go away. You give them something to eat.'

17 'We have here only five loaves of bread and two fish,' they answered.

18 'Bring them here to me,' he said. 19 And he told the people to sit down on the grass. Taking the five loaves and the two fish and looking up to heaven, he gave thanks and broke the loaves. Then he gave them to the disciples, and the disciples gave them to the people. 20 They all ate and were satisfied, and the disciples picked up twelve basketfuls of broken pieces that were left over. 21 The number of those who ate was about five thousand men, besides women and children.

Jesus walks on the water

22 Immediately Jesus made the disciples get into the boat and go on ahead of him to the other side, while he dismissed the crowd. 23 After he had dismissed them, he went up on a mountainside by himself to pray. Later that night, he was there alone, 24 and the boat was already a considerable distance from land, buffeted by the waves because the wind was against it.

25 Shortly before dawn Jesus went out to them, walking on the lake. 26 When the disciples saw him walking on the lake, they were terrified. 'It's a ghost,' they said, and cried out in fear.

27 But Jesus immediately said to them: 'Take courage! It is I. Don't be afraid.'

28 'Lord, if it's you,' Peter replied, 'tell me to come to you on the water.'

29 'Come,' he said.

Then Peter got down out of the boat, walked on the water and came towards Jesus. **30** But when he saw the wind, he was afraid and, beginning to sink, cried out, 'Lord, save me!'

31 Immediately Jesus reached out his hand and caught him. 'You of little faith,' he said, 'why did you doubt?'

32 And when they climbed into the boat, the wind died down. **33** Then those who were in the boat worshipped him, saying, 'Truly you are the Son of God.'

34 When they had crossed over, they landed at Gennesaret. **35** And when the men of that place recognised Jesus, they sent word to all the surrounding country. People brought all who were ill to him **36** and begged him to let those who were ill just touch the edge of his cloak, and all who touched it were healed.

The overall structure here is very similar to what we saw in Matthew 11–12, with negative or hostile responses to Jesus followed by Jesus withdrawing or departing to another place:

Unbelief	13:53–8 Jesus's home town 14:1–12 Herod	15:1–20 Pharisees and teachers of the law	16:1–4 Pharisees and Sadducees
Withdrawal	14:13 Withdrawal	15:21 Withdrawal	16:4 Departure
Miracles and faith	14:13–21 Feeding the five thousand 14:22–33 Peter's 'little faith' 14:34–6 More healings	15:22–8 A woman's 'great faith' 15:29–31 More healings 15:32–9 Feeding the four thousand	16:5–12 The disciples' 'little faith'

Table 14

This time, the negative responses are associated with unbelief or a lack of faith (as in 13:58), and with Jesus not doing miracles or giving signs (13:58 and 16:1–4). Each time Jesus withdraws, he moves to a place where faith can be encouraged and demonstrated through miracles, and where the little faith and doubt of his disciples can be addressed.

Matthew 14 establishes this pattern. Following a negative response to Jesus's teaching in his home town (13:53–8), the chapter begins with Herod's response to news of Jesus's miracles (14:1–12). Jesus withdraws to places where he does indeed do miracles (14:13–21, 34–6). Then, right at the heart of the chapter, is Jesus's rebuke of Peter (14:31): 'You of little faith . . . why did you doubt?'

The narrative in Matthew 14 seems at first to be non-linear.[1] We begin at about the same time as Jesus's rejection in his home town (14:1), but Matthew then takes us back in time to explain why Herod thinks Jesus is John the Baptist (14:3–12). The next episode then continues on from this flashback (14:3), and the narrative then runs in a linear fashion to the end of the Gospel. But although it is hidden in the NIV, Matthew says Jesus responds to news of John's death by withdrawing 'from there' (verse 13). The last reported location of Jesus was in his home town (13:53–8). In other words, 14:3 does not takes us far back in time. News of Jesus's miracles must have reached Herod in 14:1 at about the same time that news of John's death reached Jesus in 14:13.

Unbelief in Jesus's home town (13:53–8)

Just as he has been since 4:23, Jesus is continuing his ministry of kingdom proclamation, with its key component of 'teaching the people in their synagogue' (13:54). As before, his teaching causes amazement (compare 7:28). But, also as so often before, ultimately the response is a negative one.

This time, Jesus is teaching in the synagogue of his 'home town' (13:54). Matthew probably means us to think of Capernaum, where Jesus has been living more recently, rather than Nazareth (see 4:13). As in 12:46–50, familiarity with Jesus at a family or community level does not inevitably lead to faith. Here, in fact, familiarity acts as an impediment: those who hear him cannot understand how someone with such ordinary origins, whose family is well known (13:55–6), could speak such wisdom and do the miraculous works they have heard about (13:54). They ask the question, 'Where then did this man get all these things?' and they take 'offence at him' (13:56–7). At the very least, Matthew is suggesting they are deeply suspicious about Jesus's wisdom and powers. He may also be hinting they suspect, like the Pharisees in 9:34 and 12:24, that his powers have an occult origin.

This dishonour Jesus experiences in his home town is like the dishonour

---

[1] As noted by Terence L. Donaldson, '"For Herod Had Arrested John" (Matt 14.3): Making Sense of an Unresolved Flashback', *Studies in Religion* 28, no. 1 (1999).

experienced by the prophets when they spoke to their own people (13:57). It also foreshadows what Jesus will experience from the people as a whole in Jerusalem at the end of the Gospel.

We have already seen that Jesus's miracles are often in response to faith (8:5–13; 9:1–8, 20–22, 27–30). This goes part way to explaining why he does not do many miracles in his home town (13:58). Matthew is also perhaps suggesting Jesus chooses not to do them in a place where he knows they will be misinterpreted, and perhaps have been misinterpreted previously (compare 11:23).

The false confession of Herod (14:1–12)

Matthew then shows us the response of Herod (Antipas), tetrarch of Galilee and Perea, to news of Jesus's miracles. Like the Pharisees, Herod links the miracles to the powers of the underworld – explicitly, he thinks Jesus must be John the Baptist raised from the dead (14:1–2).[2] Herod's verdict on Jesus contrasts profoundly with Peter's at the end of this section (16:13–20). There we shall see that Peter even begins his answer to the question of Jesus's identity by saying, 'Some say John the Baptist' (16:14), reminding us of these verses, before giving his own verdict: 'You are the Messiah, the Son of the living God' (16:16). The beginning and end of the section therefore give us the kind of movement Matthew wants to bring about in his readers: from unbelief and crazy misidentification of Jesus to settled understanding and faith in his identity as the Messiah.

Matthew then gives us the background to Herod's verdict on Jesus (14:3–12). As Jesus said to the Pharisees, 'The mouth speaks what the heart is full of' (12:34). The words, 'This is John the Baptist' (14:2) originate from an incident that exposes Herod's heart as profoundly corrupt. Herod is in an unlawful relationship with Herodias and imprisons John when John tells him so (14:3–4). Herod wants to kill John and only holds back out of fear of the people (14:5). Not only is he the kind of ruler shaped by fear, but the kind who holds dubious birthday celebrations for himself and makes extraordinarily rash open promises (14:6–7). Although he is distressed by the request that comes from Herodias, he does not want to lose face before his guests and complies with it anyway (14:9–10). He

---

[2] This is similar to the Pharisees in 9:34 and 12:24. A beheaded man (as we soon discover was John's fate) 'would make a powerful ghost, highly sought after by the magicians'; Bolt, *Jesus's Defeat of Death*, 192. Hence, if 'raised', perhaps capable of doing the things that are being reported.

wanted to kill John, and now he sheds innocent blood in an extraordinarily gruesome and public manner (14:10–11).

All this serves to expose the heart attitudes behind Herod's saying, 'This is John the Baptist; he has risen from the dead' (14:2). Herod may well be terrified, thinking John (a raised ghost of some sort) has returned to torment and haunt him. But the emotional response Matthew intends from his readers at the end of the account is one of disgust. As the reader of Matthew's Gospel is repelled by Herod's wickedness, they are also encouraged to dissociate from his unbelief and his strange views on Jesus's identity.

The feeding of the five thousand (14:13–21)

When Jesus hears about John's death, he withdraws to a 'solitary place' (14:13). It seems his first intention is to be alone. Nevertheless, when crowds follow him there, he is willing to continue his ministry, exercising compassion on them by healing their sick (14:13–14). This withdrawal is very similar to his response to the Pharisees wanting to kill him in 12:14–15, and continues the pattern of moving away from intense persecution so that ministry elsewhere can continue.

Jesus's compassion continues to show when it becomes apparent that the crowds are going be hungry. Just as the events of 14:3–11 revealed Herod's true heart – undermining his false claim concerning Jesus's identity – so what Jesus does here reveals his heart, strengthening our confidence in what he has been saying about the kingdom, and giving us a true understanding of his identity. Like the other miracles we have seen, this is a window into the future, showing us what the kingdom will be like, and also demonstrating Jesus's divine authority to bring it about. It is self-consciously like the miracle Elisha performs in 2 Kings 4:42–4, amply feeding a hundred men from twenty loaves, but very much greater. The magnitude of the miracle is shown by comparing the five loaves and two fish in 14:17, the twelve basketfuls of broken pieces left over in 14:20 and the sheer number of people who have eaten in 14:21.[3] The people have 'followed' Jesus, and so Matthew is showing them as at least potential disciples. Just as the Last Supper in 26:26–9 (which shares some of the same language) points forward to Jesus's feasting with his disciples in his Father's kingdom (26:29), so here. Here, as they eat

---

[3] 'The number twelve is probably symbolic: food for all [the twelve tribes of] Israel'; Nolland, *Matthew*, 594.

and are satisfied (14:20), they serve as a picture of God's saved people enjoying a victory banquet with him. There are obvious echoes of the Lord feeding his people in the wilderness (Exodus 16). This reinforces the claim that Jesus is the Lord (YHWH).[4] But the feeding of the five thousand does more than this. It provides a foretaste of the final victory celebration over wickedness and even death itself, as foreseen by the prophet Isaiah (Isaiah 25:6–8). It makes Herod's birthday party (14:6–11) look puny, weakly self-serving and even more squalid.

'Little faith' on the water (14:22–33)

Matthew sets up the episode on the water by explaining how Jesus becomes separated from his disciples. He compels them to get into the boat and start the journey to the other side of the lake (verse 22). He waits to dismiss the crowd and then to pray alone on a mountainside through the night (verse 23). Towards the end of the night, he is still on the shore while they are in the middle of the lake, experiencing heavy weather (verse 24).

Jesus then goes out to meet them, walking on the lake (verse 25). This is of course a spectacular miracle, but as always Matthew wants us to discern its significance. The first indication comes from the disciples' reaction: terrified, they assume they are seeing a ghost and cry out in fear (verse 26). As we noted with the restoration of the two demoniacs in 8:28–34, the sea in the ancient world was considered to be a portal to the underworld, the place of the dead. It was the sort of place, then, where one might see a phantom or ghost. But Jesus has not emerged up from the underworld; he has come down from a mountainside, where he has been in prayerful communion with his Father. If anything, he is demonstrating by standing on the water his authority over the place of the dead, and the chaos and evil associated with it.

The second indication of the significance of Jesus walking on the water is Jesus's response, which is, 'Take courage! It is I. Don't be afraid.' That is (whatever Herod might think), 'I am not a ghost.' Jesus says literally and simply, 'I AM.' He uses the words the Lord God uses of himself in

---

[4] Although there are similar miracles in 1 Kings 17:9–16 and 2 Kings 4:42–4, feeding *all Israel* is something only YHWH has done. The sheer scale of the miracle here places this in a different category. The multiple allusions in this part of Matthew to the Exodus and wilderness experiences of the people of Israel also point in this direction.

the books of Exodus and Isaiah: I AM (most especially, Exodus 3:14).[5] Just as the Lord's great desire in the Exodus was that through the signs and wonders he brought about, the world and his people might know that he is the Lord, so here. This is happening so that the disciples might know that Jesus is the Lord. And like the herald of good news in Isaiah 40:9, Jesus is able to say, 'Do not fear.'

In verses 28–33, Peter asks to join Jesus on the water. For a brief moment he also walks, but begins to sink when the ferocity of the wind takes his attention away. He cries out to Jesus, is rescued and then rebuked for his little faith. They climb into the boat, the wind dies down and the disciples worship Jesus as the Son of God.

Many commentators throughout history have taken all this as an enacted parable about Christian faith in the face of difficulties. This is almost certainly Matthew's intention. But, just as with the spoken parables in the Gospel, there is an issue of how much to read into the details of what happens. For example, this is presumably not an encouragement actually to walk on water. But what, then, does walking on water represent? What about the other details? What does the wind represent? Does the boat represent the church?

We get some help from the Psalms, where the Lord rules over the sea and can calm it (Psalm 89:9). Being overwhelmed by water is used as a metaphor in the Psalms for being overwhelmed by trouble, from which only the Lord can save (Psalm 18:16–19). In Psalm 69:1–4, sinking in the miry depths is a way of talking about being hated without reason and threatened with death. David's cry is, 'Save me, O God' – just like Peter's to Jesus in verse 30. This background confirms that the sea in verses 22–33, especially when stirred by the wind into life-threatening waves, represents trouble and the threat of death.

Further interpretative control comes from looking ahead in the Gospel and noticing that what we have here in a few verses is a complete preview of what happens to Peter later on. In verse 29, he starts off boldly enough. It is an impressive act of faith to step out of a boat and expect to walk. But when trouble comes, he takes his eyes off Jesus and sinks like a stone (verse 30). In 16:16, Peter's faith will be sufficiently strong to give a true confession of Jesus's identity. But at rock bottom in the story to come, he will deny Jesus three times and call down a curse upon himself (26:69–75). It is only as he recognises that it is by Jesus

---

[5] The same phrase 'I am' appears in the LXX of Isaiah 41:4; 43:10, 25; 45:8, 18, 19, 22; 46:4, 9; 47:8, 10; 48:12, 17; 51:12; 52:6; 56:3.

alone that he can be saved that he is able to cry out and be restored, as in the sinking and saving of verse 31 here.

Once we have seen this, we can begin to see that Peter's walking on the water represents the faith that allows a disciple to participate in Jesus's authority and victory over death. Being distracted by the wind represents doubt. This is explicit in Jesus's gentle rebuke: 'You of little faith . . . why did you doubt?' We might even translate this, 'For what reason did you doubt?' The wind might be strong, but with Jesus right there beside him there were manifold reasons to keep trusting him.

When they get into the boat, the wind dies down (verse 32). The parallels with Peter's story as it unfolds in the rest of the Gospel helps us not to ascribe too much significance to the boat – as representing the church, for example, as some commentators are keen to do.[6] The safety at the end of the Gospel comes from knowing the risen Lord Jesus and his ongoing presence (28:20). Whether or not the disciples see the dying of the wind as a further miraculous act from Jesus, they have seen enough to fall down and worship him as the Son of God (verse 33).

Healings at Gennesaret (14:34–6)

When they land at Gennesaret on the other side of the lake, Jesus is recognised and word spreads (verse 35). The healings here match those in verse 14, drawing together the material from verses 13 to 36. These verses present the divine authority of Jesus in contrast to the false authority and kingship of Herod in verses 1–12. That the people of Gennesaret recognise Jesus contrasts with Herod's false identification in verse 2. The volume of healing in verses 35–6 contrasts with the lack of miracles in Jesus's home town, where he did not do many miracles 'because of their lack of faith' (13:58). The people of Gennesaret have a faith like the woman in 9:20–22, where even a touch of Jesus's cloak is enough to bring healing.

SUMMARY AND PURPOSE

Matthew's overall intentions in this section are clear. He wants his readers to move from a state of unbelief, little faith or doubt to one of secure faith in Jesus as the Lord who will secure for his people a final victory over death. He wants readers to dissociate from the unbelief of the people in Jesus's home town (13:53–8), dismayed by their small-mindedness. He

---

[6] Such as Ulrich Luz, *Matthew 8–20* (Minneapolis: Fortress, 2001), 322.

wants readers to dissociate from the superstition, false identification and self-centred moral compromise of Herod (14:1–12), deeply disgusted by the image of John the Baptist's head on a dish. He wants readers to see in Jesus the Lord at work, feeding his people, with authority over the forces of death, inviting others to participate in the victory over death he has come to secure (14:13–32).

For readers who aren't disciples of Jesus, this will naturally encourage them to become disciples of Jesus. But as usual Matthew has more in mind for those who are already disciples of Jesus – like Peter here, who serves as a representative disciple. For them, the section functions to deal with little faith and doubt (14:31). It helps them to worship Jesus and join in afresh with the confession, 'Truly you are the Son of God.' It evokes the kind of faith lacking in Jesus's home town (14:35–6), a kind of faith Jesus has commended before (9:20–22).

2. The word in Galilee: faith part 2 • Matthew 15

Matthew 15 continues the pattern established in 13:53–14:36. The Pharisees and the teachers of the law bring a further objection to Jesus (concerning rites of washing), and Jesus exposes the defilement of their hearts. Jesus then leaves, withdrawing to the region of Tyre and Sidon (verse 21). In what is Gentile territory, or near to Gentile territory, Jesus continues his ministry among more responsive people (verses 21–39). Right at the heart of the chapter is Jesus's commendation of the Canaanite woman, 'Woman, you have great faith!' (verse 28).

That which defiles

15 Then some Pharisees and teachers of the law came to Jesus from Jerusalem and asked, 2 'Why do your disciples break the tradition of the elders? They don't wash their hands before they eat!'

3 Jesus replied, 'And why do you break the command of God for the sake of your tradition? 4 For God said, "Honour your father and mother"[a] and "Anyone who curses their father or mother is to be put to death."[b] 5 But you say that if anyone declares that what might have been used to help their father or mother is "devoted to God," 6 they are not to "honour their father or mother" with it. Thus you nullify the word of God for the sake of your tradition. 7 You hypocrites! Isaiah was right when he prophesied about you:

8 ' "These people honour me with
      their lips,
   but their hearts are far from me.

⁹They worship me in vain;
  their teachings are merely
    human rules."ᶜ'

¹⁰Jesus called the crowd to him and said, 'Listen and understand. ¹¹What goes into someone's mouth does not defile them, but what comes out of their mouth, that is what defiles them.'

¹²Then the disciples came to him and asked, 'Do you know that the Pharisees were offended when they heard this?'

¹³He replied, 'Every plant that my heavenly Father has not planted will be pulled up by the roots. ¹⁴Leave them; they are blind guides.ᵈ If the blind lead the blind, both will fall into a pit.'

¹⁵Peter said, 'Explain the parable to us.'

¹⁶'Are you still so dull?' Jesus asked them. ¹⁷'Don't you see that whatever enters the mouth goes into the stomach and then out of the body? ¹⁸But the things that come out of a person's mouth come from the heart, and these defile them. ¹⁹For out of the heart come evil thoughts – murder, adultery, sexual immorality, theft, false testimony, slander. ²⁰These are what defile a person; but eating with unwashed hands does not defile them.'

The faith of a Canaanite woman

²¹Leaving that place, Jesus withdrew to the region of Tyre and Sidon. ²²A Canaanite woman from that vicinity came to him, crying out, 'Lord, Son of David, have mercy on me! My daughter is demon-possessed and suffering terribly.'

²³Jesus did not answer a word. So his disciples came to him and urged him, 'Send her away, for she keeps crying out after us.'

²⁴He answered, 'I was sent only to the lost sheep of Israel.'

²⁵The woman came and knelt before him. 'Lord, help me!' she said.

²⁶He replied, 'It is not right to take the children's bread and toss it to the dogs.'

²⁷'Yes it is, Lord,' she said. 'Even the dogs eat the crumbs that fall from their master's table.'

²⁸Then Jesus said to her, 'Woman, you have great faith! Your request is granted.' And her daughter was healed at that moment.

Jesus feeds the four thousand

²⁹Jesus left there and went along the Sea of Galilee. Then he went up on a mountainside and sat down. ³⁰Great crowds came to him, bringing the lame, the blind, the crippled, the mute and many others, and laid them at his feet; and he healed them. ³¹The people were amazed when they saw the mute speaking, the crippled made well, the lame walking and the blind seeing. And they praised the God of Israel.

³²Jesus called his disciples to him and said, 'I have compassion for these people; they have already been with me three days and have nothing to eat. I do not want to send them away hungry, or they may collapse on the way.'

33 His disciples answered, 'Where could we get enough bread in this remote place to feed such a crowd?'

34 'How many loaves do you have?' Jesus asked.

'Seven,' they replied, 'and a few small fish.'

35 He told the crowd to sit down on the ground. **36** Then he took the seven loaves and the fish, and when he had given thanks, he broke them and gave them to the disciples, and they in turn to the people. **37** They all ate and were satisfied. Afterwards the disciples picked up seven basketfuls of broken pieces that were left over. **38** The number of those who ate was four thousand men, besides women and children. **39** After Jesus had sent the crowd away, he got into the boat and went to the vicinity of Magadan.

---

a 4 Exodus 20:12; Deut. 5:16
b 4 Exodus 21:17; Lev. 20:9
c 9 Isaiah 29:13
d 14 Some manuscripts *blind guides of the blind*

The Pharisees and teachers of the law exposed (15:1–20)

Back in 9:14, the disciples of John asked Jesus why his disciples do not fast like they and the Pharisees fast. In 12:2, the Pharisees complained to Jesus that his disciples were unlawfully plucking grain on the Sabbath. Here, the teachers of the law join the Pharisees in making a similar complaint: his disciples do not wash their hands before they eat. This is breaking 'the tradition of the elders' (verse 2). This time, there is no law that commands the washing of hands before eating. (There is just Leviticus 15:11, which instructs washing hands after a 'discharge'.) But the whole Pharisaic approach as a renewal movement in Judaism meant taking laws and principles from the Law and developing traditions that went above and beyond them in an attempt to guarantee covenant fidelity.[7] In this case, John Nolland may be right when he argues that their concern was to limit the spread of impurity.[8] Food eaten with unclean hands becomes unclean; and then when eaten and taken into the stomach makes the whole person unclean. This would fit what Jesus says in response in verses 17–20.

Jesus has already hinted at the Pharisees' inadequate righteousness (5:20), critiqued their attitude to eating with sinners (9:10–13) and fasting (9:14–17), exposed their wrong understanding of the Sabbath (12:1–14), warned them about unforgivable blasphemy (12:22–32) and rebuked their unbelief (12:38–42). Here in Matthew 15, he continues to expose the failure of their approach to the Law. How absurd it is to go above and

---

[7] See the discussion on the Pharisees in the Introduction.
[8] Nolland, *Matthew*, 611–15.

beyond the laws concerning cleanliness while simultaneously breaking the fifth commandment and dishonouring their parents!

It's hard to pin down precisely what the Pharisees have been doing in verses 5–6, but it would seem that some of them are denying their parents support by declaring money or resources 'devoted [to God]'.[9] They have invented a tradition to support this. But what they say in their tradition now contradicts and trumps what God says in the commandments (verses 4 and 6). Jesus used the name 'hypocrite' back in 6:2, 5, 16 for those doing 'righteous deeds' merely to be seen and approved of by others. Here he uses the term directly of the Pharisees (verse 7). The surface 'mask' of the Pharisees is a godly one, saying money is set aside, 'devoted' or 'given' [to God]. Underneath is a desire to break the commandment, and quite possibly keep the money for themselves. Jesus applies Isaiah 29:13 to them (verses 8–9): what they are saying sounds like honour or worship to God, but their hearts are 'far from' him because of the false tradition they have set up. The Pharisees are thus like those in Jerusalem at the time of the Assyrian crisis who are blind (Isaiah 29:9–10), whose fate is sealed (Isaiah 29:11–12, and whose superficial 'worship' will not save them (Isaiah 29:13–14).

Calling a wider group to listen, Jesus then gives an authoritative understanding of cleanliness and defilement in verses 10–11: 'What goes into someone's mouth does not defile them, but what comes out of their mouth, that is what defiles them.' This sounds general, but reinforces what he said in verses 8–9 about the Pharisees. The words 'devoted [to God]' on their lips are in support of a false and dishonouring practice and therefore come from a defiled place. This is certainly how the Pharisees understand what he has said, hence the offence reported back to him by his disciples (verse 12). In his response, Jesus again implicitly warns that the Pharisees will be facing judgment: that they are not 'plants' that the Father has 'planted'; that is, they are showing themselves to be not his work, not his people (verse 13). This matches the outcome for the tares, the sons of the evil one, sown by the devil, in Matthew 13:36–42. He warns the disciples to 'leave them' (verse 14) – that is, to not follow them (or their teaching). As they encourage others to follow their traditions, they

---

[9] For example, they may be simply giving money away to the Temple to spite their parents. Or the ruse could be more sophisticated, such as making an easy-to-keep vow using a sum of money as collateral, which is then not available to help their parents. When the vow is kept and their parents have died, they have then kept the money for themselves. If making and keeping vows is then given huge moral weight, the ruse can be presented as something godly. See Nolland, *Matthew*, 617.

are 'blind guides'. When they 'fall into a pit' (that is, face the judgment of verse 13), they will take with them anyone following them.

At Peter's request, Jesus fully explains and expands the saying in verse 11 in relation to what the Pharisees have been claiming about washing hands. He begins and ends with the first half of the saying: 'What goes into someone's mouth does not defile them'. Food eaten with unwashed hands simply passes through a body (verse 17); it does not defile a person (verse 20b). Jesus then explains and expands the second half of verse 11 – 'but what comes out of their mouth, that is what defiles them' – in verses 18–20a. Jesus repeats what he said in 12:34 (also with respect to what the Pharisees have been saying): what comes out of the mouth in speech comes from the heart (verse 18). The (unclean) evil in the heart reveals itself in 'evil thoughts' – that is, evil arguments or reasoning, like those the Pharisees have been expressing verbally. The difficulty in understanding Jesus's argument here is that only the final two of the list of wicked acts in verse 19 are directly speech acts. Probably the logic is that evil in the heart – normally hidden, but revealed in speech – overflows into all kinds of wicked behaviour. That is, evil speech and evil arguments are an early indicator of internal defilement, which, when fully grown, gives birth to acts like murder, adultery, sexual immorality, etc.[10]

The great faith of the Canaanite woman (15:21–28)

In response to the hostile offence of the Pharisees to him effectively declaring them internally defiled, Jesus leaves and withdraws again (verse 21). Matthew gives us the first of three geographical markers in the chapter (the others being at verses 29 and 39). Jesus has already referred to the region of Tyre and Sidon in relation to their historic reputation for wickedness (11:21–2). Here, he also uses 'Canaanite' to describe the woman who comes out to him, with all its associations with the evil practices of the people who inhabited the Promised Land before its occupation. In other words, on the surface, this would seem like an unpromising place to find a positive response to Jesus and the proclamation of the kingdom.

And yet the response they encounter could hardly be more positive! The

---

[10] Compare James (who has much to say about the tongue): 'after [evil] desire has conceived, it gives birth to sin; and sin, when it is full-grown, gives birth to death' (James 1:15). Note that Jesus speaks very clearly about the evils of sexual immorality. It is wrong to say that he never talked about such things or had no interest in them.

woman is deferential in a way the Pharisees have failed to be, appealing to Jesus as 'Lord' throughout their encounter (verses 22, 25, 27). In this, she is like the man with leprosy in 8:2, the centurion in 8:6 and 8:8, the disciples in 8:25, the blind men in 9:28 and Peter in 14:30. Her cry, 'Son of David, have mercy on me!' (verse 22) is essentially the same as that from the two blind men in 9:27.

Her daughter is suffering greatly, like the servant of the centurion in 8:6, except this time the suffering is caused by a demon. In all previous cases like this one, Jesus has responded quickly with compassion. It is therefore quite a shock when the first response from Jesus here is silence (verse 23). Only when the disciples complain (with something like the opposite of compassion!) does Jesus explain to her that he was 'sent only to the lost sheep of Israel' (verse 24). The woman persists in her appeal, now kneeling before him (verse 25), like the man with leprosy in 8:2 and the synagogue ruler in 9:18.[11] Jesus's explanation for not responding is now deliberately shocking (verse 26). It is not just that she is outside Jesus's jurisdiction or not one of his people. If healing those of 'the lost sheep of Israel' is like a parent feeding their children, then healing a Canaanite would be like giving their food to a passing stray dog. In other words, she is from a people and place so associated with wicked hostility towards God and his people that it would actually be wrong to respond to her. It is only when she continues to persist, and in response to what she actually says in verse 27, that he grants her request. Just as the centurion's servant was healed instantly and at a distance (8:13), so it is with the woman's daughter (verse 28).

The dialogue between the woman and Jesus and the delay to the granting of her request for healing serves two related purposes. The first is to emphasise how momentous and indeed difficult it is for the blessing Jesus has begun to demonstrate among the people of Israel to flow out beyond those boundaries. Jesus is not being in any way misogynistic or racist, as is sometimes claimed. This removes entirely any sense of entitlement to God's blessing that might exist from a Gentile point of view. The second – even more so than with the centurion in 8:5–13 – is to use a Gentile (a Canaanite woman no less) to demonstrate the nature of what Jesus declares to be 'great faith' (verse 28). Faith identifies the source of blessing and mercy accurately and reverently (verses 22, 25, 27). It is in essence a desperate cry for mercy (verse 22) and help or rescue (verse

---

11 This is the same word in Greek as the one translated 'worship' used previously to describe the Magi in 2:2, 8, 11 and the disciples in 14:33.

25). It does not take offence when one's moral condition is exposed, but desperately continues to seek any help – any 'crumb' – that might be given (verses 26–7). The woman's reply in verse 27 excludes any possibility that she thinks she deserves or is entitled in any way to what she is asking for.

What the Pharisees said and argued in the previous episode came from defiled hearts, and they took offence when Jesus exposed this (verse 12). The Canaanite woman comes from a people and place hostile to God and his people, and she even accepts the label 'dog' to describe her moral condition and worthiness. But what she says comes from a heart full of 'great faith' (verse 28). This is counted to her as righteousness, as in Genesis 15:6, implicitly making her a true daughter of Abraham. As with the centurion in 8:5–13, she stands as a foretaste of the fulfilment of the promise in Genesis 12:3 that blessing will pass to all peoples on earth.

The feeding of the four thousand (15:29–39)

There are two more geographical markers in these verses, topping and tailing the feeding of the four thousand. Jesus has been in the thoroughly Gentile region of Tyre and Sidon and now he is back near the Sea of Galilee (verse 29). At the end of this episode, he travels by boat to Magadan. The location is uncertain, but may be a suburb of Tiberias on the western shore of the sea. The events of chapter 16 do seem to be more firmly set in Jewish territory. Quite how much Matthew wants to show this as a Gentile-focused version of the miraculous feast first given to a more Jewish crowd in 14:13–21 is unclear. He does not have Mark's reference to the Decapolis (Mark 7:31), for example, which would have located the event more firmly in Gentile territory. The word for 'basketfuls' in verse 37 is sometimes said to be more 'Hellenistic' than that used in 14:20, but it is not at all clear this is the case.

On the other hand, R. T. France is right to say that it is inadequate to follow some scholars and dismiss this as a 'doublet' – by which they mean an event imaginatively created by the Gospel writers to reinforce one they have already related.[12] The details in the account tell against this. There are too many differences to the feeding of the five thousand and too much of an eyewitness feel to the details for it to be dismissed plausibly as an invention.

The description of Jesus's ministry beside the Sea of Galilee deliberately echoes what Matthew has said before in 4:24; 9:35; 12:15 and 14:35–6. The

---

[12] France, *The Gospel of Matthew*, 601.

'great crowds' (verse 30) are like those of 13:2. As before, the people are amazed at what they see (verse 31). What they see is what Jesus has done before. The summary in verse 31 echoes Jesus's summary of his healing ministry in 11:5, which was in turn an echo of prophetic expectation. In contrast to the joyless practices of the Pharisees in verses 1–20, the people praise the God of Israel.

In other words, despite the hostile offence taken by the Pharisees, Jesus's ministry continues unabated, including another miraculous feast (verses 32–8). Compared to the feeding of the five thousand, this time Jesus takes the initiative and calls the disciples and himself raises the problem of there being nothing to eat (verse 32). They do not suggest sending the crowds away (as in 14:15); they just despair about the lack of bread (verse 33). They have bread and fish, as before (14:17), but different amounts (verse 34). And of course the crowd is slightly smaller (verse 38).

Taken together, the two feeding miracles serve as a double witness to the future of God's saved people, pictured as enjoying a victory banquet with him – with possible hints second time round of the many 'from the east and the west' who 'will take their places at the feast with Abraham, Isaac and Jacob in the kingdom of heaven' (8:11).

SUMMARY AND PURPOSE

Matthew's overall intentions in this section are similar to those in 13:53–14:36. He wants his readers to dissociate from the mask-wearing of the Pharisees and teachers of the law as they put on a show of religious devotion (verses 1–20), repulsed by their hypocrisy and heart attitude as one would be by other forms of defilement. Instead, he wants them to associate with the 'great faith' of the Canaanite woman (verse 28) and with those who praise the God of Israel (verse 31). He wants readers to see in Jesus the Lord continuing in his work, just as he has been earlier in the Gospel.

For readers who aren't disciples of Jesus, this will again encourage them to become disciples of Jesus. They should not be swayed by the accusations of the Pharisees and teachers of the law or afraid that becoming a disciple would make them defiled. To do so would be like blind people following the blind (verse 14).

For those who are already disciples of Jesus, the encounter with the Pharisees and teachers of the law will likewise serve to make them more resilient to certain kinds of unjust accusation and to continue as disciples of Jesus. For Jewish disciples, suspicion towards Gentiles should turn into compassion, and joy that blessing is spreading beyond the boundaries of

Israel. The overall impression by the end of the chapter is that the Lord is doing in Jesus far more than anyone might have imagined. All of this will then serve motivate and equip them as disciple-makers.

3. The word in Galilee: faith part 3 • Matthew 16:1–20

Matthew 16:1–20 repeats the pattern established in 13:53–14:36 and 15:1–39 a third and final time. The Pharisees and this time the Sadducees demonstrate their stubborn unbelief by asking (again) for a sign (verses 1–4). This ends with Jesus leaving them and going away. It is not exactly the same 'withdrawal' language as the previous sections, but likewise moves the narrative to episodes that deal with 'little faith' (verses 5–12) and then a true confession (of faith, verses 13–16). We have moved from Herod's opinion of Jesus as the risen John (14:2) to Peter's confession of him as 'the Messiah, the Son of the living God' (verse 16 here), which is then affirmed by Jesus in verses 17–20.

The demand for a sign

16 The Pharisees and Sadducees came to Jesus and tested him by asking him to show them a sign from heaven.

2 He replied, 'When evening comes, you say, "It will be fair weather, for the sky is red," 3 and in the morning, "Today it will be stormy, for the sky is red and overcast." You know how to interpret the appearance of the sky, but you cannot interpret the signs of the times.ᵃ 4 A wicked and adulterous generation looks for a sign, but none will be given it except the sign of Jonah.' Jesus then left them and went away.

The yeast of the Pharisees and Sadducees

5 When they went across the lake, the disciples forgot to take bread. 6 'Be careful,' Jesus said to them. 'Be on your guard against the yeast of the Pharisees and Sadducees.'

7 They discussed this among themselves and said, 'It is because we didn't bring any bread.'

8 Aware of their discussion, Jesus asked, 'You of little faith, why are you talking among yourselves about having no bread? 9 Do you still not understand? Don't you remember the five loaves for the five thousand, and how many basketfuls you gathered? 10 Or the seven loaves for the four thousand, and how many basketfuls you gathered? 11 How is it you don't understand that I was not talking to you about bread? But be on your guard against the yeast of the Pharisees and Sadducees.' 12 Then they understood that he was not telling them to guard against the yeast used in bread, but against the teaching of the Pharisees and Sadducees.

Peter declares that Jesus is the Messiah

13 When Jesus came to the region of Caesarea Philippi, he asked his disciples, 'Who do people say the Son of Man is?'

14 They replied, 'Some say John the Baptist; others say Elijah; and still others, Jeremiah or one of the prophets.'

15 'But what about you?' he asked. 'Who do you say I am?'

16 Simon Peter answered, 'You are the Messiah, the Son of the living God.'

17 Jesus replied, 'Blessed are you, Simon son of Jonah, for this was not revealed to you by flesh and blood, but by my Father in heaven. **18** And I tell you that you are Peter,[b] and on this rock I will build my church, and the gates of Hades[c] will not overcome it. **19** I will give you the keys of the kingdom of heaven; whatever you bind on earth will be[d] bound in heaven, and whatever you loose on earth will be[d] loosed in heaven.' **20** Then he ordered his disciples not to tell anyone that he was the Messiah.

---

a 2,3 Some early manuscripts do not have *When evening comes . . . of the times.*
b 18 The Greek word for *Peter* means *rock.*
c 18 That is, the realm of the dead
d 19 Or *will have been*

Jesus is asked for a sign – again! (16:1–4)

Since the last time the Pharisees asked for a sign in 12:38 (along with the teachers of the law), Jesus has continued to heal many people (14:14, 34–6; 15:29–31), he has fed the five thousand (and others) with five loaves and two fish (14:15–21) and he has fed the four thousand (and others) with seven loaves and a few small fish (15:32–9). The healing miracles, as we have seen before, are windows into a future where the kingdom of the heavens has filled the cosmos and swept away the shadow of death, in fulfilment of all the promises of God, but most explicitly Isaiah 35:5–7. The two great feeding miracles are foretastes of the feast that will be enjoyed with Abraham, Isaac and Jacob in the kingdom of the heavens, which many in Israel are in danger of missing out on (8:10–12). These all, then, are signs of the nearness of the kingdom and therefore of the urgent need of repentance.

The Pharisees now return to Jesus with the Sadducees (verse 1). As in 3:7, these represent the full spectrum of unrepentant religious opinion in Israel. They ask for a sign 'from heaven'. This is especially ironic given the feeding miracles and all their echoes of the bread given 'from heaven' in Exodus 16:4. It is appropriate therefore for Jesus to question their powers of perception and interpretation! They are able to look to the appearance of the sky and draw conclusions about the coming weather (verses 2–3a), but they have proved incapable of looking to what Jesus has been doing and drawing conclusions about the coming kingdom (verse 3b). He therefore says to them almost exactly what he said in 12:39: they will be given no further sign except the sign of the prophet Jonah (verse 4). As we saw above in 12:38–45, this is pointing forward to Jesus being three days preserved through death, followed by the vindication of his resurrection. This will be the ultimate sign of the nearness of the kingdom, surpassing and subsuming all the others. It will also conclusively show him to have been very much in the right, and the Pharisees and Sadducees very much in the wrong.

The disciples' 'little faith' (16:5–12)

The disparity between the evidence of the feeding miracles and the extraordinary request for a sign from the Pharisees and Sadducees in verse 1 forms the background to the awkward dialogue between Jesus and his disciples here. The request is just the latest in a long line of statements and questions from the Pharisees and others that have worked to undermine Jesus, fuelled by unbelief in his message. At the end of this section, Jesus will call this the 'teaching' of the Pharisees and Sadducees (verse 12).

The other background information we need to know to understand the dialogue is that the disciples have forgotten to bring any bread (verse 5). This was something of an oversight, given there was plenty after the feeding of the four thousand they could have kept (15:37).

The teaching of the Pharisees and Sadducees is clearly very dangerous and may well have undermined the belief of many in the crowds listening to Jesus and is likewise capable of undermining the belief of the disciples. Hence Jesus warns them about it (verse 6). He uses a metaphor to frame the warning, calling their words 'yeast' or leaven. This communicates just how dangerous their teaching is. It can get into the mind of an individual, spreading until it generates unbelief, like leaven spreading through dough. Likewise, it can spread from individual to individual in a crowd.

But the disciples do not understand the metaphor, and simply don't get what Jesus is talking about. They hear the word 'leaven', associate it with bread and wonder if it might have something to do with their mistake in having forgotten to bring enough to eat (verse 7).

It might seem an innocuous mistake, but Jesus knows it reveals a problem in their understanding. If their belief had been strong, they would have been as horrified by the request for a sign from the Pharisees and Sadducees in verse 1 as Jesus was. With their minds exercised by the corrosive words and questions coming from the Pharisees and others, the metaphor should make instant sense. As it was, their minds are on other things. In other words, the failure to understand the metaphor exposes the 'little faith' of the disciples (verse 8). Like the Pharisees and Sadducees, they have failed to fully understand the significance of the feeding miracles. So Jesus reminds them (verses 9 and 10). The sheer quantity of leftover bread should have strengthened their belief in the coming feast in the kingdom, and in Jesus as the one calling people to join him at it.

Now, when Jesus repeats the warning to be on their guard 'against the yeast of the Pharisees and Sadducees' (verse 11b), they understand him. He is warning them against the corrosive teaching of the Pharisees and Sadducees (verse 12).

The true confession of Peter (16:13–16)

That the disciples are slowing moving from 'little faith' to a more solid faith in Jesus is now confirmed when they come into the region of Caesarea Philippi. Jesus asks them, 'Who do people say the Son of Man is?' (verse 13). As before (8:20; 9:6; 10:23; 11:19; 12:8, 32, 40; 13:37, 41), Jesus uses the 'Son of Man' title to talk about himself – identifying with the one in Daniel 7 who suffers tribulation now but will be vindicated and receive the kingdom when he comes with the clouds of heaven (Daniel 7:13–14). But his question to the disciples is, 'Who do others say I am?' They answer in verse 14 that some say he is John the Baptist (like Herod in 14:2, at the beginning of this section of the Gospel), or others say he is Elijah (expected to return before the 'great and dreadful day of the LORD' according to Malachi 4:5). John the Baptist has dressed like Elijah (3:4), and he has been identified with Elijah by Jesus in 11:14.[13] Mistaking Jesus for John or Elijah is to mistake the one being heralded (the Lord or King) for the herald.

Others say, 'Jeremiah or one of the prophets.' Certainly, Jesus's words have often been received with the same unresponsive negativity as the word of the Lord through Jeremiah. But if John has been right in saying he is the one preparing the way for the Lord (3:3), Jesus has been the Lord himself speaking among them.

---

[13] Even if we know from John 1:21 that he is not literally Elijah, but was fulfilling the Elijah role from Malachi 4:5. We also know this from Matthew 17:3, where Elijah himself appears and is definitely not John.

Jesus then asks the disciples directly, 'Who do you say I am?' (verse 15). Simon Peter gives a straight answer: 'You are the Messiah, the Son of the living God' (verse 16). The disciples addressed Jesus as '[truly] the Son of God' back in 14:33. Peter now adds 'Messiah'. The Messiah, or Christ, is the title Matthew used in 1:1, 16–17, 18 and 11:2 (in relation to John). Herod used it in 2:4. Matthew linked it to the title 'son of David' in 1:1 and hence to expectations of the fulfilment of the promises to David in 2 Samuel 7. The address 'son of David' was used by Matthew of Joseph in 1:20, and by various people of Jesus in 9:27, 12:23 and 15:22. Peter also extends what was said in 14:22 by calling Jesus, 'Son of the living God'.

Jesus's response (16:17–20)

In his response to Peter, Jesus make three declarations, across each of verses 17 to 19. Each of these has three parts to it: the basic declaration followed by two explanatory expansions. This gives a 3x3 structure:

Declaration	Expansion A	Expansion B
(17) Blessed are you, Simon son of Jonah	For this was not revealed to you by flesh and blood	But by my Father in [the heavens]
(18) And I tell you that you are Peter	And on this rock I will build my church	And the gates of Hades will not overcome it
(19) I will give you the keys of the kingdom of heaven	Whatever you bind on earth will be bound in heaven	And whatever you loose on earth will be loosed in heaven

Table 15

The basic declaration at the start of verse 17 is that Peter is blessed. As previously discussed regarding 5:3–10, this is a word that declares someone to be living in a good state – living the 'good life' in some way, on the best possible path.

The first reason Jesus gives for this is that what Peter has just confessed was not revealed by 'flesh and blood' – it did not have a human source (negative statement) – but was uncovered by his Father in the heavens (positive statement). The encouragement is that his confession is evidence of the Father taking a personal interest him – the individual known as 'Simon son of Jonah' – to reveal the true identity of Jesus as Christ or Messiah, Son of the living God.

Simon (Peter) was the first of the disciples to be called by Jesus (4:18–19), and we have already seen how Matthew wants to use him as a representative disciple in Matthew 14:22–33. It is legitimate therefore to generalise Jesus's declaration to anyone able to make the confession of verse 16 sincerely, and to keep making it. Such a disciple can also take comfort and joy from the personal interest and intervention of the Father.[14]

The second reason Jesus is able to call Peter 'blessed' is that he is the 'rock' on which Jesus will build his church (verse 18). Petros, the name Simon is known by (see 4:18), is the Greek word for rock. (We can guess that Peter was not a small man!) The word Jesus uses for the rock on which he will build his church is very slightly different (feminine rather than masculine), but it seems clear that Jesus wants us to make the connection to Simon Peter.[15] But in what way will Peter be the rock on which Jesus's church is built? Verse 18 is inscribed around the dome of St Peter's Cathedral in Rome – the claim being that Peter was first bishop in the institution of what is now known as the Roman Catholic Church: an authority figure, whose authority passes down to later bishops and 'priests'. But Jesus does not say anything else about Peter having an institutional authority or authority over other disciples. It makes much more sense to take him as a representative disciple, as before. That is, the church is built out of people like Peter, disciples like Peter, who also confess what he confessed in verse 16. He stands out as different only by being the first: the pattern by which others follow.

What is more, this church (or 'assembly') will be unlike any other assembly God has called together. Unlike the assemblies of the Old Testament, which gathered for a time but then petered out and failed as the nation turned away from the Lord their God, this one will be so strong and permanent that even 'the gates of Hades will not overcome it'. Hades was the ancient Greek way of thinking about the underworld, the place of the dead. The 'gates of Hades' is therefore a way of talking about the entrance to death. Prior to this moment, any gathering or assembly of God's people would inevitably be broken up and scattered by the inevitability of death, which acted like a black hole, sucking all into its inescapable embrace. The promise here for those who, like Peter, confess Jesus as Christ and Lord is that they are being gathered into an assembly, a church, that will be victorious over death in the end.

The third reason Jesus is able to call Peter 'blessed' is the promise in

---

[14] Jesus has talked before about the special revelation coming generally to all who follow him in 11:25–30 and 13:16–17.

[15] That is not, say, just to Peter's confession, or to Jesus. He may be using the feminine version of 'rock' because the Greek word for 'church' is feminine.

verse 19. The power of the 'keys' Jesus talks about in this verse has sometimes been taken as the 'priestly' authority given to some to confer or
withhold absolution for sins – to declare to someone coming in confession, for example, 'Your sins are forgiven.' But Peter is not set up here as
a priestly figure, or even as any kind of leader with leadership authority
over others – he is merely a representative disciple. So what does Jesus
mean by these 'keys'? One commentary lists thirteen suggested possible
interpretations.[16] But which, if any, is the one Jesus intends us to make?

'Keys' to the kingdom suggests something that provides entry to the
kingdom (as opposed to entry to Hades through the 'gates of Hades' in
verse 18). But we already know a great deal about entry to the kingdom
from what we have seen so far in Matthew's Gospel. Someone like Peter,
for example, has access to the kingdom because they have heard Jesus's
proclamation of the kingdom (4:17) and believed it; they have heard Jesus's
call to follow (4:18; 11:28–30) and they have responded; they have become
a disciple of Jesus and have heard his teaching on what it looks like to
live in the light of the kingdom (chapters 5–7). Through such things, Jesus
has revealed the Father to Peter (compare 11:25–7) and the Father has
revealed the true identity of Jesus (verse 17). Such a person Jesus is able
to call blessed (as here in verse 17), and of such a person Jesus declares
'theirs is the kingdom of heaven' (5:3, 10).

Now, Peter could do all these things Jesus has been doing – proclaiming,
calling, teaching – but he is just a man, with no power or authority to
bring about entry to the kingdom, or to reveal the Father, or to reveal
the true identity of Jesus (which 'flesh and blood' cannot do, verse 17).
This, then, is the kind of authority Jesus is conferring in verse 19. As
Peter does what Jesus has been doing – proclaiming, calling and teaching
– he now has heavenly backing. As with Jesus's ministry, people may be
unresponsive, remaining 'bound' in their sin and under the shadow of
death. But by giving Peter these 'keys', this binding is now declared the
will of heaven. Likewise, some will be responsive, potentially 'loosed' from
sin and from under the shadow of death. This loosing is now declared to
be the will of heaven, and therefore will happen. What is more, as before,
what is true of Peter as representative disciple is also true for those like
Peter, able to make the same confession he made in verse 16.[17]

---

[16] W. D. Davies and Dale C. Allison, Jr., *Matthew 8–18* (London: T&T Clark, 1991),
635–9.

[17] All of which suggests that 'the keys' – as Jesus uses the term here – cover a
broader range of things than is sometimes suggested. They are not restricted to

Jesus then commands the disciples not to tell anyone he is the Messiah (verse 20). The reason for this soon becomes apparent. From verse 22 it will become obvious that not even Peter has a proper understanding of what it means for Jesus to be the Messiah. Understanding this will only come after Jesus's death and resurrection.

SUMMARY AND PURPOSE

Matthew's overall intentions across 13:53–16:20 are to move his readers away from the lack of faith in Jesus's home town (13:53–8) and the false identification made by Herod at the beginning of the section (14:2), to a more solid faith in Jesus and the true identification made by Peter (16:16).

In this section (16:1–20), he wants his readers to dissociate from the sign-seeking of the Pharisees and Sadducees (verses 1–4), horrified by what is in effect a refusal to believe, with corrosive implications. He wants his readers likewise to dissociate from the lack of understanding in the disciples, and their lack of awareness of how dangerous what the Pharisees and Sadducees are teaching is (verses 5–11). Instead, he wants them to join in wholeheartedly with Peter's confession in verse 16 that Jesus is 'the Messiah, the Son of the living God'.

The overall purpose of Matthew's Gospel is to make its readers who aren't disciples of Jesus into disciples of Jesus, and to motivate and equip its readers who are disciples of Jesus to be disciple-makers. Both aspects of this purpose are served here. For those who are already disciples of Jesus, there is further encouragement that many more like Peter will come to join the great assembly Jesus is gathering together to rescue people from death (verse 18). Furthermore, they can be assured that as they go out and multiply Jesus's proclamation of the kingdom, they have his heavenly backing as they do so.

---

church leadership or church discipline, for example. However, they do encompass church discipline, hence the similar language of binding and loosing in 18:18–20.

PART SIX

....

JESUS'S MINISTRY FROM GALILEE TO JERUSALEM

MATTHEW 16:21–20:34

II

Taking Up His Cross

MATTHEW 16:21–20:34

There is no change in location between 16:20 and 16:21, but there is a clear change in geographical focus, as Jesus declares the necessity of going to Jerusalem. Matthew also uses the time marker, 'From that time on . . .' at the start of verse 21, just as he did back in 4:17. As discussed in the Introduction, this time marker is sometimes over-emphasised in treatments of Matthew's structure. It may be best to think of it as highlighting an important transition in the narrative, between sections that are marked out in other ways. Jesus's withdrawal to Galilee in 4:12 marked the transition from John's preaching of the kingdom to Jesus's preaching of the kingdom and the start of his Galilean ministry. Similarly, 16:13–20 was a transitional section, marking the end of Jesus's Galilean ministry, with 16:21 indicating a change in geographical focus towards Jerusalem, and a transition in Jesus's teaching from an emphasis on proclaiming the kingdom to his tribulation and vindication as Son of Man.

1. Taking up his cross part 1 • Matthew 16:21–17:20

Jesus predicts his death

21 From that time on Jesus began to explain to his disciples that he must go to Jerusalem and suffer many things at the hands of the elders, the chief priests and the teachers of the law, and that he must be killed and on the third day be raised to life.

22 Peter took him aside and began to rebuke him. 'Never, Lord!' he said. 'This shall never happen to you!'

23 Jesus turned and said to Peter, 'Get behind me, Satan! You are a stumbling-block to me; you do not have in mind the concerns of God, but merely human concerns.'

24 Then Jesus said to his disciples, 'Whoever wants to be my disciple must deny themselves and take up their cross and follow me. **25** For whoever wants to save their life[e] will lose it, but whoever loses their life for me will find it. **26** What good will it be for someone to gain the whole world, yet forfeit their soul? Or what can anyone give in exchange for their soul? **27** For the Son of Man is going to come in his Father's glory with his angels, and then he will reward each person according to what they have done.

28 'Truly I tell you, some who are standing here will not taste death before they see the Son of Man coming in his kingdom.'

The transfiguration

17 After six days Jesus took with him Peter, James and John the brother of James, and led them up a high mountain by themselves. 2 There he was transfigured before them. His face shone like the sun, and his clothes became as white as the light. 3 Just then there appeared before them Moses and Elijah, talking with Jesus.

4 Peter said to Jesus, 'Lord, it is good for us to be here. If you wish, I will put up three shelters – one for you, one for Moses and one for Elijah.'

5 While he was still speaking, a bright cloud covered them, and a voice from the cloud said, 'This is my Son, whom I love; with him I am well pleased. Listen to him!'

6 When the disciples heard this, they fell face down to the ground, terrified. 7 But Jesus came and touched them. 'Get up,' he said. 'Don't be afraid.' 8 When they looked up, they saw no one except Jesus.

9 As they were coming down the mountain, Jesus instructed them, 'Don't tell anyone what you have seen, until the Son of Man has been raised from the dead.'

10 The disciples asked him, 'Why then do the teachers of the law say that Elijah must come first?'

11 Jesus replied, 'To be sure, Elijah comes and will restore all things. 12 But I tell you, Elijah has already come, and they did not recognise him, but have done to him everything they wished. In the same way the Son of Man is going to suffer at their hands.' 13 Then the disciples understood that he was talking to them about John the Baptist.

Jesus heals a demon-possessed boy

14 When they came to the crowd, a man approached Jesus and knelt before him. 15 'Lord, have mercy on my son,' he said. 'He has seizures and is suffering greatly. He often falls into the fire or into the water. 16 I brought him to your disciples, but they could not heal him.'

17 'You unbelieving and perverse generation,' Jesus replied, 'how long shall I stay with you? How long shall I put up with you? Bring the boy here to me.' 18 Jesus rebuked the demon, and it came out of the boy, and he was healed at that moment.

19 Then the disciples came to Jesus in private and asked, 'Why couldn't we drive it out?'

20 He replied, 'Because you have so little faith. Truly I tell you, if you have faith as small as a mustard seed, you can say to this mountain, "Move from here to there," and it will move. Nothing will be impossible for you.' [21] a

---

e 25 The Greek word means either *life* or *soul*; also in verse 26.

a 21 Some manuscripts include here words similar to Mark 9:29.

The structure of this next part of the Gospel from 16:21 onwards is pretty clear from the three passion-vindication predictions – of which 16:21 is the first, followed by 17:22–3 and 20:17–19. These create a familiar-looking 3x3 structure, shaping the narrative of the journey from Galilee to Jerusalem like this:

First cycle	Second cycle	Third cycle
16:21 First passion-vindication prediction	17:22–3 Second passion-vindication prediction	20:17–19 Third passion-vindication prediction
16:22–8 Exchange with disciples: the Servant pattern spelled out Peter fails to understand	17:24–18:35 Case studies raised by Peter and the other disciples: relating to the world seeking greatness dealing with stumbling (Ends with a parable: the unmerciful servant)	20:20–28 Exchange with disciples: the Servant pattern repeated James and John fail to understand
17:1–20 The Transfiguration and aftermath Listen to him!	19:1–20:16 Case studies raised by others: divorce wealth and riches (Ends with a parable: workers in the vineyard)	20:29–34 A double healing from blindness Follow him!

Table 16

Jesus's declaration is that, as Son of Man, he must suffer and die, but then be vindicated. This is the repeated refrain at the start of each cycle. This is what it will mean for him to truly be the Messiah for Israel, the Son of the living God. This is the pattern: costly suffering, and only then victory.

But the disciples don't like it. This becomes apparent in the exchanges between Jesus and the disciples at either end of the section. In the first (16:22–8), Peter challenges Jesus: surely the Messiah should never have to undergo costly suffering, only victory? In the third (20:20–28), the sons of Zebedee ask for a costless greatness. Jesus says similar things in both places. They must follow him in the path of suffering first, vindication and glory later. The last (now) will be first (later).

As previously, what Jesus is proclaiming and declaring is backed up with miracles and further teaching. At the end of the first cycle (17:1–20), three of the disciples see a foretaste of Jesus in his glory, and Jesus has to step in to heal a boy the other disciples were unable to help. At the end of the third cycle, there is a double healing from blindness that illustrates the principles of following Jesus. In the middle, filling the second cycle, is extensive further teaching. This begins with Jesus teaching in response to issues and questions raised by the disciples and relating to how they will live as a community (17:24–18:35, sometimes known as the 'church discourse'). This is followed by teaching – on divorce and wealth – following questions or issues raised by others (19:1–20:16).

The first passion-vindication prediction (16:21)

This is the first of what are often called 'passion predictions': Jesus's 'passion' being his suffering leading up to and including his execution on a cross in Jerusalem. Jesus does indeed predict this here (verse 21): going to Jerusalem, suffering many things at the hands of the elders (community leaders), chief priests (religious leaders at the Temple) and teachers of the law (educational and intellectual leaders). And then he must die. But of course this is not the end of the story. Jesus makes clear that his death will not be the end of things. On the third day, he will be raised.[1] There is a clear narrative pattern going down through suffering and tribulation and death, but then up into resurrection, life, victory and vindication. This, then, is the first of Jesus's passion-vindication predictions.

Taking up the cross (16:22–8)

What Jesus has just said does not fit Peter's understanding of what it means for Jesus to be Lord and Messiah. Extraordinarily, he rebukes Jesus (verse 22). It is a misplaced understanding of Jesus's greatness.

This sparks off the second major crisis in the mission to Israel. The first crisis was the response to Jesus's proclamation of the nearness of the kingdom, from Matthew 11 up to Peter's confession of Jesus as Messiah in 16:16. The response was mixed, and full of doubts and opposition. The people did not receive him with open arms: even John the Baptist had his doubts, and the disciples have been dim-witted in recognising him. The crisis now is that Peter (representing other disciples) cannot process the idea of a Messiah who will suffer, be humiliated and (apparently)

---

[1] It is very remarkable the number of things that happen on 'the third day' in the Bible! (There are at least four examples in Genesis alone: 22:4; 31:22; 40:20; 42:18.) But what Jesus achieved in his passion-vindication was a restoration and revival of God's people for those who will turn back to him, which is a clear fulfilment of Hosea 6:1–2.

defeated. This is very serious, because it puts Peter on a collision course with the will of God. What he wants opposes the will of God for Jesus, much as Satan opposed Jesus in the temptations back in chapter 4. Hence Jesus's reply in verse 24 to 'Get behind me, Satan!' Peter is a 'stumbling-block' – something that would cause Jesus to divert from the mandate he has taken on. Peter is thinking in worldly terms about leadership and victory: not thinking as God is thinking.

This sets the stage for the third major exhortation in Matthew's Gospel. The first was 'Repent!' (3:3; 4:17), which is what everyone should do given the closeness of the coming kingdom. The second was, from chapter 11, 'Come to me all you who are weary and burdened . . .' (11:28), which was an appeal to those struggling under the shadow of death to align themselves instead with Jesus. This is the third, and it is deeper and more serious: 'Whoever wants to be my disciple must deny themselves and take up their cross and follow me' (verse 24).

As we saw in the discussion on 10:38 above, the disciples would struggle to make much sense of the idea of taking up one's cross (verse 24), especially since Jesus does not spell out the manner of his death until the third passion-vindication prediction in 20:19. But what should be clear (as discussed in the Introduction) is that the exhortation is genuine. Denial, taking up one's cross and following Jesus is not being set up as an impossible demand. The point Jesus wants to make is not that only he can 'take up his cross' while the disciples cannot. It is true that only Jesus can die a curse-bearing death on behalf of others, but that is not the point being made here. Jesus's teaching in 16:21–20:43 is founded on the necessity of his death within his passion-vindication. This is necessary to fulfil his purpose of saving his people from their sins (1:21). Also necessary for salvation is a close identification with Jesus – unashamed, desperate dependence, placing him above all others, as in 10:32–9. Although hard, this is Jesus's expectation in verse 24: that a true disciple gives up every present claim to follow him in the pattern of suffering followed by vindication.[2]

This expectation is expanded and justified in verses 25–6. Jesus repeats the pattern he gave in 10:39 and expands it. As before, there is a simple division of time into the now and the future. There is now: the time in which someone either saves their life or loses it for Jesus's sake (verse

---

[2] As Joe Kapolyo notes, this is a necessary corrective to the 'prosperity gospel' so common across the world. That directly contradicts Jesus's teaching here, by claiming that one can save one's life now, gaining many riches now, without sacrificing life later. Kapolyo, 'Matthew', 1178.

25). At this time, someone may even gain 'the whole world' (verse 26). Then there is later, the future: the time at which someone may lose or find their life (verse 25). To lose it would be to forfeit one's soul (verse 26) – that is, to give up the very thing that gives breath and life. At such a time, there is nothing someone could give in exchange to reclaim their soul (compare Psalm 49:8).

This future is linked by Jesus to the Son of Man coming in his Father's glory with his angels to enact a judgment, rewarding people according to what they have done (verse 27). At the end of the explanation of the parable of the tares in Matthew 13, the Son of Man sent out angels to weed out all causes of sin and evil (13:40–43; also 13:49–50). Here this is described as coming 'in his Father's glory', which links it even more closely to Jesus's mandate as the Son doing the will of his Father. The language of verse 27 also echoes that of Psalm 62:12: 'You reward everyone according to what they have done.'[3]

In verse 28, the future is brought close as Jesus says that some of his disciples will not taste death before they see the Son of Man coming in his kingdom. The full picture of what Jesus is saying about the future will not be complete until the end of the Gospel, but it is worth previewing here, and can be pictured like this:

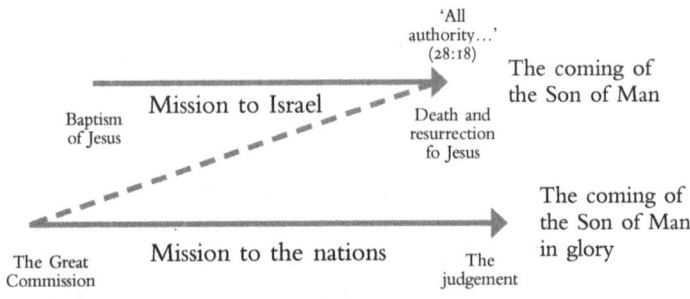

Figure 7

Talking about the coming of the Son of Man as a near event is what Jesus also did in Matthew 10:23. We said back then that Jesus was probably referring to his death and his vindication in the resurrection. The Eleven will see Jesus declare that all authority in heaven and earth has been given to him (28:18). This fits with verse 28 here: it is coming soon. As in the figure above, it is the climax of the mission to Israel (top line).

---

[3] Which is also the verse Paul seems to have in mind in Romans 2:6.

But the coming of the Son of Man also corresponds to another event. We can draw a line from the death and resurrection of Jesus, which ends the mission exclusively to Israel, to the end of the mission to all the nations.[4] This is the 'end of the age', the Parousia, the Second Advent, the end-time Judgment. And, we shall see later in Matthew, that is also called a coming of the Son of Man (unambiguously in 25:31). It is the climax of the mission to the nations (bottom line above). And that fits with verse 27 here.

Like the language of the cross in 10:38 and verse 24 here, understanding all the nuances of Jesus's language about the coming of the Son of Man will not be possible until after his death and resurrection. Here, the imprecision about what exactly Jesus is referring to actually serves his purposes. In the decision about whether to lose or save life now, with its future outcomes in saving and losing life later, Jesus wants to bring the future as close as possible. Judgment is certain and it is soon. The more weight the disciples put on this, the more likely they are to do the right thing in the present.

The transfiguration and aftermath (17:1–20)

In 16:28, Jesus promised that some of the disciples would see his coming as Son of Man before they died – his victory and vindication. (As discussed above, we discover later in Matthew that this victory is won through Jesus's death and resurrection.) Here, three of them get to see a foretaste of that future glory, a glory that prophets like Moses and Elijah longed to see. It is terrifying, and the disciples want to hide from what they see, but it guarantees what Jesus has promised.

Peter, James and John are taken by Jesus up a high mountain by themselves (verse 1). These are three of the first four disciples to be called by Jesus, and they will be taken aside again by Jesus in Gethsemane (26:37). Peter is the disciple who has misunderstood Jesus's greatness at the beginning of this section, and the sons of Zebedee (James and John) will misunderstand it at the end (see Table 16 above).

What they see at the top of the mountain is therefore an important corrective to their misunderstanding. This is the greatness they wanted to see from Jesus – and they see it clearly. But it is a future greatness. This is a glimpse into a future after the darkness of Jesus's suffering and death. We were told by Matthew that Jesus was a light coming

---

[4] Which expands, but does not replace, the mission to Israel.

into the darkness (4:16). But it is a light Matthew is setting in stark contrast to the coming darkness Jesus will face on the cross. There are many detailed points of comparison and contrast between the two accounts. Here, Jesus stands between two great prophets (verse 3). It is blindingly light. Then he will stand between two thieves, and darkness will cover everything. But, as Jesus has already predicted (16:21), after death comes resurrection. This is prefigured here in Jesus's startling appearance. His face shines like the sun, like the faces of the righteous after the judgment in 13:43. Jesus's clothes become dazzlingly white, a colour indicating not just his perfect righteousness but also the victory of perfect righteousness.[5]

The intimacy of the conversation between Jesus, Moses and Elijah (verse 3) is an indication to the disciples that what Jesus has said to them (especially in 16:21) is in close alignment with the Law and the Prophets.

Perhaps predictably, Peter misunderstands (verse 4). He recognises the mountaintop scene as one of glory and victory and is delighted to be a part of it, hence him saying, 'Lord, it is good for us to be here.' This is how he perceives Jesus as Messiah – without any of the dishonour of suffering and death Jesus has spoken about. His offer to build three shelters (literally, tents or tabernacles) may simply be because he is overwhelmed, not knowing what he is saying. Or it may be because the glory is too dazzling for him and needs to be hidden from sight, as was so for the glory of the Lord in the Old Testament Tabernacle. Or, more likely, Peter doesn't want the situation to end. He wants Jesus, Moses and Elijah to stay there. He doesn't want to leave this place, go down the mountain and see Jesus go through what he has said he must go through.

If so, then the voice from the cloud in verse 5 is a thunderous rebuke. What happens is a virtual repeat of 3:17, when the voice was a Fatherly voice commending his Son for taking on the mandate to bring forgiveness of sins to his people. Jesus had indicated his willingness to do this by getting baptised alongside sinners, 'numbered with the transgressors' in fulfilment of Isaiah 53:12. (This was therefore, from the same verse, an indication of his willingness to bear the sin of many.) In verse 5 here, the voice adds a command: 'Listen to him!' This is, of course, generally a good thing for disciples of Jesus to do. But in the context, it makes sense to link the command more specifically to what Jesus has just said in 16:21 and 24–8. They must understand that tribulation and suffering

---

[5] Compare, for example, Revelation 19:14.

come before vindication and victory – both for Jesus and for those who follow after him.

The disciples are terrified by the voice (verse 6). But immediately following this attention-grabbing exhortation comes gentle encouragement from Jesus (verse 7). He touches them and says, 'Get up' – literally, 'Be raised.' He adds, 'Don't be afraid.' The angel will say exactly the same to the women at the empty tomb in chapter 28. When they look up, they see they are alone with Jesus again (verse 8). In other words, a permanent experience of the glory they have witnessed must wait.

Jesus's command to say nothing of the glory they have seen until he has been raised (verse 9) fits with 16:20 and much of what we have said about the comprehensibility of Jesus's teaching in 16:21–8. It will only make full sense after Jesus's passion and vindication. This prompts a further question from the disciples (verse 10). They have perhaps understood that something must happen first before the coming of the Lord in glory. But, in their understanding, this should be the coming of Elijah, as per Malachi 4:5. They have just seen Elijah, but he hasn't come with them or gone ahead of them. Jesus replies that they are right that Elijah comes first (verse 11), but he adds that Elijah has indeed already come (verse 12a). The disciples understand that Jesus is talking about John the Baptist (verse 13). As he answers their question, Jesus draws them back to what remains to happen before they can see any glory: he, as Son of Man, must suffer as John suffered and die as John died (verse 12b).

As they return, a man comes to Jesus and pleads for healing for his son, as many have done before (verses 14–16). The difference this time is that Jesus's disciples have failed to heal the son, despite the authority given to them in 10:1. Jesus's rebuke in verse 17 has echoes of the anger of Moses on his return from the mountain in Exodus 32:19 and the rebuke of Deuteronomy 32:5. After the successful healing (verse 18), it becomes clear that Jesus has been rebuking the disciples for their lack of faith (verses 19–20).

The context helps us understand the severity of Jesus's rebuke. His going up to glory on the mountain (verses 1–13) has raised a further issue about the future. When Jesus is vindicated following his resurrection, the question then is: will the disciples be able to continue Jesus's ministry? The answer implied here is not unless they have sufficient faith; but if they do have faith, they will be able to do everything required of them (verse 20).

Jesus's words in verse 17 are not, then, an uncharacteristic emotional outburst. They are a genuine question: how long will Jesus have to be with his disciples to teach them (through his words and deeds) sufficient faith? In other words, there is plenty more teaching to come for the disciples before the end of the Gospel. (And even then there is a sense that Jesus will not leave them to do the ministry on their own – 28:20.)

SUMMARY AND PURPOSE

As we hear the third major imperative in Matthew's Gospel in 16:24, the focus is tightening on to those who would already be Jesus's disciples. From this section, Matthew's purpose is that the disciples would have a clear understanding that Jesus must suffer and die before his vindication and glory (16:21). Furthermore, they must follow the same pattern, with a faith that connects them both to the suffering and to the future vindication and glory (16:24–8).

The teaching in 16:24–8, the visionary experience at the top of the mountain in 17:1–8, the teaching on the way down the mountain in 17:10–13 and the incident at the foot of the mountain in 17:14–20 all serve to highlight the serious danger to the disciples of not following the path Jesus prescribes, but also the security of the outcome if they do. It is foolish to 'save' one's life only to lose it later. Foolish to fail to listen to the Law or the Prophets; even more, to fail to listen to the Father in the heavens. It is foolish to proceed apart from Jesus and without faith. But what Peter, James and John see on the mountain confirms that for the faithful disciple the outcome is certain.

2. Taking up his cross part 2 • Matthew 17:22–20:16

We are at a point in the Gospel after the moment Jesus has set his sights on Jerusalem (16:21). The wider section is framed around Jesus's three passion-vindication predictions – at 16:21, 17:22–3 and 20:17–19. Three times Jesus strongly asserts the necessity of his suffering and death as well as declaring the certainty of his resurrection. The purpose of the section as a whole seems to be to persuade the disciples, and us as later readers, of the necessity of following in the pattern of suffering followed by vindication. That is, as we shall see in this middle section, the necessity of humbling ourselves, and depending utterly 'like little children' (18:3) for the life only God can provide. Positively, Matthew is showing us the certainty of that life. Negatively, he is showing us the dangers of pushing it aside, or of stumbling on that path – or of causing others to stumble.

This is the central part of the wider section, and by far the longest. After the second passion-vindication prediction (17:22–3), Matthew relates a number of case studies raised by Peter and the other disciples, showcasing Jesus's teaching on how to relate to the world and one another within the church (17:24–18:22). This teaching ends with the parable of the unmerciful servant (18:23–35).

Jesus predicts his death a second time

22 When they came together in Galilee, he said to them, 'The Son of Man is going to be delivered into the hands of men. **23** They will kill him, and on the third day he will be raised to life.' And the disciples were filled with grief.

The temple tax

24 After Jesus and his disciples arrived in Capernaum, the collectors of the two-drachma temple tax came to Peter and asked, 'Doesn't your teacher pay the temple tax?'

25 'Yes, he does,' he replied.

When Peter came into the house, Jesus was the first to speak. 'What do you think, Simon?' he asked. 'From whom do the kings of the earth collect duty and taxes - from their own children or from others?'

26 'From others,' Peter answered.

'Then the children are exempt,' Jesus said to him. **27** 'But so that we may not cause offence, go to the lake and throw out your line. Take the first fish you catch; open its mouth and you will find a four-drachma coin. Take it and give it to them for my tax and yours.'

The greatest in the kingdom of heaven

18 At that time the disciples came to Jesus and asked, 'Who, then, is the greatest in the kingdom of heaven?'

2 He called a little child to him, and placed the child among them. **3** And he said: 'Truly I tell you, unless you change and become like little children, you will never enter the kingdom of heaven. **4** Therefore, whoever takes the lowly position of this child is the greatest in the kingdom of heaven. **5** And whoever welcomes one such child in my name welcomes me.

Causing to stumble

6 'If anyone causes one of these little ones - those who believe in me - to stumble, it would be better for them to have a large millstone hung round their neck and to be drowned in the depths of the sea. **7** Woe to the world because of the things that cause people to stumble! Such things must come, but woe to the person through whom they come! **8** If your hand or your foot causes you to stumble, cut it off and throw it away. It is better for you to enter life maimed or crippled than to have two hands or two feet and be thrown into eternal fire. **9** And if your eye causes you to stumble, gouge it out and throw it away. It is better for you to enter life with one eye than to have two eyes and be thrown into the fire of hell.

The parable of the wandering sheep

10 'See that you do not despise one of these little ones. For I tell you that their angels in heaven always see the face of my Father in heaven. **[11]** a

12 'What do you think? If a man owns a hundred sheep, and one of them wanders away, will he not leave the ninety-nine on the hills and go to look for the one that wandered off? **13** And if he finds it, truly I tell you, he is happier about that one sheep than about the ninety-nine that did not wander off. **14** In the same way your Father in heaven is not willing that any of these little ones should perish.

Dealing with sin in the church

15 'If your brother or sister b sins, c go and point out their fault, just between the two of you. If they listen to you, you have won them over. **16** But if they will not listen, take one or two others along, so that "every matter may be established by the testimony of two or three witnesses." d **17** If they still refuse to listen, tell it to the church; and if they refuse to listen even to the church, treat them as you would a pagan or a tax collector.

18 'Truly I tell you, whatever you bind on earth will be e bound in heaven, and whatever you loose on earth will be e loosed in heaven.

19 'Again, truly I tell you that if two of you on earth agree about anything they ask for, it will be done for them by my Father in heaven. **20** For where two or three gather in my name, there am I with them.'

The parable of the unmerciful servant

21 Then Peter came to Jesus and asked, 'Lord, how many times shall I forgive my brother or sister who sins against me? Up to seven times?'

22 Jesus answered, 'I tell you, not seven times, but seventy-seven times. f

23 'Therefore, the kingdom of heaven is like a king who wanted to settle accounts with his servants. **24** As he began the settlement, a man who owed him ten thousand bags of gold g was brought to him. **25** Since he was not able to pay, the master ordered that he and his wife and his children and all that he had be sold to repay the debt.

26 'At this the servant fell on his knees before him. "Be patient with me," he begged, "and I will pay back everything." **27** The servant's master took pity on him, cancelled the debt and let him go.

28 'But when that servant went out, he found one of his fellow servants who owed him a hundred silver coins. h He grabbed him and began to choke him. "Pay back what you owe me!" he demanded.

29 'His fellow servant fell to his knees and begged him, "Be patient with me, and I will pay it back."

30 'But he refused. Instead, he went off and had the man thrown into prison until he could pay the debt. 31 When the other servants saw what had happened, they were outraged and went and told their master everything that had happened.

32 'Then the master called the servant in. "You wicked servant," he said, "I cancelled all that debt of yours because you begged me to. 33 Shouldn't you have had mercy on your fellow servant just as I had on you?" 34 In anger his master handed him over to the jailers to be tortured, until he should pay back all he owed.

35 'This is how my heavenly Father will treat each of you unless you forgive your brother or sister from your heart.'

---

a 21 Some manuscripts include here words similar to Mark 9:29.
a 11 Some manuscripts include here the words of Luke 19:10.
b 15 The Greek word for *brother or sister* (*adelphos*) refers here to a fellow disciple, whether man or woman; also in verses 21 and 35.
c 15 Some manuscripts *sins against you*
d 16 Deut. 19:15
e 18 Or *will have been*
f 22 Or *seventy times seven*
g 24 Greek *ten thousand talents*; a talent was worth about 20 years of a day labourer's wages.
h 28 Greek *a hundred denarii*; a denarius was the usual daily wage of a day labourer (see 20:2).

The second passion-vindication prediction (17:22–3)

The second passion-vindication prediction says less about those by whom Jesus will suffer: here it is just that he will 'be delivered into the hands of men' (verse 22). But the repetition of the basic pattern of suffering, death and vindication in resurrection makes it emphatic. We also get a different response from the disciples this time: they are 'filled with grief' (verse 23). This indicates extreme distress and more of an acknowledgment that these things will happen to Jesus – even if not understanding of their purpose. (The same phrase is used at 18:31 and 26:22.)

The Temple tax (17:24–7)

This curious episode, unique to Matthew, has two parts to it. First, they arrive in Capernaum and the collectors of the 'two-drachma' tax ask Peter a question, and Peter gives an answer (verses 24–5a). Then, when they enter 'the house' (the same place as 13:1, 36), Jesus asks a question, Peter answers, and then then Jesus draws out some implications.

The 'two-drachma' tax was probably the Temple tax.[6] This was a tax

---

6 Davies and Allison, *Matthew 8–18*, 738–41.

levied annually on all Jewish males over the age of twenty to fund the daily sacrifice in the Temple, apparently as prescribed in Exodus 30:11–16, although, interestingly, it is not clear there that it was to be an annual event. What is clear in Exodus 30 is that the money a man gives in the event of a census is described as 'a ransom for his life' (Exodus 30:12) and as 'atonement money' (Exodus 30:16).

So will Jesus pay the Temple tax, the 'atonement money', the tax collectors ask Peter, his chief disciple. Peter thinks, yes (verse 25a): Jesus is a Jewish male over the age of twenty who depends on the sacrifices of the Temple for his life just like any other Jewish male over the age of twenty.

But are Peter and Jesus obligated to pay the tax? The implied answer this time is no, they are not. Jesus asks a question about kings and taxes (verse 25b). If a king is taxing his subjects, would he expect his own children to pay? A modern-day western answer might be 'Yes'. But in the pre-modern world (and elsewhere) the answer, as Peter knows, was definitely 'No' (verse 26).[7] Jesus says, 'Then the children are exempt' – applying the principle to the Temple tax. Jesus seems to be saying that Peter is in such a privileged position as a son or child of the kingdom (with Jesus) that he shouldn't have to pay the Temple tax.

It could be that Jesus, as Richard Bauckham argues, is saying that giving to the Temple should be voluntary, not obligatory, for those who are 'sons of the kingdom' – that is, as in 8:12, for all Israelites.[8] But the sons of the kingdom in 8:12 turn out not to be true sons of the kingdom, and are excluded. Those truly of the kingdom are Jesus's disciples, as in 5:3, 10; 13:11, 38, 43; 16:19. So it could be that by placing this episode here, Matthew wants to make a deeper theological point. What is it that makes a representative disciple like Peter exempt from the Temple tax? It may be that Matthew wants to suggest that for someone like Peter, something has replaced the Temple sacrifice and someone else pays the atonement money to ransom his life. We discover who this is later, at the end of this wider section, in Matthew 20:28.

Either way, Jesus commends paying the tax: not out of obligation, but so they 'may not cause offence' (verse 27). The word Jesus uses for 'offence' here is the same one he is about to use for stumbling or going astray in

---

[7] In Joe Kapolyo's village, one of the kinds of taxes imposed was an annual tax paid to the local chief's palace. These, he notes, 'were not paid by the chief's sons, but by those who were governed by the chief'. Kapolyo, 'Matthew', 1171.

[8] Richard Bauckham, 'The Coin in the Fish's Mouth', in *The Miracles of Jesus*, ed. David Wenham and Craig L. Blomberg, Gospel Perspectives 6 (Sheffield: JSOT Press, 1987), 219–52.

18:6–9. That is, if they were to fail to pay the tax, the perceived wrong-doing (even if unfair) might prove to be a stumbling block for someone: an obstacle to hearing the message of the kingdom and becoming a child of the kingdom. We can apply the same principle to other cultural expectations that are not wrong in themselves. On the path of the cross, following the pattern of Jesus, this is how his disciples are expected to behave towards the wider world: doing everything they can to avoid someone having an excuse to reject the message of the kingdom.

The miracle that Jesus then describes in the rest of verse 27 may seem extraordinary to us. It was perhaps not so surprising as we might think to find a coin in a fish's mouth – if coins were being used as fishing lures, for example. But it was certainly extraordinary that the very first fish would contain exactly the right amount. Like the other miracles in Matthew, this is a sign – in this case, for Peter – that Jesus remains great and powerful, despite his gentleness in not giving offence. Also, taxes are expensive and this is possibly a sign that God is more than able to provide whatever is needed for Jesus's disciples to follow his example. The implied promise is not that God will always pay our taxes for us! Nonetheless, we can trust him to provide whatever is needed in a situation to do the right thing – the right thing here being not causing offence.

The greatest in the kingdom (18:1–14)

Matthew began this wider section of the Gospel with Peter questioning how Jesus's suffering and death could be compatible with his greatness as Messiah and Son of the living God (16:22). Now the question becomes more general. The disciples ask explicitly, 'Who, then, is the greatest in the kingdom of heaven?' (18:1). This topic of who is greatest, or who is first, or to whom the kingdom belongs, will continue to be addressed in 19:13–30, 20:1–16 and 20:20–28.

Jesus's answer is: those like children are greatest in the kingdom. Indeed, it is stronger than this: being like a child is a necessary condition for entry into the kingdom (18:3). If people are not 'like little children', then they need to become so. That is, they need to start afresh – with nothing.[9] And if they do, they will be considered greatest in the kingdom of heaven (18:4).[10]

---

[9] Similar to the idea of being born again, from above or newly in John 3:7 and 1 Peter 1:3.

[10] That is, someone who is childlike now and apparently not great at all is – from

By 'like little children', Jesus is not talking about innocence or simplicity or sinlessness.[11] Probably the main thing Jesus is focusing on is a child's dependence on others: that without help, children do not survive. That was especially so in the first century, of course, but even today, children are dependent: they have nothing of their own; they are given everything. In the pre-modern world, children were also not held in high esteem. They had the lowest social status.

Jesus is beginning to show us more about what it means to be on the way of the cross. It means being utterly humbled and dependent, like a child. Not 'great' in a worldly sense at all.

Jesus now makes three important statements about the true disciple who is like a child – or, as he goes on to say 'one of these little ones' (verse 6), perhaps referring to the child he has placed in their midst. The first is that the one who welcomes one such child in his name welcomes him. This builds on what he said back in 10:40–42. Welcoming a true follower of Jesus 'in [his] name' (that is, welcoming them not merely as a person but a person identified as a follower of Jesus) is equivalent to welcoming Jesus. (Jesus will expand on this idea in 25:31–46.)

The second is the seriousness of causing a 'little one' to stumble (18:6). Here, a 'little one' is a childlike disciple who believes in Jesus even if they are not a child. To cause them to stumble is to cause them to sin or renounce their faith so badly that their kingdom entry is left in question. The millstone Jesus is talking about is literally a 'donkey-stone', one so large that it took a donkey to move it. The warning is expanded in 18:7. Here, a 'woe' expresses not just sadness or regret about the things that cause stumbling, but a desire to see such wrongdoing judged and dealt with. Things that cause stumbling will inevitably happen in the time of difficulty and tribulation before the end of all things, but they will not go unjudged.

Here we see a distinction between Jesus's gentle compassion towards those struggling with sin (e.g., in 9:36) and a severe anger towards those (leaders, teachers or others) who cause his disciples to struggle or stumble.

Jesus expands the warning in an aside. He has just taught about the dangers of causing others to stumble; now he talks about the dangers of stumbling full stop. In other words, the disciples need to be aware of the seriousness of causes of stumbling that are not just 'in the world' or external to them. Jesus is talking about stumbling in the path of the cross

---

the perspective of the kingdom – actually among the greatest of people.
[11] Davies and Allison, *Matthew 8–18*, 757.

to the path of the self – which will involve individual sins but is bigger and more serious than simply sinning. And it is worth any cost, says Jesus, to avoid falling off that path. As he said in the Sermon on the Mount (5:29–30), causes of sin need to be dealt with before they wreak havoc.

He then returns to the issue of welcoming and caring for other 'children' or 'little ones'. The third statement Jesus makes about disciples as 'little ones' is a warning not to despise them (18:10). What Jesus is referring to when he says 'their angels in heaven always see the face of my Father in heaven' has generated a good deal of discussion and speculation.[12] But the point is clear. Every single 'little one' is known to their Father and valued by him, their identity presented before him in heaven.

Jesus explains the principle we should apply with a short parable (18:12–14). The one sheep who wanders weighs more heavily on the mind of the shepherd than the ninety-nine who don't. Bringing this sheep back to safety is a moment of great happiness. He has been happy that the ninety-nine have not wandered off and have been safe, but is even more happy that this one is restored.

In other words, everyone in the community of disciples counts and is valuable. No one should be allowed to fall between the gaps. Working to restore someone who has wandered is always worthwhile.

When someone sins against you (18:15–20)

So far, disciples who are 'like little children' or 'little ones' have been held up as valuable representatives of Jesus, to be protected from stumbling. Jesus has just been encouraging the restoration of a 'little one' – a disciple – who has wandered. He now teaches more on how to do this in the case of a disciple who has sinned.

The material from 8:15 is structured around a long sequence of ifs – no fewer than eight of them in the original Greek. Up to verse 17, this is a simple code of instruction: if the situation is this, then do this. Then in verses 18 and 19 the 'ifs' play a different role, solemnly reassuring the disciples that they have divine backing if they do what Jesus says.

Jesus teaches his disciples to handle the situation very carefully. On the one hand, the sin does need to be addressed and the one who sinned restored. On the other hand, out of concern for the person who sinned, they are to give maximum opportunity for a response. If a response is not forthcoming, they are to gradually draw in more and more people

---

[12] Davies and Allison, *Matthew 8–18*, 770–72.

to call them to do so. Out of concern for the church community, they should at each stage do their best to contain the effect of the sin by as few people as possible. It is only brought before the whole church (the whole local assembly of disciples, that is) if other attempts have failed. This will no doubt be painful for everyone, but they are not to allow the sin to go undealt with.[13]

The ultimate sanction here is to treat the one who has sinned as 'a pagan or tax collector'. This is simply to treat them as an outsider – not part of the assembly or family. For that is what someone stubbornly unremorseful and unchanging in sin has effectively declared themselves to be. But even that need not be the end of the story. Like any outsider, they can then come (back) into to church through faith in Jesus, seeking forgiveness and reconciliation.

One of the reasons why many church families are slow or weak in exercising discipline is that they don't feel they have the right or authority, especially if people are aware of their own failings. So Jesus assures the disciples here that if they carefully put his teaching into practice, they have divine backing. Matthew 18:18 is almost identical to 16:19. In 16:19 Jesus was saying that if Peter does what he has been doing – proclaiming, calling and teaching – he has heavenly backing, binding some in sin if they fail to respond; loosing others if they do. Here in Matthew 18, if the disciples do as Jesus teaches when it comes to discipline, then what they decide likewise has heavenly backing. What they collectively decide, on the basis of Jesus's teaching, will be honoured by the Father (18:19). It will be effectively as if Jesus were there himself, issuing the decision (18:20).

How many times? (18:21–35)

In the previous verses (18:15–20), Jesus has taught what should happen when someone is challenged about a sin but doesn't listen or respond. If they do respond, Jesus says, 'You have won them over' (18:15). But how often can this happen? Should it happen indefinitely, over and over again?

---

[13] The pattern of responses in 18:15–17 works because it's implied that the sin is not at first publicly known; it could be known to just the sinner and one other, for example. The best outcome is then to engage with the sinner privately, and if they listen, the damage to the wider church family has been kept to a minimum. As Don Carson notes, it doesn't make sense to apply the same principle to a publicly known sin; such sins require a public response. Still less to a public debate or disagreement. D. A. Carson, 'Editorial: On Abusing Matthew 18', *Themelios* 36, no. 1 (2011): 1–3.

This could be especially hard for someone sinned against. Hence Peter's question in 18:21, 'Lord, how many times shall I forgive my brother or sister who sins against me?'

Peter's own suggestion is, 'Up to seven times?' Yet Jesus's answer is not seven times but seventy-seven times (18:22). It is unlikely Jesus is suggesting even seventy-seven times (or seventy times seven times, for that matter) as a limit. It is more likely that this is just a way of saying that our capacity for forgiveness should be unbounded. This is what Jesus has already taught in the Sermon on the Mount (6:12, 14–15).

To explain his answer, Jesus tells a parable (18:23–35). The parable allows Jesus to tell a story that is sufficiently similar to a situation where someone is sinned against and fails to forgive, but where the failure is very obviously wrong and deserving of punishment. He can then return to his answer and repeat it.

The story is simple. A servant with an unimaginably huge debt with his master has it cancelled (18:23–7). The word for 'cancelled' is the same word as 'forgive' in 18:21. A 'bag of gold', as the NIV has it, was a 'talent' and the largest monetary unit of the day. Ten thousand was the largest number people would use day by day in the ancient world. So Jesus is talking about the largest sum of money one can imagine. This same man then refuses to forgive a tiny debt in a parallel situation (18:28–30). We instinctively feel this is wrong, and agree with the outrage of the other servants (18:31). The master spells it out: the man was forgiven a debt, so, 'Shouldn't you have had mercy on your fellow servant just as I had on you?' Again, instinctively we agree, but it is worth pausing here to consider why. Certainly, the man is not imitating the generosity shown to him. Why, though, is this so wrong? The most serious thing going on here is that the man is effectively saying to his master, 'If I were you, I wouldn't have done it – you were a fool to forgive me.' That is, when a forgiven person fails to forgive, it is a slander (or, in this case, a blasphemy) against the one who forgave them.

Because of how Jesus has set up and told the story, the consequences for the unforgiving servant in 18:34 seem reasonable and just. Hence Jesus exposes the seriousness of not forgiving a brother or sister from the heart (18:35).

Two further case studies and a parable (19:1–20:16)

Matthew now relates two further case studies, this time raised by those who are not his disciples. The first is raised by some Pharisees as a test, and concerns the question of divorce (19:1–12). The second is raised by people bringing children to Jesus and a man asking about obtaining eternal life (19:13–30). This is an opportunity for Jesus to teach about kingdom entry, poverty and wealth. His teaching ends with the parable of the workers in the vineyard (20:1–16).

Divorce

19 When Jesus had finished saying these things, he left Galilee and went into the region of Judea to the other side of the Jordan. **2** Large crowds followed him, and he healed them there.

3 Some Pharisees came to him to test him. They asked, 'Is it lawful for a man to divorce his wife for any and every reason?'

4 'Haven't you read,' he replied, 'that at the beginning the Creator "made them male and female,"**a** **5** and said, "For this reason a man will leave his father and mother and be united to his wife, and the two will become one flesh"**b**? **6** So they are no longer two, but one flesh. Therefore what God has joined together, let no one separate.'

7 'Why then,' they asked, 'did Moses command that a man give his wife a certificate of divorce and send her away?'

8 Jesus replied, 'Moses permitted you to divorce your wives because your hearts were hard. But it was not this way from the beginning. **9** I tell you that anyone who divorces his wife, except for sexual immorality, and marries another woman commits adultery.'

10 The disciples said to him, 'If this is the situation between a husband and wife, it is better not to marry.'

11 Jesus replied, 'Not everyone can accept this word, but only those to whom it has been given. **12** For there are eunuchs who were born that way, and there are eunuchs who have been made eunuchs by others – and there are those who choose to live like eunuchs for the sake of the kingdom of heaven. The one who can accept this should accept it.'

The little children and Jesus

13 Then people brought little children to Jesus for him to place his hands on them and pray for them. But the disciples rebuked them.

14 Jesus said, 'Let the little children come to me, and do not hinder them, for the kingdom of heaven belongs to such as these.' **15** When he had placed his hands on them, he went on from there.

The rich and the kingdom of God

16 Just then a man came up to Jesus and asked, 'Teacher, what good thing must I do to get eternal life?'

17 'Why do you ask me about what is good?' Jesus replied. 'There is only One who is good. If you want to enter life, keep the commandments.'

18 'Which ones?' he enquired.

Jesus replied, ' "You shall not murder, you shall not commit adultery, you shall not steal, you shall not give false testimony, 19 honour your father and mother,"**c** and "love your neighbour as yourself."**d'**

20 'All these I have kept,' the young man said. 'What do I still lack?'

21 Jesus answered, 'If you want to be perfect, go, sell your possessions and give to the poor, and you will have treasure in heaven. Then come, follow me.'

22 When the young man heard this, he went away sad, because he had great wealth.

23 Then Jesus said to his disciples, 'Truly I tell you, it is hard for someone who is rich to enter the kingdom of heaven. 24 Again I tell you, it is easier for a camel to go through the eye of a needle than for someone who is rich to enter the kingdom of God.'

25 When the disciples heard this, they were greatly astonished and asked, 'Who then can be saved?'

26 Jesus looked at them and said, 'With man this is impossible, but with God all things are possible.'

27 Peter answered him, 'We have left everything to follow you! What then will there be for us?'

28 Jesus said to them, 'Truly I tell you, at the renewal of all things, when the Son of Man sits on his glorious throne, you who have followed me will also sit on twelve thrones, judging the twelve tribes of Israel. 29 And everyone who has left houses or brothers or sisters or father or mother or wife**e** or children or fields for my sake will receive a hundred times as much and will inherit eternal life. 30 But many who are first will be last, and many who are last will be first.

The parable of the workers in the vineyard

20 'For the kingdom of heaven is like a landowner who went out early in the morning to hire workers for his vineyard. 2 He agreed to pay them a denarius**a** for the day and sent them into his vineyard.

3 'About nine in the morning he went out and saw others standing in the market-place doing nothing. 4 He told them, "You also go and work in my vineyard, and I will pay you whatever is right." 5 So they went.

'He went out again about noon and about three in the afternoon and did the same thing. 6 About five in the afternoon he went out and found still others standing around. He asked them, "Why have you been standing here all day long doing nothing?"

7 ' "Because no one has hired us," they answered.

'He said to them, "You also go and work in my vineyard."

8 'When evening came, the owner of the vineyard said to his foreman, "Call the workers and pay them their wages, beginning with the last ones hired and going on to the first."

9 'The workers who were hired about five in the afternoon came and each received a denarius. 10 So when those came who were hired first, they expected to receive more. But each one of them also received a denarius.

11 When they received it, they began to grumble against the landowner. 12 "These who were hired last worked only one hour," they said, "and you have made them equal to us who have borne the burden of the work and the heat of the day."

13 'But he answered one of them, "I am not being unfair to you, friend. Didn't you agree to work for a denarius? 14 Take your pay and go. I want to give the one who was hired last the same as I gave you. 15 Don't I have the right to do what I want with my own

money? Or are you envious because I am generous?"

16 'So the last will be first, and the first will be last.'

---

a 4 Gen. 1:27
b 5 Gen. 2:24
c 19 Exodus 20:12-16; Deut. 5:16-20
d 19 Lev. 19:18
e 29 Some manuscripts do not have *or wife*.
a 2 A denarius was the usual daily wage of a day labourer.

The Pharisees and divorce (19:1–12)

In 17:24–18:35, Jesus has been teaching on a number of topics raised by his own disciples. Matthew ends this with the phrase, 'When Jesus had finished saying these things . . .' (19:1). What he has just said then joins the other long sections of teaching Jesus has given his disciples, in Matthew 5–7, 10 and 13.

In 19:2–20:16, he will teach on and address a number of topics raised by others. The first of these is a question brought by some Pharisees to test him. Is it lawful for a man to divorce his wife 'for any and every reason' (19:3)? This question may have been prompted by a debate at that time between different schools of rabbis, some of whom were teaching that Deuteronomy 24:1 allowed a man to divorce for any reason.[14] The test was perhaps to force Jesus to take sides in this debate – allowing these Pharisees to dismiss him if he showed himself on the side they disagreed with.

Jesus surprises them by giving an answer no one else was giving at

---

[14] David Instone-Brewer argues that the phrase 'any matter' in 19:3 ('any and every reason' in the NIV) is what distinguished the school of (Rabbi) Hillel from the school of (Rabbi) Shammai in the first-century debates about the interpretation of the phrase 'something indecent' in Deuteronomy 24:1, as recorded in the Mishnah, *m. Git.* 9.10. David Instone-Brewer, *Divorce and Remarriage in the Bible: The Social and Literary Context* (Grand Rapids: Eerdmans, 2002), 134–5.

the time, which was essentially, 'No.'[15] Quoting Genesis 1:27 and 2:24, he argues that men and women are created so in order to come together in marriage as one flesh and not be separated (19:4–6).

The Pharisees' response is to ask why, then, did Moses seemingly allow separation of the 'one flesh' union through the issuing of a certificate of divorce (as in Deuteronomy 24:1).

Jesus's response is to say this was a concession because of their hardness of heart (19:8). Case law like Deuteronomy 24:1–4 is there to limit the damage from messy situations like marriage breakdown and shouldn't be taken as a first-best prescription. Indeed, except in extreme circumstances, divorce is illegitimate and a further union is in fact adulterous (19:9; there is more on the exception clause below).

So when the Pharisees test Jesus about the law, they are tested by the Law – and shown to have hard, adulterous hearts. However, the disciples are also incredulous. If marriage is as permanent as Jesus suggests, surely it is better not to marry (19:10)!

We might think that in his response in 19:11 Jesus is saying not everyone can receive what he has said in 19:9 about illegitimate divorce and adultery – which is indeed what the disciples are struggling to accept. But it makes better sense to take it that he is responding to what the disciples have just said, which was, 'Well, better not get married!' Jesus says: but not everyone will be able to accept not getting married. There are various reasons why people might not get married and never express their sexuality – why they might be 'eunuchs', in other words. Some might choose this for the sake of the kingdom. But not everyone. Only those who can accept it should do it.

Who will enter the kingdom? (19:13–30)

Matthew takes us back to the running theme of being like a child, begun at 18:2. This time, people are bringing children to him (19:13). He places his hands on them and prays for them, which we may take as an act of conferring blessing on them. The disciples seem to have learned little from what Jesus taught in 18:5 and do not welcome the children. Jesus corrects them and instructs the disciples not to hinder the children coming to him, 'for the kingdom of heaven belongs to such as these' (19:14).

We should be expecting that the children are being used by Jesus as

---

[15] Although note the exception in 5:32 and here in 19:9. There is more on this below.

before to represent the kind of person who will be great in the kingdom of heaven (as in 18:3–4). What this episode adds is that childlikeness is linked is coming to Jesus (as in 11:28). A radical dependency on Jesus. The children are coming to Jesus 'empty handed' and receiving his blessing, and they represent what anyone must do to enter the kingdom of heaven. (We should note that the children are also, however, not merely a picture. In 18:1–4, the exhortation was to become 'like little children'. Here, the blessing is conferred on those who actually are children. Jesus receives and blesses them in verse 13 quite apart from any lesson he wishes the disciples and others to learn.)

This episode sets up the one that follows. There is a deliberate contrast with the man in 19:16–22. In their poverty, the children are rich. Appearances are deceptive: the 'last' are 'first', and enter the kingdom. The man who approaches Jesus in 19:16 is seeking eternal life (linked by Jesus to the kingdom in 19:23–4). In 19:22 we learn that he is very wealthy. But he walks away, with no hope of the kingdom. The 'first' will be 'last'.

The man addresses Jesus as 'Teacher' and recognises him as someone who, as a teacher of the kingdom, might give instruction on obtaining eternal life (19:16). But he seems to see in Jesus no more than this. He asks, 'What good thing must I do?' In his response, Jesus doesn't pick out the 'what must I do?' element of the question (as in much contemporary teaching of this passage). Instead, he focuses on the man asking, 'What *good* thing must I do?' Jesus begins his response with a counter-question: 'Why do you ask me about what is good?' (19:17).

This is at first glance quite puzzling! It's helpful to remember that in the background to Jesus's response is the pathway to blessing laid out in the Law, and in the book of Deuteronomy in particular. This has as its foundation the Shema: 'the Lord our God, the Lord is one' (Deuteronomy 6:4). From this follows the commandment, 'Love the Lord your God with all your heart and with all your soul and with all your strength' (Deuteronomy 6:5). Such a person will then listen to what the Lord has said and have his commandments on their hearts (Deuteronomy 6:6). On this pathway lies life and blessing (Deuteronomy 6:10–11; that is, 'it will go well' for them: Deuteronomy 5:16, 29, 31, 33; 6:2, 3, 18; 8:1; 11:8–9).

So when Jesus responds to the man, the emphasis is, 'Why do you ask me what is good?' (19:17). It has the sense, 'Why are you asking me, when you already know what the answer is from the only One who is good?' (that is, from the Lord in Deuteronomy 6, for example). Jesus then gives the man a list of commandments he should have on his heart (19:18–19).[16] These he can claim to have kept, at least more or less (19:20).

Despite the claimed obedience, it seems then man still has no confidence of life or blessing, so he asks, 'What do I still lack?' The NIV begins Jesus's answer, 'If you want to be perfect . . .' (19:21) But 'perfect' is a poor and misleading translation of the Greek word *teleios* in this verse. An English word such as 'complete' would work better. Or, as the man's question also suggests, something like, 'If you want to make up what is lacking [in your love of God] . . .' captures what Jesus is saying more accurately. If the man wants to make up what is lacking in his love of God, and feel secure on the pathway to eternal life, then he should sell his possessions, give the proceeds to the poor and then follow Jesus (19:21).

What he has taught before, Jesus is now applying to this particular man in this particular situation. Jesus taught in the Sermon on the Mount not to store treasures on earth but in heaven (6:19–20) and made it clear in that 'You cannot serve both God and Money' (6:24). The command in 19:21 here is a version of the call we had back in 16:24: 'Whoever wants to be my disciple must deny themselves and take up their cross and follow me.' Jesus has just made it more specific for this man. For this man, denying himself will mean giving up all his riches. Sadly, this is too much for the man, the cost is too great, and he goes away.

To his disciples, Jesus then states the basic principle here, emphasising that even the most apparently eligible people cannot enter the kingdom if they don't 'lose' their lives now to follow Jesus (19:23–4). By 'someone who is rich', Jesus is especially thinking of someone wanting to 'save their life' now for gain now, as in 16:25–6. For such a person to enter the kingdom is as hard as a camel going through the eye of a needle. Which is to say: it's impossible.

But the disciples are still deceived by appearances. If even such people cannot enter the kingdom, 'Who then can be saved?' (19:25). Jesus's answer points us again to the grace of God. Salvation and life, otherwise impossible, is only possible through God as he makes them possible through Jesus (19:26). What is impossible for fallen humans, however wealthy and outwardly moral, and what proved impossible for God's people in the past,

---

[16] As a list of the Ten Commandments in Exodus 20 or Deuteronomy 5, this is incomplete, and also includes the command, 'Love your neighbour as yourself' from Leviticus 19. As often noted, it doesn't explicitly include the commandment not to covet. Given the man's reluctance to give up his wealth in 19:22, this could have been another way to show what was lacking in his devotion to God. But Jesus takes a different line in 19:21.

is now made possible. But only through Jesus. What is more, following Jesus on the path of the cross is possible only through him who can bring us to stop depending on ourselves and depend entirely on Jesus. But to be a part of this does mean rich people losing their lives for Jesus (16:25).

Jesus then encourages the disciples by repeating the promise he has already made. They have endured many costs already: costs in terms of family relationships, costs in terms of land and possessions. But those who 'lose' their lives now in following him will receive many blessings (19:29).

It should be clear: don't envy those who are 'first', because they will be 'last'. Make sure you are 'last', so you will be 'first'.

WHAT HOPE FOR THE RICH?

An important application area in this section is how much to generalise 19:21. Should all disciples of Jesus give away everything to follow Jesus, as Peter and the others did at the time (19:27–9)?

We can say for sure that all disciples should 'lose' their lives (16:24–6). But what we have confirmed in the rest of the New Testament and in early Christian history is that for rich and wealthy people who deny themselves to follow Jesus, there is more than one way to lose one's life, outside the particular circumstances of 19:16–30. This is not to water down the force of what Jesus says. Selling everything to become an itinerant evangelist, for example, remains for some an excellent response to the call of 16:24. But as disciples began to be made across the Mediterranean world, forming local churches in many towns and cities, richer disciples had a role to play in providing places to meet (e.g., Acts 16:40), supporting those who led and taught (e.g., Galatians 6:6; 1 Timothy 5:17) and funding wider mission (Romans 15:24). In this light, the radical edge of 19:21 and 19:23–4 here can be reconciled with Paul's teaching in, for example, 1 Timothy 6:17–19.[17]

'CHOOSE LIFE' – MATTHEW 19 COMPARED TO DEUTERONOMY

We can see from the exchanges in Matthew 19 that 16:24 is the fulfilment of the call to life in the book of Deuteronomy. This is especially

---

[17] But to say that some disciples might be rich enough to help others and support ministry is by no means to support the 'prosperity gospel', of course. It is profoundly contrary to Jesus's teaching to claim that 'losing one's life' now is a means of investing for an earthly reward. The reward is emphatically 'in the heavens' (19:21) and in the future.

inasmuch as it builds on the call to come to Jesus in 11:28–30. The call to life in the book of Deuteronomy proved too difficult for God's people, as Moses knew it would. Their longing for gods other than the One God caused their love for him to fade, for his word to be neglected and for wickedness to overtake obedient love for God and one another. The consequence was covenant curses, and exile for any survivors. The call to life was not explicitly a call to find eternal life, but the inability of the people to love and obey denied them any kind of blessing.

The call to come to Jesus (11:28–30) and to deny oneself, take up one's cross and follow him (16:24) is in continuity with the call to life in Deuteronomy, and yet also radically different. It is in continuity because it remains a call to recognise and respond in love to the One true God with all one's heart, soul and strength (which remains the greatest commandment, as Jesus himself will confirm in 22:37–8). Jesus's identity, revealed through everything he has been saying and doing, falls clearly within the bounds of the identity of the One true God already revealed to Israel. Coming to him (in worship, 2:2, 8, 11; 8:2; 9:18; 14:33; 15:25; 20:20; 28:9, 17) is to come to the One true God. The difference now is that Jesus is a man, the Son of Man glimpsed in Daniel's vision, who can lead those who identify with him and follow him through the tribulation of life under the shadow of death to the vindication of eternal life in the kingdom. He leads as God's anointed King, the Messiah. His people and followers share in his victory and spoils, which are the spoils of life and forgiveness, won through giving himself as a ransom (20:28) and dying as a curse-bearer (as we shall see below, 27:32–8, 45–54). As he leads, he teaches; his followers show themselves his disciples as they hear what he says and put it into practice (5:19; 7:24–7). These are the things that make what was impossible for God's people in the past now possible (compare 19:26). Having said all this, a choice still has to be made. It remains necessary to 'lose' one's life by following Jesus now (16:24–6).

The last will be first (20:1–16)

Matthew 19 ended with the statement, 'Many who are first will be last, and many who are last will be first' (19:30). What has become known as 'the parable of the workers in the vineyard' (20:1–16) ends with the same claim, but in reverse order: 'So the last will be first, and the first will be last' (20:16). This means we can expect the parable in between to be illustrating, explaining or reflecting upon this claim in relation to what has just happened in the previous chapter, especially Jesus's interaction with the children in 19:13–15, the wealthy man in 19:16–22 and then with his disciples in 19:23–30.

For the disciples, the puzzle was that children (and those like them) – that is, those with the lowest status in society – and those who have 'left everything' (19:27, 29) are associated by Jesus with the kingdom and the inheritance of eternal life (19:14, 28–9). This contrasts with someone who appears much more eligible, both morally (19:20) and socioeconomically (19:22), who walks away from Jesus's offer of treasure in heaven (19:16–22). Jesus then says that those like this man cannot enter the kingdom (19:23–4).

As he did in the earlier parable in this section (18:23–35), Jesus takes the disciples into a parallel narrative setting to show the rightness and justice of what he has been saying and teaching. As in Matthew 13, when Jesus begins, 'The kingdom of heaven is like . . .', he is introducing a story that will uncover some of the secrets of the kingdom (rather than giving a complete picture of what the kingdom will be like). The setting in the story is a day in a vineyard, and the characters are a landowner and a variety of vineyard workers (20:1). The workers are distinguished by the time they start working. Those who start earlier work longer. Those who start at 'about five in the afternoon' (20:6; literally, 'the eleventh [hour]') work for just one hour (20:11). All the workers at the end of the day are paid the same one denarius (20:9–10).[18] To those hired first, this seems unjust (20:11–12), and they seem almost at the point of walking away in disgust. But the landowner reminds them that they agreed to the one denarius fee (20:2, 13). They therefore shouldn't be concerned with what the other workers receive. If they are, it shows they are envious about the landowner's generosity to others rather than considering the justice of their own pay.[19]

Jesus's offer is the same to everyone: kingdom entry and eternal life to anyone who comes to him and commits wholly to him, losing and leaving things behind to follow him. Once again, Jesus's identity falls within the bounds of the identity of the One true God, the 'landowner' of the universe, who is free to distribute what is his as he wishes (as in 20:15). The offer is given to rich and poor, old and young, relatively good and downright wicked. But the danger for those who think of themselves as 'first' in the order of things (e.g., the rich or the relatively good) end up

---

[18] This has implications for how we think about differential 'rewards' for those who enter the kingdom. See the note on 'rewards' below.

[19] Literally, their 'eye is evil' – which also helps to explain the imagery in 6:23.

being 'last' because they think they deserve privileged treatment or at least deserve more than others (e.g., the poor or those who have been wicked).

We might wonder at first how the man in 19:16–22 (or other rich people like him) corresponds to those hired first in the parable who end up grumbling against the landowner. After all, unlike those in the parable, the man says nothing about the injustice of anyone else receiving eternal life. He seems to walk away simply because he doesn't want to lose his wealth. But it may be that in the parable, Jesus is exposing his true motivation for walking away. To give away his wealth would be to deny that as a rich man he was better than others – more entitled, in his own eyes, to eternal life than those with nothing. Giving this up is what he was not prepared to do.

SUMMARY AND PURPOSE

Life as a disciple, following Jesus on the path of the cross, is not straight-forward. There are external expectations to negotiate. There is pride to deal with and stumbling blocks to avoid. Within the community of disciples, there is sin to deal with and forgiveness to give. In difficult and sensitive areas of life, like those relating to marriage and wealth, the call is to live a life that sharply challenges the attitudes of the surrounding world.

The overall purpose of Matthew's Gospel is to make its readers who aren't disciples of Jesus into disciples of Jesus, and to motivate and equip its readers who are disciples of Jesus to be disciple-makers. There are some things in this section that might attract someone who is not yet a disciple. Disciples are 'children of the King' (17:26). The parables in the section show the care of the Father (18:12–14), and God through Jesus generous in forgiveness (18:21–35) and generous in the provision of eternal life (20:1–16). This last parable follows an extraordinary promise from Jesus (19:29–30). But the main purpose of these and the rest of Jesus's teaching in this section is to help someone who is already a disciple follow through and persevere along the path that Jesus has pioneered before them. This is also what disciple-makers are to teach disciples to do.

Divorce

One of the key questions in the contemporary application of Matthew 19:1–12 is how to interpret the exception clause in verse 9. Jesus says, 'Anyone who divorces his wife, except for sexual immorality [the Greek word is *porneia*], and marries another woman commits adultery.' There was a similar exception clause in 5:32.

The Jewish rabbis often read the reason given for a divorce in the case law example of Deuteronomy 24:1–4 (which the Pharisees refer to here in 19:7) – finding 'something indecent' in a wife (Deuteronomy 24:1) – as a legitimate and lawful *reason* for divorce. In the first century, for example, the Rabbi Shammai took this to mean a husband finding his wife had committed adultery.[20] Is, then, Jesus agreeing here (against those who thought it lawful to divorce 'for any and every reason', like the Rabbi Hillel) that although the basic principle is that no one should separate what God has joined (19:6), adultery would give legitimate grounds for divorce? If so, it is strange that Jesus has not used the word for adultery rather than *porneia* – especially since he uses it later in the same sentence.

The further difficultly is that the word *porneia*, as well as being distinct from the word for adultery, covers a wide range of sexual sins, of many degrees of seriousness.[21] Is Jesus saying that something like the lustful glance of 5:28 would be legitimate grounds for divorce? But this would make the exception clause far too broad, giving in practice a legitimate reason for divorce in every marriage and going against the general tone of Jesus's answer that divorce should not be permitted. We also need to remember that the parallel accounts in Mark 10:2–12 and Luke 16:18 do not include the exception clause at all.

Some attempt to link the exception clause to the case of Joseph in 1:18–19.[22] Joseph was betrothed to Mary, and when she was found pregnant, a natural assumption would have been that she had been involved in pre-marital sex – that is, not strictly adultery, but still *porneia*. Joseph was contemplating divorcing Mary (the same word as in 19:3, 7–9), and Matthew seems to indicate that this would have been a righteous thing to do. But the links to Jesus's teaching in 19:1–12 are otherwise quite awkward. It would be odd for 19:9 to apply to a couple pledged to be married, since there are many other legitimate reasons, apart from *porneia*, to break off a betrothal, and this would have been so even in the ancient world. Similarly, 19:9 clearly applies to those who are married, and there is nothing in the exception clause to limit it to those who are merely betrothed.

My suggested solution to these difficulties is that Jesus has a specific kind of *porneia* in mind, linked to the use of the word in the Greek

---

[20] Instone-Brewer, *Divorce and Remarriage*, 111.

[21] BDAG, '*porneia*'.

[22] For example, John Piper, *What Jesus Demands from the World* (Wheaton: Crossway, 2006), 301–22.

translation of the Hebrew Scriptures, the LXX – especially its use in the Prophets. Jesus has already made a subtle allusion to the Prophets in verse 8.[23] The phrase 'your hard hearts' (translated as 'your hearts were hard' in the NIV) appears in the LXX of Jeremiah 4:4, which reads, 'Circumcise yourselves to your God and circumcise your hard hearts.' This ends a section that began in Jeremiah 3:1 that has likened the Lord God's relationship with his people to a broken marriage – one where the wife has abandoned her husband to find sexual intimacy with many others.[24] In the LXX of this section, the noun *porneia* is used to describe the behaviour of the people (Jeremiah 3:2, 9), as well as the related verb *porneuō* (Jeremiah 3:7, 8). Such behaviour gives legitimate reason for the Lord to divorce his people (Jeremiah 3:1); and in the case of Israel (the northern kingdom), the Lord has indeed already issued a certificate of divorce (Jeremiah 3:8).

This is consistent with the usage of the word *porneia* across the LXX. It is used to describe a case of individual sexual immorality just once, in Genesis 38:24. It is frequently linked to idolatry or the wickedness of idolatrous nations and cities (2 Kings 9:22 (of Jezebel); Micah 1:7; Nahum 3:4 (Nineveh); Isaiah 47:10 (Babylon), 57:9; Jeremiah 13:27). But its most common usage is in reference to the spiritual adultery of the people associated with them turning away from the Lord. In addition to Jeremiah 3, it is used this way in Numbers 14:33; Hosea 1:2; 2:4, 6; 4:11–12; 5:4; 6:10; Jeremiah 2:20; Ezekiel 16:15, 22, 25, 33–4, 36, 41; 23:7–8, 11, 14, 17–19, 27, 29, 35.

All this suggests that the meaning of the word *porneia* in the exception clauses of Matthew 5:32 and 19:9 is not directly dependent on pinning down exactly what Moses means by a matter of indecency in Deuteronomy 24:1. To take it as equivalent to an act of adultery, as in the school of Shammai and many others, generates a number of inconsistencies and actually makes the exception too broad. There are similar problems with linking *porneia* in the exception clauses with any subset of actual sexually immoral behaviour. It makes much better sense to say that the meaning is based on its use in the LXX, where it is used by the prophets as they compare the covenant relationship between the Lord God and his people to a broken marriage. The prophets are using *porneia* to describe what

---

[23] As noted by Instone-Brewer, *Divorce and Remarriage*, 145–6.

[24] The connection is a strong one. The strength of the comparison in the Prophets suggests that covenant relationship between God and his people *is* a kind of marriage. Similarly, therefore, the marriage between a husband and wife *is* a kind of covenant.

we might call 'covenantal apostasy'. The equivalent notion in a marriage setting is what we might call 'marital apostasy'. That is (parallel to Israel and then Judah turning from the Lord under the Mosaic covenant), a permanent, unrepentant turning from the marriage relationship, no doubt often involving sexual activity with someone else.

This understanding of *porneia* makes the 'exception' a genuine exception, in keeping with the overall tone of Jesus's teaching.[25] It also makes good sense in the context of Matthew's Gospel. We can see that Matthew 19:3–9 is actually a special case of the general pattern of dealing with sin within the Christian community in Matthew 18. In Matthew 18, when someone sins but seeks forgiveness, then they should always be forgiven (18:21–35). Only if they repeatedly refuse to listen are they removed from the community and treated as an outsider (18:15–17). This corresponds to the exception clause: when a sinning spouse refuses to seek reconciliation and forgiveness they are also removed from the marriage and treated as an outsider to it (that is, they are divorced). This also suggests that legitimate divorce should be accompanied by church discipline against the spouse who abandons the marriage.

1 Corinthians 7:15 is then an application of the same principle to the case of desertion by an unbelieving spouse. Paul has clearly heard Jesus's teaching on the subject of divorce (1 Corinthians 7:10–11). He then, with apostolic authority, applies this teaching to a case Jesus has not explicitly addressed: a believer married to an unbelieving spouse (1 Corinthians 7:12–16). As he does so, in my opinion it is also clear he knows about Jesus's exception clause. In this case, the general principle remains the same: they should remain married (1 Corinthians 7:12–14). The exception is when the unbelieving spouse leaves, in which case a divorce is legitimate (1 Corinthians 7:15).

In light of the background understanding of divorce in both the Old Testament and the Graeco–Roman world, Jesus and Paul probably assume we know divorce implies a freedom to remarry. The woman in the case study of Deuteronomy 24:1–4 was free to remarry (though not to her original husband). Evidence from actual certificates of divorce shows their basic purpose was to allow the divorcee to remarry.[26] The expectation in

---

[25] This is a good test of any understanding of the exception clauses. For example, Instone-Brewer, *Divorce and Remarriage*, 300–14, concludes with such broad interpretations of the exception in Matthew and 1 Corinthians that it is hard to see how divorce would not be legitimate in *any* real-life marriage.

[26] Instone-Brewer, *Divorce and Remarriage*, 20–33.

the Graeco–Roman world was that one was free to remarry after a divorce. If Paul wanted to say in 1 Corinthians 7:15 that if an unbelieving spouse leaves (that is, divorces) a believer, then the believer should *not* remarry, then he would have had to have made it explicitly clear. As it is, he says, 'The brother or the sister is not bound in such circumstances;' which would seem instead to confirm the freedom to remarry.

In short, Jesus's answer to the question, 'Is it ever permissible to divorce?' is basically, 'No. What God has joined together, let no one separate.' Except in the extreme case where a spouse abandons the marriage altogether and refuses to come back and seek reconciliation and forgiveness. In this case, a divorce is legitimate and the abandoned spouse is (almost certainly) free to remarry.

A common question at this point is, 'What about cases of domestic abuse in marriage?' Here I would follow John Frame and others in claiming that there is a point where spousal abuse becomes tantamount to the abuser renouncing his or her marriage vows. When this happens, he or she is thereby effectively divorcing their spouse in a way that is sufficiently close to the case of divorce by desertion in 1 Corinthians 7:15 for the marriage to be declared over. No doubt there will be some cases where it will be difficult to decide exactly when this point has been reached, but there will also be cases where it is entirely clear.[27]

3. Taking up his cross part 3 • Matthew 20:17–34

The wider section is framed around Jesus's three passion-vindication predictions – at 16:21, 17:22–3 and 20:17–19. Three times Jesus strongly asserts the necessity of his suffering and death as well as declaring the certainty of his resurrection. Jesus has also strongly asserted the necessity of following him in this pattern (16:24–6) and has just taught at some length what this should look like in practice (17:24–20:16). A very important part of this teaching has been on who will be greatest or first in the kingdom (18:1–4; 19:13–20:16). Jesus began the section by saying, 'Whoever wants to save their life will lose it, but whoever loses their life for me will find it' (16:25). He summed up his teaching in 17:22–20:16 by saying, 'So the last will be first, and the first will be last' (20:16).

However, it seems some of the disciples have not yet understood this

---

[27] See John M. Frame, *The Doctrine of the Christian Life* (Phillipsburg: P&R Publishing, 2008), 780–81.

principle. Just as Jesus built upon his own example in correcting Peter in 16:22–8, so here in 20:20–28. And just as a supernatural vision in 17:1–20 helped the disciples listen to Jesus, so a double healing miracle here will encourage them that Jesus can give the necessary 'sight' (that is, understanding) to follow him (20:29–34).

Jesus predicts his death a third time

17 Now Jesus was going up to Jerusalem. On the way, he took the Twelve aside and said to them, **18** 'We are going up to Jerusalem, and the Son of Man will be delivered over to the chief priests and the teachers of the law. They will condemn him to death **19** and will hand him over to the Gentiles to be mocked and flogged and crucified. On the third day he will be raised to life!'

A mother's request

20 Then the mother of Zebedee's sons came to Jesus with her sons and, kneeling down, asked a favour of him.

21 'What is it you want?' he asked.

She said, 'Grant that one of these two sons of mine may sit at your right and the other at your left in your kingdom.'

22 'You don't know what you are asking,' Jesus said to them. 'Can you drink the cup I am going to drink?'

'We can,' they answered.

23 Jesus said to them, 'You will indeed drink from my cup, but to sit at my right or left is not for me to grant. These places belong to those for whom they have been prepared by my Father.'

24 When the ten heard about this, they were indignant with the two brothers. **25** Jesus called them together and said, 'You know that the rulers of the Gentiles lord it over them, and their high officials exercise authority over them. **26** Not so with you. Instead, whoever wants to become great among you must be your servant, **27** and whoever wants to be first must be your slave – **28** just as the Son of Man did not come to be served, but to serve, and to give his life as a ransom for many.'

Two blind men receive sight

29 As Jesus and his disciples were leaving Jericho, a large crowd followed him. **30** Two blind men were sitting by the roadside, and when they heard that Jesus was passing by, they shouted, 'Lord, Son of David, have mercy on us!'

31 The crowd rebuked them and told them to be quiet, but they shouted all the louder, 'Lord, Son of David, have mercy on us!'

32 Jesus stopped and called them. 'What do you want me to do for you?' he asked.

33 'Lord,' they answered, 'we want our sight.'

34 Jesus had compassion on them and touched their eyes. Immediately they received their sight and followed him.

The third passion-vindication prediction (20:17–19)

In this third and last of the passion-vindication predictions, we get a large number of details in advance. Jesus will be betrayed, condemned and handed over. To 'hand over [someone] over to the Gentiles' is a biblical way of talking about turning Israel over to the punishment of God executed through nations hostile to them.[28] This is what happened when the nation of Israel suffered the covenant curses, with the survivors sent into exile: they were handed over to the nations. Now we get even more detail on exactly how Jesus will suffer and die: he will be mocked, flogged and crucified (verse 19). This will match the detail in 27:27–44.

Who is truly the greatest? (20:20–28)

We know that Zebedee's sons are James and John from 4:21 and 10:2. James and John have recently, along with Peter, seen a vision of the glorified Jesus on a high mountain (17:1–8). It may be this that causes them and their mother to ignore entirely what Jesus has just said in verses 17–19 about his suffering and death. Instead, they focus on Jesus's future glory, victory and vindication, which they rightly associate with his kingdom. It is not obvious why it is their mother making the request here, although it may be that James and John have noted the positive response humble women have received from Jesus before (9:20–22 and 15:21–8, for example). Like the Canaanite woman in 15:25, she kneels down in worship as she asks something of Jesus (verse 20). Jesus has encouraged the disciples to be those who freely ask of things from their Father (7:7–12), so making bold requests like this one is certainly not a bad thing in itself.

Nevertheless, Jesus does take the opportunity to address two serious errors implied by the request. The first of these is the way it ignores the suffering and death that must precede victory and glory. In 16:22, Peter was outraged by the idea of Jesus suffering and dying and could not see the necessity of it. Here, James and John cannot see the necessity of following Jesus on this path – at least, they bypass it entirely to focus on the vindication beyond it. Jesus's answer draws them back to what must happen beforehand (both for himself and for them).

Matthew has arranged the material here to set up a connection with the coming narrative of Jesus's death in Jerusalem. The 'right' and 'left' in

---

[28] Peter Bolt, *The Cross from a Distance: Atonement in Mark's Gospel* (Downers Grove; Leicester: InterVarsity Press, 2004), 56–8. This can be seen, for example, in Leviticus 26:32–3, 38; Hosea 8:10; Psalm 106:41; Ezra 9:7.

the request of verse 21 and in Jesus's answer in verse 23 will correspond to the two rebels crucified with Jesus in 27:38, one on his right and one on his left. The 'cup' in verses 22 and 23 will very clearly correspond to the cup of wine representing his blood of the covenant, poured out for many for the forgiveness of sins in 26:27–8. Similarly, Jesus will in Gethsemane, in his own request to the Father, ask for the 'cup' to be taken from him (26:39, 42, 44), referring to the extreme tribulation he will shortly suffer at Golgotha.

So when Jesus says, 'You don't know what you are asking,' in verse 22, he is implying that a request to share in his victorious rule is necessarily a request to share in his suffering. Hence, he asks, 'Can you drink the cup I am going to drink?' – asking in effect whether they are willing to do so. He knows when they answer, 'We can,' they almost certainly still do not know what they are asking for or saying yes to. But they will understand in the future, and indeed will share in his suffering (verse 23a). In the meantime, the people to be placed on the right and left of Jesus on the cross have already been chosen (verse 23b)!

If the first serious error in the request of verse 21 was to ask for a cost-free victory, devoid of suffering, the second error is implicitly to seek to exercise the wrong kind of leadership, devoid of service. When the other ten apostles hear of the request, they are 'indignant with the two brothers' (verse 24). All twelve have been promised leadership or judging roles in the kingdom (19:28). But the ten rightly discern in the brothers' request a desire to take on a higher status than them.

This wrong kind of desire for greatness in leadership is what Jesus addresses in verses 25–8. He addresses all the Twelve and makes it clear that a worldly approach to leadership characterised by lording it over others is not appropriate for those who follow him (verse 25). This is another area where the 'first shall be last' principle applies. Those who would truly be great as leaders must do so as servants and slaves (verses 26–7). Jesus himself, fulfilling the role of the Son of Man, will set the ultimate example. This is Jesus's final purpose statement in the Gospel (following those given by the angel of the Lord in 1:21 and himself in 9:13). He did not come to be served, as a Gentile leader might, but to serve, and give his life as a ransom for many (verse 28).

This also addresses a key question in 16:21–20:34, which is how ignorant and hapless people like Jesus's disciples could possibly participate in his resurrection victory. After all, more-eligible people apparently will not (19:23–4). As the disciples asked then, 'Who then can be saved?' (19:25), Jesus's answer was, 'With man this is impossible, but with God all things are possible' (19:26). But what makes the impossible possible? The answer in verse 28 here is: Jesus makes it possible. He dies as a ransom.

The word 'ransom' is the Greek word *lutron*. This is a word used for the ransom money paid to the owner of a slave to give the slave his or her freedom.[29] In the Greek New Testament, it only appears here and in the parallel verse in Mark 10:45. In the LXX, the noun appears twenty times, translating a variety of Hebrew words. One of these is the word *kopher* in Exodus 30:12. As we have already noted on Matthew 17:24–7 above, a 'ransom' in the census regulations of Exodus 30 was a payment that makes atonement for life – i.e., rescues from death. Here, it is what makes resurrection life certain for those who follow Jesus. It is an exchange that is life for life. It is for many; literally, 'instead of', 'in the place of', many. It is substitutionary. What is it a ransom from? We should have picked this up already in the Gospel. In the miracles with miscellaneous characters, for example, Jesus is taking people out from the shadow of death. Death and the shadow of death are here because of God's righteous anger at sin. So, ultimately, this is all connected to the forgiveness of sins. By achieving the forgiveness of our sins, this ransom is that which takes the righteous anger of God away.

But the main purpose of verse 28 is to set an example for the disciples to follow. It is a wonderfully countercultural picture of leadership. The kingdom of heaven will be ruled by a Servant King. A king who undertook such great service that he gave up all his natural rights and privileges to serve others. To be a ransom for them. And under this King, the kingdom will be peopled by those who have likewise learned to serve. The kingdom will not be a place of worldly excess and worldly hedonism; rather, it will be full of servants, and full of the joy which comes from that.

A double healing from blindness (20:29–34)

Jesus began this section of the Gospel calling for his disciples to deny themselves, take up their crosses and follow him (16:24) on a pathway that involves cost and loss in the near term, and vindication and glory only later (16:25–6). This pathway seems a hard one. From Jesus's teaching in this section, it means being humble, dependent, caring, forgiving, faithful and sacrificial. We might wonder how these disciples, or indeed any disciples, could be expected to manage it. Part of the answer to this has

---

[29] BDAG, '*lutron*'.

come in 19:13–30, where we saw that the pathway Jesus is pioneering is a fulfilment of the path to life laid out in the book of Deuteronomy: Jesus is making what proved impossible for God's people in the past, possible. We have also had verse 28 in this chapter: Jesus is going to die as a ransom for many. This will guarantee a resurrection life for those who do follow him.

At the end of the section, however, there still seems to be a deep problem with the disciples' understanding. Peter failed to understand the necessity of the cross (16:22), and the disciples have repeatedly failed to understand the necessity of humbly following in the same pattern. In particular, they misunderstand greatness (18:1–4; 19:13–30), culminating in the profound misunderstanding of the sons of Zebedee in 20:20–28.

But the final miracle in the section gives a note of hope. This depends on us recognising that sight is being used here as a metaphor for understanding. Back in Matthew 13:13–14, Jesus quoted from Isaiah – 'Though seeing, they do not see' – to talk about spiritual blindness – lack of understanding and faith. Physical blindness is a common picture for spiritual blindness in the Bible.

Jericho is some twenty-five kilometres northeast of Jerusalem, meaning Jesus and his followers are getting close to the place of the suffering and death he has now predicted three times. As they pass, two men correctly identify Jesus (despite their blindness) and cry out, 'Lord, Son of David, have mercy on us!' (verse 30). That there are two of them sets up a contrast with the two brothers in verses 20–28. The reaction of the crowd is similar to that of the disciples to the Canaanite woman in 15:23 and to the children in 19:13. But Jesus stops and asks them what they want (verse 32), much as he asked the mother of James and John in verse 21. Instead of asking for relative greatness, they ask for sight (verse 33). Jesus grants their request and they follow him (verse 34).

The episode highlights the supreme value of sight – which we can take to represent understanding. What is more, Jesus is able to give – miraculously – the understanding necessary to follow him.

SUMMARY AND PURPOSE

There are again some things in this section that should attract someone who is not yet a disciple of Jesus. The contrast between our normal experience of leaders – who serve themselves and lord it over others, as in verse 25 – and Jesus, the Servant leader who gives his life for others (verse 28) is particularly striking. Who wouldn't want to follow a leader like that? The simple example of the two blind men also stands out. Even if there is a cost in the short term to following Jesus, there is nothing complicated about becoming a follower.

For those who are already disciples there is much to learn: about the cup of suffering linked to true greatness (verses 20–23), about the servant nature of true leadership (verses 24–8) and the value of sight and understanding (verses 29–34). In short: the more a disciple sees and understands Jesus and what he had to do (verses 17–19), dying as a ransom for many (verse 28), the better they will be as his followers in the world, and the more effective they will be as disciple-makers.

PART SEVEN

....

JESUS'S MINISTRY COMPLETED IN JERUSALEM

MATTHEW 21–8

12

Coming to Jerusalem

MATTHEW 21–3

Finally, we arrive at Jerusalem. As Jesus enters Jerusalem to complete the mandate he took on from his Father – to bring forgiveness of sins for God's people – he does so as the Lord coming to Zion, and as the anointed King (Messiah) coming to his city. But not yet as the Lord coming in judgment – although we shall see elements of the judgment of Jerusalem prefigured and brought forward. And not as a worldly king – as a *Servant* King.

1. Coming to Jerusalem part 1 • Matthew 21:1–22

Jesus comes to Jerusalem as king

21 As they approached Jerusalem and came to Bethphage on the Mount of Olives, Jesus sent two disciples, **2** saying to them, 'Go to the village ahead of you, and at once you will find a donkey tied there, with her colt by her. Untie them and bring them to me. **3** If anyone says anything to you, say that the Lord needs them, and he will send them right away.'

4 This took place to fulfil what was spoken through the prophet:

5 'Say to Daughter Zion,
    "See, your king comes to you,
gentle and riding on a donkey,
    and on a colt, the foal of a
        donkey." ' **a**

6 The disciples went and did as Jesus had instructed them. **7** They brought the donkey and the colt and placed their cloaks on them for Jesus to sit on. **8** A very large crowd spread their cloaks on the road, while others cut branches from the trees and spread them on the road. **9** The crowds that went ahead of him and those that followed shouted,

'Hosanna **b** to the Son of David!'

'Blessed is he who comes in the
    name of the Lord!' **c**

'Hosanna **d** in the highest
    heaven!'

10 When Jesus entered Jerusalem, the whole city was stirred and asked, 'Who is this?'

11 The crowds answered, 'This is Jesus, the prophet from Nazareth in Galilee.'

Jesus at the temple

12 Jesus entered the temple courts and drove out all who were buying and selling there. He overturned the tables of the money-changers and the benches of those selling doves. **13** 'It is written,' he said to them, ' "My house will be called a house of prayer," [e] but you are making it "a den of robbers." [f]'

14 The blind and the lame came to him at the temple, and he healed them. **15** But when the chief priests and the teachers of the law saw the wonderful things he did and the children shouting in the temple courts, 'Hosanna to the Son of David,' they were indignant.

16 'Do you hear what these children are saying?' they asked him.

'Yes,' replied Jesus, 'have you never read,

' "From the lips of children and infants
you, Lord, have called forth your praise" [g] ?'

17 And he left them and went out of the city to Bethany, where he spent the night.

Jesus curses a fig-tree

18 Early in the morning, as Jesus was on his way back to the city, he was hungry. **19** Seeing a fig-tree by the road, he went up to it but found nothing on it except leaves. Then he said to it, 'May you never bear fruit again!' Immediately the tree withered.

20 When the disciples saw this, they were amazed. 'How did the fig-tree wither so quickly?' they asked.

21 Jesus replied, 'Truly I tell you, if you have faith and do not doubt, not only can you do what was done to the fig-tree, but also you can say to this mountain, "Go, throw yourself into the sea," and it will be done. **22** If you believe, you will receive whatever you ask for in prayer.'

---

a 5 Zech. 9:9
b 9 A Hebrew expression meaning 'Save!' which became an exclamation of praise; also in verse 15
c 9 Psalm 118:25,26
d 9 A Hebrew expression meaning 'Save!' which became an exclamation of praise; also in verse 15
e 13 Isaiah 56:7
f 13 Jer. 7:11
g 16 Psalm 8:2 (see Septuagint)

The Jerusalem section of the Gospel has three main parts to it. The narrative of Jesus being handed over, executed on a cross, but then raised in vindication fills chapters 26–8 (with a brief return to Galilee right at the end). Before this, Jesus gives his final speech to his disciples in chapters 24–5, teaching them about how the rest of history will unfold and how to persevere through it. Before this, in the current section, Matthew narrates Jesus coming into Jerusalem and most especially coming to the

Temple. A quotation from Psalm 118:26 – 'Blessed is he who comes in the name of the Lord!' – appears in the opening and ending episodes of the section (21:9; 23:39). Psalm 118 is a psalm of an Israelite leader, a David-like king, who has been hard pressed, almost to the point of death, but is now giving thanks for deliverance and using the psalm to encourage his people to recognise what the Lord has done and to express a similar dependence upon him. Most of the psalm is the testimony of the king, but some of it seems to be the response from the people he wishes to encourage – which in 118:26–7 is the people recognising the king as one who comes in the name of the Lord and joining him in festal procession (on the path of righteousness, 118:19–20). Other parts of the same psalm also appear in Matthew 21–23: verse 25 is picked up in the rest of 21:9; and verses 22–3 play an important role in Jesus's explanation of the parable of the tenants in 21:42–4.

What Jesus does early on in the section – driving out buyers and sellers from the Temple (21:12) – triggers a number of disputes in the Temple, and indeed the sequence of events that lead to Jesus's execution. As elsewhere in Matthew's Gospel, there would seem to be a 3x3 structure to the section. At the centre are three parables (21:28–22:14), the middle one of which is the parable of the tenants (21:33–46). This includes another quotation from Psalm 118 in 21:42. The parable and the quotation give Jesus's own interpretation of what is happening as he arrives in Jerusalem.

21:1–22 **Trial preliminaries**	21:23–22:46 **The leadership questioned and exposed**	23:1–39 **Sentence passed**
1–11 Entering Jerusalem *Blessed is he who comes in the name of the Lord*	21:23–7 The main dispute (on authority)	23:1–12 Warnings to crowds and disciples about the leadership
12–17 Figuratively shutting the Temple down, taking the Temple worship on himself	21:28–22:14 Three parables	23:13–36 Woes upon the leadership
18–22 The next morning: Figuratively(!) judging the Temple and making his own disciples the place of prayer	22:15–46 Three more disputes	23:37–39 Tears for Jerusalem *Blessed is he who comes in the name of the Lord*

Table 17

The section as a whole can be seen as Jesus putting the chief priests, the teachers of the law, the elders, the Pharisees and the Sadducees on trial. They repeatedly present themselves as those with authority, putting questions to him. He repeatedly turns the tables in his responses, showing where the true authority lies.

This opening section (21:1–22) sets things up with three sign-acts: the entry on a donkey (verses 1–11), the turning of the tables (verses 12–17) and the cursing of a fig tree (verses 18–22).

The (not very) triumphal entry (21:1–11)

This episode is often called the 'triumphal entry,' but it is not triumphal in quite the way we or the people at the time might have expected. Nonetheless, Matthew does want to depict this as the arrival of the Davidic King – that is, the Messiah – to Jerusalem (and thence to Zion).

Jesus's instructions in verses 1–3 show that he is transparently and self-consciously choosing to perform a symbolic act. It is not that he just happens to enter the city on a donkey or a colt, but that he chooses to, and he prepared for it in advance. His foresight in knowing about the donkey and colt in the village and his willingness to call himself 'Lord' in verse 3 suggest that it is also a divine choice. But how does Jesus intend the act to be interpreted? Matthew gives the key in verse 4. Jesus chooses to use these animals to fulfil what was spoken (by the Lord) through the prophet in Zechariah 9:9. That is, the main thing anyone observing Jesus entering Jerusalem on a donkey and on or with a colt should conclude is that he is the king referred to in this verse.

As Jesus approaches the city (verses 6–9), there are other signs that point to Jesus arriving as King. The crowd spreads cloaks and branches on the road before him (verse 8). This is what the people did for Jehu in 2 Kings 9:13, when he announced himself king. The crowd call Jesus the 'Son of David': the promised king in the line of David (verse 9). 'Hosanna,' they cry – meaning, 'Save us now!' – a variation of the cry to the Lord in Psalm 118:25. It's a cry that praises Jesus because it implies he is the king who can save, the one who comes in the name of the Lord. The praise is even stronger at the end of the verse: 'Hosanna in the highest heaven!'

And yet this king is very different: he subverts our expectations. It is far from being a triumphal procession like those of victorious Roman military leaders returning home. Jesus is not on a war horse. He is on a donkey. Donkeys were used by kings in the past, most notably by David himself.

But verse 5 here, as Matthew quotes from Zechariah 9:9, emphasises the gentleness, meekness or humility of the king on the donkey. The word translated 'gentle' here is the same one as in 11:29 and 5:5 and suggests someone who will not respond to antagonism by fighting back – similar to the gentleness of the Servant in 12:19–21.

It may be that Matthew is emphasising Jesus's humility even further here by having two animals feature in this scene. To have two animals is a puzzle in verse 7. Is it possible to ride on a donkey and a colt at the same time? Presumably, Jesus is riding one and the other is walking alongside them.[1] But why have two? In his quotation, Matthew rightly picks up from the Hebrew of Zechariah 9:9 that the animal the king is riding on is described in two ways. The first is a word used in, for example, 2 Samuel 16:2 of the donkeys used by the royal household. The second is a different phrase – 'a colt, the foal of a donkey' in the NIV – which perhaps suggests a younger, smaller or lesser animal, one you might put your luggage on. By having both animals in view in this section, Matthew wants us to pick up both ideas: the majesty and the humility.[2]

Matthew subverts our expectations again in verses 10–11. Our natural assumption in verse 8 is that the 'very large crowd' are people from Jerusalem. But we should remember from the end of the last chapter (20:31) that there is a crowd travelling with Jesus. In verse 10, we are told that the whole of Jerusalem in fact have no idea who Jesus is, and ask, 'Who is this?' In other words, this is far from Jerusalem welcoming her king with open arms. Verse 11 also suggests the crowd have a superficial understanding of Jesus's identity. They may just have cried out 'Hosanna to the Son of David', but their summary description is, 'This is Jesus, the prophet from Nazareth in Galilee.' That is, he is a prophet, not a king, and from some northern backwater (compare 2:23 and John 1:46).

Put it all together and we have Jesus intentionally entering Jerusalem as a humble king. He comes in the name of the Lord, but not (this time) to bring a just response to God's enemies and the final victory of his kingdom over all other kingdoms. Jerusalem does not recognise him. And he comes as the man from Nazareth, the one who will overturn the pretensions of the Jerusalem elite.

---

[1] Unless he rides one for part of the journey and then switches to the other?

[2] Similar to what we saw in 8:28 (where Matthew had two demoniacs while Mark and Luke have just the one), it's reasonable to claim that there were in fact two animals involved, that it serves Matthew's purposes to mention both of them, and that Mark and Luke chose instead to focus on the main one (Mark 11:7; Luke 19:35).

Shutting down (not cleansing) the Temple (21:12–17)

Matthew moves straight to Jesus entering the Temple and driving out the buyers and sellers, overturning tables and benches (verse 12). What Jesus does is sometimes called 'the purification of the Temple'. But there is no suggestion that after he does these things the Temple is any more purified than it was before. Matthew doesn't even suggest there was necessarily anything wrong with changing money or selling doves (although these things have perhaps taken on an excessive focus – compare John 2:16). In themselves, these activities are simply an essential part of Temple life. In driving them out, what Jesus is doing is stopping the Temple from functioning as a Temple. It is an act of judgment not on those activities but on the whole Temple – indeed, the whole nation. The Temple should be a focus of international blessing and prayer, a 'house of prayer' (verse 13, quoting Isaiah 56:7), but has clearly failed. It has been proved fruitless. Just as in the prophet Jeremiah's day, it has become 'a den of robbers' (Jeremiah 7:11). That is, it has become a place of refuge for a people who know, or should know, that they have provoked God's anger. Like the entry into Jerusalem on a donkey, this, then, is a conscious sign-act: the future of the Temple brought into the present and made visible. The Temple, the pinnacle of the nation's authority to act as a point of contact between God and humanity, is shut down and the nation judged.

But the lowly are healed and commended (verses 14–16) – here represented by the blind and lame, and then by children. This continues Matthew's theme of children in their humble and dependent state representing those of the kingdom (18:2–6, 10–11; 19:13–14). Like the crowds in verse 9, the children identify and praise Jesus as the Son of David, able to save. The chief priests and the teachers of the law are angered by both the healings and what the children are saying (verses 15–16). This indicates both envy of Jesus and a fundamental failure to recognise the one who has come in their midst. Jesus responds by commending the children's praise, as a fulfilment of Psalm 8:2 (LXX). This would anger them still further, given that the praise in Psalm 8 is directed to the LORD.[3]

The Temple is brought down: not finally – that will come later – but effectively. The blind and the lame are lifted up. Children praise Jesus as the one who can save. But, of course, this provokes huge conflict – indeed,

---

[3] YHWH our Lord (Psalm 8:2 Masoretic Text).

the central conflict in Matthew's Gospel, provoked by the coming of Jesus. We could cite this moment as the moment when Jesus's death becomes inevitable from a human point of view.

Fruitlessness judged and prayer relocated (21:18–22)

If we hadn't had so much in the Gospel about the dangers of fruitlessness, what happens next would be very hard to process and understand. In 7:16–20, fruitlessness was an indicator of a false prophet. In 12:33, bad fruit is associated with the wickedness Jesus has exposed in the Pharisees. In 13:8, 23, good fruit (or a 'crop') is associated with those who hear Jesus's word and fully understand and respond to it. In Jeremiah 8:13 (part of the oracles against Jerusalem Jesus has already quoted from in verse 13), fruit is taken away from fig trees which then wither as part of the judgment. So when on the next day Jesus sees a fruitless fig tree and then causes it to wither, it is not because he is having a bad morning. It is once again a symbolic action. Jesus finds the tree fruitless, and judges it. This is exactly what he did with the Temple the day before. (It is also exactly what he is going to do on this day with the people in the Temple, and especially the teachers of the law and the Pharisees, 21:23—22:46.)

Verses 20–22 are harder to understand and process. Not surprisingly, perhaps, the disciples fail to see any symbolism in Jesus's actions at all. They are just amazed that the tree withered so quickly (verse 20).

Jesus's response to their amazement seems to work at two levels. To begin with, if they are amazed that what Jesus said would happen does happen, then they need more trust in the power of prayer to change things. As Jesus has said before (7:7–11), because prayer connects someone with the power of God, and God can do anything he wants, nothing is outside the bounds of possibility – even mountains being thrown into the sea (verse 21). This is a possible allusion to Zechariah 14:4–5, where the Mount of Olives splits in two to allow escape from the judgment coming on Jerusalem. That is, what Jesus says is an encouragement for all kinds of prayer. But he perhaps has in mind the fundamental prayer of one of his disciples to escape the judgment he is foretelling through all these sign-acts.

At a second level, Jesus is addressing the question they should have asked. They should be more concerned about what the withering of the fig tree signifies. The days of the Temple, the 'house of prayer for all nations' (Isaiah 56:7), are coming to an end. So what happens now to the place of prayer? It is now not so much in a particular place, but in a particular kind of people: those with faith who do not doubt (verse 21). The community of faith and prayer now lies in Jesus's followers. Whatever they may have prayed for in the Temple, they can now pray by faith as followers of Jesus.

The episode with the fig tree sets up the remainder of the day in the Temple. There is judgment coming, yes, on those who have been so fruitless as to show themselves opposed to God. The days of the Temple are numbered. But prayer is not going to end just because the place of prayer is going to end. Prayer will continue – powerful prayer. God can still be trusted to answer.

SUMMARY AND PURPOSE

As mentioned above, Matthew 21–23 can be seen as Jesus putting the Jerusalem elite – the chief priests, the teachers of the law, the elders, the Pharisees and the Sadducees – on trial. The way Matthew expects his readers to process this is similar to the way they might process one of the prophets warning God's people of impending judgment in the past (we see this especially as Jesus quotes from Isaiah and Jeremiah in 21:13). That is, he expects us humbly to dissociate from the people being indicted, to call upon God's mercy and (in Jesus, following the calls of 11:28–30 and 16:24) to align ourselves with the new future God is bringing about.

To put it another way, it is rather like sitting in the public gallery in a modern-day court, watching a trial unfold – one where those accused are most decidedly guilty and where the prosecution will certainly be vindicated. Observers in such situations are not themselves directly on trial. But what they are witnessing may nonetheless have profound personal implications.

Readers or hearers of Matthew's Gospel who are not yet disciples of Jesus who recognise some of their own cold dismissiveness with regard to Jesus (or their own fruitlessness) in this section should indeed be convicted and warned. Jesus's humble and gentle entrance to Jerusalem, the 'wonderful things' (verse 14) he is doing and the possibility of powerful prayer (verses 21–2) then stand out as especially attractive.

Readers or hearers who are already disciples are warned about slipping into the wrong attitudes here. More than this, though, they are encouraged if they are being persecuted or marginalised by people like the chief priests and the teachers of the law here: that they are on the right side. They are the ones who will escape the judgment Jesus is foretelling.

2. Coming to Jerusalem part 2 • Matthew 21:23–22:46

This is the middle and (as was the case with the middle section in 16:21–20:43) the longest part of this section of the Gospel (see Table 17 above). It is structured around four disputes with the Jerusalem elite, surrounding three parables that uncover and expose the unrighteousness of those who fail to recognise Jesus's authority and respond to what God is doing through him.

The authority of Jesus questioned

23 Jesus entered the temple courts, and, while he was teaching, the chief priests and the elders of the people came to him. 'By what authority are you doing these things?' they asked. 'And who gave you this authority?'

24 Jesus replied, 'I will also ask you one question. If you answer me, I will tell you by what authority I am doing these things. **25** John's baptism – where did it come from? Was it from heaven, or of human origin?'

They discussed it among themselves and said, 'If we say, "From heaven", he will ask, "Then why didn't you believe him?" **26** But if we say, "Of human origin" – we are afraid of the people, for they all hold that John was a prophet.'

27 So they answered Jesus, 'We don't know.'

Then he said, 'Neither will I tell you by what authority I am doing these things.'

The parable of the two sons

28 'What do you think? There was a man who had two sons. He went to the first and said, "Son, go and work today in the vineyard."

29 ' "I will not," he answered, but later he changed his mind and went.

30 'Then the father went to the other son and said the same thing. He answered, "I will, sir," but he did not go.

31 'Which of the two did what his father wanted?'

'The first,' they answered.

Jesus said to them, 'Truly I tell you, the tax collectors and the prostitutes are entering the kingdom of God ahead of you. **32** For John came to you to show you the way of righteousness, and you did not believe him, but the tax collectors and the prostitutes did. And even after you saw this, you did not repent and believe him.

The parable of the tenants

33 'Listen to another parable: there was a landowner who planted a vineyard. He put a wall round it, dug a winepress in it and built a watchtower. Then he rented the vineyard to some farmers and moved to another place. **34** When the harvest time approached, he sent his servants to the tenants to collect his fruit.

35 'The tenants seized his servants; they beat one, killed another, and stoned a third. **36** Then he sent other servants to them, more than the first time, and the tenants treated them in the same way. **37** Last of all, he sent his son to them. "They will respect my son," he said.

38 'But when the tenants saw the son, they said to each other, "This is the heir. Come, let's kill him and take his inheritance." **39** So they took him and threw him out of the vineyard and killed him.

40 'Therefore, when the owner of the vineyard comes, what will he do to those tenants?'

41 'He will bring those wretches to a wretched end,' they replied, 'and he will rent the vineyard to other tenants, who will give him his share of the crop at harvest time.'

42 Jesus said to them, 'Have you never read in the Scriptures:

' "The stone the builders rejected
   has become the cornerstone;
the Lord has done this,
   and it is marvellous in our
      eyes"[h]?

43 'Therefore I tell you that the kingdom of God will be taken away from you and given to a people who will produce its fruit. **44** Anyone who falls on this stone will be broken to pieces; anyone on whom it falls will be crushed.'[i]

45 When the chief priests and the Pharisees heard Jesus's parables, they knew he was talking about them. **46** They looked for a way to arrest him, but they were afraid of the crowd because the people held that he was a prophet.

The parable of the wedding banquet

22 Jesus spoke to them again in parables, saying: **2** 'The kingdom of heaven is like a king who prepared a wedding banquet for his son. **3** He sent his servants to those who had been invited to the banquet to tell them to come, but they refused to come.

4 'Then he sent some more servants and said, "Tell those who have been invited that I have prepared my dinner: my oxen and fattened cattle have been slaughtered, and everything is ready. Come to the wedding banquet."

5 'But they paid no attention and went off – one to his field, another to his business. **6** The rest seized his servants, ill-treated them and killed them. **7** The king was enraged. He sent his army and destroyed those murderers and burned their city.

8 'Then he said to his servants, "The wedding banquet is ready, but those I invited did not deserve to come. **9** So go to the street corners and invite to the banquet anyone you find." **10** So the servants went out into the streets and gathered all the people they could find, the bad as well as the good, and the wedding hall was filled with guests.

11 'But when the king came in to see the guests, he noticed a man there who was not wearing wedding clothes. **12** He asked, "How did you get in here without wedding clothes, friend?" The man was speechless.

[13] 'Then the king told the attendants, "Tie him hand and foot, and throw him outside, into the darkness, where there will be weeping and gnashing of teeth."

[14] 'For many are invited, but few are chosen.'

Paying the poll-tax to Caesar

[15] Then the Pharisees went out and laid plans to trap him in his words. [16] They sent their disciples to him along with the Herodians. 'Teacher,' they said, 'we know that you are a man of integrity and that you teach the way of God in accordance with the truth. You aren't swayed by others, because you pay no attention to who they are. [17] Tell us then, what is your opinion? Is it right to pay the poll-tax[a] to Caesar or not?'

[18] But Jesus, knowing their evil intent, said, 'You hypocrites, why are you trying to trap me? [19] Show me the coin used for paying the tax.' They brought him a denarius, [20] and he asked them, 'Whose image is this? And whose inscription?'

[21] 'Caesar's,' they replied.

Then he said to them, 'So give back to Caesar what is Caesar's, and to God what is God's.'

[22] When they heard this, they were amazed. So they left him and went away.

Marriage at the resurrection

[23] That same day the Sadducees, who say there is no resurrection, came to him with a question. [24] 'Teacher,' they said, 'Moses told us that if a man dies without having children, his brother must marry the widow and raise up offspring for him. [25] Now there were seven brothers among us. The first one married and died, and since he had no children, he left his wife to his brother. [26] The same thing happened to the second and third brother, right on down to the seventh. [27] Finally, the woman died. [28] Now then, at the resurrection, whose wife will she be of the seven, since all of them were married to her?'

[29] Jesus replied, 'You are in error because you do not know the Scriptures or the power of God. [30] At the resurrection people will neither marry nor be given in marriage; they will be like the angels in heaven. [31] But about the resurrection of the dead – have you not read what God said to you, [32] "I am the God of Abraham, the God of Isaac, and the God of Jacob"[b]? He is not the God of the dead but of the living.'

[33] When the crowds heard this, they were astonished at his teaching.

The greatest commandment

[34] Hearing that Jesus had silenced the Sadducees, the Pharisees got together. [35] One of them, an expert in the law, tested him with this question: [36] 'Teacher, which is the greatest commandment in the Law?'

[37] Jesus replied: ' "Love the Lord your God with all your heart and with all your soul and with all your mind."[c] [38] This is the first and greatest commandment. [39] And the second is like it: "Love your neighbour as yourself."[d] [40] All the Law and the Prophets hang on these two commandments.'

Whose son is the Messiah?

41 While the Pharisees were gathered together, Jesus asked them, **42** 'What do you think about the Messiah? Whose son is he?'

'The son of David,' they replied.

43 He said to them, 'How is it then that David, speaking by the Spirit, calls him "Lord"? For he says,

44 ' "The Lord said to my Lord:
    'Sit at my right hand
  until I put your enemies
    under your feet.' "ᵉ

45 If then David calls him "Lord", how can he be his son?' **46** No one could say a word in reply, and from that day on no one dared to ask him any more questions.

---

h 42 Psalm 118:22,23

i 44 Some manuscripts do not have verse 44.

a 17 A special tax levied on subject peoples, not on Roman citizens

b 32 Exodus 3:6

c 37 Deut. 6:5

d 39 Lev. 19:18

e 44 Psalm 110:1

The disputes all follow a standard format and work in the same way. We have seen similar confrontations before (e.g., in 12:1–8; 15:1–10; 19:3–9, etc.). Each time we find three basic steps: a situation that provokes a conflict, an aggressive question, then an answer or counter-question from Jesus which turns the tables on his opponents.

The dispute in 21:23–7 opens the section and begins the foundational conflict between Jesus and the chief priests and the elders. This is followed by three parables, the central one of which (the parable of the tenants, 21:33–46) exposes most explicitly what is going on in the conflict and what is at stake. The final three disputes draw in the Pharisees and Sadducees (22:15–46).

Who has authority? (21:23–7)

Jesus has entered Jerusalem and gone to the Temple at the heart of the city. He has turned over the tables of the Temple money-changers and the benches of those selling doves. He has found the nation fruitless and is declaring an end to the Temple as a point of contact between God and his people. It is perhaps unsurprising, then, that when Jesus returns to the Temple the following day, he is greeted with an obvious question. The chief priests and elders ask him (verse 23), 'By what authority are you doing these things . . . And who gave you this authority?'

Jesus promises he will answer if they answer his counter-question about John's baptism and where it came from (verses 24–5a). Did it come from heaven or was it merely of human origin?

The counter-question traps the chief priests and elders. They are questioning Jesus's authority and where it comes from. Implicitly they are claiming they are the ones with true authority – over the Temple and over the people – and that this authority comes from God. But their unwillingness to answer, 'From heaven' (which is the true answer) shows they do not have an authority from God. If they did, they would have known its authenticity and would have responded appropriately (verse 25b). And their unwillingness to say it had a human origin shows that they have no real authority over the people. If the baptism was a false one, then they should have had the courage to say so, and to have led the people away from falsehood. As it is, they are afraid of the people (verse 26). The answer, 'We don't know' (verse 27a) undermines their own claims to authority.

Jesus responds to their question in much the same way that he responded to the request from the Pharisees and Sadducees for a sign in 16:1 – that is, with a refusal. In part we may say this is because the kind of authority Jesus has does not need to be defended – it is self-authenticating. Also, as with 16:1, his opponents have graciously been given multiple signs of his authority already (prominent examples are 9:1–8 and 15:29–39).

The exchange with the chief priests and elders has exposed them as people who have heard the preaching of John about the kingdom but have not believed it. They have not subsequently been convicted of their sins and shown it by seeking his baptism. They have not listened to John about the one coming after him. They want to hold on so stubbornly to what authority they have that they are blind to the one who comes in the name of the Lord, with true authority, when he stands before them.

The parable of two sons (21:28–32)

These failures of the chief priests and elders, along with the similar failures of the Pharisees and Sadducees, are then further uncovered and exposed to view in three parables. In the first of these, a man has two sons and commands them both to go and work in the vineyard (verse 28). The first son said no, but then changed his mind and went (verse 29). The second son said yes, but then did not go (verse 30).

Like Nathan with David (2 Samuel 12:1–6), in this parable and the next Jesus gets his listeners to indict themselves.[4] Here he asks which of the two did the will of his Father. The answer within the narrative world

---

[4] Samson Uytanlet notes that in a shame-dominant culture, parables can be

of the parable is very obvious: it was the first one (verse 31).

Then we get the interpretation: Jesus says to them, 'Truly I tell you, the tax collectors and the prostitutes are entering the kingdom of God ahead of you.' In other words, the tax collectors and prostitutes are like the first son. They came from a place of wrongdoing, set against God, but they changed their minds. And theirs is the kingdom.

The implication is that the Jewish leaders are like the second son. They say they will do their Father's will, but they do not. Jesus continues (verse 32): 'John came to you to show you the way of righteousness,' and called you to repent, but 'you did not believe him, but the tax collectors and the prostitutes did. And even after you saw this, you did not repent and believe him.'

In other words, Jesus is saying to them exactly what John said to them. If someone refuses to believe the news of the kingdom, to repent and change their minds about their condition before a holy God, and if they show no fruit in keeping with repentance, then they show themselves at odds with the will of the Father and not on the way of righteousness.

The parable of the tenants (21:33–46)

The second parable is a story about a vineyard, with many Old Testament resonances. In the Prophets, the vineyard is a picture of the place where God blesses his people (e.g., Isaiah 5:1–7). Here, the owner leaves it in the charge of some tenants. It becomes clear that these tenants represent the corrupt human leadership of God's people, like the chief priests and teachers of the law questioning Jesus back in verse 23. To these we should also now add the Pharisees, who are present as Jesus speaks. When Jesus has finished the story and its explanation, the chief priests and the Pharisees know full well that he has been talking about them (verse 45).

The tenants are 'bad guys' in the story because they want the blessings and produce on their own terms – without having to acknowledge or include the owner. Every overture from the owner is rejected, and each messenger shamefully treated (verses 34–6). Finally, verse 37, the owner sends his son. They should respect his son, surely? But, verse 38, they take it as an opportunity to seize permanent ownership of the vineyard by killing the heir. Which is what they do (verse 39).

---

an effective way of indirectly exposing a sin: 'parables can be a discreet way of confronting a sin'. Uytanlet and Kwa, *Matthew*, 182. That is true here, although it also should be noted that Jesus doesn't hold back in driving home his point!

It was an absurdly irrational thing for the tenants to do, and we wonder how on earth they thought they could get away with it. And this is indeed the point. As with the previous parable, Jesus makes those listening to him indict themselves. He asks them what the owner will do (verse 40). Within the narrative world of the parable, the owner will inevitably act with severe retribution against the tenants. Those listening actually go further and add, 'He will rent the vineyard to other tenants, who will give him his share of the crop at harvest time' (verse 41).

Again, Jesus gives an explanation (verses 42–4). This time it is based on Psalm 118:22–3, a part of the psalm where the king was reflecting on his deliverance from enemies who came close to destroying him. The enemies had discarded him, just like builders rejecting a stone during the construction of a building. But he became the stone that shaped or kept the building together. That is, the enemies were thwarted and he was the one vindicated – by the Lord himself (Psalm 118:23). Jesus implicitly links this to the moment in the parable when the tenants reject and discard the son of the vineyard owner (verse 38). Like the enemies in the psalm, they too will be thwarted in their attempt to seize control. He then clearly links the tenants to those listening to him, applying their own verdict against them: the kingdom of God will be taken away from them and 'given to a people who will produce its fruit' (verse 43).

The other part of their verdict back in verse 41 was that before this, the owner 'will bring those wretches to a wretched end'. In verse 44, Jesus links this also to Psalm 118 and the image of a rejected stone, and by saying 'this stone' strongly implies he is talking about himself. He is not someone who can simply be ignored, discarded or rejected. Those who attempt to do that with this stone this will find themselves tripping and broken to pieces or crushed under its weight.

At this point, Jesus is moving on from the narrative world of the parable. In the parable, the son simply dies and the owner is the one who brings retribution against the tenants. But in Psalm 118, the rejected ruler or king survives and is the one through whom the Lord cuts down his enemies (Psalm 118:11–12). By quoting from the psalm, Jesus is communicating to those listening that even if they kill him, he is the one who nonetheless will end up vindicated and victorious against them.

As we noted earlier, the chief priests and the Pharisees know full well that Jesus is speaking this parable (and the previous one) against them (verse 45). It is a measure of their hardness of heart that they still fail to respond to the warning, to feel any conviction of their sin or to show any fear of either Jesus or the Father. Instead (verse 46), their desire to arrest him increases, and the only fear they exhibit is a fear of the crowd.

The parable of the wedding banquet (22:1–14)

As previously, when Jesus says, 'The kingdom of heaven is like . . .' (verse 2), he is indicating that the parable will reveal otherwise hidden secrets about the kingdom of the heavens – here, concerning who will be there and who will be excluded. The story this time is of a king preparing a wedding feast for his son. In the narrative world of the parable, the question is: who will respond to the invitation, and who will be excluded?

The parable is in three parts. In the first part, the king sends servants to collect those who have been invited (verse 3). When they refuse to come, he sends more (verse 4), but these are ignored (verse 5), mistreated or killed (verse 6). The king then sends his army, and brings retribution on those who dishonoured him and mistreated or killed his servants (verse 7).

In the second part of the story, the servants are sent out with a new invitation (verse 8), to 'anyone you find' (verse 9). This results in a wedding hall full of guests (verse 10).

In the third part of the story, the king arrives at the feast. He finds someone inappropriately dressed (verses 11–12), who is then cast outside (verse 13).

Jesus's final comment is, 'For many are invited, but few are chosen' (verse 14).

Many have found this parable puzzling, although we should pick up easily that it is not good to ignore an invitation from a king (or God, for that matter), mistreat his servants or turn up to one of his banquets under-dressed![5] But the punishment of the man without wedding clothes, for example, does at first seem a little harsh.

The key to interpreting the parable is to realise that it traces a similar historical overview to that in the parable of the tenants at the end of Matthew 21. The first part of the parable of the tenants, from 21:33–6, corresponded to the past history of Israel, when the Lord sent multiple prophets who were then ignored and mistreated. The second part corresponded to the present, 21:37–9, when the Lord sent his Son. Then Jesus asked about what would happen in the future (21:40–41).

There is a similar historical overview in this parable. The first part (22:2–7) likewise corresponds to the past history of Israel, when the

---

[5] Indeed, we should be able to see that showing up ill-dressed 'is as contemptuous as actively dismissing the king's invitation'; Uytanlet and Kwa, *Matthew*, 279.

Lord's invitation to life and blessing was ignored by the people, who mistreated his servants the prophets. This ended with the covenant curses coming upon the people, and upon Jerusalem. In the story, this is when the murderers are destroyed and their city burned (22:7).

The second part (22:8–10) corresponds to the present situation, when the invitation to life and blessing in the kingdom has been thrown open (to all who are 'weary and burdened', 11:28). Many have responded, even tax collectors and sinners.

The third part (21:11–13) corresponds to the future. It should remind us of the moment in 7:21–3 when Jesus was teaching about the future Day of Judgment and who will enter the kingdom. Many on that day will claim to know the Lord, but their lawlessness and fruitlessness will prove otherwise (7:23). Or we might be reminded of 8:10–12, when Jesus said that many will come to the feast in the kingdom of heaven, 'but the subjects of the kingdom will be thrown outside, into the darkness, where there will be weeping and gnashing of teeth' (using very similar words to 22:13 here). In other words, this is the moment in the parable when Jesus is speaking especially against his opponents in the Temple courts, warning them that although they might presume to be welcome at the feast in the kingdom, they might well find themselves excluded. There are many people around Jesus at this moment invited to the feast, but few of them will find themselves chosen to stay and enjoy it (22:14).

A dispute with the Pharisees (22:15–22)

After these three parables, directed pointedly at those opposed to him in the Temple courts, Jesus now fields three sets of questions. The first comes from the Pharisees, along with the Herodians. Matthew makes it very clear that it is their intent to trap Jesus (verse 15). This helps us process what at first sound like flattering language in verse 16. What they say is true, but it seems unlikely they fully believe it! The presenting issue in this dispute is allegiance to Caesar: 'Is it right to pay the poll-tax to Caesar or not?' (verse 17). If Jesus says 'no', the Herodians especially will have material to take to the Roman authorities to condemn him. If he says an unqualified 'yes', he risks seeming less zealous than the Pharisees. Caesar claimed divinity, so paying taxes to him could therefore be seen as denying the first commandment against worshipping other gods, using coins that potentially break the second commandment against images of things to worship.

As in his dispute with the chief priests and elders in 21:23–7, Jesus's counter-question turns the tables (22:18–20). The coin bears Caesar's image; Caesar demands taxes in the coinage he has issued.

Jesus uses this to redirect the dispute on to the issue of his questioners' devotion to God. That is, never mind whether they are paying taxes to Caesar, what about what they should be giving to God? This is the main issue. Jesus suggests it is right to pay taxes in this situation, but that is a secondary issue. By finishing by telling them to give 'to God what is God's' (22:21), Jesus is strongly suggesting that this is what his questioners are *not* doing – like the tenants in the parable of the tenants (21:34–41).

Jesus says paying your taxes is giving back to Caesar what is his and is not in conflict with giving to God what is God's. It would be wrong therefore to build too much on, 'Give back to Caesar what is Caesar's' (22:21), as some have tried to do. Whole systems of social theology have been built on these verses![6] But Jesus doesn't give any detail about why it is right to pay taxes in this instance. He's just confirming that when they pay their taxes, which they should, they are not breaking the first or second commandments.

Having said this, we can see that paying the tax is quite consistent with what Jesus has taught previously. It is simply a continuation of the principles of interaction Jesus has been teaching about since the Sermon on the Mount. His disciples should be light in a hostile world (5:16), going the extra mile under Roman coercion (5:41), paying religious taxes so as not to give offence (17:27). It is no surprise that they should also pay the imperial tax.

A dispute with the Sadducees (22:23–33)

Jesus now clashes with the final party in the religious establishment: the Sadducees. Matthew tells us all we need to know about the Sadducees here. The important thing about them is that they say 'there is no resurrection' (22:23).

The question the Sadducees ask Jesus comes after a story. The story is based upon instructions from Moses in the book of Deuteronomy about what to do when a man dies childless: the dead man's brother should marry his wife (Deuteronomy 25:5–10). The story is pure mockery. What if, say the Sadducees, such marriages happen many times – seven times, say? The question is, 'Now then, at the resurrection, whose wife will she

---

[6] For example, Abraham Kuyper, *Lectures on Calvinism* (Peabody: Hendrickson Publishers, 2008).

be of the seven, since all of them were married to her?' (22:28).

The Sadducees are taunting Jesus (and others who believe in the resurrection) with how easily they can come up with scenarios that apparently show the concept of resurrection to be full of holes and contradictions. But Jesus's answer is clear. They are in error because they 'do not know the Scriptures or the power of God' (22:29).

He deals first with their lack of understanding of the power of God. They should know that at the resurrection, God will be powerful to order things differently. People will not marry one another, but will be 'like the angels in heaven' (22:30). Probably the key thing Jesus wants them (and us listening in) to infer from this is that those raised will be like the angels of heaven in that they will not die.[7] God will have powerfully and permanently swept away death. If people don't die, then the need for marriage is very much lessened. Marriage is the appropriate place for procreation, which is what is needed when people keep dying. (In particular, the sorts of marriages the Sadducees are talking about aren't necessary when people don't die.)

Jesus then deals with their lack of understanding of the Scriptures. Jesus quotes from Exodus 3:6: 'I am the God of Abraham, the God of Isaac, and the God of Jacob.' Jesus takes it as obvious from this quotation that God is not the God of the dead, but of the living (22:32). At one level, Jesus simply seems to be saying that if Abraham, Isaac and Jacob had died and that was the end of them (with no hope of resurrection), why would God talk about them as if he's continuing to be their God? Wouldn't he make it clear that he 'once was' their God, or something like that? God is not the God of the dead! So Abraham, Isaac and Jacob must be part of the resurrection to life.

This is comprehensible even if someone knows nothing at all about Abraham, Isaac and Jacob. But for those who do, there is more we can say. These are the key characters at the beginning of God's great story about bringing life back into a dead world. Indeed, they are the ones to whom God promised blessing and life, beginning with one family but spilling out into the whole world (Genesis 12:1–3). As the writer to the Hebrews comments, in believing those promises, Abraham, Isaac and Jacob were showing belief in 'a better country – a heavenly one'. That is, they were believing in the resurrection (Hebrews 11:8–22).

Matthew comments again that the crowds are 'astonished' at Jesus's teaching, that he has dealt with an apparently clever argument so quickly

---

[7] This is even more explicit in Luke's version of the dispute, Luke 20:34–6.

and decisively. The crowds and others have been astonished before at Jesus's teaching (7:28; 13:54), or otherwise amazed (8:27; 9:33; 15:31; 21:20; 22:22). It seems to be Matthew's way of prompting his readers to be likewise amazed, but then to follow through to a deeper reflection on Jesus.

A further dispute with the Pharisees (22:34–46)

The Pharisees respond to Jesus silencing the Sadducees by gathering around him again. This could well be a positive move, given their own views on the resurrection. One of them asks which is the greatest commandment (22:36). Again, this could be positive: some of the Pharisees taking Jesus more seriously. If he teaches wisely on the law in one area, can he be trusted on the Law more generally? But it could also be a trick question, and might be seen that way by at least some of those listening in. The danger is that if Jesus picks one particular law, then he may be seen to be dividing the Law, pitting one part against another.

Jesus's answer is perfectly balanced. He cites from the *Shema*, Deuteronomy 6:5, on loving God with everything one has, above all things. And then he quotes from Leviticus 19:18 (which he has before at 5:43 and 19:19) on loving one's neighbour. This second is like the first. That is, it is an implication of the first and a means of fulfilling the first. Importantly, Jesus has answered the question without pitting one part of the Law against another. All the Law and the Prophets 'hang on these two commandments'. That is, they may be derived from them. As Jesus said in the Sermon on the Mount, he has not come to abolish the Law or the Prophets, but to fulfil them (5:17).

But the question then is: as those professing a concern for the Law and the Prophets, do the Pharisees have a correct understanding from the Scriptures of how God will fulfil the Law and the Prophets? This leads to Jesus's counter-question in 22:41 about the Messiah and whose son or descendant he is. The question reveals that at the time there was some expectation of a Messiah figure who would somehow restore the nation's fortunes. The prophetic expectation was of a restoration of the house of David (e.g., Ezekiel 37:25; Hosea 3:5; Amos 9:11; Zechariah 12) – hence the Pharisees' answer, 'The son of David'. But what did David have to say about the one who in the future would crush God's enemies? In Psalm 110:1, David (speaking by means of the Spirit) calls this one 'Lord' (22:43–4), apparently contradicting the answer 'his son' (22:45).

Were the Pharisees then wrong when they gave the answer, 'The son of David'? No, but the answer was inadequate, in that it ignored another important stream of prophetic expectation, which was that the Lord (YHWH) himself would come to restore his people, defeat his enemies and fulfil his purposes (e.g., Isaiah 40:3–5, 66:15–24; Ezekiel 34:12–24; Zechariah 14; Malachi 4). That is, the one to restore all things would be far greater than David. This is what David himself was looking forward to in Psalm 110.

There is strong dramatic irony at this moment. That is, we as readers know more than the key characters – the teachers and the law and the Pharisees – at this point. Unlike them, we know that Jesus is the 'son of David' they expect as Messiah. Matthew began his Gospel with this: Jesus is the promised Messiah (or Christ) in David's line (1:1, 17). He has been frequently addressed as 'Son of David' (12:23; 15:22; 21:9). Even every one of the blind people in Matthew's Gospel, for example, has seen that he is Son of David and called upon his mercy (9:27; 20:30–31). But Matthew has also been showing us Jesus as one greater than David: even the Lord (YHWH) himself. For example, compare 3:3 and 3:13. What is more, he comes displaying actions and words that can only be compatible with a divine identity (e.g., 8:23–7; 9:1–8; 11:27; 12:8; 14:13–33; 15:32–9). That the Messiah is also the Lord is what Jesus confirms here in 22:41–5.

As Jesus speaks, he does not look like one just about to have his enemies placed under his feet. Matthew has made clear that those enemies include those he has just interacted with in the Temple courts, and the next chapter will confirm that the teachers of the law and the Pharisees are especially in his sights. But quite how Jesus will bring about an unexpected victory against his enemies (and much more) and for the fulfilment of God's promises and purposes we have yet to see.

SUMMARY AND PURPOSE

We have seen that in Matthew 21–23 Jesus is putting the Jerusalem elite on trial. As we watch on, Matthew expects us humbly to dissociate from those in this section who oppose Jesus but have the tables turned on them in the disputes here, and have their motives and wickedness exposed in the three central parables. Like the prophets in the past exposing the sin of Israel's leaders, he is encouraging us instead to call upon God's mercy, and to align ourselves with the new future God is bringing about.

Readers or hearers of Matthew's Gospel who are not yet disciples of Jesus who feel, like the chief priests and elders, that their authority or autonomy is under threat from Jesus, should be convicted by this material. Likewise, anyone who, like the chief priests and Pharisees, senses that the parables are spoken against people like them. Or, indeed, anyone who, like the Pharisees or Sadducees, thinks they can outsmart Jesus.

Readers or hearers who are already disciples are warned about slipping into these wrong attitudes. More than this, though, they are affirmed and encouraged again that if they are being persecuted or marginalised by people like the chief priests, elders, Pharisees or Sadducees here, that they are on the right side.

3. Coming to Jerusalem part 3 • Matthew 23

In the previous section, Jesus was strongly hinting that the religious establishment was like the second son in the first of the three parables from 21:28–22:14. That is, they were like the son who said he would follow the father's instruction, but then did not. He was strongly suggesting that the religious establishment were like the tenants in the second parable: attacking and rejecting the owner's messengers, and then killing his son. He was strongly suggesting that they were like the people who were invited to the banquet in the third parable, but chose not to go. Then, when the invitation was sent out to a wider group, they were like those presuming to be a part of the banquet but turning up unprepared.

A warning against hypocrisy

23 Then Jesus said to the crowds and to his disciples: **2**'The teachers of the law and the Pharisees sit in Moses' seat. **3**So you must be careful to do everything they tell you. But do not do what they do, for they do not practise what they preach. **4**They tie up heavy, cumbersome loads and put them on other people's shoulders, but they themselves are not willing to lift a finger to move them.

5'Everything they do is done for people to see: They make their phylacteries[a] wide and the tassels on their garments long; **6**they love the place of honour at banquets and the most important seats in the synagogues; **7**they love to be greeted with respect in the market-places and to be called "Rabbi" by others.

8'But you are not to be called "Rabbi", for you have one Teacher, and you are all brothers. **9**And do not call anyone on earth "father", for you have one Father, and he is in heaven. **10**Nor are you to be called instructors, for you have one Instructor, the Messiah. **11**The greatest among you will be your servant. **12**For those who exalt themselves will be humbled, and those who humble themselves will be exalted.

Seven woes on the teachers of the law and the Pharisees

13'Woe to you, teachers of the law and Pharisees, you hypocrites! You shut the door of the kingdom of heaven in people's faces. You yourselves do not enter, nor will you let those enter who are trying to. [14] b

15 'Woe to you, teachers of the law and Pharisees, you hypocrites! You travel over land and sea to win a single convert, and when you have succeeded, you make them twice as much a child of hell as you are.

16 'Woe to you, blind guides! You say, "If anyone swears by the temple, it means nothing; but anyone who swears by the gold of the temple is bound by that oath." 17 You blind fools! Which is greater: the gold, or the temple that makes the gold sacred? 18 You also say, "If anyone swears by the altar, it means nothing; but anyone who swears by the gift on the altar is bound by that oath." 19 You blind men! Which is greater: the gift, or the altar that makes the gift sacred? 20 Therefore, anyone who swears by the altar swears by it and by everything on it. 21 And anyone who swears by the temple swears by it and by the one who dwells in it. 22 And anyone who swears by heaven swears by God's throne and by the one who sits on it.

23 'Woe to you, teachers of the law and Pharisees, you hypocrites! You give a tenth of your spices – mint, dill and cumin. But you have neglected the more important matters of the law – justice, mercy and faithfulness. You should have practised the latter, without neglecting the former. 24 You blind guides! You strain out a gnat but swallow a camel.

25 'Woe to you, teachers of the law and Pharisees, you hypocrites! You clean the outside of the cup and dish, but inside they are full of greed and self-indulgence. 26 Blind Pharisee! First clean the inside of the cup and dish, and then the outside also will be clean.

27 'Woe to you, teachers of the law and Pharisees, you hypocrites! You are like whitewashed tombs, which look beautiful on the outside but on the inside are full of the bones of the dead and everything unclean. 28 In the same way, on the outside you appear to people as righteous but on the inside you are full of hypocrisy and wickedness.

29 'Woe to you, teachers of the law and Pharisees, you hypocrites! You build tombs for the prophets and decorate the graves of the righteous. 30 And you say, "If we had lived in the days of our ancestors, we would not have taken part with them in shedding the blood of the prophets." 31 So you testify against yourselves that you are the descendants of those who murdered the prophets. 32 Go ahead, then, and complete what your ancestors started!

33 'You snakes! You brood of vipers! How will you escape being condemned to hell? 34 Therefore I am sending you prophets and sages and teachers. Some of them you will kill and crucify; others you will flog in your synagogues and pursue from town to town. 35 And so upon you will come all the righteous blood that has been shed on earth, from the blood of righteous Abel to the blood of Zechariah son of Berekiah, whom

you murdered between the temple and the altar. **36** Truly I tell you, all this will come upon this generation.

37 'Jerusalem, Jerusalem, you who kill the prophets and stone those sent to you, how often I have longed to gather your children together, as a hen gathers her chicks under her wings, and you were not willing. **38** Look, your house is left to you desolate. **39** For I tell you, you will not see me again until you say, "Blessed is he who comes in the name of the Lord." **c'**

---

a 5 That is, boxes containing Scripture verses, worn on forehead and arm
b 14 Some manuscripts include here words similar to Mark 12:40 and Luke 20:47.
c 39 Psalm 118:26

One way of reading Matthew 23 is to realise that all Jesus is doing is confirming what he has previously implied. These are people who say one thing and do another. These are people who reject God's messengers and even his Son. These are people who effectively turn down the kingdom, even while they presume they will be a part of it.

Many commentators find what Jesus says here too strong.[8] They would do well to remember the answer to the question Jesus asked in 21:40: 'When the owner of the vineyard comes, what will he do to those tenants?' Those from the religious establishment condemned themselves, answering, 'He will bring those wretches to a wretched end' (21:41). What Jesus says in chapter 23 is no stronger than what they have said themselves.

In some treatments of the structure of Matthew's Gospel, the woes here in verses 13–36 are matched with the Beatitudes in 5:3–10. But a woe is not the exact counterpart to a Beatitude, which – as we noted above – should not be taken as a declarative 'blessing'. What is more, the numbers and content do not match convincingly. Having said this, the connections between this chapter and the Sermon on the Mount in Matthew 5–7 as a whole are very strong. What Jesus called his disciples to do there, the Pharisees and teachers of the law are shown here not to be doing. Instead, what the disciples were warned against, the Pharisees and teachers of the law are shown to be doing – and worse. This confirms Jesus's warning in 5:20 that the disciples' righteousness (that is, their actual moral behaviour) must prove superior to the Pharisees and teachers of the law if they are to be a part of the coming kingdom. There are also connections with other judgment warnings in 11:1–20:34. In Matthew 23, all these are brought together and summarised one last time.

---

[8] Recently, for example, Adela Yarbro Collins, 'Polemic against the Pharisees in Matthew 23', in *The Pharisees*, eds. Joseph Sievers and Amy-Jill Levine (Grand Rapids: Eerdmans, 2021), chapter 8.

In other treatments of the structure of Matthew's Gospel, this chapter is taken along with chapters 24–5 as one long final speech or discourse from Jesus.[9] There is something to be said for this, in that chapter 23 is an unusually long and unbroken example of speech from Jesus. There are also some connections with the material in Matthew 24–5. However, the quote from Psalm 118:26 in verse 39 forms a convincing inclusion with 21:9, binding chapters 21–3 as one long trial scene, with chapter 23 as the final sentencing (see above). There is also no change of scene between Jesus speaking in 22:46 and 23:1. On the other hand, Jesus leaving the Temple in 24:1 is an important break, as we shall argue later.

Like the other sections in Matthew 21–3, this one has a three-part structure. First, there are instructions to the crowd and the disciples about how to relate to the teachers of the law and the Pharisees: their teaching and practice (verses 1–12). Next are the seven woes on the teachers of the law and the Pharisees (verses 13–36). Finally, there is a lament for Jerusalem (verses 37–9).

Relating to corrupt leadership (23:1–12)

Jesus turns now to address the crowds and his disciples (verse 1). He has just been talking to a group of Pharisees (22:41–6), so we can take that what he says is very much in their hearing.

The warnings and woes throughout Matthew 23 are consistently concerning 'the teachers of the law and the Pharisees' (verses 2, 13, 15, 23, 25, 27, 29). It is perhaps surprising that the other antagonists of Matthew 21–2 – the chief priests, the elders and the Sadducees – don't get a mention. We can take it that the teachers of the law and the Pharisees are representative of the wider group in their attitudes. It also serves Matthew's purposes to focus on the anti-Christian rivals his first readers would have known and encountered in cities like Antioch, and in their travels around the Mediterranean.

The basic instruction to the crowds and the disciples is in verses 2–3. The teachers of the law and the Pharisees 'sit in Moses' seat' (verse 2). Jesus has previously implied (in 5:21–48) that their teaching of the Law and the Prophets has been deficient, and he has given authoritative teaching on a number of areas where they had got things badly wrong. In 16:5–12, Jesus warned his disciples against the teaching of the Pharisees.

---

[9] For example, Jason Hood, 'Matthew 23–25: The Extent of Jesus's Fifth Discourse', *Journal of Biblical Literature* 128, no. 3 (2009).

Nonetheless, what they teach is the Law as given through Moses. With this in mind, Jesus says, 'So you must be careful to do everything they tell you' (verse 2a). Jesus is effectively saying, 'Do everything Moses tells you'. But don't do what the teachers of the law and the Pharisees *do*, because they do not do what they say (verse 2b).

What they do, Jesus outlines in verses 4–6. First, they burden people through their teaching without helping them (verse 4). Previously, Jesus has rebuked the Pharisees for both going beyond the Law (e.g., on fasting, 9:14, the Sabbath, 12:1–14, and cleansing, 15:1–9) and not caring for people (12:9–12; 15:3–6). Second, they do everything for show (verses 5–6). This builds on Jesus's critique of the 'hypocrites' in 6:1–18. Wide phylacteries (boxes worn on the hand and forehead containing passages of Scripture) would have been a very literal and pedantic application of Deuteronomy 6:8, signalling constant fidelity to the Law. Likewise, long tassels would signal someone who is remembering the commandments, based on Numbers 15:37–41. Jesus knows there is no reality behind these implied claims. They also love the high status assigned to the pious at important events and on public display (verses 6–7a). And they love to be known and respected as a teacher or 'Rabbi' (verse 7b).[10]

Jesus instructs the crowd and disciples to dissociate from such practices, filling out what it means to 'not do what they do' (verse 3), tackling them in reverse order. To begin with, they are not to join those seeking to be called by the title 'Rabbi' (verse 8), or the similar title 'Father' (verse 9, used by some rabbis as a mark of special respect).[11] They are likewise not to be seen as or called 'instructors' (verse 10), who would have been some kind of private tutor. All this would be incompatible with what Jesus has shown them and taught them about being his disciples. As his disciples they have one Teacher (who is the one source for them teaching others, 5:19), who has drawn them together as equal brothers (verse 8; compare 12:49), with one Father in the heavens (verse 9; compare 6:9), and one leader to gather them as one and guide them, who is the Messiah (verse 10; compare 16:18–19). If they were to follow the attention-seeking pattern of the teachers of the law and the Pharisees, they would, in short, cease to be disciples and become instead distractions and sources of disunity.

---

[10] This desire for leadership status has lasted long beyond the first century, of course, and in every culture. Joe Kapolyo comments, 'Many Christian leaders in Zambia today are consumed with symbols of their status: titles such as apostle, bishop, reverend and pastor are much sought after.' Kapolyo, 'Matthew', 1186.

[11] Jesus is not attacking calling one's own father, 'Father'. Similarly, using 'Father' as a term of respect towards an older person is probably not in view.

Finally, the disciples are not to be those who burden people without helping them (compare verse 4). Instead, as Jesus has taught before, being great means being a servant (verse 11; compare 20:25–8). The pathway to exaltation is not through self-exaltation like the teachers of the law and the Pharisees; it is through humbling oneself (verse 12; compare 18:3; 19:30; 20:16).

Woes upon the leadership (23:13–36)

Jesus has pronounced woes against people before. In 11:21, the tone was something like a grieving lament that Chorazin and Bethsaida were in such a miserable state caused by their unresponsiveness, foolishly doing nothing about the judgment coming their way. In 18:7, the tone was more pointed, more like, 'May woe come to the world because of the way it causes people to stumble.' There is judgment coming, and because of the damage done by those being judged, they more than deserve it. The tone is similar here in Matthew 23: the teachers of the law and the Pharisees deserve judgment not just because of their own unrighteousness, but also because they have harmed others and led them astray. (Having said this, when Jesus turns to lament the state of the whole city in verses 37–9, the tone is similar to the laments against Chorazin and Bethsaida.)

The phrase 'Woe to you' (verses 13–16, 23, 25, 27, 29) is directed towards the teachers of the law and the Pharisees. It has the sense: may judgment come upon you because of what you have done, especially the harm you have inflicted. But it is said very deliberately in the hearing of the crowds and disciples (verse 1). Jesus expects these observers to process and respond to what he is saying here.

Verses 13–15, Woes 1 and 2: against false missionaries
The first two woes are against what we might call false missionaries. The teachers of the law and the Pharisees are hypocrites, representing themselves as those who can provide access to the kingdom. But, in reality, this is just a mask: they cannot themselves enter, and cannot therefore provide entrance to anyone else (verse 14). They travel large distances to win people to their camp (and at the time Matthew was writing, would indeed have been travelling around the Mediterranean, much like the early Christians). But they make them twice as much a 'child of hell' as they themselves are. Jesus has used the language of hell or Gehenna before (5:22, 29–30; 10:28; 18:9) as a way of talking about the fiery destruction that will come alongside the kingdom in judgment. To be a child or

son of hell is therefore to be one destined for destruction, and perhaps spreading destruction to others.

Verses 16–24, Woes 3 and 4: against 'blind guides'

The third and fourth woes are against 'blind guides', a description that appears both at the beginning (verse 16) and end (verse 24). Jesus has used this phrase before back in 15:1–20 against the Pharisees and the teachers of the law to describe them as they teach and set an example on washing, defilement and how they treat their parents. Here, Jesus focuses first on their teaching and example when it comes to making oaths (verses 16–22), building on what he taught the disciples in 5:33–7. Here, he again exposes the absurdity of the distinctions the teachers of the law and Pharisees are making between different kinds of oaths, which are very clearly attempts to avoid making good on one's word (verses 16–18). Jesus teaches that, on the contrary, all oaths are equally binding (verses 19–22).

He then turns to their example when it comes to tithing (verses 23–6). As with the issue of washing in 15:1–20 (and likewise with fasting in 9:14–17), this is a case where excessive 'hedging' of one part of the Law is hiding a severe deficiency in another. There is nothing wrong per se with tithing one's herbs and spices. Indeed, Deuteronomy 14:22–3 encourages giving a tenth of all the produce of one's fields, in order to hold a feast to the Lord. Tithing even herbs and spices looks like a meticulous obedience to this. But it means nothing if a person is disobedient to the central requirements of the Law: 'justice, mercy and faithfulness' (verse 23). The final word here is actually the same word as 'faith' throughout Matthew's Gospel, and may mean this here also – along the lines of Micah 6:8, where the requirement of the law is described as 'to act justly and to love mercy and to walk humbly with your God' (compare also Deuteronomy 10:12–13). Jesus is not averse to using dark humour to describe the perversity of what they are doing: it is like straining gnats from a drink but then being happy to swallow a camel (verse 24; compare the 'speck' and the 'plank' in 7:1–5).

Verses 25–8, Woes 5 and 6: against outward show

The fifth and sixth woes are also against a deceptive outward appearance. Jesus again calls the teachers of the law and the Pharisees 'hypocrites' – here, putting on a mask of cleanliness to hide a corrupt and unclean inner reality. The starting point alludes to similar practices to the excessive washing in 15:1–20. Here, Jesus uses that as part of a metaphor. They are keen on washing what can be seen (the 'outside of the cup and dish', verse 25), but do nothing about the 'inside' – the unseen greed and self-indulgence that is actually driving all their behaviour. They should deal with this first, before anything lesser (verse 26). Similarly, verse 27, they are like 'whitewashed tombs'. The outward appearance is righteous; the inner reality is deceptive and wicked (verse 28).

Verses 29–36, Woe 7: against those who murder God's prophets
The final woe is against the teachers of the law and Pharisees in their affinity with those who murdered the prophets in the past (verses 29–36). This links with what Jesus has said in the parables. In the parable of the tenants, the tenants beat, kill and stone the servants the owner of the vineyard sent (21:38). This represented the prophets sent by the Lord to his people in the past, but was in part a parable told against the chief priests and Pharisees listening to Jesus tell it (21:45). There was similar mistreatment and murder of servants in the parable of the wedding banquet (22:6). Here in Matthew 23, Jesus challenges the claim of the teachers of the law and the Pharisees to be on the side of the prophets. They are again hypocrites (verse 29). They put on an appearance of honouring the deaths of the prophets (verse 29) and they attempt to dissociate themselves from those who killed them (verse 30). But this is just a mask. They have admitted that they are descendants of those who murdered the prophets, and Jesus knows they are of the same kind and mind (verse 31).

Jesus knows therefore that the same will happen again. He will send prophets and sages and teachers, just as God has before (verse 34), and they will be killed, crucified, flogged and pursued (verse 35). (This is in itself a huge implied claim about himself from Jesus, doing the task ascribed to the Lord previously. What he says will happen to the messengers also fits what he has said to the disciples in 10:16–25.) The teachers of the law and Pharisees will demonstrate themselves in a long line of those who have shed innocent blood (the sin that sealed the covenant curses for Judah according to 2 Kings 21:16; 24:4) – from the shedding of the blood of Abel in Genesis 4 to the shedding of the blood of the prophet Zechariah according to popular tradition.[12] Strikingly, concerning Zechariah, Jesus says 'you murdered' him (verse 35). Their affinity with those who actually did the deed is so strong that they are personally held culpable.

This persecution of Jesus's messengers will happen within a generation (verse 36) – and will of course begin with Jesus himself being flogged and

---

[12] Which is a tradition Jesus supports here.

crucified in, as Jesus has said (20:19) and Matthew will relate in 27:27–44. Jesus may also be implying that the punishment of those who so persecute his messengers will also take place (or begin) within a generation.

In the past, the people of God rejected him and the messengers he sent to call them back to himself, and brought upon themselves the curses of the covenant. For all their claims to be those restoring Israel through meticulous covenant obedience, and their presumption that their righteousness with respect to the Law will secure them blessing and a part in God's coming kingdom, the teachers of the law and the Pharisees are just the same. They are hypocrites and deceivers ('snakes' and 'vipers', verse 33) to pretend otherwise. Jesus therefore asks them (verse 33): if they brought a curse upon themselves, 'How will you escape being condemned to hell?'

Tears for Jerusalem (23:37–39)

Jesus ends his teaching of the crowds and disciples against the teachers of the law and the Pharisees with a lament. The lament now extends to the whole city of Jerusalem (verse 37). Jerusalem as a whole, not just the teachers of the law and the Pharisees, is now accused of killing the prophets and stoning those sent their way. The city should have recognised him as one reaching out with love and protection, and responded appropriately. Jesus speaks of himself here using language closely related to that ascribed to the Most High, the Almighty, the Lord (that is, YHWH) in Psalm 91:4: 'how often I have longed to gather your children together, as a hen gathers her chicks under her wings'. But Jerusalem was not willing to be gathered.[13] The consequence will be judgment (verse 38) – including against her 'house' (that is, as we shall see, the Temple). When Jesus says they will not see him until they say, 'Blessed is he who comes in the name of the Lord' (verse 39; forming an inclusion with 21:9), this should not therefore be taken as a positive outcome. There will be a time in the future when 'all will acknowledge him'.[14] But for those who remain resistant to him, this will not be a happy time.

Again, the purpose for the disciple of Jesus is to dissociate strongly

---

[13] There is no warrant for generalising this to say that the resistance of people to what God (or Jesus) in some sense wants for them always dictates what then actually happens, as if God were helpless against such hostility. If God were helpless against human resistance, there would be no hope for any of us! God is perfectly powerful to take hostile people, even those eager to stone Jesus's disciples, and reveal his grace to them – the apostle Paul being a graphic example (Acts 9:1–18).
[14] D.A. Carson, *Matthew, Chapters 13 through 28* (Grand Rapids: Zondervan, 1995), 487.

from such hostility to Jesus. When Jerusalem turns on them to stone them (as in Acts 7:54–8), Jesus's lament will also reassure them of their eventual vindication and that justice will come against their persecutors.

SUMMARY AND PURPOSE

We have seen that Matthew 21–3 can be seen as Jesus putting the Jerusalem elite – the chief priests, the teachers of the law, the elders, the Pharisees and the Sadducees – on trial. If so, then Matthew 23 is somewhat like the trial sentencing. The seven woes at the centre of the chapter especially suggest an unfavourable verdict on the teachers of the law and the Pharisees.

We should note that Matthew is relating Jesus's judgment against his opponents in Jerusalem and the Temple in part to show a decisive moment in history. These are those who are part of God's historic people, who would self-identify as Israelites. But Jesus has exposed them as in the same line as those who turned from the Lord in the past, rejected and persecuted his prophets and used their religion to cover over wicked hearts and behaviour – the people who brought down the covenant curses on the nation. Just as before, judgment is therefore coming against the Temple and Jerusalem (hence the lament at the end of the chapter). The difference this time, as we shall see in the next chapters of the Gospel, is that this time the Temple will be permanently destroyed.

I have argued that the way Matthew expects his readers to process this is similar to the way they might process one of the prophets warning God's people of impending judgment in the past. That is, he expects his readers humbly to dissociate from the people being indicted, and to align themselves with the new future God is bringing about through Jesus.

Readers or hearers of Matthew's Gospel who are not yet disciples of Jesus who with his help begin to see the dangerous superficiality of the religion of the teachers of the law and the Pharisees (or are perhaps convicted of such things in themselves) should be drawn to the humility and service Jesus commends in verses 8–12.

Readers or hearers who are already disciples are warned about slipping into the wrong attitudes detailed at length here. More than this, though, they are again encouraged if they are being persecuted by people like the teachers of the law and the Pharisees here: that they are on the right side. They are the ones who will escape the Judgment Jesus is foretelling. In missionary contexts, this is also an encouragement to protect people from the example and influence of the teachers of the law and the Pharisees.[15]

In times and places where the readers of Matthew would no longer be encountering this group, the teachers of the law and the Pharisees still provide a reference point to dissociate from. This – all that is described in chapter 23 – is what not to be like and what not to do. But just as they are representative of a wider group of Jesus's opponents here, so they are in general. Throughout Christian history there have been plenty of prominent and influential leaders and teachers fitting their description in one way or another.

---

[15] The apostle Paul in Galatians being a good example of this.

13

The Final Briefing

MATTHEW 24–5

This is the start of Jesus's final speech to his disciples – the last block of extended teaching he gives in the Gospel – which is something of a final briefing to them before the events of Matthew 26–28 and the task they are given for the nations in 28:16–20. The background is Jesus's entry into Jerusalem as a Davidic king who has gone straight to the Temple to pronounce judgment, culminating in the woes and lament of Matthew 23.

1. The final briefing part 1 • Matthew 24:1–35

The destruction of the temple and signs of the end times

24 Jesus left the temple and was walking away when his disciples came up to him to call his attention to its buildings. **2** 'Do you see all these things?' he asked. 'Truly I tell you, not one stone here will be left on another; every one will be thrown down.'

3 As Jesus was sitting on the Mount of Olives, the disciples came to him privately. 'Tell us,' they said, 'when will this happen, and what will be the sign of your coming and of the end of the age?'

4 Jesus answered: 'Watch out that no one deceives you. **5** For many will come in my name, claiming, "I am the Messiah," and will deceive many. **6** You will hear of wars and rumours of wars, but see to it that you are not alarmed. Such things must happen, but the end is still to come. **7** Nation will rise against nation, and kingdom against kingdom. There will be famines and earthquakes in various places. **8** All these are the beginning of birth-pains.

9 'Then you will be handed over to be persecuted and put to death, and you will be hated by all nations because of me. **10** At that time many will turn away from the faith and will betray and hate each other, **11** and many false prophets will appear and deceive many people. **12** Because of the increase of wickedness, the love of most will grow cold, **13** but the one who stands firm to the end will be saved. **14** And this gospel of the kingdom will be preached in the whole world as a testimony to all nations, and then the end will come.

15 'So when you see standing in the holy place "the abomination that causes desolation,"ᵃ spoken of through the prophet Daniel – let the reader understand – **16** then let those who are in Judea flee to the mountains. **17** Let no one on the housetop go down to take anything out of the house. **18** Let no one in the field go back to get their cloak. **19** How dreadful it will be in those days for pregnant women and nursing mothers! **20** Pray that your flight will not take place in winter or on the Sabbath. **21** For then there will be great distress, unequalled from the beginning of the world until now – and never to be equalled again.

22 'If those days had not been cut short, no one would survive, but for the sake of the elect those days will be shortened. **23** At that time if anyone says to you, "Look, here is the Messiah!" or, "There he is!" do not believe it. **24** For false messiahs and false prophets will appear and perform great signs and wonders to deceive, if possible, even the elect. **25** See, I have told you in advance.

26 'So if anyone tells you, "There he is, out in the desert," do not go out; or, "Here he is, in the inner rooms," do not believe it. **27** For as lightning that comes from the east is visible even in the west, so will be the coming of the Son of Man. **28** Wherever there is a carcass, there the vultures will gather.

29 'Immediately after the distress of those days

' "the sun will be darkened,
  and the moon will not give its
    light;
the stars will fall from the sky,
  and the heavenly bodies will be
    shaken."ᵇ

30 'Then will appear the sign of the Son of Man in heaven. And then all the peoples of the earthᶜ will mourn when they see the Son of Man coming on the clouds of heaven, with power and great glory.ᵈ **31** And he will send his angels with a loud trumpet call, and they will gather his elect from the four winds, from one end of the heavens to the other.

32 'Now learn this lesson from the fig-tree: as soon as its twigs become tender and its leaves come out, you know that summer is near. **33** Even so, when you see all these things, you know that itᵉ is near, right at the door. **34** Truly I tell you, this generation will certainly not pass away until all these things have happened. **35** Heaven and earth will pass away, but my words will never pass away.

ᵃ 15 Daniel 9:27; 11:31; 12:11
ᵇ 29 Isaiah 13:10; 34:4
ᶜ 30 Or *the tribes of the land*
ᵈ 30 See Daniel 7:13-14.
ᵉ 33 Or *he*

In 24:1–2, Jesus leaves the Temple and, when his disciples point out the buildings, declares, 'Truly I tell you, not one stone here will be left on another; every one will be thrown down.' This then prompts the disciples' question in 24:3, to which the speech in Matthew 24–5 is a very long answer.

We can divide Jesus's answer into two parts, giving an overall structure for Matthew 24–5 like this:

24:1–2 **The Temple's days are numbered**

24:3 **The disciples' question:** Tell us when these things will happen and what will be the sign of your coming and of the end of the age?

24:4–35 **The answer part 1:** Don't worry about when these things will happen; just make sure you are not deceived by lies among the coming tribulation (which may include the tribulation associated with the destruction of the Temple, or tribulation like it). But be assured that vindication will surely come, and it will be absolutely clear when it does.

24:36–25:46 **The answer part 2:** Indeed, you cannot know when these things will happen, but make sure you are vigilant and diligent in service while waiting for the return of your master, because these will be tested when he comes in judgment. (That is, because you do not know the day or hour of the coming of the Son of Man, keep watch).

We shall address the second part of Jesus's answer later. The first part is complex enough in its own right!

The explanatory parable in 24:32–4 is a good starting point for seeing the overall structure of Jesus's answer. Jesus says, when you see the leaves, then comes the summer. So we can expect Jesus's answer in 24:4–31 to have something of the form, when you see things A, then will come the thing B. The things A are the various forms of tribulation described in verses 6 to 28. The thing B that follows is the vindication described in verses 29–31 (the coming of the Son of Man). This is what will surely follow the tribulation, as summer follows seeing leaves on a fig tree.

But Jesus makes it clear from the very start of his answer that the reason why he is telling them this is not so they can start making predictions about the timing of the end or the vindication. He is telling them so that in the midst of tribulation they will not be deceived by events that are not in fact the end. And he is telling them so they can endure the tribulation in a state of readiness and expectation, knowing that vindication is near (much as the kingdom is near, 3:2; 4:17; 10:7) – on which he will have more to say in the second part of his answer (24:36–25:46).

We can also divide the kinds of tribulation Jesus warns about into two kinds. The first is the general tribulation that will fill the world the disciples inhabit all the way to the end (verses 6–14). The second is a specific kind of tribulation, an especially extreme one, that requires a special response (verses 15–28).

Putting all these things together suggests that the first part of Jesus's answer to his disciples is structured like this:

(4–5) Headline warning: 'Watch out that no one deceives you. For many will come in my name, claiming, "I am the Messiah," and will deceive many.'	
(6–8) General warnings of global tribulations which are only the birth pangs.	(15–22) Specific warning of a great tribulation in Judea and a command to flee (compare 10:23).
(9–13) Warnings of hatred and lies from false prophets, and an appeal to endure.	(23–6) Warnings about false messiahs and prophets.
(14) The gospel will be preached in all the world, and then the end will come.	(27–8) Even this is not the end. The end will be perfectly clear when it comes.
(29–31) Vindication (the coming of the Son of Man) will surely follow this tribulation.	
(32–5) It will come as surely as summer follows leaves on a fig tree.	

Table 18

Jesus's teaching in Matthew 24–5 builds on and develops many things he has already said in the speech of Matthew 10. This is especially so in 24:9–14, which basically repeats many things Jesus said back then. Back in 10:23, Jesus said, 'When you are persecuted in one place, flee to another. Truly I tell you, you will not finish going through the towns of Israel before the Son of Man comes.' We shall see this is very important background for understanding Jesus's answer here.

Leaving the Temple (24:1–3)

Jesus had left the Temple and was walking away from it when his disciples drew his attention to the building (verse 1). Leaving the Temple could in itself be taken as a significant act: compare the glory of the Lord leaving the Temple in Ezekiel 10; 11:22–4. The disciples are perhaps remarking on the buildings much as the psalmist does in Psalm 48:12–14, where the buildings of Zion are meant as an encouragement of the enduring presence of the Lord until the end. But Jesus reinforces the impression that the Temple is under the judgment of God again by predicting that the stones of the Temple building will all be thrown down (verse 2).

This prompts the disciples' question in verse 3: 'Tell us . . . when will this happen, and what will be the sign of your coming and of the end of the age?'

We could say that there are two or three questions here. The first is, 'When will this happen?' Or, more precisely, 'When will these things be?' (the things that will lead to the Temple being in ruins, for example).

The second is, 'What will be the sign of your coming?' This is an unusual word (from which we get the term 'Parousia', which is often used to talk about the second coming of Jesus). Jesus used a different word to talk about the coming of the Son of Man back in 10:23. In 16:27–8, Jesus similarly told the disciples about the Son of Man coming in his Father's glory with his angels to bring a judgment, rewarding each person according to what they have done. He also calls this event 'the Son of Man coming in his kingdom', and indicates it will happen soon, before all of those he is speaking to die (16:28).

The third (related) question is, 'And [what will be the sign of] the end of the age?' Jesus will use this same phrase, 'the [very] end of the age' in 28:20. In his answer, Jesus will simply talk about 'the end' (verses 6, 13–14). The only time he has used this word before was back in 10:22, where he said the same as verse 13 here: 'But the one who stands firm to the end will be saved.'

The disciples seem to think these last two events might be connected, but are unsure how they might connect with what Jesus has just said about not one stone of the Temple being left on another. We can expect Jesus's answer to make some of these connections. We shall see, however, that Jesus also wants to take the disciples' concern away from the Temple. The Temple is no longer important and will shortly be disabled (27:51), prefiguring the ruin Jesus has just predicted. What matters is 'the end'. And here, Jesus wants to take the disciples' focus off the precise timing of the end, such as looking for signs that the end is just about to happen, and to put their focus instead on persevering faithfully through to the end – regardless of its timing, which is not their concern.

General warnings (24:4–14)

Jesus begins his answer to the disciples' question with a general warning against being led astray (verse 4, 'Watch out that no one deceives you'; verse 6, 'See to it that you are not alarmed'). This sets the tone for everything that follows. Many will come claiming to be the Messiah, and many will wrongly believe them (verse 5). Many things will happen that may look like the end – wars, for example – but 'the end is still to come' (verse 6). International conflicts, famine and earthquake are but 'the beginning of birth-pains' (verse 8).

The most straightforward reading of 'the end' in verse 6 (and verses 13 and 14) is that it refers to 'the end of the age' raised in the disciples' question.

The general warning is followed by a call to long-term endurance (verses 9–14), which repeats much of what Jesus said to his disciples back in Matthew 10. The difference this time is that Jesus seems to be presupposing the international witness that will follow the Great Commission at the end of the Gospel. For example, Jesus says, 'you will be hated by all nations because of me' (verse 9). The disciples need to endure, because 'the one who stands firm to the end will be saved' (verse 13). What is more, 'the end' is delayed, so that the gospel of the kingdom can be proclaimed throughout the whole world (verse 14)

The abomination: some possibilities (24:15–28)

Looking ahead, one possibility at this point in Jesus's teaching is to take verse 29 to be referring specifically to the particular tribulation or distress described in these verses (verses 15–28). That is, the verses describe a particular period of distress that is to take place immediately before the 'Son of Man' events described in verses 29–31. But if we then take the events of verses 29–31 to be the same as the 'coming of the Son of Man' event Jesus teaches on from verse 36 to the end of Matthew 25 (as seems reasonable and as verse 36 suggests), this would create a problem. It would sit oddly with what Jesus goes on to say from verse 36 about the timing of this somewhere-in-the-future event – that no one can know when it is going to happen; it will come at an unexpected time. If the coming of the Son of Man (in glory, at 'the end') comes immediately after a specific event, then when that event happens, those seeing it would know the timing of the end (giving us a contradiction).

Nevertheless, the language of 'those days' in verses 19, 22 and 29 does seem to tie verses 15–28 quite closely to verses 29–31. (We shall come back to this below.)

The abomination as a specific warning

The more consistent way to relate the different elements of these verses begins with noting how comprehensive verses 4–14 are, taking us all the way through to 'the end'. Given this, it makes most sense to take the distress of verses 15–28 as a specific instance of the general distress described in verses 4–14. It could in principle happen at any time in the period between Jesus speaking here in Matthew 24 and 'the end', rather than simply being fixed at the end of this period. (The events of the coming of the Son of Man in verses 29–31 then come immediately after the whole of this period.)

Like the general distress, Jesus is clear that whatever it is should not be mistaken for 'the end'. Jesus encourages the disciples not to be deceived by messiahs and false prophets (verses 23–6) – just as he did in verses 4–5 and 11. The difference this time is that the distress is so severe that those experiencing it should do something specific: that is, flee to the mountains (verse 16). In the context of global mission (verse 14), this repeats the logic of 10:23, when Jesus told the disciples in their mission to the lost sheep of Israel that if they were persecuted in one place, they should flee to another.

The intense period of distress Jesus raises (within the general pattern of distress) begins with them seeing 'standing in the holy place "the abomination that causes desolation" spoken of through the prophet Daniel' (verse 15). By adding 'let the reader understand', Matthew is encouraging us to understand this phrase as it is used in the book of Daniel, where we find it in Daniel 9:27, 11:31 and 12:11. In these verses, the 'abomination that causes desolation' is linked with the destruction of the Temple sanctuary, its profanation and the end of Temple sacrifices. Daniel's prophecies built upon Jeremiah's prophecy of judgment and return (Daniel 9:2), and Jeremiah's preaching (like Jesus's in Matthew 21–3) was focused on the fruitless Temple (Jeremiah 7:1–8:3; 8:13; compare Ezekiel 5:11–15) announcing the destruction of the whole city, an event fulfilled on a 'Day of the Lord' in 586/7 BC. It is understandable, therefore, that many commentators suppose Jesus is talking about something terrible that will happen to the Temple and also perhaps Jerusalem, especially given that this is an event that takes place in Judea (verse 16).

The Temple and city had already been profaned and damaged by

Antiochus Epiphanes in 167 BC, in what became known as the Maccabean crisis. This is what the 'abomination' in Daniel's visions may refer to in the first instance. But looking back from later in history, we also know that similar events of profaning and destroying took place in AD 70 and AD 135. It is reasonable to suppose that is what Jesus was referring forward to in verses 15–22. In particular, readers after AD 70 might well associate the 'abomination' with the corruption and destruction of the Temple which happened in that year (as with the clearer allusion in Luke's account, Luke 21:20).

Alternatively, we need to keep in mind that in that in Matthew, Mark and Luke, the Temple effectively ends when Jesus dies and its curtain is torn (Matthew 27:51, Mark 15:38, Luke 23:45). The cross is also an end-time event. Indeed, it is the key end-time event: it is God coming in judgment in a manner that prefigures his judgment at the final end – but this time, on the Son of Man (27:51–4). It is therefore possible that we should include the cross as part of the complex web of interrelations and allusions in this chapter.

Either way, what is described in verses 15–22 is the only event in 24:4–28 we can link with the prediction of 'not one stone will be left on another' in verse 2. However, the link is not explicit. The warning about the 'abomination' seems to be deliberately ambiguous. It could be a way of talking about any future severe persecution or tribulation facing Jesus's disciples. Whatever these are, they should not be mistaken for the end. As Davies and Allison note, Jesus is speaking in the language of 'eschatological events to come' (compare, for example, verse 21 to Dan 12:1).[1] While it was common to use such language in Old Testament accounts of divine judgment that were not the end (e.g., Isaiah 13 on the destruction of Babylon by the Medes; note also similar language to verse 21 in Exodus 9:18, 11:6), it may well be that Jesus is using such language to show that this event at least prefigures the end.

What is clear is that Jesus is saying that no one should be unduly distracted by the 'abomination' event. In verses 23–6, Jesus returns to the exhortation not to be led astray by false messiahs and false prophets, forming an inclusion with verses 4–8. The end of the Temple (if that is in view) is hugely significant, as is made clear in 21:12–13; 24:1–2; 27:51 – its end makes way for the 'vineyard' to be given to others (21:41). Nevertheless, it is, literally, not the end of the world! Rather than be distracted, disciples at the time, or disciples facing similar great tribulation,

---

[1] W. D. Davies and Dale C. Allison, Jr., *Matthew 19–28* (London: T&T Clark, 1997), 331.

can take comfort that such tribulation is cut short by God (verse 22) and that vindication will always come to those who remain faithful.

In these verses, Jesus helps the disciples not to be deceived by false messiahs and prophets by saying that the coming of the Son of Man will be an event of a completely different order of magnitude from someone saying, 'There he is,' or, 'Here he is' (verse 26). It will be like lightning, visible from east to west (verse 27). In other words, there is no warrant to be distracted by things that are not the end, or people who have nothing to do with the end. This is because when the Son of Man does come, it will be plainly and immediately obvious to the whole world, from east to west. The same idea is probably also the meaning of the proverb in verse 28. A corpse can also be seen from east to west because of the vultures that gather over it. (The association of the coming of the Son of Man with death and mourning is also suggested in verse 30 – see below.)

The sign and coming of the Son of Man: some possibilities (24:29–35)

If we insist that 'the distress of those days' (verse 29) must refer specifically to verses 15–22, and that these must refer to the tribulation preceding AD 70, then we are led to a reading along the lines of R. T. France.[2] Verses 29–35 would then be describing the events of AD 70. Similarly, if verses 15–22 refer to the tribulation preceding the cross in the coming narrative of Matthew 26–8, then we are led to a reading along the lines of the one suggested by Peter Bolt.[3] In this understanding, Jesus would be speaking predominantly about his coming suffering and death. In both these cases, the vindication in verses 26–30 would be a partial vindication, and the gathering of the elect in verse 31 would mark the *start* of the mission to the nations (compare 28:18–20). Notice that the timing fits Peter Bolt's reading better.

However, if 'the distress of those days' refers more generally to all the kinds of tribulation described in verses 4–28 (with AD 70 as a possible special instance), then we are led to a reading along the lines of Davies and Allison, or Don Carson.[4] In this case, the vindication of verses 26–30 would be the final vindication of God's purposes, and verse 31 would mark the gathering at the *end* of the age (compare 25:31–46, which uses very similar language).

---

[2] France, *The Gospel of Matthew*, 885–967.
[3] Peter Bolt, *Matthew: A Great Light Dawns* (Sydney: Aquila Press, 2014), 209–15.
[4] Davies and Allison, *Matthew 19–28*, 326–433; Carson, *Matthew 13–28*, 488–523.

Or there could be a deliberate ambiguity, resolved in the narrative of Matthew 26–8 – which is the interpretation I would favour here. Both particular and general instances of tribulation are followed by vindication. (But the emphasis in this case would be on final vindication. After all, final judgment and final vindication has been the repeated emphasis in Matthew from the beginning, and we would expect to see that here too.)

The sign and coming as encouragement

Whatever period of distress Jesus has in mind here, we can be clear from these verses that after tribulation and distress comes vindication. The time of vindication is marked by darkened sun, falling stars and shaking (verse 29). These are familiar images across the Scriptures of the Lord coming in divine judgment to vindicate his name and make himself known (e.g., Isaiah 13:10; 34:4; Joel 2:10, 3:15–16). In verse 30, Jesus talks about both the appearance of the 'sign of the Son of Man in heaven' and 'the Son of Man coming on the clouds of heaven, with power and great glory'. Back in verse 3, the disciples asked about the *sign of* his coming. Here we get an answer, but Jesus basically presents the sign of the coming of the Son of Man and the coming of the Son of Man as the same event. This reinforces what he said in verses 27–8. The coming of the Son of Man will not need a separate sign.

The peoples of the earth (who have set themselves up against the Lord and his anointed) will mourn when the Lord is vindicated at his coming (verse 30). But for the elect, it will be a great day of gathering (verse 31).

The mini-parable about the fig tree in verses 32–3 most likely explains the relationship between 24:4–28 and 24:29–31. On a fig tree, leaves are an indication (Jesus doesn't use the word 'sign') that summer is near. Likewise, seeing 'all these things' is an indication that the coming of the Son of Man is near.

Jesus talks about 'all these things' again in verse 34 – again referring to the tribulations in 24:4–28: he says all of them will be seen within the current generation. This part of Jesus's final long speech to his disciples ends with him assuring them that his words about the nearness of the end are absolutely faithful (verse 35).

If Jesus is saying that the end is near, because from this point on his disciples will be in the final period of distress and tribulation before the end, then the nearness of the end is 'near' as in the kingdom being 'near' in 3:2 and 4:17. That is, the end is imminent, next on God's agenda, already present in some partial sense but not necessarily temporally immediate (as we see in the parables of chapter 13). The final timing is known only by the Father, as we see in the next section, from verse 36.

SUMMARY AND PURPOSE

As with the other speeches in Matthew, which are also teaching directed at those already following Jesus as his disciples, there are nonetheless things here that might persuade a non-disciple to become one. In particular, Jesus is claiming that salvation and vindication are certain for those who follow him and remain faithful and undeceived until the end. Salvation from the distress of the days to come does not come any other way.

For the reader or hearer who is already a disciple, my claim here is that the speech in Matthew 24–5 is not nearly as difficult or as complicated as it is often made out to be, so long as we focus on the main imperative and recognise the basic pattern Jesus is setting out. The main imperative in this first part of Jesus's answer is 'watch out' ('that no one deceives you', verse 4). All the others follow from this: 'see to it you are not alarmed' (by things that are not the end, verse 6) and 'do not believe' (in false messiahs, verse 23). Then there are the imperatives connected with the 'abomination': 'let the reader understand' (the connection with Daniel's visions, verse 15), 'flee to the mountains' (verse 16), 'let no one . . . go down' or 'go back' (to get anything, verses 17–18), and 'pray' ('that your flight will not take place in winter or on the Sabbath', verse 20).

The basic pattern in this first part of Jesus's answer is that there will be tribulation and distress, but this will inevitably and surely be followed by vindication. The vindication is described using the terminology of Daniel 7 as 'the Son of Man coming on the clouds of heaven, with power and great glory' in verses 29–31. Reading on, we see this is the same event described as 'the coming of the Son of Man' from verse 36 onwards. This second part of Jesus's answer will end with a vision of final Judgment, a moment described as 'when the Son of Man comes in his glory' in 25:31. It is therefore the same final event as 'the end' Jesus talks about in 24:6, 13–14.

The purpose so far is therefore for the disciples to persevere to the end through distress and tribulation, not to be deceived by people or events that the end has come when it has not, but firmly convinced that vindication will come. This even applies to an event so distressing that it is 'unequalled from the beginning of the world until now' (verse 21). In such a case, it would be appropriate to flee (verses 15–16; compare 10:23 and Jesus's example of withdrawing from persecution earlier in the Gospel). But even in such a case, the exhortation is not to be deceived that the end has come (verses 23–8).

We should also note, however, that Jesus deliberately initially leaves the timing (and relative timing) of the great distress (verses 15–28) and the vindication of verses 29–31 quite imprecise. What verses 29–31 are referring to only becomes explicitly clear in the second part of Jesus's answer. The imprecision is helpful, because it allows the narrative from Matthew 26 to strengthen the disciples' conviction that vindication will surely follow the tribulation they are about to enter. What they observe in Matthew 26–8 is Jesus as Son of Man experiencing a distress 'unequalled from the beginning of the world until now' (verse 21; compare 27:3–10, 32–8). But even within this, in the conflict between him and those in the Temple, he is the one vindicated, as the Temple curtain is torn from top to bottom (27:51). Jesus's curse-bearing work on behalf of others is then vindicated in his resurrection and as he declares that he has been given all authority in heaven and earth (28:18).

Those disciples in Jerusalem later on observing the war, siege and destruction of AD 66–70 will see another period of great distress associated with the Temple, and a further vindication of Jesus and everything he has said. The judgment prefigured in 27:51 will then be publicly confirmed, fulfilling the warning of 24:2.

To see Jesus, the Son of Man, so clearly vindicated in these events (one of which, the resurrection, happens soon after this; the other, the siege of Jerusalem, within a generation) strengthens his promise to those who follow him that they too will be vindicated in good time.

ESCHATOLOGY

I have argued in the comments above that in answering his disciples' question, Jesus does not give an explicit, precise programme of future events. There is a degree of referential ambiguity and obscurity in Jesus's answer – but it is deliberate and controlled. By withholding precise information on the referentiality of certain events (such as the abomination in 24:15) and by withholding information on the timing of 'the end', Jesus keeps his followers alert to multiple possible distractions and constantly 'awake'.

Instead of a programme, Jesus sets out a basic pattern – one that will unfold historically in more than one way. The pattern is that turmoil and tribulation will inevitably be followed by vindication. They are the (ironically) comforting signs that vindication is 'near', just as leaves on a fig tree are signs that summer is near (24:32). Therefore, in the midst of turmoil and tribulation, do not mistake the signs for what they signify and thereby be deceived and led astray. Vindication will be clear when it comes. But also, because the timing of vindication is open, keep awake.

Matthew also gives the clues we need to see this pattern working out in identifiable historical events. As we see this, it strengthens the conviction of disciples suffering in the present that future vindication is secure.

The first time we encounter the paradigm in action lies within the narrative of Matthew itself. In his suffering and death, Jesus experiences 'great distress, unequalled from the beginning of the world' (24:21). From a superficial perspective, it will look like his enemies in the religious establishment have been victorious and he has been defeated. We shall see that the reverse is true. Jesus is the one fully vindicated, made clear to us first in his resurrection and then in the declaration of 28:18: 'All authority in heaven and on earth has been given to me.' However, it is also clear as this unfolds that it anticipates future events. In particular, as Jesus dies, it will be like (and look like) the end-time Judgment brought into the present. Jesus's enemies are judged, signified by the tearing of the Temple curtain (27:51). People holy to God are vindicated, signified by the opening of the tombs in 27:52–3.[5]

A disciple witnessing the siege of Jerusalem and fall of the Temple in AD 70 will also see the pattern in action. (The same applies to later readers looking back on those events.) There will be great tribulation in Jerusalem, and Jesus's followers will be under extreme pressure. They will need to flee if they can (24:16). Nevertheless, they will be publicly vindicated in their choice. It is those who fail to recognise Jesus as Christ who will be judged, and the Temple at the centre of their opposition will finally be destroyed.[6]

These historical expressions of vindication following tribulation give weight and credibility to the promise that vindication will follow the tribulation faced by later disciples. Within a generation of Jesus speaking, instances of every example he has talked about in 24:4–31 will have taken place – including foretastes of the final vindication itself! His word is trustworthy (24:35). Therefore, keep going: do not be led astray; keep awake.

If the basic pattern claimed by Jesus in the speech is that tribulation will be followed by vindication, then the view of the future implied by

---

[5] Meier describes the death and resurrection of Jesus as a 'proleptic parousia'. That is, anticipating something future using present-tense language. John P. Meier, *Matthew* (Dublin: Veritas 1980), 289.

[6] This is the line of thought highlighted by Luke in his account of Jesus's teaching on the future – Luke 21:20–24. Luke is historically more straightforwardly concrete than Matthew, partly because he has the luxury of addressing the situation of post-resurrection readers directly in the book of Acts.

the speech is one that does not strongly distinguish between different possible instances of future tribulation or different possible instances of future vindication. However, we at this point may build upon the observation above that the first time we encounter the paradigm in action lies within the narrative of Matthew itself. We can argue that this provides a distinction between future events that Jesus held back from giving in the speech itself. That is, events that have apparently been portrayed as contemporaneous are teased out and shown to be separate by the subsequent narrative.

We have seen something like this in Matthew before. In 3:7–12, John the Baptist presented a view of the near future in which the coming of a mightier one after him (3:11) was not distinguished from the coming of the end-time, separating Judgment. However, what happened next served to update John's expectations. Jesus came as the mightier one after John, but he did not bring wrath or a judgment of fire for the unrepentant. Indeed, he continued to proclaim the Judgment as a future event (e.g., 7:21–3; 10:32–3; 11:22–4). We can say that the implied future as it stood at the end of 3:12 has been temporally resolved by the arrival of Jesus in 3:13–17.

We can now argue that just as we saw a 'temporal resolution' in Matthew 3, as the one coming after John came without judgment, so here. We have already seen the ways in which Jesus uniquely experiences in himself in the narrative of Matthew 26–8 the tribulation–vindication pattern he has outlined previously, including the speech of Matthew 24–5. In other words, by the end of the Gospel, the Son of Man has been through both tribulation and vindication, such that in some significant sense we may say that he has come. As Jesus promised, 'all these things' happen within the current generation (compare 24:33). However, it is also clear at the end of the Gospel that 'the end' has not yet come. The global proclamation has only just begun (28:19–20; compare 24:14) and 'the very end of the age' lies in the future (28:20).

What this suggests in particular is that by the end of the Gospel, Matthew wants his readers to separate 'the coming of the Son of Man' into two events, temporally distinct but nevertheless retaining a tight connection. There is the vindication of the Son of Man – in the sense that he is vindicated. And there is the vindication of the Son of Man – in the vindication he will enact for others in the separating Judgment of the whole world. Nevertheless, these remain tightly connected. The first event confirms and guarantees the second:

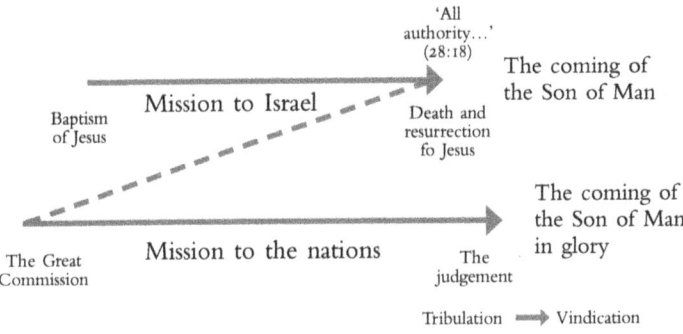

Figure 8

2. The final briefing part 2 • Matthew 24:36–25:46

This is the second part of Jesus's answer to the disciples' question in 24:3. Jesus has just said of the Temple, 'not one stone here will be left on another; every one will be thrown down' (24:2). The disciples then asked, 'Tell us . . . when will this happen, and what will be the sign of your coming and of the end of the age?' (24:3). I argued above that the first part of Jesus's answer could be summed up like this:

> 24:4–35 The answer part 1: Don't worry about when these things will happen; just make sure you are not deceived by lies among the coming tribulation (which may include the tribulation associated with the destruction of the Temple, or tribulation like it). But be assured that vindication will surely come, and it will be absolutely clear when it does.

We now come to the second part of Jesus's answer.

The day and hour unknown

36 'But about that day or hour no one knows, not even the angels in heaven, nor the Son,[f] but only the Father. **37** As it was in the days of Noah, so it will be at the coming of the Son of Man. **38** For in the days before the flood, people were eating and drinking, marrying and giving in marriage, up to the day Noah entered the ark; **39** and they knew nothing about what would happen until the flood came and took them all away. That is how it will be at the coming of the Son of Man. **40** Two men will be in the field; one will be taken and the other left. **41** Two women will be grinding with a hand mill; one will be taken and the other left.

341

⁴²'Therefore keep watch, because you do not know on what day your Lord will come. ⁴³But understand this: if the owner of the house had known at what time of night the thief was coming, he would have kept watch and would not have let his house be broken into. ⁴⁴So you also must be ready, because the Son of Man will come at an hour when you do not expect him.

⁴⁵'Who then is the faithful and wise servant, whom the master has put in charge of the servants in his household to give them their food at the proper time? ⁴⁶It will be good for that servant whose master finds him doing so when he returns. ⁴⁷Truly I tell you, he will put him in charge of all his possessions. ⁴⁸But suppose that servant is wicked and says to himself, "My master is staying away a long time," ⁴⁹and he then begins to beat his fellow servants and to eat and drink with drunkards. ⁵⁰The master of that servant will come on a day when he does not expect him and at an hour he is not aware of. ⁵¹He will cut him to pieces and assign him a place with the hypocrites, where there will be weeping and gnashing of teeth.

The parable of the ten virgins

25 ¹'At that time the kingdom of heaven will be like ten virgins who took their lamps and went out to meet the bridegroom. ²Five of them were foolish and five were wise. ³The foolish ones took their lamps but did not take any oil with them. ⁴The wise ones, however, took oil in jars along with their lamps. ⁵The bridegroom was a long time in coming, and they all became drowsy and fell asleep.

⁶'At midnight the cry rang out: "Here's the bridegroom! Come out to meet him!"

⁷'Then all the virgins woke up and trimmed their lamps. ⁸The foolish ones said to the wise, "Give us some of your oil; our lamps are going out."

⁹'"No," they replied, "there may not be enough for both us and you. Instead, go to those who sell oil and buy some for yourselves."

¹⁰'But while they were on their way to buy the oil, the bridegroom arrived. The virgins who were ready went in with him to the wedding banquet. And the door was shut.

¹¹'Later the others also came. "Lord, Lord," they said, "open the door for us!"

¹²'But he replied, "Truly I tell you, I don't know you."

¹³'Therefore keep watch, because you do not know the day or the hour.

The parable of the bags of gold

¹⁴'Again, it will be like a man going on a journey, who called his servants and entrusted his wealth to them. ¹⁵To one he gave five bags of gold, to another two bags, and to another one bag,^a each according to his ability. Then he went on his journey. ¹⁶The man who had received five bags of gold went at once and put his money to work and gained five bags more. ¹⁷So also, the one with two bags of gold gained two more. ¹⁸But the man who had received one bag went off, dug a hole in the ground and hid his master's money.

19 'After a long time the master of those servants returned and settled accounts with them. 20 The man who had received five bags of gold brought the other five. "Master," he said, "you entrusted me with five bags of gold. See, I have gained five more."

21 'His master replied, "Well done, good and faithful servant! You have been faithful with a few things; I will put you in charge of many things. Come and share your master's happiness!"

22 'The man with two bags of gold also came. "Master," he said, "you entrusted me with two bags of gold: see, I have gained two more."

23 'His master replied, "Well done, good and faithful servant! You have been faithful with a few things; I will put you in charge of many things. Come and share your master's happiness!"

24 'Then the man who had received one bag of gold came. "Master," he said, "I knew that you are a hard man, harvesting where you have not sown and gathering where you have not scattered seed. 25 So I was afraid and went out and hid your gold in the ground. See, here is what belongs to you."

26 'His master replied, "You wicked, lazy servant! So you knew that I harvest where I have not sown and gather where I have not scattered seed? 27 Well then, you should have put my money on deposit with the bankers, so that when I returned I would have received it back with interest.

28 ' "So take the bag of gold from him and give it to the one who has ten bags.

29 For whoever has will be given more, and they will have an abundance. Whoever does not have, even what they have will be taken from them. 30 And throw that worthless servant outside, into the darkness, where there will be weeping and gnashing of teeth."

The sheep and the goats

31 'When the Son of Man comes in his glory, and all the angels with him, he will sit on his glorious throne. 32 All the nations will be gathered before him, and he will separate the people one from another as a shepherd separates the sheep from the goats. 33 He will put the sheep on his right and the goats on his left.

34 'Then the King will say to those on his right, "Come, you who are blessed by my Father; take your inheritance, the kingdom prepared for you since the creation of the world. 35 For I was hungry and you gave me something to eat, I was thirsty and you gave me something to drink, I was a stranger and you invited me in, 36 I needed clothes and you clothed me, I was ill and you looked after me, I was in prison and you came to visit me."

37 'Then the righteous will answer him, "Lord, when did we see you hungry and feed you, or thirsty and give you something to drink? 38 When did we see you a stranger and invite you in, or needing clothes and clothe you? 39 When did we see you ill or in prison and go to visit you?"

40 'The King will reply, "Truly I tell you, whatever you did for one of the

least of these brothers and sisters of mine, you did for me."

41 'Then he will say to those on his left, "Depart from me, you who are cursed, into the eternal fire prepared for the devil and his angels. **42** For I was hungry and you gave me nothing to eat, I was thirsty and you gave me nothing to drink, **43** I was a stranger and you did not invite me in, I needed clothes and you did not clothe me, I was ill and in prison and you did not look after me."

44 'They also will answer, "Lord, when did we see you hungry or thirsty or a stranger or needing clothes or ill or in prison, and did not help you?"

45 'He will reply, "Truly I tell you, whatever you did not do for one of the least of these, you did not do for me."

46 'Then they will go away to eternal punishment, but the righteous to eternal life.'

------

f 36 Some manuscripts do not have *nor the Son.*

a 15 Greek *five talents . . . two talents . . . one talent;* also throughout this parable; a talent was worth about 20 years of a day labourer's wage.

The second part of the answer can be summarised like this:

> The answer part 2: You cannot know 'when', but make sure you are vigilant and diligent in service while waiting for the return of your master, because these will be tested when he comes in judgment.

Or, to put it another way (as Davies and Allison put it), because you do not know the day or hour of the coming of the Son of Man, keep watch.[7]

The section begins with Jesus's assertion about not knowing the day or hour (24:36), and ends with a picture of what the day will be like (25:31–46). In between, there are parables encouraging the disciples to be ready for that day, emphasising either vigilance (watchfulness) or diligence (service) and arranged like this:

(36) Headline issue: 'About that day or hour, no one knows, not even the angels in heaven, nor the Son, but only the Father.'	
(37–44) Three short parables exhorting vigilance: Like the days of Noah . . . Like one taken, one left . . . Like a thief in the night . . .	(25:1–13) A long parable exhorting vigilance: (The parable of the virgins)

------

7 Davies and Allison, *Matthew 19–28,* 376–7.

(45–51) A parable exhorting diligence: (The parable of the servant) Ends with: '. . . where there will be weeping and gnashing of teeth'.	(25:14–30) A parable exhorting diligence: (The parable of the talents) Ends with: '. . . where there will be weeping and gnashing of teeth'.
(25:31–46) A picture of final Judgment	

Table 19

The parables repeat the truth that the hour is unknown (24:42, 44, 50). They also suggest it will be delayed (24:48; 25:14, 19) and will come suddenly (24:27–9, 39, 43–4, 50). This reinforces our conclusion in the first part of Jesus's answer that the coming of the Son of Man in 24:29–31 comes without a special sign preceding it, and comes suddenly at the end of the whole period of tribulation described in 24:4–28.

Even before the picture of final Judgment in 25:31–46, some of the parables describe a division into two groups (24:37–41, 45–51; 25:14–30). This is another way to exhort the disciples to persevere to the end. They need to ensure they find themselves on the right side of this divide.

Concerning that day or hour (24:36)

Apart from the Father, no one knows 'that day or hour'. It does seem most natural to take 'that day or hour' to refer back to the 'Son of Man coming on the clouds of heaven' in verse 30, hence Jesus repeating the phrase 'the coming of the Son of Man' in verses 37 and 39 (with a similar expression in verse 44). In the parables that follow, and in the final scene in 25:31–46, it also seems fairly clear that from this point we are concerned with 'the end' (as in 24:6, 13–14) and with eschatological Judgment.

Not even the Son knows the day or hour. It is unlikely that Jesus wants us to hear 'Son' as shorthand for 'Son of Man' here. He doesn't do this anywhere else. 'Son' appears in the same sentence as 'Father', so Jesus is talking about himself as the (unique) Son of the Father.

I began to argue in the Introduction that, like Mark and Luke, Matthew's presentation of Jesus is that he is fully part of the divine identity. It is true that his identity is uncovered gradually rather than all at once, beginning with Jesus as the promised human descendant of David, called Messiah, who will save and rescue God's people, leading them to victory. But from the very beginning we get suggestions, hints and implications that Jesus is much more than a merely human king like David. And we shall see that, by the end of the Gospel, we do see the identity fully revealed, as

Jesus is given a full, divine authority over heaven and earth (28:18). If this is right, then it's a puzzle that Jesus the Son does not know what the Father knows about the day or hour of the coming of the Son of Man.

It is most likely that the ignorance of the Son in verse 36 is out of a pastoral concern for the disciples. As we shall observe in the parables to come in this section, it is very important – for their own benefit – that the disciples do not know the day or hour. We can take it, then, that the ignorance of the incarnate Son here is a voluntary ignorance: part of the mandate he has taken on from his Father to save people from their sins. Salvation comes from following Jesus, coming to Jesus, being his disciple, persevering to the end. This close relationship could be coloured somewhat if his disciples knew he was keeping something from them. Hence, he chooses not to know.

Three short parables on vigilance (24:37–44)

A comparison with the days of Noah begins three parables encouraging watchfulness and vigilance.

Verse 37 begins with 'For' (missing from the NIV), linking what follows to the uncertainty of 'that day or hour' in verse 36. Like the judgment at the time of Noah, the coming of the Son of Man (the final Judgment) will burst in unexpectedly and many will be caught off guard (verses 37–8).

This is followed by two examples, in perfect parallelism, of one taken, one left (24:40 and 41). Back in verse 39, those being 'taken' were being taken in judgment by the flood. The Greek word is different in verses 40 and 41, but it makes sense to assume a similar idea (especially since the word for 'leave' can mean 'pardon'). Some will be taken in judgment; some will be left, and survive.[8] The implication is: be ready, and make sure you are on the right side of the division. Or, as Jesus puts it in verse 42, 'Therefore keep watch.' Just as 'Watch out that no one deceives you' set the tone for the first part of Jesus's answer (24:4–36), so now, 'Therefore keep watch,' or, 'Be on the alert,' sets the tone for the second part of Jesus's answer (24:36–25:46). The reason is 'because you do not know on what day your Lord will come'.

· In the next parable, the coming of the Son of Man is compared to the uncertain timing of a thief coming in the night. The application is,

---

[8] That is, the pattern is opposite to, and speaks against, popular rapture theology, where those 'taken' are not taken in judgment but taken to meet the Lord in the air and thence to heaven.

'So you also must be ready' (verse 44). The reason is 'because the Son of Man will come at an hour when you do not expect him'.

We are beginning to see, then, just how important is for disciples not to know the day of Jesus's coming. If they did know the temptation would be to wait until the day approached before doing anything. Not knowing brings about watchfulness, focus and vigilance

A parable on diligence (24:45–51)

The parable of the servant (24:45–51) imagines a situation where a master has left a servant in charge of feeding the other servants (24:45). The question is: will he do it? If the servant is diligent, then he is a faithful and wise servant (24:45) and will be appropriately rewarded (24:47). If the servant uses the delay of his master to indulge in self-serving activity, he is a wicked servant (24:48–9), and when the master returns (24:50) will be severely punished (24:51).

As with other parables, this one uses an analogy to expose how wrong it is to be given a task and then to not do it. In the familiar world of households, masters and servants, it's obvious that the servant caught abusing his position and not doing a given task will be punished. However, the rewards and punishments in the story are far more extreme than we would expect in any household (24:47, 51)! This is a reminder that what Jesus has in view is the task he is leaving his disciples to do, and the Judgment that will take place at his return in glory. The implied argument, then, is, if diligence is right behaviour in a household setting, then how much more is it for you as my disciples, awaiting my return?

The parable of the servant continues the idea of an unexpected coming: 'The master of that servant will come on a day when he does not expect him and at an hour he is not aware of' (24:50). We are seeing, then, further reasons for how important it is for disciples not to know the day of Jesus's coming. If they did know and the timing was distant, what a disciple did today would feel distant from the future occasion on which their behaviour will be judged. Not knowing keeps the day close as an ever-present possibility, helping the disciples to serve diligently.

A parable on vigilance (25:1–13)

In the parable of the wise and foolish virgins, the scene is a wedding celebration. This is a classic five-act story. In the setting of the story, five wise virgins take oil for their lamps and five foolish virgins do not

(25:1–4). Then the͟ cond scene) a complication: the bridegroom is
delayed (25:5). A ͟ then arises in the middle of the night from an
unexpected deve͟ ͟t. The arrival of the bridegroom is announced
and the foolish ͟ ask for oil from the wise virgins, but there is
none to spare (͟). Then the bridegroom arrives and only the wise
virgins go in to͟ marriage feast (25:10). Afterwards, in the final act, the
foolish virgins ͟ denied entry (25:11–12). Jesus gives the application in
25:13: 'There͟ keep watch, because you not know the day or the hour.'

This is not strictly an allegory, but there are elements of allegory here.
Jesus has already made the equation Jesus = Christ = bridegroom (9:15),
drawing on Old Testament precedents equating the Lord God to a bridegroom. The virgins clearly represent disciples, wise or foolish, but it is
probably too far of a stretch to suppose their virginity is highly significant
(as Augustine did).[9] David Garland suggests the oil represents 'evidential
works of righteousness'.[10] This is possible, but also probably going too far.
As Carson says, 'It is merely an element in the narrative showing that the
foolish virgins were unprepared for the delay and so shut out in the end.'[11]

As with other parables, this one uses an analogy to expose wrong
behaviour. The world of weddings, bridegrooms and wedding banquets
would be familiar to the disciples Jesus is addressing. To them, it would
be obvious (as in the other wedding parable in 22:1–14) that being
unprepared for the celebration would be dishonouring to the bridegroom and therefore it would feel right that the foolish virgins are
excluded. As with the parable of the servant (24:45–51), some things
within the story world of the parable seem excessively harsh – such as
the refusal to share oil in 25:9 or the response of the bridegroom, 'I
don't know you,' in 25:12. But these things make sense if we remember
that again he has in view his own return in glory. This will be a time
when qualities such as watchfulness and living in anticipation of his
return will not be easily transferable from one person to another, like
lamp oil. And people will be rightly judged on whether they have lived
in relation to him or not – as in 7:23, where Jesus uses very similar
words to those who claim to know him but, in reality, do not. The
implied argument this time is, if watchfulness and vigilance are right

---

9 More likely, the story has ten 'virgins' – that is, unmarried relatives or friends
– because young females like this would indeed have played a similar role in an
actual marriage ceremony at the time.
10 David E. Garland, *Reading Matthew: A Literary and Theological Commentary on the
First Gospel* (New York: Crossroad, 1993), 241.
11 Carson, *Matthew 13–28*, 512.

behaviour in a wedding setting, then how much more is it for you as my disciples, awaiting my return?

Another parable on diligence (25:14–30)

Compared to the other parables in this section, the (even longer) parable of the talents lacks the elements of unexpected and sudden return and the call to watchfulness. Rather than there being a delay, the master is simply away 'for a long time' (25:19). The focus is more on faithfulness and productivity while awaiting his return.

There are three scenes. In the first scene (25:15), a master entrusts property to three servants: five 'bags of gold' to one, two to a second and one to a third. (As in 18:21–35, a 'bag of gold', as the NIV has it, was a talent, the largest monetary unit in use in the ancient world.) In the second scene (25:16–18), the master departs and the servants carry out their business: the first makes five more 'bags of gold', the second two more and the third simply buries what he was given. In the third and final scene (25:19–30), the master returns and settles accounts. There is reward for the one who made five talents, reward for the one who made one talent and punishment for the one who buried his talent.

Despite there being three servants, this is still a separation into two groups. The reward for the first two servants is identical: 'Well done, good and faithful servant! You have been faithful with a few things; I will put you in charge of many things. Come and share your master's happiness! (25:21, 23). The punishment for the third servant is severe (25:26–30).

What does the third servant do so wrong? He tries to blame the master for his actions and slanders him, saying, 'I knew that you are a hard man, harvesting where you have not sown and gathering where you have not scattered seed' (25:24). That is, he was afraid of losing his money, which is why he buried it (25:25). His words and actions betray a 'fear which is the opposite of love and trust'.[12] It is for this hatred and lack of faith that he is judged. As before, the punishment is severe. Being thrown outside 'where there will be weeping and gnashing of teeth' (25:30) is how Jesus previously described eternal judgment in 8:12; 13:42, 50; 22:13; 24:51. As with the earlier parable of the servant (24:45–51), the implied argument is, if good use of time and resources is right behaviour in a household setting, then how much more is it for you as my disciples, awaiting my return?

---

[12] Garland, *Reading Matthew*, 242. The opposite, then, of the fear of God that is the beginning of wisdom (e.g., Psalm 111:10; Proverbs 9:10).

This is a parable especially in need of careful application. The third servant does not correspond to a disciple with faith but unwilling, say, to use some of the 'gifts' he has been given. Someone, for example, who is otherwise faithful but reluctant to help with the children's ministry in a local church would not correspond to the third servant. For such a person, the punishment of 25:30 would indeed be disproportionate! We need to be clear: the third servant here *does not have faith*: he despises the master and tries to keep everything he has been given for himself.

Having said this, the parable is nonetheless an encouragement for Jesus's disciples to use all the resources and opportunities he gives them to do the task he has left them with. In Matthew's Gospel, this servant task is summarised in the Great Commission: go and make disciples in all the nations. Making good use of what we might call 'gifts' (as in the lists of Romans 12:3–8, 1 Corinthians 12:4–11 or 1 Peter 4:7–11) does come into this, but much more besides. Trust, love and diligent service is the key purpose of the parable.

A picture of final judgment (25:31–46)

The final scene uses the image of a shepherd dividing his flock to portray the Judgment of the nations, when the Son of Man finally appears in his glory. (A similar phrase to 'Son of Man comes', and the words 'glory' and 'angels' also appeared in 24:29–31, supporting the idea that those verses were also concerning the final return of the Son of Man in judgment.) Davies and Allison helpfully describe this as 'a word-picture of the Last Judgment', rather than a parable.[13]

This is a conventional judgment scene. The scene is set in 25:31–3, with the nations gathered before the King, who will separate them into two groups, 'as a shepherd separates the sheep from the goats'. The King speaks first to those on his right (25:34–40) and then to those on his left (25:41–5). Jesus concludes: the second group will go away to eternal punishment; the first to eternal life (25:46).[14]

---

[13] Davies and Allison, *Matthew 19–28*, 418. Among other things, the future tenses make it very unlike a parable.

[14] Both punishment and life are 'eternal' (compare also 'eternal fire' in 25:41 and 18:8). Some argue that 'eternal' (*aiōnios*) should be translated as 'in the age to come', based on Jesus's use of a related word *aiōn* in Matthew 12:32 (e.g., France, *The Gospel of Matthew*, 485, 683, 966–7). If this is right, then it leaves open the possibility of a punishment that destroys and then ceases, with no conscious experience to follow, as in the view known as 'annihilationism'. But it is more usual

The two speeches follow an identical pattern. The King speaks, declaring reward or punishment on the basis of whether or not the group gave him food or drink, welcomed him, clothed him, visited him when he was sick or came to him in prison (25:34–6, 41–3). Each group then asks when these things happened (25:37–9, 44). The King responds, 'Truly I say to you, whatever you did (not do) for one of the least of these (brothers and sisters), you did (not do) for me' (25:40, 45).

This criterion almost certainly builds on the test of worthiness in chapter 10. In chapter 10:9–15, when a messenger with nothing greets a household, whether he is welcomed and heard dictates whether or not that household is 'worthy'. As David Garland notes, this is generalised at the end of chapter 10: 'If anyone gives even a cup of cold water to one of these little ones who is my disciple, truly I tell you, that person will certainly not lose their reward' (10:42). 'Brothers' ('brothers and sisters' in the NIV) is a term used exclusively of Jesus's disciples in Matthew (12:49–50; 23:8; 28:10). 'Little ones' is used of those who believe in Jesus (10:42; 18:6, 10, 14). How you treat the messenger shows how you respond to the message; and how you treat the 'brothers' and 'little ones' shows how you treat Jesus and the one who sent him (compare 10:40). The Greek word used in 25:40, 45 and translated 'the least of these' is different from the one translated 'little ones' in 10:42; 18:6, 10, 14, but the sense is much the same. Garland concludes, 'The nations are judged according to the way they treated Jesus's humble brethren who represented Christ to them.'[15]

Garland also notes that this judgment scene 'has often been used to emphasise the Christian's obligation to the down and out in society' – and, we might add, thus makes such activity a primary condition of salvation.[16] This requires the 'brothers and sisters' in 25:40 and 'the least of these' in 25:45 to be the materially needy in general. In 25:35–6 and 25:42–3, Jesus would then be identifying intimately with many people who are *not* his disciples – something we don't find him doing anywhere else in the New Testament. But, as already noted, we *do* find him identifying intimately with 'one of these little ones who is my disciple' in 10:40–42 – what one does to such a person is what one does to him. (Acts 9:4–5 is another

---

to take *aiōnios* simply to mean 'a period of unending duration' (as in BDAG). This suggests Jesus is warning about a future punishment that is conscious and without end (although it is hard to be absolutely certain about this). The important pastoral point to make is that the punishment is something *to be avoided at all costs*.

[15] Garland, *Reading Matthew*, 243.

[16] Garland, *Reading Matthew*, 244.

example of Jesus identifying intimately with persecuted disciples – such that what Paul does to them, he does to Jesus.)

As Don Carson (along with many others) observes,[17] there is a consistent concern in the Bible for the poor and oppressed (e.g., Deuteronomy 15:11; Proverbs 14:31; 19:17; 21:13; 22:9, 22; 28:3, 8, 27; 29:7; 31:9, 20; Isaiah 58:6–7; Ezekiel 18:7; Galatians 2:10). However, without negating the scriptural call to attend to the needy in general, it would seem that the purpose of this scene lies elsewhere. In part, this is again to encourage the disciples to be on the right side of the division (with the sheep, as it were). This will in turn encourage them to be those who look after their fellow disciples in the midst of suffering, persecution and tribulation. But also, as they themselves undergo such hardships, it will be encouraging to know that the future judgment of the nations will vindicate them, since it will be on the basis of how they have been treated.

SUMMARY AND PURPOSE

As with the first part of Jesus's answer to his disciples, which was also teaching directed at those already following Jesus as his disciples, there are nonetheless things here that might persuade a non-disciple to become one. In particular, Jesus is claiming that he will come as Son of Man in a final vindication, and will do so suddenly and unexpectedly, dividing people into those who will be saved from eternal punishment for eternal life and those who will not. Anyone who believes this should be persuaded to do everything they can to be a part of the first group.

But the primary purpose of this section is directed towards those who are already disciples. In multiple ways, the message is simple: to be watchful and vigilant, living in constant anticipation of the return of Jesus in glory (24:37–44 and 25:1–13). And then in the meantime to be diligent in service (24:45–51 and 25:14–30), like servants awaiting the return of their master. The kind of servant activity Jesus hints at here includes feeding other servants (24:45) and looking after them in every way (25:31–46). But by the end of the Gospel, we know that the main task of the servant will be to join Jesus in making disciples in all the nations (28:16–20) – which will encompass teaching them and looking after them.

Rewards

In the 'parable of the talents' (or 'bags of gold' as it is in the NIV, 25:14–30), the first two servants put the gold to work and are rewarded

---

[17] Carson, *Matthew 13–28*, 522.

when the master returns and settles accounts with them. The language of rewards comes up repeatedly in Matthew's Gospel. The noun *misthos* – meaning wages, reward or recompense – is used in 5:12, 46; 6:1, 2, 5, 16; 10:41–2; 20:8. The verb *apodomi* – meaning to give, pay out, return, reward or recompense – is used in 6:4, 6, 18; 16:27. But the concept of reward comes up in other ways. For example, it's implied that storing treasure in heaven will result in a future return or reward (6:20). And the reward for losing life now is finding life later (16:24–7). The question is: what kind of reward is being talked about in each case? And how does it function to motivate the disciples in the present?

In the Sermon on the Mount, the reward for being persecuted as a disciple because of Jesus (5:11) is the reward of being people of the kingdom (5:3, 10), with all the future benefits described in 5:4–9. This is an encouragement to be and keep going as a true disciple. It makes sense to take the reward given by the Father to those giving, praying and fasting in secret (6:1–18) to be essentially the same. (Although the contrast with the immediate reward experienced by the 'hypocrites' suggests that the reward to a faithful disciple might also include an element of Fatherly approval or praise.) Similarly, 'treasure(s) in heaven' (6:20; 19:21) is life that lasts, in contrast to a life that doesn't. In 19:21, 'treasure in heaven' is a way of talking about getting or entering into life (19:16–17).

When Jesus talks about people being called 'least' or 'greatest' in the kingdom (5:19; compare 11:11) he is most likely talking about a (future) kingdom perspective on present behaviour. As we saw in the commentary on 5:17–20, he probably means that when the kingdom comes, those who enter will look back on the teaching being done now and see clearly that some was harmfully bad and some was good. Those whose teaching is harmfully bad do not enter the kingdom.[18] So this is not a distinction between people in the future, but people in the present.

In Matthew 10:41–2, the 'prophet's reward' and the 'righteous person's reward' (10:41) follows on from finding life in 10:39.

Similarly, in Matthew 16:24–7, the reward for those who 'lose' life now is to 'find' life in the future (16:25). This is what Jesus means when he says the Son of Man 'will reward each person according to what they have done' (16:27).

In the parable of Matthew 20:1–16, the whole point is that the reward to each of the labourers is exactly the same. There is a strong warning

---

[18] Compare 18:3–4, where the criterion for kingdom entry and the criterion for being 'greatest' in the kingdom is the same.

to those who feel entitled to greater reward for greater work, who are in danger of walking away in disgust.

It's only in the parable of Matthew 25:14–30 that we find any suggestion of a long-term difference of reward to those who are faithful to their master to the end. The bag of gold wasted by the third servant is given to the first servant (and not to the second). In the similar but not identical parable in Luke 19:11–27 the differences are greater: the first servant is given charge of ten cities; the second, charge of five cities. What are we to make of these differences? I personally agree with Craig Blomberg that it would be unwise to make much of them.[19] One would have to take the parable as a very precise allegory to draw any conclusions from the differences in reward to the first and second servants. Even then, it's far from obvious what 'taking charge of ten cities' would correspond to in the kingdom of the heavens, and far from obvious how to square this with the parable in Matthew 20:1–16. More likely, these details are simply to reinforce the main difference between the first and second servants on the one hand and the third servant on the other. Importantly, in the parable, the first and second servants are not motivated by possible differential rewards; they are motivated by their love for the master and the general prospect of sharing in the master's praise and happiness.

Again, this is not to deny the possibility of *some* kind of differentiation between those saved at the Judgment. In 1 Corinthians 4:5, Paul says that at the Judgment, when all is revealed (including the motives of the heart), 'At that time each will receive their praise from God.' This could perhaps be a uniform statement, as in Jesus's parable, 'Well done, good and faithful servant.' But it could be that the praise is individually tailored. (We noted this as a possibility in 6:1–18.) But, again, we should be careful not to overstate this. The reward of salvation and eternal life is a frequently used motivation across the New Testament. Loving the Lord our God and seeking his praise and approval are likewise encouraged. But differential eternal rewards, relative to other believers, are *never* used as a motivation. Again, although it's hard to be certain, I find myself inclined to agree with Craig Blomberg: 'I do not believe that there is a single NT text that, when correctly interpreted, supports the notion that believers will be distinguished one from another from all eternity on the basis of their works as Christians.'[20]

---

[19] Craig L. Blomberg, 'Degrees of Reward in the Kingdom of Heaven?' *Journal of the Evangelical Theology Society* 35, no. 2 (1992): 168.

[20] Blomberg, 'Degrees of Reward?', 160.

14

Mission Completed (and Commissioned)

MATTHEW 26–8

We have reached the final section of the material in Matthew's Gospel that is located in Jerusalem. Jesus has entered his city as a humble king, as one who comes in the name of the Lord (chapters 21–3). He has effectively put the leadership in Jerusalem on trial and found it fruitless and wanting. He has then prepared his disciples to persevere through the coming tribulation with faithful vigilance and diligence (chapters 24–5). Chapters 26–8 will now narrate Jesus being handed over and executed on a cross, but then raised in vindication.

This is all in fulfilment of Jesus's passion-vindication predictions in 16:21, 17:22–3 and 20:17–19. The final prediction was this:

The Son of Man will be delivered over to the chief priests and the teachers of the law. They will condemn him to death and will hand him over to the Gentiles to be mocked and flogged and crucified. On the third day he will be raised to life! (Matthew 20:18–19)

The three parts to this prediction provide the overall three-part structure for Matthew 26–8:[1]

26:1–56 The Son of Man will be delivered over to the chief priests and the teachers of the law	(A) Jesus's opponents plot against him, and his disciples desert him
	(B) But Jesus is determined to complete the task he's been given
26:57–27:54 They will condemn him to death and will hand him over to the Gentiles to be mocked and flogged and crucified	(A) People shown to be under curse for their own actions, or (in the case of Jesus) for the sake of others
	(B) Jesus condemned and mocked for his claims of kingship and divine sonship
27:55–28:20 On the third day he will be raised to life!	(A) The resurrection of Jesus is witnessed and uncovered for the whole world . . .
	(B) He cannot remain buried and hidden

Table 20

1. Mission completed (and commissioned)
part 1 • Matthew 26:1–56

The plot against Jesus

26 When Jesus had finished saying all these things, he said to his disciples, **2**'As you know, the Passover is two days away – and the Son of Man will be handed over to be crucified.'

3Then the chief priests and the elders of the people assembled in the palace of the high priest, whose name was Caiaphas, **4**and they schemed to arrest Jesus secretly and kill him. **5**'But not during the festival,' they said, 'or there may be a riot among the people.'

Jesus anointed at Bethany

6While Jesus was in Bethany in the home of Simon the Leper, **7**a woman came to him with an alabaster jar of very expensive perfume, which she poured on his head as he was reclining at the table.

8When the disciples saw this, they were indignant. 'Why this waste?' they asked. **9**'This perfume could have been sold at a high price and the money given to the poor.'

10Aware of this, Jesus said to them, 'Why are you bothering this woman?

---

[1] The structure suggested here is strongly influenced (with some adaptations) by that in John Paul Heil, *The Death and Resurrection of Jesus: A Narrative–Critical Reading of Matthew 26–28* (Minneapolis: Fortress Press, 1991).

She has done a beautiful thing to me. **11** The poor you will always have with you,^a but you will not always have me. **12** When she poured this perfume on my body, she did it to prepare me for burial. **13** Truly I tell you, wherever this gospel is preached throughout the world, what she has done will also be told, in memory of her.'

Judas agrees to betray Jesus

14 Then one of the Twelve – the one called Judas Iscariot – went to the chief priests **15** and asked, 'What are you willing to give me if I deliver him over to you?' So they counted out for him thirty pieces of silver. **16** From then on Judas watched for an opportunity to hand him over.

The Last Supper

17 On the first day of the Festival of Unleavened Bread, the disciples came to Jesus and asked, 'Where do you want us to make preparations for you to eat the Passover?'

18 He replied, 'Go into the city to a certain man and tell him, "The Teacher says: my appointed time is near. I am going to celebrate the Passover with my disciples at your house."' **19** So the disciples did as Jesus had directed them and prepared the Passover.

20 When evening came, Jesus was reclining at the table with the Twelve. **21** And while they were eating, he said, 'Truly I tell you, one of you will betray me.'

22 They were very sad and began to say to him one after the other, 'Surely you don't mean me, Lord?'

23 Jesus replied, 'The one who has dipped his hand into the bowl with me will betray me. **24** The Son of Man will go just as it is written about him. But woe to that man who betrays the Son of Man! It would be better for him if he had not been born.'

25 Then Judas, the one who would betray him, said, 'Surely you don't mean me, Rabbi?'

Jesus answered, 'You have said so.'

26 While they were eating, Jesus took bread, and when he had given thanks, he broke it and gave it to his disciples, saying, 'Take and eat; this is my body.'

27 Then he took a cup, and when he had given thanks, he gave it to them, saying, 'Drink from it, all of you. **28** This is my blood of the^b covenant, which is poured out for many for the forgiveness of sins. **29** I tell you, I will not drink from this fruit of the vine from now on until that day when I drink it new with you in my Father's kingdom.'

30 When they had sung a hymn, they went out to the Mount of Olives.

Jesus predicts Peter's denial

31 Then Jesus told them, 'This very night you will all fall away on account of me, for it is written:

' "I will strike the shepherd,
    and the sheep of the flock will
        be scattered." ^c

³²But after I have risen, I will go ahead of you into Galilee.'

³³Peter replied, 'Even if all fall away on account of you, I never will.'

³⁴'Truly I tell you,' Jesus answered, 'this very night, before the cock crows, you will disown me three times.'

³⁵But Peter declared, 'Even if I have to die with you, I will never disown you.' And all the other disciples said the same.

Gethsemane

³⁶Then Jesus went with his disciples to a place called Gethsemane, and he said to them, 'Sit here while I go over there and pray.' ³⁷He took Peter and the two sons of Zebedee along with him, and he began to be sorrowful and troubled. ³⁸Then he said to them, 'My soul is overwhelmed with sorrow to the point of death. Stay here and keep watch with me.'

³⁹Going a little farther, he fell with his face to the ground and prayed, 'My Father, if it is possible, may this cup be taken from me. Yet not as I will, but as you will.'

⁴⁰Then he returned to his disciples and found them sleeping. 'Couldn't you men keep watch with me for one hour?' he asked Peter. ⁴¹'Watch and pray so that you will not fall into temptation. The spirit is willing, but the flesh is weak.'

⁴²He went away a second time and prayed, 'My Father, if it is not possible for this cup to be taken away unless I drink it, may your will be done.'

⁴³When he came back, he again found them sleeping, because their eyes were heavy. ⁴⁴So he left them and went away once more and prayed the third time, saying the same thing.

⁴⁵Then he returned to the disciples and said to them, 'Are you still sleeping and resting? Look, the hour has come, and the Son of Man is delivered into the hands of sinners. ⁴⁶Rise! Let us go! Here comes my betrayer!'

Jesus arrested

⁴⁷While he was still speaking, Judas, one of the Twelve, arrived. With him was a large crowd armed with swords and clubs, sent from the chief priests and the elders of the people. ⁴⁸Now the betrayer had arranged a signal with them: 'The one I kiss is the man; arrest him.' ⁴⁹Going at once to Jesus, Judas said, 'Greetings, Rabbi!' and kissed him.

⁵⁰Jesus replied, 'Do what you came for, friend.'ᵈ

Then the men stepped forward, seized Jesus and arrested him. ⁵¹With that, one of Jesus's companions reached for his sword, drew it out and struck the servant of the high priest, cutting off his ear.

⁵²'Put your sword back in its place,' Jesus said to him, 'for all who draw the sword will die by the sword. ⁵³Do you think I cannot call on my Father, and he will at once put at my disposal more than twelve legions of angels? ⁵⁴But how then would the Scriptures be fulfilled that say it must happen in this way?'

55 In that hour Jesus said to the crowd, 'Am I leading a rebellion, that you have come out with swords and clubs to capture me? Every day I sat in the temple courts teaching, and you did not arrest me. **56** But this has all taken place that the writings of the prophets might be fulfilled.' Then all the disciples deserted him and fled.

---

a 11 See Deut. 15:11.
b 28 Some manuscripts *the new*
c 31 Zech. 13:7
d 50 Or *'Why have you come, friend?'*

The rapid-fire narrative progression in this section of the Gospel is accentuated by the contrast between adjacent episodes. As Heil observes, the first thread of the pattern in 26:1–56 (marked A in Table 21 below) emphasises 'the theme of opposition to and separation from Jesus on his way to death'.[2] So the Jewish leaders plot his arrest and death (26:3–5), Judas plans to hand him over (26:14–16), the betrayal is predicted by Jesus at the Passover meal (26:20–25), Jesus further predicts his abandonment by the disciples (26:30–35) and then, finally, the arrest, betrayal and abandonment take place (26:47–56).

The second thread (marked B in Table 21 below), interwoven with the first, seems to emphasise Jesus's determination to prepare for and embrace the events leading to his death – events that are necessary to complete his Father's mandate. So Jesus willingly interprets an anointing as a preparation for burial (26:6–13). He then arranges preparation for the Passover meal (26:17–19) and at the meal itself he embraces his death (26:28) as that which will bring forgiveness of sins for many (26:26–9). Finally, in prayer at Gethsemane he faces up to his death (26:39; compare 20:22–3) and the scale of the task he has been given, but submits to the will of his Father (26:36–46).

(A) Jesus's opponents plot against him, and his disciples desert him	26:1–5 Chief priests and elders	26:14–16 Judas	26:20–25 Jesus foretells betrayal	26:30–35 Jesus foretells desertion	26:47–56 Betrayal and desertion
(B) But Jesus is determined to complete the task he's been given	26:6–13 Jesus anointed for burial	26:17–19 Jesus arranges Passover meal	26:26–9 Words at Lord's Supper	26:36–46 Gethsemane	

Table 21

---

[2] Heil, *Death and Resurrection*, 54.

The chief priest and elders plot (26:1–5)

Jesus has been talking about many things in Matthew 21–5, and we concluded above that the most important of those stretches deep into the future. But in Matthew 26 he brings us back to the current crisis in Jerusalem, precipitated by his conflict in the Temple with the chief priests and the elders of the people back in Matthew 21.

Even in these few words, Jesus is beginning to interpret his death for us, reminding us that all this happens at the time of Passover (verse 2). The nation will be remembering how the Lord God ransomed them from slavery and death in Egypt, how he rescued them and brought them victory. This is going to be happening all over again – but this time in a quite unexpected way, through the handing over of the Son of Man for crucifixion.

In assembling and plotting to arrest and kill Jesus (verses 3–4), the chief priests and elders are showing themselves to be just the sort of 'tenants' Jesus said they would be (back in 21:38). Their continuing fear of the people (verse 5) is a reminder of the lack of genuine authority they have as leaders, which Jesus exposed in 21:23–7.

Jesus prepared for burial (26:6–13)

The next scene is set in Bethany, at the home of Simon the Leper (verse 6). Simon, who was once a leper, is presumably known to Matthew and perhaps more widely among early Christians. But we still might wonder why Matthew has drawn attention to him, especially given that Matthew doesn't name Jesus's hosts like this elsewhere in the Gospel. The only person cleansed from leprosy in the Gospel was the man in 8:1–4, the very first miracle described by Matthew. It may be that the man in Matthew 8 was indeed Simon, or that Simon is mentioned here to remind us of that episode. The striking thing about that miracle was that with a touch, which would normally have made him unclean, Jesus was able to cleanse the man, absorbing a disease that made people resemble a walking corpse. This is a striking background to Jesus announcing his own upcoming burial (verse 12), where he will experience an uncleanliness that wealthy people would attempt to mask with the kind of perfume in the jar of verse 7. The one who showed himself able to solve the uncleanliness of death is about to embrace the uncleanliness of death.

But the principal character in these verses (apart from Jesus himself) is the unnamed woman in verse 7 who pours a jar of expensive perfume

over his head. This is presumably a very shocking and socially embar-
rassing thing to do, but what upsets the disciples most is the expense of
the perfume apparently thrown away (verses 8–9).

In contrast, Jesus strongly commends the woman (verse 10): 'She has
done a beautiful thing to me.' Jesus reinterprets what she has done as an
anointing – an anointing in preparation for burial (verse 12) – a burial
preparation fit for a king. What she uncovers here is the hidden value of
Jesus's coming death, pointing forward to a kingly burial. The value of his
death will be so high that, shockingly, even the anointing associated with
it is worth more than providing for the poor (verses 9 and 11).

Jesus thus begins a sequence of events where he can be seen preparing
for his death, determined to complete the task he has been given to do
(continued in verses 17–19, 26–9 and 36–46).

Meanwhile, at the beginning of Matthew 26–8, the woman demonstrates an exemplary faith-response to Jesus. In contrast to the chief priests
and the elders of the people in verses 3–5 (who want him dead), she
shows how worthwhile it is to give everything for him (compare 13:44–6).
When the gospel about him and his death is proclaimed, with a world-
wide impact, it will include the amazing story of this woman (verse 13).

Judas plots (26:14–16)

Judas was introduced by Matthew as the one who would betray him
(10:4), but here he becomes a foreground character, joining the chief
priests in their plot to kill Jesus. This continues the stream of episodes
dealing with the future handing over, betrayal and desertion of Jesus
(continuing in verses 20–25, 30–35 and 47–56). Judas will represent the
full horror of what it means to stumble or go astray (compare 18:7–9;
24:4). Here he accepts thirty pieces of silver as a bribe in order to hand
over an innocent person to death (verse 15). This is explicitly singled out
as worthy of curse in Deuteronomy 27:25.

Jesus prepares for the Passover (26:17–19)

We continue the preparations for Jesus's death, part of which will be a
Passover meal. This will be so important that it requires preparation of its
own, briefly described here. The repetition of words denoting preparation
for the Passover in verses 17 and 19 highlights just how important this
meal will be. The preparation consists of going to a certain (unnamed)
man in the city to let him know the meal will be held in his house.

But this is an opportunity to remind us that beyond the meal lies the time for Jesus to fulfil the task he has been given by his Father. There is a deep sense of expectation and imminent crisis: 'My appointed time is near,' says Jesus (verse 18).

Betrayal foretold (26:20–25)

We fast-forward to the evening and the meal itself (verse 20). The meal is a reminder of the outpouring of blessing from covenant membership at the Exodus, and eating together should be an occasion of joyful solidarity. But Jesus turns immediately to speak of his forthcoming betrayal. One of the Twelve will betray him (verse 21). Matthew has already told us this will be Judas (10:4; verses 14–16 above). But this is where Matthew shows us that Jesus knows about his betrayal in advance.

The language of eating intimately with his betrayer in verse 23 picks up on that of Psalm 41:8–10, which is also about the horror of someone close to the King betraying him, but also hints at the King's eventual victory.

The betrayal will be an integral part of Jesus as the Son of Man going into the intense tribulation of crucifixion and death (verse 24a). But by warning Judas in advance about the severe consequences of betraying innocent blood (verse 24b), and by making it public that he knows what Judas is planning (verse 25), Jesus is giving Judas every opportunity – humanly speaking – to turn from the path he has set out on. Judas is not driven by a fatalistic compulsion to betray Jesus. He is fully culpable and morally responsible – as he himself will come to acknowledge in 27:3–10.

Jesus prepares the disciples (26:26–9)

Matthew then takes us to a different moment in the meal (verse 26). Once again, this is Jesus preparing for and interpreting his coming death.

These words come in the context of a meal where eating the roasted body of a lamb was a reminder of the lamb whose blood was shed (and painted around the doors of houses) to avert the angel of the Lord in Exodus 12 from bringing death to the firstborn in each household. It prompted the Lord to pass over that house, as death came to all the other firstborn in Egypt. Large quantities of blood were also used at the covenant ratification ceremony of Exodus 24. We should take it that the significance of the blood in Exodus 24 is already established by the significance of the blood in Exodus 12. Just as the firstborn needed a substitute death for death to pass over in Exodus 12, so do all the people in Exodus 24; and the need and necessity of this is vibrantly displayed in red.

Also in the background are Jesus's words at 20:28: 'the Son of Man did not come to be served, but to serve, and to give his life as a ransom for many'.

As Jesus gives thanks for and hands around bread and then wine, his words take the focus of the meal away from the Passover lamb and on to himself. The bread represents his body (verse 26). (I say 'represents' because Jesus's actual, physical body is right there: he is not the bread or somehow in the bread; he is handing it out.) The wine in the cup Jesus passes round represents the 'blood of the covenant' (verse 28). (Again, I say 'represents' because Jesus's blood is very much inside his body at this point.) Spilled blood represents death throughout the Bible (including Exodus 12 and 24), and so it does here. The blood of the covenant is 'poured out for many for the forgiveness of sins'. These help us, then, to interpret the significance and relevance of Jesus's coming death. His blood will be poured out (that is, he will die, giving his life as a ransom, as in 20:28) for many, achieving the forgiveness of their sins.

We see here the fulfilment of the Passover sacrifice. Jesus's death will be like the Passover (averting death), but much greater: averting death permanently, for many. We see also the fulfilment of the 'blood of the covenant' of, for example, Exodus 24. Jesus's blood (that is, death) will be like the covenant ratification of Exodus 24, but much greater: sealing a more accessible, permanent and stable covenant. And we see how the task Jesus took on at the beginning of the Gospel – to bring the forgiveness of sins, 1:21; 6:12; 9:1–13; 12:32 – will be fulfilled in the coming events of his crucifixion.

In the flow of the narrative, this is the moment when the disciples are invited to do something that connects them to Jesus and his death on their behalf, through the act of eating and drinking. The act is essentially an act of faith. The connection means they participate in and benefit from his death. As readers, we are also helped to interpret the meaning and relevance of Jesus's death. Matthew's purpose here doesn't seem to extend to commanding the disciples to repeat this act in the future, or to give any details on what this should look like. On this, we need to remember that when Matthew was writing, the practice of meeting to eat 'the Lord's Supper' was already well established (as we know from 1 Corinthians 11:17–34). He does not need to defend it or re-establish it. But in giving this 'origin story' of the Lord's Supper, he is helping those who take it to know more precisely what they are remembering, and to recognise that they too are engaging in a 'faith-act' that strengthens and assures them of their connection to the death of Jesus and its benefits.

Now it is relative to Jesus and his sacrificial death that covenant membership is defined. This will be the event that truly and finally brings in the kingdom – and the kingdom in all its fullness is something that is next on God's agenda. The Supper was the final experience of physical closeness and companionship between Jesus and his disciples; like many moments of communal closeness, it was marked by eating together, gladdened by wine. Jesus now says that the next time this happens will be when all things are completed (verse 29). Jesus will not celebrate until not only his own his own distinctive work of providing atonement is completed, but also the task and suffering of his disciples is completed and they can celebrate together in the kingdom of their Father.

Desertion foretold (26:30–35)

Jesus's prediction is solemn: he will be struck and all his disciples will disobey the call to follow him by falling away and scattering (verse 31, quoting Zechariah 13:7; compare 4:19; 16:24). However, there is hope: he will rise after being struck, and lead them to Galilee (verse 32).

Peter makes a heartfelt promise not to fall away (verse 33). This begins a very important component of the narrative in Matthew 26–8, highlighting the incapability of the disciples before Jesus has rescued and ransomed them through his death and resurrection. We shall see this incapability displayed by Peter, James and John in Gethsemane (26:36–46), and then especially in Peter (26:57–8, 69–75). What we learn here is that the incapability is far from a surprise to Jesus (verse 34). He knows precisely how Peter will betray him; and his prediction will prove correct. Peter will deny Jesus before the morning. Peter, on the other hand, has much to learn about his own incapacity and the necessity of Jesus dying first (verse 35). As Jesus will shortly comment in Gethsemane, his spirit is willing, but his flesh will prove weak (verse 41).

Jesus prays (26:36–46)

From the house where they have been eating the Passover meal together, Jesus takes the disciples to 'a place called Gethsemane' (verse 36). From verse 30 we can see that this is likely on the Mount of Olives, especially since the name means something like 'The Oil Press'. Jesus leaves most of the disciples while he goes to pray, but takes Peter and the sons of Zebedee (James and John) with him (verse 37). The tone is set by Matthew's comment: 'he began to be sorrowful and troubled'. As with Jesus's words at the Lord's Supper (verses 26–9 above), this episode is profoundly important in Matthew's strategy for helping us interpret and understand Jesus's coming death.

In the background lies the prayer at the centre of the Sermon on the Mount – the so-called Lord's Prayer (6:9–13). This was a prayer through which Jesus taught his disciples to be focused on their Father in the heavens – to pray for his name, his kingdom and his will to be done on earth as in heaven. Here we see that attitude modelled perfectly in the most testing of circumstances. Verse 39: 'Yet not as I will, but as you will.' Verse 42: '. . . may your will be done'.

Also in the background is the encounter on the mountain of transfiguration in Matthew 17. The same three disciples – Peter, James and John – were taken up a mountain with Jesus. As with this incident at Gethsemane, there was an encounter with the Father. In Matthew 17, Jesus had recently said he must suffer, die and be raised: something Peter in particular was struggling to grasp (16:22). The word from the Father to the disciples was, 'This is my Son whom I love; with him I am well pleased. Listen to him!' In 20:20–28, the sons of Zebedee were also struggling to accept the necessity of suffering before vindication. In Gethsemane, the issue is the same. In his anguished encounter with his Father in prayer, Jesus faces up to the inevitability of his death, proving as he does so that, yes, he must suffer and die. This time the exhortation is to join Jesus in watching and praying (verses 38 and 41) – with which all three disciples fail to comply.

Matthew has flagged up these exhortations as important already. In the recent background is another interaction between Jesus and his disciples on the Mount of Olives: Jesus's last block of extensive teaching in 24:3–25:46. Jesus taught: as trouble comes, don't be deceived or led astray (24:4–5, 23–4). As you wait for vindication, keep watch (24:42; 25:13).

The remainder of the episode is structured into three cycles, carefully numbered by Matthew (verses 42, 44), as Jesus prays three times to his Father: verses 38–41, 42–3, 44–6. The first of these is the longest, beginning with Jesus sharing with Peter, James and John his anguish and calling them to join in watching with him (verse 38). While the same verb in 24:42 and 25:13 was used to call the disciples to be (wakefully) ready for the return of their Master, here Jesus is calling Peter, James and John to join with him as he prayerfully prepares for his coming tribulation and death. Jesus rightly looks ahead to this in prayer (verse 39), but they can't keep awake (verse 40). Jesus then repeats the exhortation (verse 41). The second and third cycles (verses 42–3 and 44–6) act as intensifiers, multiplying our awareness of Jesus's anguish and our despair at the disciples' failure.

From Jesus's prayers to his Father, we learn more about the magnitude of what he is just about to experience on behalf of many, its necessity, and his ultimate willingness to follow through on what he has taken on. In verse 39, Jesus asks his Father for 'this cup' to be taken from him – but only if this is possible and in line with his Father's will or intentions. What is 'this cup'? The Scriptures do occasionally speak of the cup of blessing or salvation (e.g., Psalm 16:5; 116:13), but there is a much larger stream of Old Testament prophecy that talks about the 'cup' of God's wrath or judgment – something he pours out in punishment in response to sin and wickedness (e.g., Psalm 75:8; Jeremiah 25:15–29; 49:12; Isaiah 51:17–23). Alternatively, we can simply look back to 20:22, when Jesus asked 'Can you drink the cup I am going to drink?' He seems in the context to be talking about his coming suffering and death. These two ways of thinking about the 'cup' are the same. After all, ultimately, the punishment for sin in the Bible is death (Genesis 2:16–17). Hence the 'cup' here is death, poured out by God as a punishment for sin.

Three times Jesus prays to his Father, whom he knows loves him, for this cup to be taken away if at all possible. Jesus falls to the ground to pray in verse 39, and that he prays for essentially the same thing three times is a sign of great earnestness. This is showing us the profound, unimaginable magnitude of the suffering he is just about to bear. This takes away any thought that because of his nature or status as Son or Son of God, suffering and death will be easy for Jesus. His prayers reveal that his anticipation is that he will be feeling the full force of human suffering.

Jesus prays for the cup to be taken away if possible under God's purposes and intentions, but the cup is not taken away. We should conclude from this that it was not possible under God's purposes and intentions. It is necessary for Jesus to face suffering and death through crucifixion. The will of God for his Son is for him to save his people from their sins (1:21) – to solve the background crisis facing Israel and indeed the whole world. That is the mandate Jesus took on in his baptism – identifying with sinners so that he can save them (see commentary on 3:13–17). He has said three times that he must suffer, die and be raised (16:21; 17:22–3; 20:17–19). Now we have seen three times that it is not possible for the cup of death to be taken away. His death is necessary if God's will is to be done.

It would be a mistake to suppose Matthew is depicting Jesus and his Father at odds with one another here, or that Jesus is somehow being coerced into going to his death. Indeed, one of the po that by the end of the episode we can be sure that Jesus an er are in complete alignment and that Jesus goes willingly to the y are of one will. But we are not listening in here to a convers. ween the Father and the *pre-incarnate* Son. This episode is *part of* rrative of Jesus completing *as a man* the mandate given to *him* at aptism, bringing salvation as the Servant of the Lord. As in *4:1-11, 16* and later at 27:38–44, this is Jesus battling to complete this task. The b e here is especially emotional and intense for Jesus, but *he perseveres through it* so he can bring salvation to others (compare Hebrews 5:7–10). In *doing* so, he also identifies with his disciples' future struggle to persevere, showing them the way (Hebrews 2:18). All of which means that, as John Frame puts it, 'In this time of prayer, the eternal agreement of Father and Son becomes a temporal process, in which the elements of agreement come together in time.'[3]

From the commands to watch and pray and the disciples' failure to follow and obey, we learn that only Jesus is able to face the future anguish set before him and complete the purpose of the Father, whatever the disciples may have claimed about themselves in verse 35. Matthew clearly wants us to dissociate from the sleepy prayerlessness of the three disciples here, and we should be strongly reminded of the foolish virgins in 25:3 – with the associated warning of being shut out in 25:12. The failure of the disciples is theologically crucial as it puts the focus exclusively on Jesus as the only one able to complete the Father's will and bring salvation and forgiveness. But the pattern will be repeated. Once Jesus's unique task is complete and his vindication in resurrection clear and public, there is a parallel call to post-resurrection disciples to watchfulness and prayerfulness, as they await their Master's return. This time, failure has been dealt with and accommodated, and the pathway to vindication and life is clear and the future secure, and Jesus's expectation for his disciples is that they will comply with the call to keep watch.

The whole thrust of the Gethsemane episode has been pointing forward. The final cycle of Jesus praying (verses 44–5a) is recounted very concisely, quickening the pace of the narrative. All this places a strong emphasis on Jesus saying, 'Look! The hour has come' (or 'has drawn near', verse 45b). Likewise, he says 'Look!' again in verse 46 (missing in the NIV), 'Here comes my betrayer' (or 'My betrayer has drawn near'). The first stage of Jesus's passion–vindication predictions has begun to be realised.

---

[3] John M. Frame, *The Doctrine of God* (Phillipsburg: P&R, 2002), 695 n14.

Betrayal ...rtion (26:47–56)

Jesus pred... would be betrayed and abandoned. Now it happens. No on... out of this well apart from Jesus. Judas betrays him with a kis... of love (verses 48–9). In this case, the sign is a lie, since its intent... to betray. Jesus knows the intent and allows himself to be se... and arrested (verse 50). A disciple (unnamed by Matthew) shows ... swashbuckling bravado with a sword and cuts off the ear of the servant of the high priest (verse 51). Jesus rebukes him (verse 52). Jesus has already called his disciples to meekness (e.g., 5:5) — that is, to be those who do not physically fight for position or retaliate when struck (5:39), because they are trusting in the ultimate care and protection of their Father in the heavens. Here he warns, 'For all who draw the sword will die by the sword.' Meekness, after all, is the pathway Jesus himself is pioneering. We saw in Matthew 3 that he came not with wrath, an axe or the fire of judgment, but with a willingness to stand alongside sinners — ultimately for their salvation. He is the 'gentle' (meek, 11:29) one, who entered Jerusalem as one 'gentle' (meek again, 21:5) on a donkey. He could call on 'twelve legions of angels' (verse 53). But then the Scriptures (plural) would not be fulfilled (verse 54). We do not need to point to particular Scriptures here, but to the Hebrew Scriptures as a whole as they point forward to the rescue, salvation and vindication Jesus came to bring.

The armed crowd has come to arrest him out of public sight, probably aware of the injustice they are caught up in, and in fear of a public backlash. Jesus exposes this in verse 55. 'This has all taken place,' he says, verse 56, 'that the writings of the prophets might be fulfilled.' As with verse 54, this could be a reference to the writings of the prophets in general. But the particular events unfolding of betrayal, arrest and abandonment suggest he may have especially the Scripture he quoted earlier in verse 31 in mind: that the shepherd would be struck and the sheep scattered. Zechariah 13:7–9 describes the partial destruction of God's people following the striking down of their leader. But there is restoration: one third are refined through suffering.

We dissociate both from the explicit betrayal, in all its sleazy reality, and from the implicit betrayal as Jesus is abandoned with such haste and cowardice (verse 56). The abandonment is so universal that hope lies only in depending on the obedience of Jesus, who therefore must die to take God's wrath on their behalf (compare 20:28), but who will rise to lead his people again (26:32).

SUMMARY AND PURPOSE

The overall purpose of Matthew's Gospel is to make its readers who aren't disciples of Jesus into disciples of Jesus, and to motivate and equip its readers who are disciples of Jesus to be disciple-makers.

There are many things in this section that should persuade someone who is not yet a disciple. The stream A material in Table 21 above portrays those who plot to kill Jesus, those who hand him over for money and those who betray or desert him in such a bad light that a natural response is to want to have nothing to do with such attitudes. Interwoven with this, the stream B material portrays Jesus in the best possible light. He is making a clear choice to face the hostility and hatred, to endure the betrayal and cowardice, and to not depart from the pathway he has embarked upon, which is heading towards crucifixion. The Gethsemane episode presents the difficulty of this pathway at its most intense, but also Jesus's final determination to follow the will of his Father. Yet the pathway is also clearly not just an example of calm bravery: it is also meaningful for others. This is shown most clearly as Jesus shares bread and wine at the Last Supper. All these different elements work together to help a reader of the Gospel to dissociate from those who hate Jesus and instead embrace him and the forgiveness of sins he died to provide for many.

But the main purpose in this section is to build on Jesus's teaching in Matthew 24–5: to help someone who is already a disciple follow through and persevere along the path that Jesus has pioneered before them. Now the encouragement comes through the narrative. It is clear as this unfolds that only Jesus is able to do the task the Father has set, and all else fail. But we already know this is a pattern Jesus expects his disciples to follow him on. After the success of the cross, then, secure in the forgiveness and hope Jesus secures, the true disciple is encouraged to identify with the woman who anointed Jesus and to give everything for him. And with eyes opened to the realities of what Jesus went on to do, they can follow Jesus's example in Gethsemane, entrusting themselves to the one 'who judges justly' (compare 1 Peter 2:23). What proved impossible for Peter, James and John then becomes possible, and they can face the difficulties coming their way through earnest prayer and watchfulness, as Jesus has already taught them to do. And then they get on, through every difficulty, with the task they will be given to do: which is to make disciples in all the nations.

2. Mission completed (and commissioned)
part 2 • Matthew 26:57–27:54

This section corresponds to the middle of Jesus's final prediction in 20:17–18: 'They will condemn him to death and will hand him over to the Gentiles to be mocked and flogged and crucified.'

Jesus before the Sanhedrin

57 Those who had arrested Jesus took him to Caiaphas the high priest, where the teachers of the law and the elders had assembled. **58** But Peter followed him at a distance, right up to the courtyard of the high priest. He entered and sat down with the guards to see the outcome.

59 The chief priests and the whole Sanhedrin were looking for false evidence against Jesus so that they could put him to death. **60** But they did not find any, though many false witnesses came forward.

Finally two came forward **61** and declared, 'This fellow said, "I am able to destroy the temple of God and rebuild it in three days."'

62 Then the high priest stood up and said to Jesus, 'Are you not going to answer? What is this testimony that these men are bringing against you?' **63** But Jesus remained silent.

The high priest said to him, 'I charge you under oath by the living God: Tell us if you are the Messiah, the Son of God.'

64 'You have said so,' Jesus replied. 'But I say to all of you: from now on you will see the Son of Man sitting at the right hand of the Mighty One and coming on the clouds of heaven.'**e**

65 Then the high priest tore his clothes and said, 'He has spoken blasphemy! Why do we need any more witnesses? Look, now you have heard the blasphemy. **66** What do you think?'

'He is worthy of death,' they answered.

67 Then they spat in his face and struck him with their fists. Others slapped him **68** and said, 'Prophesy to us, Messiah. Who hit you?'

Peter disowns Jesus

69 Now Peter was sitting out in the courtyard, and a servant-girl came to him. 'You also were with Jesus of Galilee,' she said.

70 But he denied it before them all. 'I don't know what you're talking about,' he said.

71 Then he went out to the gateway, where another servant-girl saw him and said to the people there, 'This fellow was with Jesus of Nazareth.'

72 He denied it again, with an oath: 'I don't know the man!'

73 After a little while, those standing there went up to Peter and said, 'Surely you are one of them; your accent gives you away.'

74 Then he began to call down curses, and he swore to them, 'I don't know the man!'

Immediately a cock crowed. **75** Then Peter remembered the word Jesus had spoken: 'Before the cock crows, you will disown me three times.' And he went outside and wept bitterly.

Judas hangs himself

27 Early in the morning, all the chief priests and the elders of the people made their plans how to have Jesus executed. **2** So they bound him, led him away and handed him over to Pilate the governor.

3 When Judas, who had betrayed him, saw that Jesus was condemned, he was seized with remorse and returned the thirty pieces of silver to the chief priests and the elders. **4** 'I have sinned,' he said, 'for I have betrayed innocent blood.'

'What is that to us?' they replied. 'That's your responsibility.'

5 So Judas threw the money into the temple and left. Then he went away and hanged himself.

6 The chief priests picked up the coins and said, 'It is against the law to put this into the treasury, since it is blood money.' **7** So they decided to use the money to buy the potter's field as a burial place for foreigners. **8** That is why it has been called the Field of Blood to this day. **9** Then what was spoken by Jeremiah the prophet was fulfilled: 'They took the thirty pieces of silver, the price set on him by the people of Israel, **10** and they used them to buy the potter's field, as the Lord commanded me.'[a]

Jesus before Pilate

11 Meanwhile Jesus stood before the governor, and the governor asked him, 'Are you the king of the Jews?'

'You have said so,' Jesus replied.

12 When he was accused by the chief priests and the elders, he gave no answer. **13** Then Pilate asked him, 'Don't you hear the testimony they are bringing against you?' **14** But Jesus made no reply, not even to a single charge – to the great amazement of the governor.

15 Now it was the governor's custom at the festival to release a prisoner chosen by the crowd. **16** At that time they had a well-known prisoner whose name was Jesus[b] Barabbas. **17** So when the crowd had gathered, Pilate asked them, 'Which one do you want me to release to you: Jesus Barabbas, or Jesus who is called the Messiah?' **18** For he knew it was out of self-interest that they had handed Jesus over to him.

19 While Pilate was sitting on the judge's seat, his wife sent him this message: 'Don't have anything to do with that innocent man, for I have suffered a great deal today in a dream because of him.'

20 But the chief priests and the elders persuaded the crowd to ask for Barabbas and to have Jesus executed.

21 'Which of the two do you want me to release to you?' asked the governor.

'Barabbas,' they answered.

22 'What shall I do, then, with Jesus who is called the Messiah?' Pilate asked.

They all answered, 'Crucify him!'

23'Why? What crime has he committed?' asked Pilate.

But they shouted all the louder, 'Crucify him!'

24When Pilate saw that he was getting nowhere, but that instead an uproar was starting, he took water and washed his hands in front of the crowd. 'I am innocent of this man's blood,' he said. 'It is your responsibility!'

25All the people answered, 'His blood is on us and on our children!'

26Then he released Barabbas to them. But he had Jesus flogged, and handed him over to be crucified.

The soldiers mock Jesus

27Then the governor's soldiers took Jesus into the Praetorium and gathered the whole company of soldiers round him. **28**They stripped him and put a scarlet robe on him, **29**and then twisted together a crown of thorns and set it on his head. They put a staff in his right hand. Then they knelt in front of him and mocked him. 'Hail, king of the Jews!' they said. **30**They spat on him, and took the staff and struck him on the head again and again. **31**After they had mocked him, they took off the robe and put his own clothes on him. Then they led him away to crucify him.

The crucifixion of Jesus

32As they were going out, they met a man from Cyrene, named Simon, and they forced him to carry the cross. **33**They came to a place called Golgotha (which means 'the place of the skull'). **34**There they offered Jesus wine to drink, mixed with gall; but after tasting it, he refused to drink it. **35**When they had crucified him, they divided up his clothes by casting lots. **36**And sitting down, they kept watch over him there. **37**Above his head they placed the written charge against him: THIS IS JESUS, THE KING OF THE JEWS.

38Two rebels were crucified with him, one on his right and one on his left. **39**Those who passed by hurled insults at him, shaking their heads **40**and saying, 'You who are going to destroy the temple and build it in three days, save yourself! Come down from the cross, if you are the Son of God!' **41**In the same way the chief priests, the teachers of the law and the elders mocked him. **42**'He saved others,' they said, 'but he can't save himself! He's the king of Israel! Let him come down now from the cross, and we will believe in him. **43**He trusts in God. Let God rescue him now if he wants him, for he said, "I am the Son of God."' **44**In the same way the rebels who were crucified with him also heaped insults on him.

The death of Jesus

45From noon until three in the afternoon darkness came over all the land. **46**About three in the afternoon Jesus cried out in a loud voice, *'Eli, Eli,*^c *lema sabachthani?'* (which means 'My God, my God, why have you forsaken me?').^d

47When some of those standing there heard this, they said, 'He's calling Elijah.'

48Immediately one of them ran and got a sponge. He filled it with wine vinegar, put it on a staff, and offered it to Jesus to drink. **49** The rest said, 'Now leave him alone. Let's see if Elijah comes to save him.'

50 And when Jesus had cried out again in a loud voice, he gave up his spirit.

51 At that moment the curtain of the temple was torn in two from top to bottom. The earth shook, the rocks split **52** and the tombs broke open. The bodies of many holy people who had died were raised to life. **53** They came out of the tombs after Jesus's resurrection and**e** went into the holy city and appeared to many people.

54 When the centurion and those with him who were guarding Jesus saw the earthquake and all that had happened, they were terrified, and exclaimed, 'Surely he was the Son of God!'

---

e 64 See Psalm 110:1; Daniel 7:13.

a 10 See Zech. 11:12,13; Jer. 19:1-13; 32:6-9.

b 16 Many manuscripts do not have *Jesus*; also in verse 17.

c 46 Some manuscripts *Eloi, Eloi*

d 46 Psalm 22:1

e 53 Or *tombs, and after Jesus's resurrection they*

The pattern of two sequences of material forming an alternating pattern seems to continue into this next group of episodes (see Table 22). The first sequence (A) focuses on a series of witnesses to the arrest, trial and execution of Jesus. These people are all somewhat removed from direct involvement in the mainline events (mostly described in the second sequence), but respond to and comment on them. First there is Peter, across two episodes (26:57–8, 69–75), then Judas (27:3–10), the crowd (27:15–26) and, in the climax of the sequence (27:45–54), there are both bystanders (27:47) and the centurion (and 'those with him', 27:54).

The second sequence (B) also has an internal integrity. In this case, the focus is on Jesus in his interaction with Jewish and Gentile leadership. This begins with the trial before the high priest and scribes and elders (26:57–68), followed by the trial before Pilate, across two episodes (27:1–2, 11–14), and ends with the execution of the sentence (27:27–44), within which agents of both the Gentile leadership (the soldiers in 27:27–31) and Jewish leadership (the chief priests, scribes and elders in 27:41–44) openly mock the crucified Jesus as 'King of the Jews' and 'King of Israel'.

(A) People shown to be under curse for their own actions, or (in the case of Jesus) for the sake of others	26:57–8 Peter	26:69–75 Peter	27:3–10 Judas	27:15–26 Crowd	27:32–8 Guards (Jesus crucified)	27:45–54 Centurion (Jesus dies)
(B) Jesus condemned and mocked for his claims of kingship and divine sonship	26:59–68 Before high priest	27:1–2 Led to Pilate	27:11–14 Before Pilate	27:27–31 Mocked by guards	27:39–44 Mocked by bystanders	

Table 22

The A stream in the previous section (26:1–56) was narrating the betrayal, arrest and abandonment of Jesus by various parties. This time, the A stream narrates various responses to what is happening to Jesus. The B stream in the previous section showed Jesus willing and determined to complete the task given to him by his Father, and his theological interpretation of coming events. The B stream here continues this, but now focuses on the identity of Jesus. There is dramatic irony here: we know Jesus is the Son of God, the King of Israel. He *is* the Messiah. His claims under questioning and in the face of mockery are correct. But he is the Messiah of Psalm 22: forsaken now, awaiting vindication later.

As before, the two narrative streams work together. Inasmuch as the characters in the A stream distance themselves from Jesus, they implicitly side with those putting him to death, and Matthew shows them under a curse. Only towards the end of this stream do we see how the curse might be taken and lifted, and we finally get an exemplary positive response – from a surprising source, the centurion 'and those with him' (27:54).

Peter (26:57–8)

As Jesus is taken to Caiaphas the high priest (26:57), Peter follows (26:58). This is setting up a contrast between Jesus and Peter that will come back to focus on Peter in 26:69–75. But even at this stage the confidence Peter expressed in 26:33 and 35 seems to have evaporated. He is following at a distance, and instead of standing in solidarity with Jesus, passively sits with the guards to see the outcome.

Jesus before the high priest (26:59–68)

The key elements of a trial scene are here: witnesses are called (26:59–61), the accused is questioned (26:62–3), he answers (26:64), and there is some sort of unruly verdict (26:65–7).

Matthew, however, makes it very clear in the opening scene that the chief priests and the whole Sanhedrin are intent not on seeking truth or justice but on putting Jesus to death, and so are seeking false evidence (26:59). While they don't fabricate evidence, they do struggle to find any apart from a claim that Jesus said he would destroy the Temple and rebuild it in three days (26:60–61).[4]

The high priest seems to take this as evidence of a claim to deity (or something close to it), and hence (in his eyes) blasphemy – 26:62. God is the one who can declare the end of the Temple (Jeremiah 7:14–15) and he is the one associated with its rebuilding (e.g., Ezekiel 40–48) – moreover, 'three days' implies a supernatural event of some sort. As he will be in 27:14, Jesus is silent (26:63a). Even if the testimony is broadly correct (he has said something like this), the implication of blasphemy is not.

The high priest then asks Jesus directly, 'I charge you under oath by the living God: Tell us if you are the Messiah, the Son of God' (26:63b).

Jesus is clear: 'You have said so' (26:64a). Jesus's agreement is not yet an explicit claim to deity (although it is a claim to extraordinary greatness). The high priest is thinking about 'Son of God' here in relation to 'Messiah' or 'Christ'. As in Psalm 2, the Son, the Anointed One (Messiah), is the King set on Zion (Psalm 2:6) who will bring victory over the kings of the nations. It's what Jesus adds to this that tips the high priest over into rage. First, Jesus builds on what he has already said about himself as the 'Son of Man'. He is the one with human form in Daniel's vision (Daniel 7) who survives tribulation under the beasts but will be seen 'coming on the clouds of heaven' (26:64; compare Daniel 7:13), vindicated by the Ancient of Days and given an everlasting kingdom (Daniel 7:14). To this, Jesus adds 'sitting at the right hand of the Mighty One'. Now Jesus is building on what he said about Psalm 110 in 22:41–6. He is the one greater than David, whom David calls 'Lord', who will sit at God's right hand, equal in status and glory to God, victorious over God's enemies (Psalm 110:1, 5–7).

---

[4] Matthew doesn't record Jesus saying these words (although see John 2:19). In Matthew, Jesus has symbolically shut down the Temple (21:12–13), announced its destruction (24:2) and alluded to or spoken about his resurrection after three days (12:40; 16:4, 21; 17:23; 20:19).

This is enough for the high priest to conclude that Jesus is claiming to be equal to God.[5] In his eyes the claim is so obviously false that it amounts to outrageous blasphemy (26:65). The others there agree – he deserves to die (26:66). The mismatch between the claim and Jesus's appearance is so stark that alongside the outrage there is also vicious mockery (26:67).

The dramatic irony, of course, is that the claims are true. What is more, we should be able to see Jesus beginning to bring to completion the Servant role both he and Matthew have linked him with. He has no obvious beauty or majesty to reveal his status (Isaiah 53:2), he is 'despised and rejected' (Isaiah 53:3), and 'as a sheep before its shearers is silent, so he did not open his mouth' (Isaiah 53:7).

Even more than this, the further irony is that this has been the high priest, the teachers of the law and the elders on trial, not Jesus. As he did many times in Matthew 21–3, Jesus has turned the tables on his questioners. They just don't know it yet. But Jesus gives the verdict in 26:64 – from now on, after Jesus's death and resurrection, they will see Jesus vindicated and exalted and (by implication) themselves condemned.

Peter under a curse (26:69–75)

The scene of Jesus before the high priest (26:59–67) contrasts sharply with what now happens to Peter. Jesus is questioned by the high priest; Peter is questioned by some servant girls. Jesus tells the truth; Peter tells lies that get worse and worse. Jesus faces three stages of false witness and hostile questions, ending with him making a full confession (26:63b–4), provoking a striking event (the high priest tears his clothes) and a final verdict (26:66–8). In contrast, Peter is a false witness. Peter also faces three rounds of hostile questioning, but this ends with him making an emphatic final denial (26:74a), provoking a striking event (a cock crows) and a final recognition.[6]

As he describes Peter's responses to questions from the two servant girls (26:69–72), Matthew uses the same word for 'deny' used by Jesus in 10:33, where he said, 'Whoever disowns me before others, I will disown

[5] Compare John 5:18, where implicitly claiming equality with God also results in the Jewish leaders wanting to kill Jesus.

[6] A pattern noted by B. Gerhardsson, 'Confession and Denial before Men: Observations on Matt. 26:57–27:2', *Journal for the Study of the New Testament* 13 (1981): 50–51.

before my Father in heaven.' The seriousness of Peter's position is reinforced by the detail of his final denial, in which he begins 'to call down
curses, and he swore to them' (26:74). Some commentators take this to
be an implied cursing of Jesus.[7] But it is more likely that Peter is backing
up his oath with what is called a 'conditional self-imprecation'. That is,
Peter is effectively saying, 'May I be cursed [by God] if this is not true.'[8]
But it does not really matter in the end whether Peter is cursing Jesus
or calling curses on himself. As John Nolland observes, 'In either case, in
yet another way Peter is condemning himself here.'[9]

The contrast with Peter's earlier claim in 26:35 ('Even if I have to
die with you, I will never disown you') could not be more pronounced.
Rather than an alignment with Jesus even to death, Peter shows himself
here firmly aligned with his enemies. Given 10:33, if Peter has denied
Jesus, then he can expect Jesus to deny him before his Father in heaven.
Jesus has already spelled out what this will mean at the Judgment. In
7:23 it meant hearing Jesus say, 'I never knew you. Away from me, you
evildoers!' In 25:41, it meant hearing the words, 'Depart from me, you
who are cursed, into the eternal fire prepared for the devil and his angels.'
By renouncing his discipleship, Peter has renounced any claim to the
forgiveness of sins Jesus has come to bring (26:28; compare 1:21). As he
becomes aware of this, he goes outside and weeps bitterly. This perhaps
recalls Jesus's repeated refrain in the Gospel to describe those left outside
under the separating judgment of God – a place of 'weeping and gnashing
of teeth' (8:12; 13:42, 50; 22:13; 24:51; 25:30).

Jesus led to Pilate (27:1–2)

Matthew emphasises once again the intention of the Jewish leadership –
here, the chief priests and elders of the people – to have Jesus executed
come what may (27:1). For this to happen, they need the cooperation
of the Roman governor, so he is handed over (27:2). The language of
'handing over' echoes Jesus's in his third passion-vindication prediction

---

[7] Including Gerhardsson, 'Confession', 54–5; Ulrich Luz, *Matthew 21–28* (Minneapolis:
Fortress, 2005), 546; France, *The Gospel of Matthew*, 1034–5; Davies and Allison,
Matthew 19–28, 548–9.

[8] So J. P. Louw and E. A. Nida, *Greek–English Lexicon of the New Testament: Based
on Semantic Domains* (2 Volumes) (New York: United Bible Societies, 1996), §33.472.
In Acts 23:12–22, the same verb is used fairly straightforwardly in a conditional
self-imprecation.

[9] Nolland, *Matthew*, 1142.

(20:19) – he is being handed over to the Gentiles. (As noted above, this is what happened to the people of Israel when the covenant curses were triggered – they were sent into exile for their sin and handed over to their enemies, Ezekiel 39:23.)

Judas under a curse (27:3–10)

Judas sees that Jesus was condemned (to death) and is 'seized with remorse' (27:3). He knows full well that Jesus has not done anything remotely deserving of death, and he would know Deuteronomy 27:25, where the people call out curses against 'anyone who accepts a bribe to kill an innocent person'. Hence the remorse. The word Matthew uses here is similar in meaning to the one he has used earlier in the Gospel to talk about the change of mind and remorse John and Jesus call for when they call the people to 'repent' (3:2; 4:17). Matthew most likely uses a different word here to indicate that Judas's change of mind is insufficient: he doesn't follow through by doing the right thing, which would be to return to Jesus and plead for forgiveness. Instead, he returns to the Temple, perhaps thinking he can reverse what he has done. He confesses his sin (27:4) but finds no atonement, just a dismissive, 'That's your responsibility.' Matthew then very tersely tells us that he throws the bribe money back into the Temple and goes away and hangs himself (27:5).

What does Matthew want us to make of this? Many suggestions have been made.[10] Most plausible is to infer that what Judas does is somehow related to the case law about 'hanging for exposure' in Deuteronomy 21:22–3. This regulated what happened after an execution for a capital crime, where (like many cultures across history) it was customary in Israel to expose the executed criminal by hanging them on something. The verses make clear that the criminal has died under the curse of God (Deuteronomy 21:23). To show and ensure that the curse is limited to the offender, the body is taken down before the end of the day, so as to not defile the Land.[11]

Given this, it seems reasonable to suppose that when Matthew says 'he went away and hanged himself', he is indicating that Judas took

---

[10] See the suggestions in Luz, *Matthew 21–28*, 472–3.

[11] There is more on this in Ben Cooper, 'That Cursed Messiah: The Curse-Bearing Death of Jesus in Matthew 26:57–27:54', in *Listen to Him: Reading and Preaching Emmanuel in Matthew*, ed. Peter Bolt (London: Latimer Publications, 2015), including biblical examples of the practice.

matters into his own hands and, as Ulrich Luz puts it, 'applied to himself the appropriate punishment'.[12] Death by hanging satisfied Deuteronomy 21:22–3 in his mind by providing both the punishment of death and the hanging for exposure. His precise motivation for doing this remains unspoken. But whatever the motivation, it does seem reasonable to suggest that by telling us about his chosen manner of death, Matthew is reinforcing the conclusion that Judas died under the curse of God.[13] If so, then the allusion to Deuteronomy 21:22–3 suggested by Judas's death by hanging is important background for understanding the hanging for exposure of Jesus on a cross in 27:32–8.

At this stage of the narrative, then, both Peter and Judas are both shown in a 'cursed' state. We shall return to consider their ultimate and final condition below. Matthew's more immediate concern is to implicate the chief priests and elders in Judas's betrayal, his sin, his blood-guilt and therefore his cursed state. The chief priests and elders attempt to distance themselves from Judas's blood-guilt by saying, 'What is that to us? . . . That's your responsibility' (27:4). They keep the returned coins away from the Temple treasury, for fear of contamination (27:6). However, by showing that they know it is 'blood money', Matthew is making it clear that this attempt is unsuccessful. The purpose of Matthew's comment in 27:7 coupled with the fulfilment formula in 27:8–10 is probably then to reinforce their culpability in the betrayal of innocent blood. Matthew gives a quotation apparently based on Zechariah 11:13 but attributes it to Jeremiah. Matthew may be alluding to both prophets to indict the chief priests and elders here. Like the false shepherds of Zechariah 11, they think they can be rid of God for the price of thirty silver coins. And just as the potter's jar Jeremiah is commanded to break in Jeremiah 19:10–11 stands as testimony that Israel's leaders have filled the valley of Ben Hinnom (near the Potsherd Gate) with the blood of the innocent (Jeremiah 19:1, 4), so the 'Field of Blood' purchased by the chief priests from a potter here in Matthew stands as an enduring testimony to their shedding of innocent blood.

---

[12] Luz, *Matthew 21–28*, 473.

[13] This is not at all to say that death by hanging (or suicide in general) implies in itself the curse of God. The person hung for exposure in Deuteronomy 21:22–3 is under the curse of God because of the (unatoned-for) capital crime they have committed. Likewise Judas here, for the (unatoned-for) betrayal of innocent blood (Deuteronomy 27:25).

Jesus before Pilate (27:11–14)

This is a second episode with elements of a trial scene. Pilate asks one question and Jesus answers it (27:11). The chief priests and elders then throw accusations, and Jesus is silent (27:12). Pilate asks a final question, and still Jesus does not reply (26:13–14).

Previously, the high priest asked Jesus if he was 'the Messiah, the Son of God?' (26:63). On the lips of Pilate, a Gentile outsider, this becomes, 'Are you the king of the Jews?' (27:11). This may well be what the Jewish leaders have told Pilate that Jesus has claimed to be, and is therefore a threat to social order and quite possibly Roman authority. Jesus's answer is similar to the one he gave before: 'You have said so.' But he is then silent: this is all he has to say, even under further accusation and questioning (27:12–14). This amazes Pilate, but Jesus is the Servant King and his work is to suffer for the sake of God's people, not to field false accusations from people with questionable authority. In other words, yet again, there is heavy irony here. We readers can see through to the truth of the title, even if those using it do not, and Matthew is going to exploit that. Jesus is tried, mocked and dies as 'King of the Jews' (27:29, 37).

We should acknowledge that at this moment Jesus does not look like a king. All power and authority seem to lie with Pilate. The king of the Jews from a Jewish perspective is the one who will free God's people from bondage and oppression. But Jesus here seems to be under the oppressor. And this may be what the chief priests and the elders tell the crowd in the next scene: how could he be the Christ?

Matthew is reinforcing the dramatic irony. Not only do we know that the title 'King of the Jews' is a true one, but we also can see how it fits with the appearance. Again, we see Jesus living out the Servant role of Isaiah 53, and especially Isaiah 53:7: 'He was oppressed and afflicted, yet he did not open his mouth.'

The crowd under a curse (27:15–26)

Matthew comments that was a custom for the governor 'at the festival to release a prisoner chosen by the crowd' (27:15). Pilate gives the option of 'Jesus Barabbas' or 'Jesus who is called the Messiah' (27:17). Encouraged by the chief priests, the crowd insist on Jesus Barabbas (27:21). Barabbas is released and Jesus (who is called Messiah) is handed over to be crucified (27:26).

It is very unlikely that Matthew wants to use this event to present the innocent Jesus acting as a substitute for the guilty Barabbas in order to save him. Nothing in the detail of the account points in this direction. In particular, although Barabbas is released, there is no hint or suggestion that he was ever saved or had his sins forgiven. This is not to deny that Jesus died a substitutionary death. Indeed, we shall see shortly that Matthew presents Jesus dying a curse-bearing death on behalf of (as a substitute for) 'holy ones' who thereby have the curse of death lifted from them.

The purpose of the scene is much more to show the culpability of all the parties involved (Jew and Gentile) in the betrayal of innocent blood. Like Judas in 27:3–10, they are thereby – all of them – shown deserving of the curse of God.

To begin with, we are reminded that Jesus is indeed clearly innocent. Pilate knows he has been handed over 'out of self-interest', not for any real crime (27:18, 23). He has also been told by his wife, 'Don't have anything to do with that innocent man' (27:19). A Gentile woman can see the evil of condemning an innocent (literally, 'righteous') man even if the chief priests and elders, the crowd and Pilate cannot. (In this, Pilate's wife is much like the Gentile Magi – also spoken to in a dream – who put to shame the chief priests and scribes in 2:1–12.)

Matthew then shows us that, even though everyone knows Jesus is innocent, they want to kill him anyway, or are happy to let him be killed to avoid 'an uproar' (27:24). Pilate's efforts to follow the advice of his wife and absolve himself of blood-guilt are as futile as those of the chief priests and elders in 27:3–10. He has the power to stop the execution of Jesus but chooses not to. Matthew has him use the same expression, 'It is your responsibility!' (27:24), as the chief priests and elders used in 27:4 in their failed attempt to distance themselves from the blood-guilt of Judas. Pilate washes his hands in front of them.[14] But Matthew has made it clear from Jesus's teaching that external washings cannot remove real inner defilement (15:1–20).

While Pilate cannot wash away his involvement, he is at least expressing some reluctance to be involved in the death of an innocent man. In contrast, the chief priests and elders put huge energy into encouraging the death of an innocent man by inciting the crowd (27:20). And the crowd go along with this, despite the absence of any good reason (27:21–3). Finally, 'all the people' cry out, 'His blood is on us and on our children!'

---

[14] This is a ritual reminiscent of that prescribed in Deuteronomy 21:1–9 to absolve a city of blood-guilt. But the elders in that passage *really are* innocent, while Pilate is clearly not.

(27:25). At the very least, this is accepting the consequences for handing over Jesus – which, if he is transparently innocent, are to be under a curse, according to Deuteronomy 27:25.[15]

Matthew 27:25 has a notorious history in anti-Semitism.[16] Matthew would be horrified. As we shall consider below, the final state of Peter (who is, of course, a Jew and just as culpable as the people in 27:25) shows that there is always forgiveness for sins and cleansing of the shame of betrayal for those who would turn or return to Jesus and depend on his 'blood of the covenant' (26:28). The verse functions here as part of a picture Matthew is building of the whole of humanity under the curse of God for disowning Jesus or betraying innocent blood. Jesus's disciples (represented by Peter and Judas) are under the curse. The Jewish leadership is under the curse. 'Gentile sinners' would automatically have been considered under the curse of God anyway, but this is reinforced here by the involvement of Pilate and his soldiers. The involvement of 'all the people' simply completes the picture.

Jesus mocked by the guards (27:27–31)

These are the governor's soldiers (27:27), and we can take it that what they do implicitly has his approval. One of the key points of execution by crucifixion was to bring as much shame on the person to be crucified as possible, and this began straight away. When Jesus was gathered before the high priest and others in 26:57–68, the outcome was both outrage at his claims to be the Messiah who will be seated at the right hand of the Mighty One and derision. The Roman response is pure mockery, with a whole company of soldiers involved. They dress him as a caricature of a king (27:28–9a), pay mock homage to him (27:29b) and then straightforwardly abuse him physically (27:30).

As before, the dramatic irony is that what the soldiers are saying as they pay mock homage is true. Jesus is the King of the Jews, worthy of honour. Again, we see Jesus living out the Servant role of Isaiah 53:2, 3 and 7.

---

[15] While this may not be an explicit 'self-curse' (as Davies and Allison argue it is not), it is at least a 'qualified self-curse' (as Luz argues) and places the people in a similar accursed state to Judas according to Deuteronomy 27:25. Davies and Allison, *Matthew 19–28*, 591; Luz, *Matthew 21–28*, 502. According to Luz, the qualification is that 'curse' is not to be understood as a verbal curse that the people pronounce on themselves but as the curse the people bring upon themselves by their actions.
[16] For a (thankfully) limited survey see Luz, *Matthew 21–28*, 506–8.

Jesus under God's curse part 1 (27:32–8)

The A stream storyline of those who are observers of the trial, death and execution of Jesus continues with the soldiers who lead him out to crucify him. They force (compel, as in 5:41) a man called Simon from Cyrene to carry the cross bar.

What this does in Matthew's narrative is establish an identification between Jesus and those who will follow after him (compare 10:38 and 16:24). Jesus's followers bear or carry (either literally or metaphorically) something that identifies them with Jesus, as he bears something for them. (As we shall see: as he bears the curse due to them because of their sin, thereby releasing them to live to God.)

The main activity here, though, is done by the soldiers who crucify and keep watch over Jesus. On the one hand, these are Pilate's soldiers (27:27), caught up in Pilate's culpability, sharing in the mocking of Jesus and instrumental in the execution of an innocent man. Even as Gentiles, they too implicitly stand under curse according to the terms of Deuteronomy 27:25. Their actions here are at first malicious, offering Jesus wine mixed with bitter gall (27:34) – perhaps as a cruel practical joke, intended either to fool Jesus into thinking he was getting a sedative or (worse) fooling him into thinking he was being given poison to cut short his suffering. They are then selfish and greedy, as they cast lots for his clothing (27:35). This is a continuation of Matthew's portrait of the whole world set against Jesus.

Having said this, it is worth noting that these are the same soldiers who are among the group who respond more positively to the signs in 27:51–4. Matthew sets this up in 27:36. They sit and keep watch, and see everything that happens as Jesus dies.

But the main role the soldiers play here is to do things that show Jesus fulfilling what he came to do as the Messiah, the one who is truly King of the Jews. When they offer drink and Jesus tastes it, he refuses to drink it (27:34). This may not be because of its bitterness, but simply because he realises it is wine. Recall that in 26:29 he promised his disciples that he wouldn't drink wine until he does so with them in the kingdom. This is not that day: he has work to finish first. When the soldiers cast lots for his clothing (27:35), they should remind us of those who opposed King David in Psalm 22:18, taking him deep under the shadow of death. (Like 27:42 below, this then prepares us for hearing the cry in 27:46.) When the soldiers put up the written charge in 27:37, we have confirmed that all this is indeed happening to the King of the Jews. (And since this is a true statement, we are reminded that Jesus is being executed as an innocent man.) When the soldiers place him between two 'rebels' or bandits (27:38), they remind us that Jesus has been 'numbered with the transgressors' like the Servant of Isaiah 53:12, and will thereby bear the sin of many.

They have brought Jesus to Golgotha, 'the place of the skull' (27:33). As Heil notes, the translation into Greek provided by Matthew 'projects the ghastly aura of death'.[17] It may also imply uncleanness and shame.[18] We have already seen in Matthew 8–9 Jesus saving people from the curse and shadow of death. Now, as the bystanders will note shortly (27:42), instead of rescuing others from the shadow and curse of death, he is facing it himself.

Moreover, the main thing the soldiers do in these verses is crucify Jesus (27:35, 38). Matthew has already highlighted Judas's chosen means of suicide by hanging (27:3–10). This should (as argued above) raise in our minds the text of Deuteronomy 21:22–3. Crucifixion combined a means of execution with the practice of hanging for exposure dealt with by these verses in Deuteronomy. Crucifixion was commonly associated with being under the curse of God.[19] Moreover, by noting the time at which Joseph of Arimathea asked for Jesus's body ('As evening approached', 27:57), Matthew is indicating the general presumption among those involved that this was a situation to which Deuteronomy 21:22–3 applied.

The evidence is strong, therefore, that in depicting Jesus hung on a cross to die, mocked and accused by men, his body removed and buried by sunset, Matthew is depicting Jesus under God's curse, as implied by the contemporary understanding of Deuteronomy 21:22–3.

Jesus mocked by bystanders (27:39–44)

Now we have further mockery, probably from those who were at the gathering before the high priest in 26:57–68. This mocking scene is topped and tailed by two references to the robbers: verses 38, 44. This places the other mockers here in the same wicked camp.

---

[17] Heil, Death and Resurrection, 79.

[18] Davies and Allison, Matthew 19–28, 612; compare Hebrews 13:13.

[19] For more on this, see D. W. Chapman, Ancient Jewish and Christian Perceptions of Crucifixion volume 244, Wunt Ii (Tübingen: Mohr Siebeck, 2008), 57–66. Also Davies and Allison, Matthew 19–28, 616.

The first group 'hurled insults at him' (26:39) and repeat the claim attributed to Jesus in 26:61 that that he would destroy the Temple and then rebuild it in three days (26:40). The second group are the leaders mentioned in 26:57 – chief priests, teachers of the law and elders – who have come now to mock him (27:41).

The insults and mockery all have the same pattern to them. There is a claim or observation about Jesus and then an inference intended to undermine the claim or example. The pattern is reminiscent of that used in the taunting and testing by the devil/Satan in 4:1–11. It is therefore fair to call this Jesus's 'last temptation'.

Each taunt reveals a false understanding of the claim or observation. Someone able to destroy and rebuild the Temple would, under a false understanding, necessarily save themselves from crucifixion (27:40a). The 'Son of God' would definitely get down from the cross (27:40b). Someone able to save others would surely be able to save himself (27:42a). The 'king of Israel' would get down from the cross (27:42b). A 'Son of God', who trusts God would certainly be rescued by him (27:43). (This final taunt echoes the taunt of David's enemies in Psalm 22:8.)

The Jewish leaders use these (false) inferences as an excuse for unbelief (27:42c).

Again, the dramatic irony is that all the claims and observations are true. Knowing that we know this, Matthew is steering us towards a correct understanding of what Jesus is doing on the cross. To rebuild after three days (27:40a) means a delay before salvation: destruction comes first. To be the 'Son of God' (27:40b), approved and beloved by the Father for taking on the role of Servant (3:17; 17:5), means completing this mandate and not getting down from the cross. Jesus is able to save others (27:42a) *because* he is not saving himself (compare 20:28). Not getting down from the cross and enduring the taunts of those who see him not being rescued (27:42b–3) is therefore actually evidence that he is Son of God, and the Psalm 22, David-like king of Israel.

And indeed, Jesus doesn't save himself, he doesn't get down from the cross and God doesn't rescue him at this particular moment. Matthew's intention is that this doesn't lead to unbelief (as in 27:42c) but to a deep and dependent belief.

Jesus under God's curse part 2 (27:45–54)

The sign of midday darkness reinforces the impression of Jesus dying under the judgment, wrath or curse of God. Darkness is a familiar sign of God's judgment across the Hebrew Scriptures (Exodus 10:21–2; Isaiah 59:10), especially darkness at midday (Job 5:14; Jeremiah 15:9; Amos 8:9–10).

After three hours of midday darkness, Jesus cries out, 'My God, my God, why have you forsaken me?' (27:46). It is a huge mistake to read this as indicating some kind of hostile division between Father and Son, or some kind of rift in the Trinity. Not only would this be a profound misunderstanding of the Trinity (an absurdity, in fact), but we already know by the end of the Gethsemane episode (26:36–46) that Father and incarnate Son are fully in agreement and alignment concerning his death. Jesus does not say, 'My Father, why have you forsaken me?' He does not even use original words, but the very human words of David in Psalm 22:1. What is more, the point of view in these verses is not on Jesus's subjective experience. It is external, with the focus on what the witnesses made of what they saw and heard. Those who mishear Jesus suppose that he is seeking help through Elijah (27:47–9) – presumably, salvation from his unhappy (even cursed) state.[20] Those who correctly hear what Jesus says, however, should simply hear from the cry that this is a man who feels desperately forsaken by God. This reinforces what Matthew wants us to understand: Jesus was indeed dying as a man under the wrath or curse of God. He was dying as a sin-bearer, taking upon himself the curse of death (compare Isaiah 53:12). As Peter Bolt puts it (commenting on the parallel verse in Mark 15:34), 'In the cry of dereliction we hear Jesus crying out in solidarity with our own Godforsaken mortality.'[21]

That the words Jesus cry out are from a psalm is also significant. The psalms in general associate forsakenness with the wrath of God (for example, Psalm 27:9; compare Psalms 38:1, 21). The basic assumption in the Psalms is that the Lord in his covenant faithfulness will not forsake his people (e.g., Psalms 9:11; 16:10; 27:10; 37:25, 28, 33; 94:14). So when forsakenness takes place, it makes sense to conclude that the covenant has been broken, with those forsaken under curse rather than blessing.

---

[20] This should remind us of two other significant events in the Gospel (also accompanied by signs) where Elijah is either alluded to or features significantly: the baptism of Jesus (3:4, 13–17) and the Transfiguration (17:1–13). At the first, Jesus takes on a mandate from his Father, and at the second the mandate is confirmed. At the crucifixion, we shall see the mandate fulfilled.

[21] Bolt, *Cross from a Distance*, 141. In saying we should not separate Father and Son as Jesus dies, we also need to be careful not to divide the Son. This is the cry of the one Lord Jesus Christ, fully God and fully man. Hence Paul is able to say to the Ephesian elders in Acts 20:28, 'Be shepherds of the church of God, which he bought with his own blood.'

Because this is a cry from Psalm 22, however, there is already a hint of hope and greater purpose here. The words of forsakenness are uttered by David, the Lord's Anointed, and the psalm ends not in despair but in his vindication (Psalm 22:22–31).

In 27:50, Jesus actually dies. Matthew does not tell us the content of this second cry as Jesus 'gave up his spirit' (that is, consciously and voluntarily gave up his life). Most likely, he records it as a simple reminder of the sheer awfulness and suffering Jesus was experiencing at the point of death. This makes it all the more surprising that the signs after Jesus cries out are uniformly signs of vindication. The tearing of the Temple veil in 27:51a signifies God's judgment against those who have been clear enemies of Jesus at least since conflicts in the Temple (Matthew 21–2), conspiring to execute him despite his innocence.[22] As David Garland notes, earthquakes (27:51b) frequently signify vindication against the enemies of God's people.[23] Moreover, this vindication is demonstrated as the earthquake breaks open the tombs of 'holy people' and they are raised to life (27:52–3). This curious detail has long puzzled readers of Matthew. The most obvious allusion is to Ezekiel 37:12–13, where the Lord declares to Israel in exile that he will 'open your graves', in a vision of the vindication of the nation and an end to covenant curse.

The key witnesses provided by Matthew to help us interpret these events are the centurion and those with him in verse 54. As mentioned earlier, this group may well overlap with the soldiers who crucified Jesus. Dramatic signs were often associated with the death of kings and great people, but the signs here are much greater.[24] They see what happens and naturally conclude that a great one has died – even a (or the) son of God. They may have also picked up a sense of anger poured out from the heavens – anger that a great one has died unjustly. The signs thus vindicate the one who has been wrongly executed.

---

[22] It is common to read more into the significance of the torn curtain. It opens access to God, or opens the heavens, as in D. M. Gurtner, *The Torn Veil: Matthew's Exposition of the Death of Jesus* (Cambridge: Cambridge University Press, 2007), 201. But Matthew does nothing to set up such a reading, and it does not fit the context well. It seems much simpler to say that the torn curtain signifies not 'heaven is open' but simply that 'the Temple is judged and the Lord is not here' (compare Ezekiel 10).

[23] Garland, *Reading Matthew*, 260, citing Judges 5:4–5; 2 Samuel 22:8; 1 Kings 19:11; Psalm 68:8; Isaiah 13:13; 24:18–23; 29:6; Jeremiah 10:10; Ezekiel 38:18–19; Joel 3:16; Nahum 1:5–6.

[24] See Garland, *Reading Matthew*, 260, and the references cited there.

The death of Jesus according to Matthew therefore fulfils the pattern Jesus set out in his final speech in Matthew 24–5. Tribulation will certainly be followed by vindication for the faithful. Matthew shows him hung and exposed on a cross, shrouded in darkness, crying out in God-forsaken mortality. But that is not the end of the story. Matthew also shows him vindicated against his enemies, his life-giving ministry vindicated, this vindication seen and recognised by the world, and even experienced by some as the shadow of death is lifted from them.

SUMMARY AND PURPOSE

The overall purpose of Matthew's Gospel is to make its readers who aren't disciples of Jesus into disciples of Jesus, and to motivate and equip its readers who are disciples of Jesus to be disciple-makers.

There are many things in this middle section of Matthew 26–8 that should persuade someone who is not yet a disciple. The B stream of material shows Jesus attractively clear and resolute about his identity and mandate, contrasted with unattractive and irrationally hostile or mocking responses to him. This is interwoven with the A stream material, which portrays people either distancing themselves from Jesus (like Peter), or implicitly joining those scheming to execute him. Not only are these people portrayed by Matthew as dishonourable or unattractive, but they are also shown under the curse of God in danger of judgment. We are naturally led to dissociate from their behaviour. Finally, we are shown an attractive, model response – one we should want to associate with, even as a rank outsider. The centurion and those with him see Jesus dying a death that actually reflects a high kingly or even divine status (a 'Son of God', 27:54). Seeing past the shame of crucifixion, they see him dying a noble, kingly death. Matthew has helped us to understand this as Jesus dying a kingly, Davidic death on behalf of his people, taking their curse upon himself.

The same mechanism also helps those who are already disciples to persevere in their faith, especially if, like Peter, they have wavered under pressure to acknowledge or confess Jesus – or have been tempted to waver. A disciple in this situation is reminded of the dangers. And they are also offered a way back: humbly following the example of the centurion and those with him, to confess Jesus openly and to depend exclusively on his curse-bearing death. Again, the encouragement comes through the narrative rather than direct, explicit teaching: showing rather than telling.

Like the other Gospel writers, Matthew portrays what Jesus does in his Servant, curse-bearing work as utterly unique and impossible to replicate.

Nevertheless, Jesus is also setting his followers (those who also 'take up their crosses', 10:38; 16:24) an example of steadfastness to a God-given task under extreme opposition. From the beginning of the section, Jesus sets his sights beyond the immediate suffering he's facing to the vindication to come (26:64), and this is an encouragement for his disciples to follow the same pattern.

3. Mission completed (and commissioned) part 3 • Matthew 27:55–28:20

The pattern of two threads of material forming an alternating pattern continues in this section, although the alternation is more rapid, with short sections, making it perhaps less distinct than previous sections.

55 Many women were there, watching from a distance. They had followed Jesus from Galilee to care for his needs. 56 Among them were Mary Magdalene, Mary the mother of James and Joseph, **f** and the mother of Zebedee's sons.

The burial of Jesus

57 As evening approached, there came a rich man from Arimathea, named Joseph, who had himself become a disciple of Jesus. 58 Going to Pilate, he asked for Jesus's body, and Pilate ordered that it be given to him. 59 Joseph took the body, wrapped it in a clean linen cloth, 60 and placed it in his own new tomb that he had cut out of the rock. He rolled a big stone in front of the entrance to the tomb and went away. 61 Mary Magdalene and the other Mary were sitting there opposite the tomb.

The guard at the tomb

62 The next day, the one after Preparation Day, the chief priests and the Pharisees went to Pilate. 63 'Sir,' they said, 'we remember that while he was still alive that deceiver said, "After three days I will rise again." 64 So give the order for the tomb to be made secure until the third day. Otherwise, his disciples may come and steal the body and tell the people that he has been raised from the dead. This last deception will be worse than the first.'

65 'Take a guard,' Pilate answered. 'Go, make the tomb as secure as you know how.' 66 So they went and made the tomb secure by putting a seal on the stone and posting the guard.

Jesus has risen

28 After the Sabbath, at dawn on the first day of the week, Mary Magdalene and the other Mary went to look at the tomb.

2 There was a violent earthquake, for an angel of the Lord came down from heaven and, going to the tomb, rolled back the stone and sat on it.

3 His appearance was like lightning, and his clothes were white as snow. **4** The guards were so afraid of him that they shook and became like dead men.

5 The angel said to the women, 'Do not be afraid, for I know that you are looking for Jesus, who was crucified. **6** He is not here; he has risen, just as he said. Come and see the place where he lay. **7** Then go quickly and tell his disciples: "He has risen from the dead and is going ahead of you into Galilee. There you will see him." Now I have told you.'

8 So the women hurried away from the tomb, afraid yet filled with joy, and ran to tell his disciples. **9** Suddenly Jesus met them. 'Greetings,' he said. They came to him, clasped his feet and worshipped him. **10** Then Jesus said to them, 'Do not be afraid. Go and tell my brothers to go to Galilee; there they will see me.'

The guards' report

11 While the women were on their way, some of the guards went into the city and reported to the chief priests everything that had happened. **12** When the chief priests had met with the elders and devised a plan, they gave the soldiers a large sum of money, **13** telling them, 'You are to say, "His disciples came during the night and stole him away while we were asleep." **14** If this report gets to the governor, we will satisfy him and keep you out of trouble.' **15** So the soldiers took the money and did as they were instructed. And this story has been widely circulated among the Jews to this very day.

The great commission

16 Then the eleven disciples went to Galilee, to the mountain where Jesus had told them to go. **17** When they saw him, they worshipped him; but some doubted. **18** Then Jesus came to them and said, 'All authority in heaven and on earth has been given to me. **19** Therefore go and make disciples of all nations, baptising them in the name of the Father and of the Son and of the Holy Spirit, **20** and teaching them to obey everything I have commanded you. And surely I am with you always, to the very end of the age.'

---

f 56 Greek *Joses*, a variant of *Joseph*

The mainline sequence (marked A in Table 23 below: 27:55–6, 61; 28:1, 5–10, 16–20) depicts the uncovering of Jesus's resurrection: a progression of reliable witnesses to the resurrection of Jesus, all people who have known him, the first of whom have seen his death. The women who have followed Jesus from Galilee witness his death (27:55–6), witness his tomb sealed (27:61), come to see the tomb on the first day of the week (28:1), see the stone rolled away, the angel of the Lord and then Jesus himself (28:5–10). The eleven disciples then go to Galilee and see the risen Jesus for themselves (28:16–20). Matthew describes the women watching and looking (27:55; 28:1) and then tells how they will see Jesus (28:6–7, 10, 17) to describe this pattern of sight which contrasts with the kingdom-blindness we noted earlier in the Gospel. This sequence completes the fulfilment of Jesus's passion-vindication predictions. It also completes the portrait of Jesus as vindicated Son of Man who has completed his particular mandate as the Servant of the Lord. This sets the stage for a derivative servanthood for his disciples and a future vindication for them at the end of the age.

The background (inner) sequence (marked B below: 27:57–60, 62–6, 28:2–4, 11–15) depicts events that involve, in different ways, attempts to hide Jesus – ultimately futile attempts (innocent or otherwise) to restrain him in death. Thus Jesus is laid in a sealed tomb (27:57–60), which is then secured further and guarded (27:62–6). An angel of the Lord then exposes the inability of the stone and the guards to contain Jesus (28:2–4). Finally, Matthew exposes an attempt to hide the truth about the resurrection: the lie that the body was stolen (28:11–15).

(A) The resurrection of Jesus is witnessed and un-covered for the whole world . . .	27:55–6 At cross (first day)	27:61 At tomb (first day)	28:1 At tomb (third day)	28:5–10 See Jesus (third day)	28:16–20 See Jesus The Great Commission
(B) He cannot remain buried and hidden	27:57–60 Burial	27:62–6 Guards posted (second day)	28:2–4 Tomb opened; guards stunned	2:11–15 False report exposed	

Table 23

Witnesses of Jesus's death (27:55–6)

First, then, Matthew wants us to know as surely as we can that Jesus was definitely dead and that the same Jesus who was seen to die was the one shortly to be buried in Joseph's tomb.

Matthew establishes the women watching from a distance as those who know Jesus well (27:55). They would have known him in Galilee and have travelled with him to Jerusalem. Matthew names two of them and clearly identifies a third (27:56). These were presumably known to him or by others, making their testimony verifiable.

We can presume that the women saw Jesus crucified (27:35), heard his cry (27:46) and heard and saw him give up his spirit (27:50). They would have seen the earthquake and the other things that happened, just as the centurion and those with him did (27:54). These women then provide a link to the verses that follow.

Jesus is hidden in burial (27:57–60)

Joseph's concern to remove Jesus from hanging on the cross and bury him before sunset (27:57) confirms what we said above about the background understanding of crucifixion falling under the regulations of Deuteronomy 21:22–3. Jesus is a 'hanged man' and 'under God's curse'. But because he is buried the same day as his death, he will not defile the land. This point is reinforced by Joseph wrapping Jesus's body in a clean cloth and placing him in a new (and therefore clean) tomb (27:60). This is also a mark of Joseph's deep respect for Jesus, as one of his disciples (27:57). Like the woman who anointed Jesus for burial in 26:6–13 (but at the other end of the social spectrum), Joseph stands out as someone prepared to face public shame for his association with Jesus and willing to give up much that seems superficially valuable (in this case, a private tomb).

The clean linen and fresh tomb are also perhaps a hint that, far from defiling the land, Jesus is in fact through his death and resurrection going to be a power for cleansing a world under the shadow of death.

This episode begins the B stream of material in the structure in Table 23 above. We begin this stream with Jesus's body firmly hidden: wrapped in a cloth (29:59), placed in a tomb cut into the rock, with a big stone placed over the entrance (29:60). The location of the body is also clear and known. It has been placed there by a reputable man with Pilate's permission – in a recognisable tomb, not a common grave.

Witnesses of his burial (27:61)

Continuing the thread begun in 26:55–6, Mary Magdalene and the other Mary (the mother of James and Joseph) are watching all this. The women then serve as reliable, faithful witnesses of Jesus's death and secure burial, and add further confirmation of the location of his burial (26:61).

Jesus is guarded in the tomb (27:62–6)

The next day, the chief priests and the Pharisees go to Pilate and express their worries that Jesus's disciples will come and steal his body so they can falsely claim that Jesus's promise to be raised after three days has been fulfilled (26:62–4). Pilate allows them to make the tomb as secure as they can, by sealing the stone and posting a guard (26:65–6).

This reinforces the hiddenness of Jesus's body at this stage of Matthew's resurrection account. Jesus can't get out. His disciples can't get in.

It also begins to address the attempt to 'conceal' (that is, hide the truth about) Jesus's risen body that comes to light later in the narrative, when the chief priests and elders will plot to spread the idea that the disciples came in the night to steal the body (27:11–15). The sealing of the tomb and the presence of the guard make this a harder story to promote.

The witnesses at the tomb on the third day (28:1)

The women have been faithful witnesses of Jesus's death and burial. Now, at dawn on the first day of the week, they will be faithful witnesses of the empty tomb and his resurrection.

Jesus is not there! (28:2–4)

The earthquake in 28:2 should remind us of the one in 27:51. That one accompanied the death of Jesus – a sign of God intervening, with echoes of judgment through earthquakes in the past. But it also broke open many tombs and exposed signs of the life for others, which the death of Jesus achieved. This one will expose and show us the empty tomb. In other words, this one will show us the origin of that life.

This earthquake is caused by an angel of the Lord moving the stone from the entrance of the tomb. The appearance of the angel (28:3) should remind us of both the Ancient of Days in Daniel 7:9 (linked to the vindication of one like a Son of Man, Daniel 7:13–14) and then the angelic being of Daniel 10:6, at the beginning of the visions that end with general resurrection and judgment (Daniel 12:1–4).

Unlike those witnessing the earthquake in 27:54, the guards do not confess, but are filled with fear (28:4). Instead of being released from death by the earthquake like the holy people in 27:52–3, they 'became like dead men'. They would seem to represent those opposed to God's purposes and who therefore only experience the negative implications of Jesus's death and resurrection.

Witnesses of Jesus's resurrection (28:5–10)

Just as an angel imparted privileged information back in 1:20–21, so here at the end. Back then, the angel told Joseph to give Mary's son the name Jesus 'because he will save his people from their sins'. Now, in chapter 28, once Jesus's task is finished, the angel of the Lord reappears to declare the job done.

What the angel says in 28:5–7 divides into two parts, both concerned with the news that Jesus has risen. The first part communicates the news to the women. With the stone rolled back and the tomb open in front of them, the angel addresses their fear, knowing they are looking for Jesus, whom they saw crucified (28:5). The good (victorious) news is that he is not in there; he has risen, and the angel invites them to see the empty tomb (28:6). In the second part, the angel commissions them to communicate the news that Jesus has risen to the other disciples, sending them back to Galilee, where they will see him (28:7). The angel's final, 'Now [or 'Behold!'] I have told you,' completes his task of communicating the news.

The women depart with fear and the same great joy experienced by the Magi at the beginning of the Gospel (2:10). The message they take with them heightens our expectation of what will happen in Galilee.

On the way, they meet the risen Jesus (28:9). He greets them, and they fall down, grasping his feet in worship. (Again, this is like the Magi in 2:11.) But they are not to stay with him. Jesus repeats what the angel sent them to do (28:10). On his lips, the message for the disciples is extraordinary given the way they scattered and abandoned him (and, in Peter's case, denied him) before his death. After his death and resurrection, he is able to call them 'brothers' and arrange to meet them. His mandate is completed. Again, we are looking forward to what will happen in Galilee.

A false report exposed (28:11–15)

It is obviously very important to Matthew to persuade his readers that the resurrection is genuine historical fact. The story seems to have been circulating as he was writing that the disciples had stolen Jesus's body from the tomb for their own gain – and this is why the tomb was empty (28:15). Notice that nobody denies that the tomb was empty. In these verses, Matthew explains the story that's circulating. The guards reported what happened to the chief priests (28:11) and they devised a plan for the guards to spread the rumour that the body had been stolen

(28:12–13). In return, the guards get payment and protection (28:12, 14). In other words, the reality behind the false story was that much of what the disciples were being accused of – seeking personal gain by telling a lie – was actually true of the guards. It was the guards who were seeking personal gain, and it was they who told the lie (with full funding and support from the religious establishment).

Witnesses commissioned (28:16–20)

Finally, we return to Galilee. This is what Jesus promised in 28:7, 10 and back in 26:32, before he was arrested. We should also remember this is where his ministry began (4:12–16).

These five verses at the end of Matthew's Gospel have become known as the 'Great Commission', and are worthy of much attention in their own right. They also, however, complete the narrative sequence begun at 27:55. In the mainline A stream of material in this section (see Table 23), these verses show the complete uncovering of the risen Jesus. His authority over the entire cosmos is announced and unveiled, and many can now come to know the risen Jesus as his disciples across the world. In the overall plot of Matthew's Gospel, this is a classic 'dénouement', in that it shows that the basic problem raised at the start of the narrative has been addressed. This is what is able to happen once the main action of the plot is complete. With the crisis of death dealt with at such a fundamental level, disciples of Jesus can be made in every nation.

Matthew begins by telling us that 'the eleven disciples went to Galilee' (28:16a). This is significant, because it means Peter is included. As we noted earlier, the key difference between Peter and Judas in their self-cursed states was that, while Judas pursued atonement by himself, Peter stayed with the other disciples and benefited from the curse-bearing death of Jesus.

Matthew calls the Eleven 'disciples', rather than 'apostles' (compare 10:2). This too is significant. This may be in part because Jesus is just about to re-send them out into a global mission, but it also establishes a close connection with the command to 'make disciples' in verse 19. Disciples are to make disciples, and then to teach them what Jesus has commanded (28:20) – teaching that culminates with the command to make disciples. This expands the command beyond the Eleven to all disciples.

It is also clear that we are up a mountain again (28:16b), like the mountain in 5:1. Like Sinai in the Old Testament, Matthew is expecting us to see this as a contact point between heaven and earth. In both chapters 5–7 and here, he is saying that this is like that foundational moment in the past, but new and greater. In Matthew 5–7, Jesus began his teaching that was the fulfilment of the Law and the Prophets, and here in Matthew 28 he completes it. Now is the time to put the teaching into practice and spread it across the nations.

The disciples are people who know Jesus and know who he is. Matthew says that when they see him, they recognise him and worship him (28:17). That is, they express in attitude or gesture a complete dependence on or submission to him as a divine figure, quite possibly by falling down and prostrating themselves before him.

And yet: some doubt. Are those who doubt different from those who worship? Possibly, but it's more likely that Matthew is showing in the disciples' reaction a mixture of worship and doubt. That is, at least some of those worshipping disciples also doubt. It is even possible to translate 28:17 simply like this: 'When they saw him, they worshipped, but they doubted.' In other words, perhaps they all doubted!

This is striking, because it means the doubt and little faith besetting the disciples throughout the Gospel has survived all the way to the end. Even seeing the risen Jesus hasn't quenched it. And, of course, the uncomfortable co-existence of worship and doubt has survived beyond this moment on the mountain in the experience of disciples ever since. But doubt is not the note on which the Gospel ends! Jesus now comes to them and says something that addresses their doubt: a declaration, a command and a promise (28:18–20).

The declaration
The declaration is in 28:18. Jesus declares, 'All authority in heaven and on earth has been given to me.' This is a declaration of vindication, fulfilling the vision of Daniel 7:14:

> He was given authority, glory and sovereign power; all nations and peoples of every language worshipped him. His dominion is an everlasting dominion that will not pass away, and his kingdom is one that will never be destroyed.

I have argued that the kingdom of the heavens in Matthew's Gospel has the kingdom language of Daniel in the background and refers to the coming of a kingdom from the heavens that will fill heaven and earth, reuniting them under one dominion. Jesus's declaration in 28:18 is that the first part of Daniel 7:14 has been fulfilled: authority, glory and sovereign power has been given to him.

This addresses the disciples' doubt because it explains the significance of seeing the risen Jesus. It is not just an isolated supernatural wonder, but signifies a task completed. The task was given to Jesus even in his naming as he was born of Mary by the Holy Spirit: to save God's people from their sins. At his baptism, Jesus publicly showed his willingness to take the task on. In the narrative that followed, his authority to forgive sins and give life by the Spirit was revealed. In the final chapters of Matthew's Gospel we have learned that the forgiveness of sins and life have been enabled through the death and resurrection of Jesus. And because that work is done, finished, now the Father gives the Son 'all authority in heaven and on earth'. He has been given the right to rule in heaven and on earth and the power to progress his purposes, which (as we see in the command of 28:19–20) are to make disciples in all nations and so to bring about worship in 'peoples of every language' (Daniel 7:14). All this means that the kingdom of the heavens is not simply 'near' (as in 3:2, 4:17, 10:7) but 'right at the door' (as Jesus put it in 24:33).

We should also recall the final temptation in 4:8–9. From a mountain, the devil showed Jesus all the kingdoms of the world and their splendour, and then said, 'All this I will give you . . . if you will bow down and worship me.' Jesus refused, saying, 'Away from me, Satan! For it is written: "Worship the Lord your God, and serve him only."' Here in Matthew 28, Jesus is given the world by his Father, not by Satan; his patient faithfulness is now vindicated and rewarded. The consequence will be worship – not of the devil, but of the Lord God, in the worship of the risen Jesus.

The command

The command and commission Jesus gives his disciples is in 28:19–20 follows as a consequence of the authority given to Jesus in the previous verse. It begins with, 'Therefore go and make disciples in all nations . . .' The construction is the same as 9:13 ('Go and learn . . .') In the Greek text, there is a participle followed by an imperative: 'Going, make disciples . . .' There is some debate about how much weight to put on the 'going' idea, and whether it should be treated as an imperative, just like 'make disciples'.[25] The answer to this lies not so much in the syntax of the verse but in the context. In 9:13, Jesus's command is effectively to take some time out to learn something: the idea of 'going' to do this doesn't

---

[25] That is, taking the participle as a 'participle of attendant circumstances' rather than, say, a temporal participle. (A temporal participle would suggest, 'When (or as) you go, make disciples . . .')

seem to have much weight behind it. But in 28:19, the command is to make disciples in all nations – for which it will be necessary for at least some of the disciples to go to the nations. So, in this case, to go is very much part of the command.

Again, this addresses any doubt the disciples might have, further explaining the significance of seeing the risen Jesus. It is not just an isolated supernatural wonder, but signifies a task commissioned. There is reason and purpose behind the appearance: it begins a process through the disciples of making disciples that will last until the end of the age.

The disciples earlier in Matthew were 'made' by hearing and accepting the news of the kingdom preached by John and Jesus (3:2; 4:17), then by being called to follow Jesus (4:19, 21; 9:9) and then by being taught by Jesus – teaching that began in Matthew 5–7 and ends here in Matthew 28. This is the task the disciples are now drawn into, multiplying it much as they multiplied the preaching of the kingdom in Matthew 10. 'Make disciples of [or 'in'] all nations,' says Jesus. The phrase '. . . of all nations' is similar to the phrase 'all the nations' in 25:32, where it was used in the context of universal global judgment – that is, Jew and Gentile. The mission to Israel in Matthew 10 is expanded, not replaced.

After saying, 'Go and make disciples of all nations,' Jesus continues, 'baptising them in the name of the Father and of the Son and of the Holy Spirit, and teaching them to obey everything I have commanded you.' There could be a three-step order here: disciples are made, then baptised and then taught. Or, much more likely,[26] it could simply be that baptism and teaching expand (in two steps) what it means to 'go and make disciples'.[27]

If this right, then 'baptising them in the name of the Father and of the Son and of the Holy Spirit' would be some way of marking the first stages of making a disciple: for a person who has acknowledged the reality of the coming kingdom, been convicted of their sin and responded to Jesus's call to follow him. Whatever it is, like teaching in 28:20, it's something that the disciples actually do to new disciples; it's not a figurative way of talking about them becoming a disciple. Apart from baptising in the Spirit (which is something unique to Jesus, 3:11), the only other references to baptism in Matthew's Gospel are to water baptism, so this is almost certainly what Jesus has in mind. Indeed, we should be reminded in particular of Jesus's water baptism in 3:13–17, which

---

[26] Given that 'make disciples' is the main verb, and 'baptising' and 'teaching' are participles.

[27] O'Brien, 'The Great Commission', 76–7.

Christology and commission

It is right at the end of his Gospel that Matthew's presentation of the person and identity of Jesus (his 'Christology') comes into full focus.

Matthew began his Gospel with Jesus as the Messiah the son of David (1:1). That is, he began with Jesus as the promised *human* descendant of David, called Messiah, who will save and rescue God's people, leading them to victory. Also very early in the Gospel, the voice from the heavens in Matthew 3:17 says of Jesus, 'This is my Son . . .', echoing Psalm 2:7, where the 'son' is also the Messiah who will crush the enemies of the Lord and inherit the nations.

Throughout the Gospel, Jesus's favoured way of talking about himself has been as 'Son of Man', beginning at 8:20. In Daniel 7, the one like a son of man is vindicated by the Ancient of Days and given an everlasting kingdom.

We saw these two strands come together at Jesus's trial before the high priest in 26:59–68. The high priest asks Jesus directly, 'Tell us if you are the Messiah, the Son of God' (26:63b). Jesus is clear: 'You have said so' (26:64a). He then adds, 'From now on you will see the Son of Man sitting at the right hand of the Mighty One and coming on the clouds of heaven' (26:64b). This connects the Messiah and Son of God to the 'one like a son of man' in Daniel 7:13, *and also* to the 'Lord' greater than David in Psalm 110 (which Jesus has spoken of in 22:41–6). There have been many hints throughout the Gospel that as 'Son', Jesus is much more than a human king, and has a unique kind of relationship with the Father. And Jesus himself has said many things about himself as Son of Man that suggest he shares the divine identity. But it is these words from Jesus in Matthew 26 that bring the high priest to conclude that Jesus is claiming to be equal to God, and therefore (in his eyes) speaking blasphemy (26:65).

When Jesus says, 'All authority in heaven and on earth has been given to me,' in 28:18 he is saying not only has he been vindicated as Son of Man but also that he now sits in this exalted status appropriate only for God himself. That is, it is clear by the end of the Gospel that Jesus is Lord as well as Messiah (compare Peter in Acts 2:36).

The second way Matthew introduced Jesus at the start of the Gospel was as 'son of Abraham' (1:1). The promise to Abraham was that through his descendants, blessing would flow to 'all peoples on earth' (Genesis 12:3). According to Isaiah, this 'light' will flood out to the nations through one called the Servant (of the Lord, Isaiah 42:6; 49:6). At first this seems to be the nation of Israel descended from Abraham (Isaiah 41:8–9; 44:1, etc.), but then the Servant is portrayed by Isaiah as one who will suffer and bear the iniquity and sin of many (Isaiah 53:4–12). Matthew has been clear from the beginning that we should associate Jesus with this Servant figure (this is most explicit at 12:18–21). As we saw above, he has also been very clear to portray Jesus dying a curse-bearing death on behalf of others. But with this particular aspect of Jesus's Servant ministry completed, there is still much to do: taking the light of salvation out to the nations.

Hence the declaration in 28:18 is followed by command and commissioning. The call to the disciples is essentially a gracious invitation to join in and participate in what Jesus will now do among the nations. The follow-up command to baptise and the 'Trinitarian' formula in 28:19 should remind us of Jesus's baptism in 3:13–17, where Father, Son, and Holy Spirit were all involved as Jesus took up the mandate of Isaiah's Servant figure. This suggests that baptism marks the incorporation of a disciple into the same programme. That is, Jesus is issuing a derivative mandate to the one he received.

Contemporary Christian institutions and local churches frequently put enormous energy into setting a compelling 'vision' for themselves. But this is to ignore the fact that we already have been given a vision in Matthew 28:16–20, and it is far greater and more exciting and motivating than any we could invent for ourselves. This motivation should, according to Jesus, flow into a desire to learn and then teach all he has commanded (28:20). This should take those who have been made disciples back to the beginning of the Gospel, eager to read it again and be trained as disciple-makers. And they have Jesus's promise that he is with them as they do so, leading them and training them, until the end of the age.